Customer Relationship Management

We work with leading authors to develop the strongest educational materials in marketing, bringing cutting-edge thinking and best learning practice to a global market.

Under a range of well-known imprints, including Financial Times Prentice Hall, we craft high-quality print and electronic publications which help readers to understand and apply their content, whether studying or at work.

To find out more about the complete range of our publishing, please visit us on the World Wide Web at:
www.pearsoned.co.uk

Customer Relationship Management

Ed Peelen

An imprint of Pearson Education
Harlow, England • London • New York • Boston • San Francisco • Toronto
Sydney • Tokyo • Singapore • Hong Kong • Seoul • Taipei • New Delhi
Cape Town • Madrid • Mexico City • Amsterdam • Munich • Paris • Milan

Pearson Education Limited
Edinburgh Gate
Harlow
Essex CM20 2JE
England

and Associated Companies throughout the world

Visit us on the World Wide Web at:
www.pearsoned.co.uk

This translation of Ed Peelen: Customer Relationship Management, 1st edition is published by arrangement with Pearson Education Benelux BV, Amsterdam.

ISBN 0 273 68177 X

British Library Cataloguing-in-Publication Data
A catalogue record for this book is available from the British Library

Library of Congress Cataloging-in-Publication Data
Peelen, Ed.
[Customer relationship management. English]
Customer relationship management / Ed Peelen.
p. cm.
Includes bibliographical references and index.
ISBN 0-273-68177-X
1. Customer relations—Management. I. Title.

HF5415.5.P44 2005
658.8′12—dc22

2005040020

10 9 8 7 6 5 4 3 2 1
09 08 07 06 05

Typeset in 10/12pt Times by 35
Printed by Ashford Colour Press Ltd., Gosport

The publisher's policy is to use paper manufactured from sustainable forests.

Contents

Supporting resources
Visit **www.pearsoned.co.uk/peelen** to find valuable online resources

For instructors
- Complete, downloadable Instructor's Manual
- PowerPoint slides that can be downloaded and used as OHTs

For more information please contact your local Pearson Education sales representative or visit **www.pearsoned.co.uk/peelen**

Preface

CRM from the start . . .

It was twenty years ago when I was confronted for the first time with relationship marketing. The newly founded Lester Wunderman Institute approached me with a request to initiate a study on the subject. Freshly graduated as an economist with a marketing specialisation, it was a challenge and the beginning of an interesting discussion with marketing specialists. Following the publication of my first article, marketers began to react. Nobody had ever applied theories and concepts from social psychology to relationships between individual consumers and sellers in the field of marketing. Initial doubts were replaced by enthusiasm in a fairly short time. A demand for relationship marketing took off. In Scandinavia, Gummesson, Grönroos and Håkansson, in the UK, Payne, and in Canada, Berry played major innovative roles right from the beginning; thus relationship marketing was born.

The popularity of relationship marketing has not been the same in all European countries through the years. Some have started slowly or late; for others the interest in it was directly related to the economic climate; and some have shown continuous commitment. But everyone who became involved with relationship marketing discovered that the field was more difficult than at first expected. The necessary data were lacking as most organisations were still more product- and market- than customer-oriented. Acquiring customers had a higher priority than retaining them and the need to redesign processes was apparent.

In the 1990s, people became more aware of the development of buyer–seller relations and realised that these relations had consequences for entire organisations. Customer relationships were no longer just a marketing issue, but everybody in the organisation played a direct or indirect role in customer contact. Relationship marketing was implemented in organisations and affected company culture, communication patterns and reward systems. Organisations that had previously been built around factories had to be rebuilt around customers. Conquering markets and achieving market leadership was no longer a company's primary concern; instead activities within the organisation had to be orchestrated to ensure they contributed to the development of mutually profitable relationships with the right customers.

Improved understanding of the organisational consequences brought both advantages and disadvantages to the discipline. It was good to increase knowledge; however, organisations realised that it was difficult to achieve short-term results with relationship marketing playing an integral role in every aspect of the organisation. Initial enthusiasm in several countries and organisations evaporated. Management ambitions were not realised and clients complained that, as customers, they were being treated shabbily by companies.

> ***Customer satisfaction rates in the US are at an all-time low.***
>
> ***When we talk to people about their life as consumers, we do not hear praise for their so-called corporate partners. Instead, we hear about the confusing, stressful, insensitive, and manipulative marketplace in which they feel trapped***

and victimized . . . Customers cope . . . They tolerate sales clerks who hound them with questions . . . They muddle through the plethora of products that line grocery store shelves . . .

***Source*: Fournier, Dobscha and Mick (1998). Preventing the premature death of relationship marketing, *Harvard Business Review*, January–February, 42–52.**

In several countries and companies CRM might have disappeared completely had it not been for the information technology industry which introduced CRM systems with great promises. Ambitions regarding buyer–seller relations sky-rocketed again and it seemed that previous negative experiences were forgotten within days. The economic climate was prosperous, and visionary people grabbed our attention. Relationship marketing, now named CRM, was again high on the agenda of top management. Technology would enable us to communicate at low costs with large numbers of individual customers, educate them, deliver customised solutions to them, engage and bind them. Customers themselves would play a major role in the transition of product- or market-oriented organisations into customer-oriented ones. Customers would take the lead and would force organisations to build their processes around consumers.

Reality again, however, was less glossy than the initial thoughts. Changing daily routines and structures is not as easy as it seems. The positive economic climate throughout the 1990s changed. But this time it is not appropriate to announce the next 'premature death of relationship marketing'. There is too much at stake. Information technology can enable the dialogue between (large groups) of individual customers and their suppliers in an efficient way, independent of time and place. To some extent, there is recognition of the value of individual customer knowledge. The business case in which the retention of existing customers is more profitable than the continuous acquisition of new ones is still appealing. The idea to increase entry barriers for competition by increasing customer loyalty remains a worthy goal.

The promise of this book

In today's world, most organisations ask, 'What do we want to achieve with CRM, and how?' The period of hype is over; reality is here and experience helps us grow. The need for a serious CRM approach exists. What should our business strategy be? How do we adapt the organisation? How do we translate the CRM business strategy into marketing? How will we build our analytical CRM and enable our processes? Which CRM systems are needed and how are we going to implement them? This book addresses these subjects and examines the entire scope of CRM, including strategy, organisation, marketing and information technology.

The book opens with an introduction to the topic of buyer–seller relations and then addresses the organisational and strategic aspects of CRM. Part II covers marketing aspects of CRM. Part III examines CRM as the domain of database managers and Part IV explores operational CRM – the work area of channel managers. Part V looks at the implementation of CRM systems and concludes with a glimpse into the future.

Old and new experiences are brought together in this book. The lessons of the direct marketer, database managers, project managers, strategists, change masters, Internet ad specialists, and call and contact centres are combined. To achieve a thorough discussion of all aspects of CRM, the book blends together theory and practice to convey a full understanding of the subject.

The target audience

This book is geared to MBA students and undergraduate students in the later years of their study, as well as those attending courses on CRM, direct marketing, relationship marketing, database management or business intelligence. It is also appropriate for graduate students in information management attending courses on CRM and participants in specific CRM/database management courses. Students reading this book should have basic knowledge of marketing management.

Pedagogy

To help reinforce key learning points, each chapter includes the following;

- Questions that the reader should be able to answer after studying the chapter.
- Sections and sub-sections break up the main text to help students digest and retain the information.
- Tables, figures and other illustrative material help the reader grasp the essential facts.
- Boxes throughout the text with practitioner's insights, CRM illustrations and CRM definitions reinforce concepts.
- Case studies provide a basis for class discussion or assessment in depth on a set of issues.
- Review questions provide a basis for self-assessment by the students or revision topics at the end of the programme.

While the book can be read from cover to cover, it has also been structured so that parts can be read independentally from one another. For example, Part III (with the exception of the first and last chapters) on analytical CRM can be omitted from the undergraduate syllabus as this section primarily addresses people with a database management specialisation.

Instructor learning resources

Visit www.pearsoned.co.uk/peelen to access an Instructor's Manual and PowerPoint slides. For the Dutch educational market, in addition to end-of-chapter cases, a case library has been developed. For further information, please e-mail the author at ed.peelen@icsb.nl or e.peelen@nyenrode.nl.

Acknowledgements

I would like to thank many people for their pleasant cooperation and support during the past few years and during the writing of this book. First, I extend thanks to Allison Klein for assisting with the English translation and to Professor Susan Hart at University of Strathclyde, Scotland, for her participation as super-reviewer. Also helpful and pleasant to work with were both the Pearson publishers, Thomas Sigel in the UK office and Vanessa van Kempen in the Benelux office. Thanks also go to editorial assistant Peter Hooper and desk editor Mary Lince. The following reviewers also provided insight and suggestions for this project: Dr Stephen Tagg, University of Strathclyde, Scotland; Caroline Tynan, University of Nottingham, England; and John Oliver, University of Bournemouth, England.

I would also like to mention the initiators of this project, HEO-ICT and the insurance company Centraal Beheer Achmea. I also extend thanks to several of my students, as well as Philip Waalewijn's students who wrote their theses on CRM and were a great help. In particular, I thank Wouter Niks, Wouter van der Schans, Hans Swinkels, Kees Ekelmans and Leontine Brandt. It is Pieter Vijn who introduced me to this subject almost twenty years ago. He, as well as Gerard Wolfs, Cees den Hollander, Jeffrey Berend, Frank Slisser, Rob Beltman, Pauline van Esterik-Plasmeijer, Wojtek Kowalczyk, Wim Kwakernaat and many others have been a great inspiration.

Ed Peelen
Rotterdam/Breukelen
Autumn 2004

About the author

Ed Peelen is Professor of Direct Marketing at the Center for Supply Chain Management and the Executive Management Development Center at Nyenrode University, The Netherlands.

He specialises in direct marketing, customer relationship management, account management and marketing in general. He organises several programmes on these topics at Nyenrode for managers and specialists and is the academic supervisor of several PhD students. He has written fifteen books and numerous managerial and academic journal articles.

Professor Peelen is Chairman of the jury of the CRM Award, on award presented to the company with the best results in the field of CRM. He is an editorial board member of the *Journal of Interactive Marketing* and the *Tijdschrift voor Marketing* as well as a partner in ICSB, marketing and strategy consultants.

He completed his PhD in 1989 at Erasmus Universiteit Rotterdam, on relationship marketing and was one of the first to introduce this topic to The Netherlands.

Publisher's acknowledgements

We are grateful to the following for permission to reproduce copyright material:

Table 2.1 from 'After the Sale is Over' in *Harvard Business Review*, September/October (Levitt, T., 1983), Figure 3.2 from 'Why Satisfied Customers Defect' in *Harvard Business Review*, November/December, pp. 88–100 (Jones, T.O. and Sasser Jr, W., 1995, Boston, MA) Copyright © 1995 by the Harvard Business School Publishing Corporation, Figures 3.3 and 3.4 from *The Loyalty Effect* (Reichheld, F.E., 1996, Boston, MA) Copyright © 1996 by the Harvard Business School Publishing Corporation, Figure 4.3 from 'Putting the Service-Profit Chain to Work' in *Harvard Business Review*, March–April, pp. 164–174 (Heskett *et al.*, 1994) Copyright © 1994 by the Harvard Business School Publishing Corporation and Tables 14.2, 14.3 and 14.4 *Customer Equity: Building and managing relationships as valuable assets* (Blattberg, R.C., Getz, G. and Thomas, J.S., 2000, Boston, MA) Copyright © 2000 by the Harvard Business School Publishing Corporation, all reprinted by permission of the Harvard Business School Publishing Corporation; Figure 7.3 from 'Customizing Customization', *Sloan Management Review*, Autumn, pp. 21–29 (Lampel, J. and Mintzberg, H., 1996). Copyright 1996 by Massachusetts Institute of Technology. All rights reserved. Distributed by Tribune Media Services; Figure 8.4 from *The relation oriented organization*, Universiteit Nyenrode, Beukelen (Peelen, E., 1989); Figures 9.1 and 9.2 from *Mentality: Sociographics in Marketing*, from the Motivaction International BV website www.motivaction.nl (Sprangenberg, F. & Liebregts, L., 1999); Tables 11.1 and 11.3 from *Optimal Database Marketing, Strategy, Development and Data Mining* (Drozdenko, R.G. & Drake, P.D., 2002) © 2002 by Sage Publications, Inc., reprinted by permission of Sage Publications, Inc.; Table 11.2 from *Elements of Direct Marketing* (Baier, 1983), reproduced with permission of the McGraw-Hill Companies; Figure 11.2 from *CHAID Analysis for a discounter*, ICSB, Rotterdam (Peelen, E., 2002); Figure 11.3 from 'CART: A recent advance in tree-structured list segmentation methodology', *Journal of Direct Marketing*, Vol 5, No 1, pp. 35–47 (Thrasher, R.P., 1991) and Figure 17.2 from *Sell it by mail, making your product the one way they buy* (Lumley, J.E.A., 1986), © John Wiley & Sons, Inc., used by permission of John Wiley & Sons, Inc.; Figure 13.1 from *Performance Selling*, pp. 142–145 (Mertens, F. and Heilijgers, B., 2002) with permission from the authors; Table 14.1 from *Direct Marketing Management* (Roberts, M.L. and Berger P.D., 1999) available for download at www.marylouroberts.info; Figure IV.1 used with the permission of QCi Assessment Ltd; Figure 15.2 used with the permission of Belloni Business Consultancy Contact Centers B.V.; Figure 16.1 used with the permission of Capgemini Nederland B.V.; Figure 17.1 from *Het direct mail pack* (Zuiderduin, J., 2003) used with the permission of Tias Business School.

We are grateful to the Financial Times Limited for permission to reprint the following material:

Reaping the benefits of customer insight, FT.com, © *Financial Times*, 8 June 2004.

We are grateful to the following for permission to use copyright material:

Ville Saarikoski for Secrets of success for going mobile, from FT.com, *The Financial Times Limited*, 9 June 2004, © Ville Saarikoski; Kluwer B.V. for an extract from the 'Interview with Gerard Wolfs' published in *Tijdschrift voor Marketing* 2001, and an extract from 'Shell and CRM: One database for 20 million customers' published in *Tijdschrift voor Marketing* April 2004; The Independent for an extract from the article 'Airlines told to end price discrimination' by Stephen Castle published in *The Independent* on 8th June 2004 © The Independent; Human Inference Enterprise B.V. for an extract from 'Euro 2000 Case Study' published in *Memo* Volume 13, No. 3; and The Institute of Direct Marketing for an extract from 'Garnier – the beauty bank, IDM Business Performance Award 2003' and an extract from 'Pampers, IDM Business Performance Award 2002', published on www.theidm/bpa.

In some instances we have been unable to trace the owners of copyright material, and we would appreciate any information that would enable us to do so.

1

Introduction

CRM has far-reaching implications for organisations. A great deal of experience has been gained when it comes to the formulation and implementation of CRM strategies, but we still have a long way to go in travelling along this learning curve. Acknowledging this provides reason enough to examine further in this book all aspects of CRM and to share the experiences and research results we have obtained.

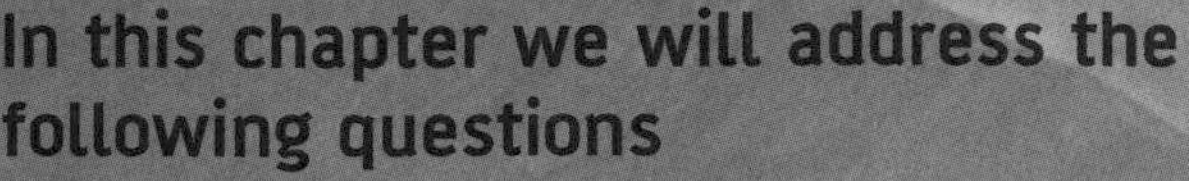

In this chapter we will address the following questions

- What is the meaning of customer relationship management (CRM)?
- What is CRM as a business strategy?
- What are the elements of CRM?
- What are CRM processes and systems?
- What influences the success of CRM?

Practitioner's insight

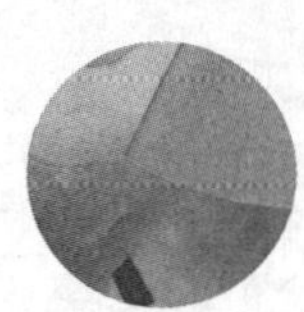

Customer relationship management (CRM) is, or at least appears to be, due to the efforts of the information technology (IT) industry, a topic that is high on the agenda of many general, commercial and IT managers. Great promises were made in the late 1990s. Thanks to the deployment of information and communication technology, organisations would become accessible to large groups of customers: people who companies would get to know individually, and whose individual needs could be served. Permanent relationships could be developed with these customers for a relatively low price, and these could function as barriers to keep out the competition: customers would become so loyal to the organisation that they would not consider switching to another supplier. Under these circumstances, it should naturally also be possible to perform better financially. Now, at the start of the twenty-first century, we are discovering that achieving success with CRM is more difficult than we had expected. The promises made have yet to be fulfilled. The realisation of an infrastructure that enables customer and supplier to communicate with one another, freed from the constraints of place and time, remains a formidable challenge. Increasing customer knowledge by recording the right data in databases, updating them, enriching them and using them appears to be no small task either. Formulating and implementing a marketing strategy that is aimed at the development of long-lasting relationships with customers is new to many. The strategy that is most suitable will have to be discovered through trial and error. Gradually, we finally also discover that CRM requires organisational adjustments; a customer-oriented organisation will have to be created which incorporates the appropriate culture, structure and procedures.

1.1 Definition

In spite of the progress that is being made, there is still some confusion about the meaning and implications of CRM. In order to illustrate the differences in views, we will present two extreme and two 'standard' definitions.

One of these definitions originates from the Metagroep, which, in 2000, defined CRM as 'the automation of horizontally integrated business processes involving front office customer contact points (marketing, sales, service and support) via multiple, interconnected delivery channels'. In this description, CRM is positioned in the 'IT corner'. Technology facilitates or makes customer contact possible between employees from different departments via the Internet, telephone and the 'face-to-face' channel. On the Internet, technology essentially replaces people, and a human–machine interaction arises. In telephone and face-to-face contact, IT plays a more supportive role and makes sure that the supplier's employees are in a better position to help the customer.

According to this definition, a company is engaged in CRM if it ensures, for example, that customers are recognised during contact via the Internet, by telephone or personal contact. A customer who orders a book on the Internet from an online bookstore may afterwards contact this supplier by telephone to obtain additional information. The operator can check the computer system and see that this purchase has been completed, plus has access to additional information on the delivery, the product, payment, etc. The customer does not need to provide his or her entire contact history; the dialogue may proceed without obstacles because the delivery channels have been connected with one another – perhaps even in 'real time'.

An entirely different definition suggests that CRM is 'a process that addresses all aspects of identifying customers, creating customer knowledge, building customer relationships, and shaping their perceptions of the organisation and its products'. The role of technology is not even mentioned in this definition. CRM is still referred to as a process, or rather a sequence of activities; however, this definition does not specifically state that IT is necessary to perform these activities. At the same time, this definition requires that more attention be paid to the customer and the goal one hopes to achieve *vis-à-vis* the customer. We would like to get to know the customer and develop a relationship with him or her: we are not only interested in closing a deal. We feel it is important that the customer's and supplier's interest in one another covers a longer period of time than simply the moment of the transaction, and that this interest also goes deeper than the purchase and sale. At any rate, we consider it important for the customer to get an impression of the company as a whole and the products it manufactures and for the supplier to get to know the customer more as a person rather than just as a buyer.

With this definition, we examine in more detail the reasons why the online bookstore should implement the 'interconnected delivery channels'. It is important here for the communication travelling through the various channels to be recorded in databases, thus allowing us to identify customers and get to know them. We can analyse how customers differ from one another. This essentially involves insights which may be used in order to better cater to customers' wishes. Customers may be given buying recommendations; a certain book by a certain author will be recommended because it appears that many customers with a similar profile were also interested in that particular title. The customer may even look up information to find what the other customers thought about that title, receive additional background information on the writer, and so forth. And, should they prefer to be spared from receiving these types of recommendations, they may always notify the supplier of this fact; the bookstore will not contact them without permission. Through this individualised and proactive approach, customers are afforded a different impression of the organisation. The image is created that they are recognised as a customer and thus respected, but mostly that they will receive special attention and care.

The Gartner group's definition from 2004 goes a step further. This research agency describes CRM as 'an IT enabled business strategy, the outcomes of which optimise profitability, revenue and customer satisfaction by organising around customer segments, fostering customer-satisfying behaviours and implementing customer-centric processes'. In comparison with the previous definition, CRM is not postulated as a process but instead as a *business* strategy. The intention that organisations have in mind for CRM is made explicit: on the one hand, the goal is to increase revenue and profit, and on the other, it is to improve customer satisfaction. The road which must be travelled in order to achieve this goal is also the subject of attention. In doing so, the achievement of the maximum amount of customer satisfaction may not occur at the expense of efficiency, and the deployment of technology and people must go hand-in-hand.

If we are to project this definition onto our example, then we will have to delve deeper into the reasons why we have built the network of channels and what we hope to achieve by doing so. Let's say that the online bookstore would like to expand its availability for customers. The bookstore is interested in creating a delivery channel that is available 24/7 (24 hours a day, 7 days a week). Customers may contact it from the comfort of their own homes, or from any other location. Customers will be recognised and they are given the opportunity to help themselves in an efficient manner. Or they will be served personally by qualified and motivated personnel who are available to communicate with the customer and also make optimum use of the technology. The underlying strategy of the bookstore is to develop a long-term mutually profitable relationship with the customer. The goal is to encourage the customer to make its future purchases from this store and to reduce the share of purchases being made from the competition. Due to the fact that individual customer knowledge is being accumulated, it will have to be more difficult for the competition to be able to offer a similar proposal.

Finally, the most sweeping definition of CRM is the one provided by Regis McKenna, who has adapted the concept of 'real time marketing' for these purposes. He recognises that CRM targets the building of an infrastructure which may be used to develop long-term customer–supplier relationships. However, at the same time, he emphasises that as a result of this infrastructure, the walls between company and customer are torn down. Whereas it was once impossible to enter the other's domain at one's own convenience, nowadays this is a great deal easier. On the one hand, customers are able to have a look into the records to determine whether or not a specific product is in stock, track the status of the delivery, and read other buyers' opinions of the product. They may be involved as a 'lead user' in the development of new products and share confidential information. They obtain access to areas of the company which were previously hidden and which could, at the very most, only be entered or accessed under supervision and after having made an appointment. Viewed from the other side, it becomes much easier for suppliers to gather information from customers and to contact them. In other words, customer and supplier activities are integrated with one another. The privacy of both parties may easily be violated and both will have to consider carefully what is and what is not desirable in this area. On the other hand, at the same time it will be possible to cater to one another's wishes quickly, in 'real time'.

In this book, we subscribe to Gartner's definitions and concur with McKenna's forward-looking vision. As McKenna so aptly puts it, as organisations progress in the implementation of the infrastructure, people will automatically start to discover that this not only requires a new (marketing) strategy, but actually calls for an adjustment in the organisation itself. Customer and company move closer to one another; each will have to react to and anticipate the other's actions more directly. Each will have to exercise more openness and provide insight into one another's affairs. Organisations will have to adjust their cultures and will have to learn how to operate in a more customer-oriented manner. Processes will have to be of high quality because customers will now be 'having a look in the supplier's kitchen', defects or irregularities will quickly be discovered and companies will not want to allow the potential advantages of long-term customer–supplier relationships to slip through their fingers. What is perhaps even wiser is not to discover the true implications of the new infrastructure along the way or after the fact, but to formulate a vision and strategy at the very outset which points the way for the entire CRM programme. This way, investments in systems, databases, strategy and organisational adjustments which ultimately fail to be profitable may be prevented. In short, it is preferable for CRM to be regarded as a business strategy from the start, one that is aimed towards developing long-term, mutually profitable, individual customer–supplier relationships and is based on an IT infrastructure to be developed, one that enables well-defined and controlled processes, and places capable personnel in a position to function optimally.

1.2 CRM as a business strategy

CRM is a business strategy and therefore more than a functional strategy alone. It affects the organisation as a whole: marketing, IT, service, logistics, finance, production and development, HR, management, etc. The CRM strategy will have to provide direction to each department or employee that maintains contact with customers. The employees' and managers' customer-oriented approach will have to improve. However, the back office, whose task it is to fulfil the promises made by the front office, will ultimately have to learn to cater for individual customers. Processes will have to become well defined, and will have to be executed flawlessly and efficiently, because after all, the customers are 'watching'. The fact that IT plays a role here goes without saying and requires no further explanation. These individuals must build the new 'infrastructure', but will also have to realise that it is the strategy and not the technology that is a determining factor during the design of the CRM programme.

The question is whether or not a CRM strategy is suitable for every company and whether or not there is an unequivocal CRM strategy to be defined. Is it possible for a bank, an energy distribution company, a public transport company, a small-scale or large-scale retailer, a restaurant and a tax authority to implement successfully *one* of the many or the *only* CRM strategy? Or is a CRM strategy only recommended for certain organisations in certain market situations? The opinions on this topic are extremely varied (Peelen, 1999; Hoekstra, 2001).

In practice, when it comes to CRM, many companies' strategies focus on increasing efficiency and reliability. For example, self-service grants customers continuous access, and the back office also remains spared from all sorts of customer questions. These days, train passengers look up their own train schedules, and taxpayers can file their returns electronically. This type of system is friendlier, but also more efficient. In order to realise self-service with a high level of quality, the underlying processes – such as the booking of and delivery of tickets, receipt of payment and processing of the tax return – will have to be perfectly defined and controlled. An experienced person with the necessary talent for improvisation to compensate for errors in the system, or to make adjustments to the process in order to be able to satisfy varying customer needs, is not available.

This is only one of many examples which demonstrate that CRM can be focused on the achievement of 'operational excellence': excellent, efficient processes must result in satisfied customers and a competitive advantage.

However, it is primarily researchers who justifiably raise for discussion the issue of whether this involves the *true* CRM strategy. Does a strategy which focuses on the achievement of operational excellence deserve the designation 'customer relationship management'? It is reasonable to expect that a business/corporate strategy whose goal is the development of long-term, mutually profitable customer–supplier relationships, would place the customer in a more central position. Who is this customer and what does he or she want? What types of solutions, not which products or services, should the organisation provide to make the customer more successful or satisfied? How can the organisaton develop and deliver these, together with the customer?

Prior to the 'information age', this was all defined as relationship marketing and account management and it would seem strange suddenly to deviate from all of that now.

In this book, we take a rather 'strict' approach and do justice to history by proposing that as a business strategy, CRM's goal is a so-called customer intimacy. The development of relationships requires that both parties get to know one another, and help, trust and make a commitment to one another for the long term. By working together in this way, both parties are capable of achieving lasting success in a competitive environment.

We do not wish to imply in any way here that a strategy geared towards the achievement of operationally excellent processes is unsuitable. It could be a quite sensible strategy, the realisation of which is, for a large part, dependent upon the use of the same IT systems as those used for a CRM strategy. However, we do not agree with the idea of equating the application of the technology and the definition of processes that go along with it to a CRM strategy. We would also prefer not to rule out the fact that companies, once they have reached the stage of operational excellence, might get ambitions when it comes to achieving customer intimacy. For them a new era will begin – one in which customers may be served in a reliable and efficient manner. The back office is perfect! The current system also offers the opportunity to further expand customer knowledge and to develop a broader differentiation in the customer approach. In addition, the organisation is capable of supplying customisation. In other words, the time has come when the supplier can fulfil the promise of *customer intimacy*.

1.3 Elements of CRM

The realisation of a CRM strategy depends on a number of components or competencies. Perhaps the most obvious competency is related to the ability to create the infrastructure referred to by McKenna, which makes it possible for customer and supplier to recognise one another and to be able to interact in 'real-time'. However, in this book we do not wish to place priority on this. After all, it is not the technology but the business strategy which must lead or provide guidance. The manner in which we aim to achieve a lasting competitive advantage in our industry is the primary matter of importance.

The four cornerstones of CRM which must be mentioned first are:

1 Customer knowledge.

2 Relationship strategy.

3 Communication.

4 The individual value proposition.

Customer knowledge

Knowledge of the individual customer is essential in order, ultimately, to develop a long-term relationship and to supply customisation. Customers, but also prospects, must be identifiable; it has to be possible to determine who someone is. Is that John, Peter or Pauline on the other side of the proverbial counter? At the same time, the customer's profile must also be known. What has the customer purchased, how does he or she prefer to communicate and how may he or she be characterised further? Without this type of knowledge, it would be unthinkable to attempt to build a long-term relationship with the customer.

Companies must develop the competency or capability to develop this type of individual customer knowledge for a large number of customers. Databases will have to be filled with correct and current data which will be transformed by analyses into individual customer information. Individual customer data will have to be supplemented by the outcomes of anonymous (qualitative) market research so that a more complete image of the customer may be created. In the expansion of the customer information, economic considerations and manageability factors will have to play an important role. Although it is actually quite interesting to gather as much data and obtain as much customer information as possible, one must not lose sight of the ultimate goal. The aim is still to develop long-term relationships that are mutually profitable. The information must result in companies being better able to help customers on time, in a more targeted manner, and with more appropriate solutions. Data that do not contribute to the achievement of this goal are not worth registering and storing.

Relationship strategy

The individual customer information must be used to develop a long-lasting customer–supplier relationship. In other words, a marketing or other type of strategy must be implemented which truly differs from a strategy which merely focuses on the stimulation of transactions and thus requires other competencies. Companies that concentrate on the stimulation of sales become proficient in the art of 'seduction' (Levitt, 1983). They have a certain means of communication, a short-term horizon and a limited interest in the customer. They measure their success by their sales and the number of completed transactions. Market share represents a very important criterion for success. On the other hand, organisations with a relationship strategy in place have a longer-term horizon, 'tell' and 'listen' more than they 'sell', and have a broader and deeper interest in the right customers. Their interest in individual customers does not end at the moment the transaction is completed. On the contrary, the purchase only marks the beginning of the relationship in which trust and commitment must grow. The supplier has also traced out the contours of a policy necessary to further develop this relationship with the customers.

Communication

In the communication between customer and supplier, the relationship strategy will have to prove itself to a great extent. Is the supplier capable of carrying on a dialogue with individual customers? On the surface, it may seem like a simple task, yet every consumer who recalls experiences with suppliers will quickly arrive at the conclusion that the quality of conversation generally taking place between customer and supplier is somewhat basic. It consists primarily of the most urgently necessary functional remarks and is not very spontaneous in nature. And those moments which do occur that are favourable to engaging in a dialogue of any true substance often end up being rather disappointing. For example, it suddenly appears to be very difficult to respond to a simple request for information or to remedy a complaint because in order to do this, one must deviate from the prescribed procedures, and the computer system will not accommodate such deviation.

Many companies have no experience in carrying on a dialogue of any substance. The situation becomes even more complicated if we involve the role of information and communication technology. A so-called multichannel environment or better yet, a network of communication channels, must be developed through which it is possible to communicate 'anywhere, any time, any place'. Even while walking through town, a customer must be capable of finding a financial institution using his or her mobile telephone in order to consider the available options for a personal loan. The customer is on the brink of making a major purchase and would first like certainty about the financing of this purchase. After having received an initial confirmation by telephone from the credit provider, the customer would like to have a look at a few things on the Internet from home. At the point that the customer still has unanswered questions, he would like to establish contact by phone once again in order to receive further information. Should certain factors still remain unclear, he will most likely want to arrange a face-to-face meeting with an adviser. A dialogue will take place, hopefully without repetition and reiteration of the identification ritual: who are you and what would you like? Shifts are made between the various channels and the transitions between them appear to proceed smoothly. The conversation takes place, independent of time and location.

The individual value proposition

An organisation that takes the initiative to get to know an individual customer, to develop a relationship with him or her, and to carry on a dialogue with him or her really cannot avoid also offering these customers an individual proposition. The physical product, service, and also the price are all adapted to the individual circumstances. The organisation has built up the capability to supply customisation in one form or another. Together with the customer, for example, the company may design his or her ideal product. The company will then have an efficient method of producing this design; for instance, the custom product might be composed from standard modules produced on a large scale and for which 'only' the assembly needs to be flexible. Apart from the physical product, in interaction with the customer, the service may also be geared towards his or her specific wishes, as may the price, naturally. The supplier must not allow opportunities to implement revenue management pass him by. Adapting the price to the value that the proposition represents for an individual customer at a certain time and at a certain location offers the supplier an interesting prospect for increasing sales and profits.

One of the pitfalls involved in the development of the *customised propositions* is that companies create a complexity which is too large. An attempt is made to combine this large-scale aspect with flexibility. Companies do not wish to sacrifice the benefits associated with economies of scale; the advantage of the low costs and the consistent and high level of quality are vital in order to rise above the competition in any way with standard products. The result is that, in many cases, a great deal of investment must be made in order to make the production machines flexible: to be able to switch from one product to the next and incur very few costs in the process. However, we have learned in practice that operating in this manner sometimes results in the creation of a great deal of complexity that is difficult to control. Van Asseldonk (1998) describes just such an outcome in a physical distribution operation for a retailer. This particular retailer had developed a very complex operating system for the loading and route planning of delivery lorries. Many of the lorries had to find their way to the branches and in order to guarantee regular and timely delivery of goods, the lorries had to be loaded with colourful packages of diverse goods in small quantities. The cargo had to be delivered to different destinations and therefore had to be loaded into the lorries in the correct sequence. In order to steer the whole operation in the right direction, an elaborate system was developed which was ultimately only barely controllable. A complexity had been created that, upon further consideration, was deemed to be completely unnecessary. Ultimately there were just as many vehicles on the road as there were branches, and a very simple solution became obvious: a lorry for each branch with its own simple operating system.

The development of these four competencies must occur in a step-by-step, balanced manner. It is not desirable for one of the four to move ahead of the others in its development. The unavoidable situation then arises in which too much is invested in one of the sub-elements; the expected yield – financial as well as in terms of activity – will fail to materialise and frustration will develop. The creation of the CRM strategy will be delayed and in this unfortunate scenario, top management's commitment to the CRM strategy falls away and a modified strategy is likely to materialise.

1.4 CRM processes and systems

In many situations, the achievement of the four competencies is to a great extent dependent on IT. The system must make it possible for customer knowledge to be developed in an efficient manner, for the relationship strategy to be implemented, for a dialogue to be conducted, and for customisation to be supplied.

It is only in situations in which relationships must be maintained with a small number of customers, the organisation is small and manageable, and each of the customers represents sufficient value to justify an individual approach that CRM may be realised without an elaborate IT system. This involves idyllic situations in which the guild master still knows his customers personally and maintains relationships with them, both professionally as well as socially, through face-to-face contact. He still makes each product to measure and with craftsmanship.

As soon as relationships must be maintained with a larger group of customers, a portion of which represents a low value to the supplier, then the use of IT becomes inevitable. This might only be because some of the modern-day customers prefer to communicate with the supplier through modern means.

The construction of the appropriate IT system presents a real challenge. Many companies first find themselves confronted with what is known as a 'legacy' problem: a large part of their computer system is outdated and, above all, developed to fulfil a goal other than that of implementing the CRM strategy. The system may have been designed to maintain product administrations: for example, who is carrying which type of insurance, who has paid and who must receive an allowance as a result of submitted and approved expense reports. The transactions entered for the data are processed in 'batches'; during the day various people input the changes into the system and at night the computer incorporates them into the files. These are systems in which customers are difficult to identify. It is not easy to determine which different members of a household have purchased which different products over the years. In order to find this out, an extensive search will have to be performed. The results of this 'query' are, however, questionable; the probability is actually rather high that customers are registered in a variety of ways and that it is not known which persons should be considered to be part of a certain household.

Among other things, the systems which are developed specifically for the creation of the CRM strategy involve the Internet as a channel, the call centre and sales information systems for account managers and sales personnel. Usually these systems are developed independently of one another and it is a challenge now to link them together. Linking is the only way to integrate channels, which is necessary in order for customer and supplier to conduct an ongoing dialogue with one another independent of the aspects of place and time.

This dialogue will only be satisfying if the front office is linked to the back office. The front office with its channels of communication must be linked to the product administration in the back office: for example, in order to be able to supply product information, to take out insurance policies, and to distribute allowances. Systems which vary in age and do not dovetail well with one another must be linked. In many cases, this cannot be done without installing a middle layer: the 'middleware' or midoffice. This can exist of one or several data warehouses in which data involving customers and prospects are compiled from different databases. For customers and prospects, for instance, this may be used to determine who they are, how they have been communicating, and which transactions they have performed.

The midoffice functions act not only as a binder, but also as a buffer ensuring that the safety and stability of the entire system remain intact. The prevention of fraud remains possible, as does keeping the system 'on air'. This is possible because many users are prevented from gaining 'real-time' access to a system that was not built for this purpose and which contains data critical to the company.

The integration of the front and rear sections is a 'moment of truth' for many companies. Previously, one had people to fall back on as the binder between the front and back offices. If a customer asked a question which deviated from the standard, the employee involved was able to come up with a solution thanks to his or her talent for improvisation. However, system integration has reduced the role of the human element in this respect. Processes involved in acquisition, ordering, payment, remittance, complaints, information queries, etc. will have to be described perfectly and give the customer what he wants. The process descriptions form the input for the IT systems to be developed; these are the processes which are automated and supported by the CRM systems.

1.5 Entrance, applications and success of CRM

The term 'CRM' seems to be new and the concept witnessed only in the last five years. After all, it is the software suppliers that brought the concept to life through marketing efforts designed to stimulate demand for their solutions. In terms of its actual content, CRM obviously involves a much older principle. As long as companies have been in existence, customer–supplier relationships have been the goal of a number of them, at the very least. The old guild masters knew their customers and made sure that they received customised products. They engaged in CRM in an authentic manner. Perhaps it was due to the Industrial Revolution that the distance between producer and consumer grew and the interest in CRM within consumer markets dissipated, but during those times there were always small-scale and specialised companies which did maintain close relationships with their customers. Prime examples include the fresh bakery, the butcher, the handyman, the hairdresser, the automobile garage, the doctor and so forth.

The attention for individual customer–supplier relationships began to grow in the late 1980s and early 1990s. The concept of relationship marketing began to gain in popularity and was advanced as an alternative to transaction marketing. The awareness grew that marketing literature had dedicated a great deal of attention in previous years to the stimulation of sales transactions and less to the development of customer–supplier relationships (Arndt, 1979). At the same time, an analysis proved that a large number of cooperative relationships between customer and supplier are of a long-term nature. Knowledge of the dynamic in relationships and the manner in which parties influence one another in a relationship could thus often be more effective than the simple stimulation of sales alone.

In several European countries, relationship marketing was nonetheless incapable of holding companies' attention. Too many companies encountered problems in the implementation of relationship marketing. Individual knowledge of customers was lacking and the costs of a differentiated customer approach were perceived to be too high. In addition, there was doubt on the part of management regarding the yield produced by relationship marketing. Keeping customers and developing a relationship with them does not yield its first actual return until some point in the future, and the acquisition of a customer must be viewed as an investment. It was precisely during a period in which the economy experienced a downturn that people were less willing to listen to or invest in this type of strategy.

However, once the economy began to rally, relationship marketing was given a second chance. Calculations of customer values had since been made and had demonstrated that keeping customers was more profitable than simply attracting them. The calculations performed by Frederick E. Reichheld (1995) in particular resounded well, paving the way for relationship marketing. At the same time, during this period of revitalisation, the realisation had sunk in that relationship marketing would have far-reaching organisational consequences. The pursuit of developing individual customer–supplier relationships requires customer-oriented instead of product-oriented enterprises. The position of the so-called customer managers would improve whereas that of product managers would be more likely to erode. Managers and employees would have to be judged on the basis of other standards than those used in the past. The crux of the matter was no longer selling as many newly developed products as possible, but keeping customers and increasing customer satisfaction.

The current IT applications for CRM also emerged at the same time that relationship marketing resurged. Solutions for call centres, Internet and websites, e-commerce, the data warehouse, campaign management and so forth all developed and spread throughout the market among users.

Experiences with these systems were not always positive. According to diverse sources, the percentage of successful CRM 'projects' is estimated at just over 30 per cent (Hoekstra, 2001). This is not entirely surprising. CRM is a strategy that affects the entire company. Product-oriented organisations will have to transform themselves into customer-oriented ones. Investments will have to be made in an infrastructure that makes it possible to communicate with customers through a variety of channels. Organisations will have to learn how to conduct a dialogue with these customers. They will need to develop individual customer knowledge and formulate a marketing strategy that targets the development of the relationship instead of the stimulation of transactions. CRM is more than just the sum of a number of innovative IT projects and will also have to be approached as such. Companies will have to implement the necessary changes in a well-balanced manner and will need to grow into a relationship-oriented organisation, step by step, provided this fits within their overall strategy. Patience is a prerequisite. It shouldn't surprise us to hear that the management of a certain company indicates that it actually took the first steps in the area of CRM back in 1990, and is convinced that it still has a long way to go before implementation is complete. But these are years that have certainly not been wasted. On the contrary, such good groundwork was laid during that period that the company in question, Siemens, even won the 2001 CRM Award.

In general terms, it would be wrong to use the current disappointing examples of CRM as a reason to recommend that companies forgo choosing and implementing CRM as a business strategy. It may be viewed as a positive development that the period has now ended in which CRM had almost reached 'hype' proportions and was desired by everyone, yet it would also be going too far to bid CRM farewell at this point. What is much more important is to recognise the true meaning of the strategy and its implementation so that companies may once again take up the old adage 'doing the right things right'.

1.6 Contents of this book

The objective of this book is to contribute to the gaining of insight into CRM so that a CRM strategy is chosen in the appropriate situations and implemented efficiently and successfully. In order to accomplish this, the next chapter is dedicated to customer–supplier relationships; after all, these relationships form the core of CRM. These relationships and how they develop will also be examined from a social-psychological angle.

Part I starts in Chapter 2 with the treatment of these customer–supplier relationships and then focuses on the consequences of CRM for the business strategy and the organisation. In Chapter 3, the CRM strategy is described as a customer intimacy strategy, which is one of Treacy and Wiersema's (1996) three strategies. The conditions under which this strategy may be chosen and the advantages which are associated with this strategy are also examined. Chapter 4 discusses the organisational consequences of CRM. The customer-oriented organisation and the corresponding culture are also studied. An analysis is performed demonstrating how 'customer ownership' may be established and how the deployment of resources for customers may be orchestrated within the organisation.

In Part II of the book, the focus is on the marketing aspects of CRM. Chapters 5 through to 8 illustrate the concepts of customer knowledge, communication in a multi-channel environment, offering and achieving an individual value proposition, and formulating a relationship strategy. What would we ultimately like to know about customers and to what extent is it useful to invest in this knowledge? How can we make the specific dialogue with customers meaningful, independent of time and place? How can we individualise the products offered to customers, while still retaining economies of scale and profit margins? And how will we ultimately need to develop the relationship with the right customers, step by step? These main questions will be addressed in Part III of the book. There will be less focus on *how* we accumulate the customer knowledge, conduct the dialogue and so forth. We consider it more important first to address the marketing-related issues so that we may obtain a clear view of what we intend to accomplish with CRM in the market. In this way, we can prevent technology from dominating the implementation of CRM.

In Parts III and IV of the book, the attention shifts from the marketing to the information-related topics. In Part III, what is known as analytical CRM will be examined first. Analytical CRM concentrates on the creation of an unambiguous image of the customer. This involves the segmentation and profiling of customers, identifying customers' needs, selecting interested parties in cross-sell activities, predicting customer churn, customers' reactions to marketing promotions, and customers' value to the organisation. Part IV will also focus on the tools provided by IT systems which aid in solving these types of problems. One example is data mining.

Operational CRM is the central topic in Part IV. We zoom in on one of the four marketing aspects, namely marketing communication and the contact cycle which represent the heart of operational CRM. How do we ensure that we develop customer traffic, interest and inform customers, convince them to make a purchase, complete transactions and get customers to commit? How should we implement the IT system to achieve what we have devised in Part III? Three separate chapters will be dedicated to the tools of the telephone, Internet and e-mail.

Part V deals with the implementation of the CRM strategy. Chapter 18 considers what the different CRM systems are, and how we choose a CRM supplier. In the next chapter in this part, Chapter 19, we discuss the implementation of CRM.

The book is concluded in Chapter 20 with a glance into the future. How will the creation of the new communication infrastructure change the traditional division of roles between customer and supplier? Will we succeed in controlling technology or will technology control us? When the traditional borderlines between producer and consumer fade, how will topics such as privacy and information property be approached and resolved? The vision of leading experts on these topics will be presented and used to determine the direction CRM will take in its development. After all, it is an illusion to assume that the end of the formulation and implementation of CRM is already in sight. It is a continuous process.

1.7 Conclusion

At the end of the 1990s, CRM ended up high on the agenda of many a top manager, thanks to the marketing efforts of software companies, as well as other factors. Their IT systems enable companies to interact with large groups of customers on an individual basis and at a relatively low cost. As a result, companies may accumulate individual customer knowledge which they may use in offering customised solutions and in developing long-lasting, mutually profitable relationships. On the one hand, these solutions improve the operational excellence of organisations' front offices, and on the other, they offer the potential to develop a long-lasting relationship with customers. To date, companies' experiences with CRM are somewhat disappointing, and this may be for a variety of reasons. Too many CRM initiatives are still dominated by technology, and the strategic and organisational aspects of CRM tend to fall by the wayside. Insufficient attention is focused on the interpretation of the marketing strategy: who are the right customers and what do they want, how do we conduct a meaningful dialogue with them, and offer them what they want? And how do we develop a relationship with them? On the other hand, too much energy is invested in the creation of the communication infrastructure and the orchestration of the dialogue with the aid of IT. The objective of this book is to expand the insight into CRM and to deepen it so that, for the right companies, CRM will grow and blossom to become a system of 'doing the right things right'.

Case study

We have got a huge success on our hands

Cristina Zanchi, CRM director KLM

Despite difficult market circumstances the number of KLM Flying Dutchmen (FD) members grew in a little less than six months by 20 per cent; the number of e-mail addresses of FD members tripled. This triumph was the reason for KLM winning the Gartner CRM Excellence Award 2004. CRM director Cristina Zanchi loves to show these glorious figures, especially to Air France. The two companies share the same CRM vision and that opens a window of opportunity for the future. 'I am so impatient because I have the evidence of a huge success in my hands.'

Zanchi: 'The award is a recognition for our team. I really pushed them. There are few airlines that are so focused on CRM – Continental, Lufthansa and Southwest Airlines make good progress – and there is certainly no airline that implemented CRM the way we did it. I wanted to leap forward; speed these days is as important as quality. And, yes, I am an impatient person.' This personality trait of the Italian is her greatest strength. 'If people think something is too complex, they slow down. Some people warned me of a mission impossible. Why would KLM pursue CRM while all flights are full? Well, then I learned to say: the chairs of Sabena and Swiss Air were also occupied, but see what happened.

If you cannot enlarge your capacity you should think of another solution. You can increase the revenues per customer and that is something you achieve when you utilise your customer insight to improve the service. In interaction with customers you intensify the customer experience and therefore also the turnover.'

Delay

The reason why many airlines postpone CRM is clear to Cristina Zanchi. CRM requires large investments and the current margins in the airline industry are low. In the meantime the financial effects of CRM are vague. Several years ago KLM also withdrew a CRM initiative. 'In 1997 KLM performed a very valuable CRM study, but the system never got implemented then. CRM-software was much more expensive then and probably the organisation was not up to it.'

But between 1997 and 2002 – the year the first building block of an integral CRM vision was constructed – the airline industry changed dramatically. Competition is heavy. 'Internally, I had a good reason to sell CRM as a way to distinguish ourselves. As each airline offers a seat, staff and service for a price, it became our ambition to differentiate ourselves on emotional elements. We wanted to realise our positioning of reliability and comfort with a personal touch.'

The ambition of Zanchi to implement CRM quickly seems to contradict the opinion of many that CRM implementation above all requires a steady approach. But do not confuse this eagerness with a lack of propriety. In Zanchi's approach hard facts play a crucial role. From the beginning she involved financial management and asked for frequent reports. Transparency is key to success and at KLM's headquarters there is a panel the size of a man, showing all key indicators. Little planes mark the status and target: below target – on target – above target. 'To get an overview of CRM in one shot is impossible. It was my intention to split up our plan in pieces; a plan in three phases – change management, customer database and campaign management – with underlying steps. Phase one is ended and we are far beyond the start of phase two now. Almost with one snap of my finger I can show you the total overview, the results we realised and the plans we have for 2005 and 2006.'

CRM targets are defined as a sort of acronym: CARE, Customer acquisition, Activation, Retention and Extension. The entire KLM organisation is organised around these objectives; everyone has his target. From August 2003 onwards KLM applied the first instruments of E.piphany's CRM suite. The centralised customer database became operational in December 2003. The software company presented a solution that was as ingenious as it was simple: build a software layer above the current systems – ranging from booking, checking-in to customer complaint handling – and import the data you need to fill your virtual customer model. As a consequence employees will not only see the check-in data on their screen, but also directly get information about past customer behaviour and preferences.

Zanchi: 'The turnaround in airline marketing is that we do not sell flights any more, but processes. We sell lounges, gates, websites, seat environments . . . We need to understand our customers and their wishes. The database allows us to get a complete view, no matter if it is about the lounge or about onboard facilities – real time at the end of this year. A simple example. Among our Flying Dutchman members there are several people with a height of 1.95–2.05 metres. Every time they make a reservation they have to ask for a seat with additional space. Why can an airline not remember this? Or, why would you not reassure a customer with a bad luggage experience during check-in that his baggage has been checked-in properly? KLM check-in stewards will get a signal on their screen that the customer previously had a problem and needs reassurance. The screen will give indications on the way to start a dialogue. Customer satisfaction has risen sharply since we give customers this type of attention.'

Incubation

KLM's next step is to identify individual customers and customer wishes to introduce one-to-one marketing. Mass marketing through television has been replaced by focused 'dialogue marketing' in which use is made of customer profiles. Flying Dutchman members are categorised based upon age, customer profitability, recency (date of the last flight) and frequency of flying. For passengers who have not flown with KLM in the last twelve months a re-activation campaign has been developed: 'if you fly with us between now and the coming six months you can double your Flying Dutchman points'. Also campaigns are adapted to customers' wishes and hobbies, such as golf and sailing.

Another objective is to win new FD members. 'The Flying Dutchman programme is our starting point, we have to be able to identify our customer. A new customer, however, has no past. So we start with an incubation period; we start broad. If this new FD customer did not fly for a month, he will receive an e-mail with opportunities. If he does fly, he will receive different information after four weeks. We start a dialogue with the customer tailoring information to his segment, profitability and behaviour.'

In the past seven months the database with e-mail addresses tripled. 'Of course, we strive towards online communication. The costs are lower and besides that the response is higher than offline; between 5 and 12 per cent.'

At the moment the customer experience is being improved. Flying Dutchman Platinum and Gold members are printed separately on the boarding lists and get a label 'special and valuable'. Employees are trained in master classes to improve their service towards FD members even further. Changing the mindset will take years, says Zanchi. It sounds uncommon for an airline with a cabin crew that has a service orientation by nature. 'The difference is we enable our people with tools now.' Besides that, additional attention is given to complaint handling. 'Complaints are a gift. A complaining customer gives you another chance. We think we should respond to customers if in their eyes something goes wrong; within five working days we react. Letters are being signed by the CEO, Leo van Wijk. In doing so we give the customer the opportunity to give feedback and new customer information.' Within less than a year the number of FD customers increased by 20 per cent and the profit by 5 per cent. The payback time of the CRM tools was less than Zanchi expected initially. Under the current circumstances, with SARS, the war in Iraq, this is tremendous. Cristina Zanchi will miss no opportunity to present these results, especially to Air France. The partner shares the same vision and in some situations the same tools are applied or existing systems can be integrated. But the new alliance and new decision procedures mean a slight delay for CRM. 'I am so impatient because I have the proof of a mega success in my hands. In the future the database will count twelve million customers. Twelve million. A world of opportunities.'

Next year she hopes to make her big bang, although she makes a correction to this statement. Maybe she is too fast. 'First the training programme, the alliance with Air France and the cultural changes. Then the opportunities are almost unlimited.'

Source: Connie Wiering (2004), *Tijdschrift voor Marketing*, April, 48–50.

Questions

1 If you were a member of the CRM Award Jury, what would be the reason(s) for you to choose KLM as the winning company of this global award?

2 Where do you criticise KLM's CRM approach?

3 What are the major risks for KLM's CRM future?

Questions

1 Give a description of CRM in your own words.

2 In your opinion, is a discounter capable of implementing a successful CRM strategy? Provide an example to explain your answer.

3 What are the core elements of CRM?

4 Choose one of your service providers and reconstruct the dialogue you have conducted with this organisation. How could the content of this dialogue be improved so that you would become more loyal to this service provider?

5 Why is CRM more than simply an IT project?

6 Why do 70 per cent of the CRM projects fail, according to companies' perceptions?

7 Are there causes which may be cited for the failures of relationship marketing (at the end of the 1980s and beginning of the 1990s) which differ from the failure of CRM projects in the past two to three years? Explain your answer.

8 How would you explain the resurgence of CRM in the past three to five years?

9 What were the causes of relationship marketing's loss of popularity in the mid-1990s?

10 What are the differences within a CRM implementation project between a mail-order company and a company that supplies electronic products in the consumer and the business markets?

References

Arndt, John (1979) Toward a concept of domesticated markets, *Journal of Marketing*, **32**, Autumn, 69–75.

Asseldonk, Ton G.M. van (1998) *Mass Individualisation: Business strategies applying networked order to create economic value in heterogeneous and unpredictable market*, TVA Management, Veldhoven, The Netherlands.

Hoekstra, Janny, C. (2001) *Direct Marketing*, 2nd edn, Wolters-Noordhoff, Groningen.

Levitt, Theodore (1983) *The Marketing Imagination*, The Free Press, New York.

McKenna, Regis (1995) Real-time marketing, *Harvard Business Review*, July–August, 87–95.

Peelen, Ed (1999) *The Relation Oriented Organization*, Nyenrode University, Beukelen.

Reichheld, Frederick, E. (1995) *The Loyalty Effect*, The Free Press, New York.

Treacy, M. and F. Wiersema (1996) *The Discipline of Market Leaders*, Harper Collins, New York.

Wiering, Connie (2004) KLM viert CRM triomfen in moeilijke marktomstandigheden, *Tijdschrift voor Marketing*, April, 48–50.

Part I

Strategy and Organisation of CRM

This first part of the book will start with an examination of the meaning of customer–supplier relationships from a social-psychological viewpoint. Before elaborating further on a CRM strategy, the corresponding organisation, the tactical policy and the systems involved, we will first need to define what it is we are talking about. Next, the strategy will be discussed and after that, we will examine the relationship-oriented organisation. An indication will be given as to the types of situations in which the application of a CRM strategy is suitable, and those in which a long-term competitive advantage may be achieved. The implications for an organisation actually developing relationships with customers will also be considered. The company will need to be designed around customers and not around products.

2

Customer–supplier relationships

This chapter starts with a short historical overview: when and where did the focus on customer–supplier relationships begin (Section 2.1)? The concept will then be further defined (Section 2.2); a number of core elements such as reciprocity and interactions, trust and commitment will be examined further. A very real element in relationships will be then explored, namely the dynamic: which pattern do relationships follow in their development (Section 2.3)?

In this chapter we will address the following questions

- When and how did the relationship orientation arise within marketing?
- What are the differences between a transaction-based and a relationship-based orientation in marketing?
- What is the meaning of buyer–supplier relationships?
- What types of buyer–supplier relationships can we distinguish, including the customer pyramid?
- How can we describe the interactions and reciprocity in relationships?
  - What are Foa and Foa's objects of exchange?
  - What is the Bales' interaction process analysis?
- What are the meaning and forms of commitment (and loyalty)?
- What is trust?
- How can we describe the dynamic of relationships; the relationship life cycle?
- What are communities and social structures?

Practitioner's insight

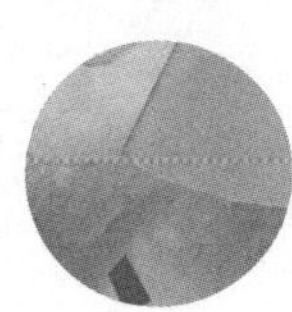

CRM stands for customer relationship management, or the relationship between customer and supplier. Before examining the strategic, technological and organisational aspects of CRM, it would seem appropriate first to discuss the nature of relationships, and in particular, the relationship between a customer and a supplier. It is quite easy for people in an organisation to speak of their relationships with customers, but further inquiry always reveals they give different meanings to it. For one it is the delivery of quality and service, for another it is to listen and to be customer friendly, and for yet another it is commitment. Building a common understanding of buyer–seller relationships is a prerequisite for CRM.

2.1 History

Within marketing theory and practice, 'there has been a long-standing and clear tendency . . . to focus on the sale, the single event of a transaction, as the objective of marketing activity and the dependent variable for analysis' (Webster, 1992).

Levitt has illustrated this concept quite clearly (Table 2.1). Apart from indicating the salesman's strong focus on the transaction, he demonstrates what the consequences are for the feelings of the salesman as well as the buyer during the purchase and use process. It would seem obvious that a better synchronisation of emotions is a precondition for both customer and supplier in order to arrive at the development of a long-term relationship.

Table 2.1 The transaction orientation

Stage of the sale	*Salesman*	*Buyer*
Before transaction	'Real hope'	'Vague need'
Romance	'Hot and heavy'	'Teasing and hopeful'
During transaction	'Fantasy – bed'	'Fantasy – bored'
After transaction	'Looks elsewhere for next sale'	'You don't care'
A long time afterwards...	'Indifferent'	'Can't this be made better?'
Next transaction	'How about a new one?'	'Really?'

Source: Levitt (1983). Reprinted by permission of *Harvard Business Review*. From 'After the Sale is Over' by Theodore Levitt, September/October 1983. Copyright © 1983 by the Harvard Business School Publishing Corporation; all rights reserved.

Levitt's black-and-white depiction is hardly flattering, however, some level of differentiation is appropriate here. First of all, his example focuses on salesmen and not on marketing in general, and second, one must not forget that the objective of transaction marketing is to make customers happy. The expectation is that this happiness will translate into future repeat purchases. Within transaction marketing, the process between two or more transactions is neither analysed nor influenced. The attention for the relationship and the investments in the relationship is lacking.

In recent years, an increasing number of market situations have witnessed a shift in the focus on the transaction to the relational aspects of the exchange (Arndt, 1979). Arndt said that 'many earlier competitive markets are structured as a result of voluntary, long-term, binding commitments among the organizations involved. In such arrangements transactions are planned and administered instead of being conducted on an ad hoc basis.'

As Bruhn (2003) describes in his book *Relationship Marketing*, in the literature the origins of relationship marketing are diverse. We basically follow his historical analysis here. Bagozzi (1974, 1975) contributed in the mid-1970s when he defined marketing as an exchange process between buyer and seller, and thereby formed the basis for the subsequent conceptualisation of relationship marketing. Accepting the view that a customer relationship comprises various exchange processes, the question arises as to how the relationship changes over time. In this regard, one recognises several relationship phases that first came under discussion in the early 1980s (Dwyer, Schurr and Oh, 1987; Peelen, 1989). The possibility of delineating phases within a relationship makes it necessary to design relationship marketing explicitly. In the early 1980s this was seen for the first time in the field of service marketing (Berry, 1983). It is in the field of service that significant contributions have been made to relationship marketing: the so-called Nordic school, with founders Evert Gummesson and Christian Grönroos, was the first explicitly to define relationship marketing and contrast it with transaction marketing, its marketing instruments and organisation. Zeithaml, Parasuraman and Berry (1990) constructed ServQual, a method to measure the (thus) so far intangible subject of service.

Around 1990, the International Marketing and Purchasing Group with, among others, Håkansson (1983) designed a conceptual model for relationship marketing in business-to-business markets. The interaction and networking between buyers and sellers became the subject of research of this international group.

At the beginning of the 1990s, as Bruhn (2003) notes, an after-effect of analyses and discussion on customer relationships was that customer retention and lifetime values entered the stage of marketing research (Reichheld, 1995). Relationship marketing, with its origin in the service industry and business-to-business markets, was in this period also applied to the consumer markets for branded goods (Fournier, Dobscha and Mick 1998).

In the 1990s, diverse relationship constructs, such as commitment and trust (Morgan and Hunt, 1994), were developed and the issue of relationship termination, whose essence is the breaking-up and recovery of relationships, was increasingly considered (Boshoff, 1997).

2.2 Description of customer–supplier relationships

General

The word 'relationship' conjures up thoughts of the feelings that two people have for one another: mutual attraction and respect, consideration, dependency and the like. These are aspects which will only appear if certain conditions are met. Relationships, after all, 'imply some sort of intermittent interaction between two or more persons, involving interchanges over an extended period of time' (Hinde, 1979). Poeisz and van Raaij (1993) describe this in more detail as follows:

- Interactions must take place between at least two parties; characteristic of interactions is that the activities of one of the parties influence those of the other, and vice versa.
- A certain degree of continuity must be present in a relationship since interactions from the past influence present and future interactions; relationships will also have to extend over a longer period of time.
- The effects of interactions are dependent upon the actual events and the subjective approach to these events.

Within the field of psychology, a distinction is made between primary and secondary relationships (Tolboom, 1996). The first type of relationship involves basic long-term interpersonal relationships which are based primarily on emotional bonds and the feeling of mutual obligation towards one another. Primary relationships, such as the love relationship between a man and a woman, are, unlike secondary relationships, rather diffuse and comprise many roles, behaviours and situations. Normally they are not limited by strict rules governing contact, and the people involved generally know one another extremely well. In primary relationships, one person cannot automatically be replaced by another. Secondary relationships, such as those between customer and supplier, are by contrast relatively short-term interpersonal relationships with a limited degree of social interaction, fairly clear rules of etiquette and reasonably well-defined social roles. In contrast with primary relationships, deep emotional involvement rarely occurs; the various players may be more easily replaced in general. The transitional area between secondary and primary relationships is rather large.

Customer–supplier relationships

The relationships between customer and supplier may be present at a variety of levels and in various compositions (Peelen *et al.*, 1996; Rowe and Barnes, 1998); they may be secondary in nature, but may also lie somewhere in the transitional area between secondary and primary relationships. An example of a primary relationship is the bond a customer has with the local bakery shop; this is the place where Bob gets fresh bread from John every morning, bread which represents a guarantee that his day will get off to a good start. The two men have got to know and value one another over the years and are involved with one another. This is different from the relationship between the

Figure 2.1 Pyramid of relationships

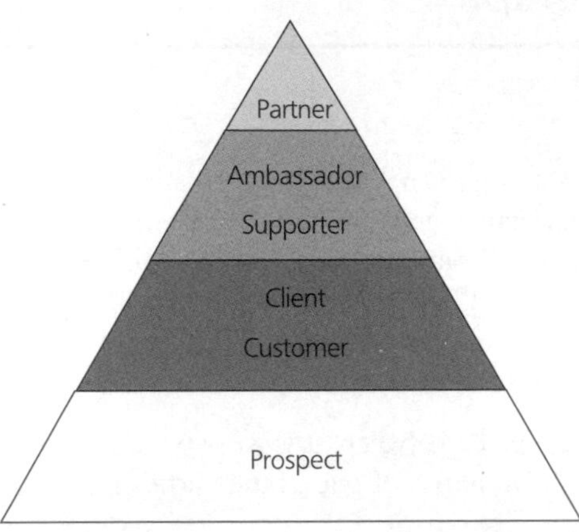

cashier at the supermarket and the customer. Even if the customer shops there regularly and has been buying groceries there for quite some time, it is highly likely that the supplier and the customer do not know one another by name and that their conversation is extremely limited and not very varied.

A variety of supplemental classifications have been created to further clarify the differences between the parties involved in customer–supplier relationships. These classifications indicate (see Figure 2.1; including Peelen, Ekelmans and Vijn, 1989; Payne, 1995; Schijns, 1998):

- Whether or not a transaction has already been completed: from prospect to customer.
- If a long-term orientation is present which extends further than that one transaction: from customer to client.
- To what degree the relationship is felt by both parties: from supporter to ambassador.
- To what degree both parties take an active position in the relationship: from ambassador to partner.

Alternatively the categories describe to what degree the following are present (Tolboom, 1996):

- Cooperation or competition: competition occurs in a relationship if a customer plays a number of suppliers off against one another and ultimately chooses the one with the best offer. Cooperation may be considered to be present if both work together well to achieve that result which is best for both parties: for example, while setting an appointment the customer takes the supplier's schedule into account as well.
- Equal or unequal distribution of power: although a balanced distribution of power is a characteristic of a close relationship, it is not something we will encounter often. An unequal distribution of power is often seen in knowledge- and skill-oriented services where the customer's fate depends upon the expertise of the service provider. An imbalance of power also frequently exists between producers

and distributors because one of them is dependent on the other for a substantial portion of its turnover, and for which other alternatives do not exist. It is not unusual for a large supermarket chain to be responsible for some 30 per cent of the turnover of a brand-name manufacturer within a certain national market.

- Dependence or independence: this involves an aspect of relationships that is inversely proportional to the balance of power; the powerful party is the independent one, and the other party is the dependent one.
- A task or social-emotional orientation: are the interactions between both of them heavily task-oriented, such as in the case of the supermarket, or is there room for social interaction, such as in the case involving the local baker?
- A formal or informal form of contact: the contact between a customer and his or her solicitor will be much more formal than the contact with his or her hairdresser.

In analysing the quality of the relationship, attention is also drawn to aspects such as commitment, fairness, loyalty and trust (Dwyer, Schurr and Oh, 1987; Peelen, 1989; Moorman, Zaltman and Deshpandé, 1993). Some relationships are continued because there are no better alternatives available and because terminating the relationship would invite a great number of problems (for example, Jackson, 1985; Peelen, 1989). In these types of relationship it is the negative rather than the positive considerations which result in continuity. Take, for example, a company which has made an investment in a certain operating system for its computer and feels obligated to equip newly purchased computers with this system as well and to choose application software which will run on this particular operating system.

Other situations may be characterised by more positive aspects which bind both parties to one another. The car dealer is a representative of your favourite make of car, takes extremely good care of your car, makes sure that you feel special, and is always available. What keeps two parties together may differ from one relationship to another and even within relationships themselves. As the examples above demonstrate, the bond may be for financial, personal as well as structural reasons.

A profile is shown in Table 2.2 for the two most extreme types of relationship; many of the aspects mentioned above were used in the creation of the profile for the weak and close relationships.

Although customer–supplier relationships may be described on the basis of a multitude of aspects, there seems to be general agreement on the central role assigned to interactions and reciprocity, commitment and trust in the formation of relationships (Morgan and Hunt, 1994). Without a reciprocal basis, there is no relationship. The meaning of commitment and trust were also recently demonstrated empirically in Garbarino and Johnson's study (1999). They determined that the intention to continue a relationship in close relationships is dependent upon commitment and trust. In situations of a more transactional nature, it appears that it is particularly customers' general contentedness with the organisation and its products and services that determines whether repeat purchases will be made.

Interactions and reciprocity

According to social exchange theories, reciprocity forms the basis for relationships. The views on reciprocity have been around for quite some time. In 1925, Mauss had

Table 2.2 Profile of close and weak customer–supplier relationships

Lacking/weak relationships	*Close relationships*
Concrete agreements have been made regarding reciprocation.	There are few agreements concerning reciprocation.
Agreements have a short-term horizon.	Of the few agreements that do exist, many have a long-term horizon.
Initiative for interaction is taken primarily by one party.	The initiative for interaction is distributed evenly among the parties.
A limited number of topics are raised for discussion.	A multitude of topics are raised for discussion.
Topics are treated in a limited degree of depth.	Topics are treated in a high degree of depth.
Both parties present themselves as separate individuals/entities to the outside world.	Both parties present themselves as one entity to the outside world.
Each of the parties pursues its own interests.	Each of the parties pursues its own interests and takes the other's satisfaction/fate to heart.
Intentions regarding the continuation of the relationship are present to a limited degree.	The intention exists to continue the relationship in the long term, in spite of changes in the environment.
There are few barriers to ending this relationship and to starting another one.	There are many barriers to ending this relationship and starting a new one.
The parties consider, and may experiment with, alternative partners.	With respect to alternative partners, the adage 'look but do not buy' applies.

Source: Peelen *et al.* (1996).

already suggested that three rules apply in a primitive society: giving, receiving and giving again. Something must be received for which something is given in return which then creates the obligation to give something again. It is referred to as a 'calculated return' in association with reciprocity. A positive gift is returned with another positive gift; a negative gift is returned with a negative one. This last theory describes a negative form of reciprocity. Receiving something creates the obligation to give something, and a never-ending cycle is thus begun, even in a negative respect. Generally speaking, reciprocity assumes the following:

- A moral norm exists to give something back when something is received.
- A precise return is not desirable. Exchanges do not need to be in balance immediately as long as an equilibrium is created in the long run.
- Reciprocity occurs in all cultures; it is universal.
- Reciprocity makes interaction possible because the norm of return applies; people are willing to take a chance with someone because of the valid norm.

- According to anthropologists, the goal of reciprocity is the survival of the group, but according to an individual psychological explanation, the goal is to better oneself in an economic sense.

All sorts of things may be exchanged in relationships. On the basis of an extensive empirical study, Foa and Foa (in Peelen, 1989) suggest that an adult is capable of distinguishing between six 'resources': love, services, status, information, goods and money. There are two dimensions by which these 'resources' may be specified:

1 The personal aspect of the resources: if the value of a resource is dependent upon the person providing it, then there is a personal aspect involved. This is the case with love, for example. People do not receive love from a stranger or an enemy. The opposite of this occurs with money: individuals are usually indifferent with respect to the person who makes the money available.
2 The tangibility of the resources: goods are characterised as the most concrete type of resource – they are tangible. Status and information consist of verbal or non-verbal behaviour and have the least amount of tangibility.

In addition to resources, Foa and Foa also differentiate between costs. The costs of resources vary. The giving of love does not have to entail costs; it may even imply benefits. By providing information, people do not become poorer in terms of information. The handing over of goods on the other hand leads to a direct loss of the resource concerned.

The personal nature of resources and tangibility of resources are set off against one another in Figure 2.2. The exchange relationship is typified by the types of resources which are exchanged (Hinde, 1979). Loose relationships with little commitment will generally be characterised by the exchange of few personal resources, whereas in close relationships, in addition to resources found under the diagonal, more personal objects are also exchanged.

Objects of exchange

Figure 2.2

With personal resources, similar resources are exchanged
The greater the difference between the resources, the lower the chance of exchange

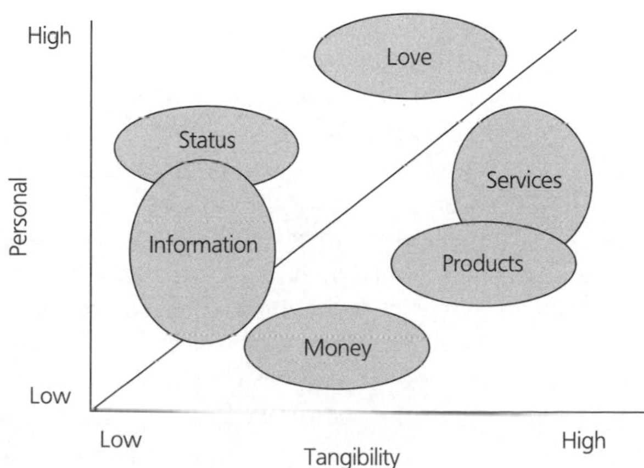

Source: Foa and Foa (in Peelen, 1989).

Bales' interaction process analysis

In 1950, Bales had already developed an observation method to analyse interactions in small groups which could also be applied to the interactions between customer and supplier. Bales identifies a number of categories into which interactions may be divided:

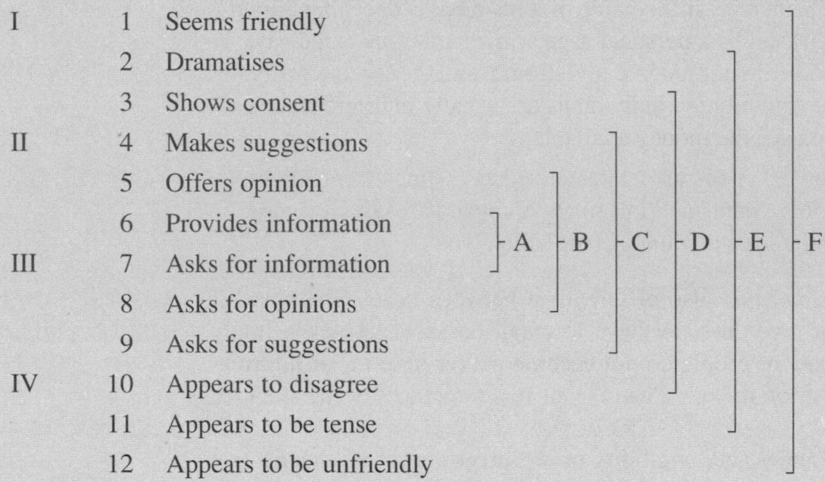

Key:

A – orientation problem
B – evaluation problem
C – control problem
D – decision-making problem
E – tension problem
F – integration problems

I – positive reactions
II – answers
III – questions
IV – negative reactions

II and III: task-area; I–IV: social-emotional area

Categories II and III comprise the task area and consist of questions and answers. The two external areas form the social-emotional area in which the parties display the positive and negative aspects of their characters. When two parties, for example a customer and a supplier, perform their task, social-emotional reactions arise. The attention may then be focused on these reactions; people express their feelings and try to keep the parties together and to integrate them.

A successful interaction process will be characterised by a certain symmetry. For each category under the centre, there is a corresponding category above this centre (i.e., 6 corresponds with 7 and 4 with 8, and so forth). Bales assumes a tendency towards equilibrium. For example, an answer follows a question. In order to preserve the balance, it is important to solve communication, evaluation or control problems immediately.

It can prove interesting for the customer–supplier relationship to describe the interaction process on the basis of Bales' method. The results may be shown in a table as follows:

1 Seems friendly									
2 Dramatises				2–1					
3 Shows consent									2–1
4 Makes suggestions									
5 Offers opinion					1–2				
6 Provides information	1–2		1–2						
7 Asks for information		2–1							
8 Asks for opinions						1–2			
9 Asks for suggestions								1–2	
10 Appears to disagree							2–1		
11 Appears to be tense									
12 Appears to be unfriendly									

The number 1 indicates the supplier, 2 the customer. The party who is named first addresses the other. The interaction begins with the supplier who provides information to the customer; the customer then asks for further information which he receives, etc.

Source: Bales (1950).

Commitment

The exchange of resources will influence the level of commitment present in the relationship. Commitment is defined as 'an enduring desire to maintain a valued relationship' (Moorman, Deshpandé and Zaltman, 1993; Morgan and Hunt, 1994). Within this framework of commitment, the objective is to continue the relationship, producing outcomes which are as beneficial as possible for both parties (in Peelen, 1989).

Johnson (1991) is critical of the way in which many people treat the concept. Many go beyond the future orientation in their measurements and then others measure only one of the forms of commitment. In order to address the points of criticism mentioned above, Johnson identifies three different forms of commitment, namely personal, moral and structural. *Personal commitment* is demonstrated by the will that someone displays in continuing a relationship. The satisfied customer at a car dealership will want to continue his relationship with that company. In the case of *moral commitment*, people feel a sense of obligation; they feel that they are supposed to continue the relationship. The small independent fresh baker has a difficult time just to stay in business, and people feel that after all these years, they really can't just go and buy their bread elsewhere, even if it is better or cheaper somewhere else. The *structural form* involves the perception that 'there is no escaping it'. Investments have been made in that operating system and it cannot be done away with without having to make substantial investments in new software, training programmes and undergoing a difficult transitional period. Clear differences may be seen between these three forms. Some of them are experienced as a limitation to freedom of movement, others are based on a voluntary choice. Some are

CRM definitions

Loyalty

Should we talk about loyalty or commitment at this point? Is there any difference between the two concepts? A comparison of definitions may automatically produce differences; however, you might ask yourself whether the discrepancies are purely semantic in nature or whether they also have an actual meaning. After thorough preparation, Oliver (1996) formulated the following definition:

> *Loyalty is a deeply held commitment to rebuy or repatronize a preferred product/service consistently in the future, thereby causing repetitive same-brand or same brand-set purchasing, despite situational influences and marketing efforts having the potential to cause switching behavior.*

With this definition, he also removes any doubt that this could possibly involve different concepts. Oliver restricts the definition's application to the area of brands.

Table 2.3 Characteristics of the three forms of commitment

	Structural	*Moral*	*Personal*
Choice/limitation	Limitation	Limitation	Choice
External/internal	External	Internal	Internal

Source: Johnson (1991).

the result of the individual's own decision and others are imposed from the outside. Table 2.3 shows how the three forms score in terms of the aspects indicated.

Of the three forms, personal commitment is the only one which is felt both internally and originates from a personal choice. The choice may be seen as an attitude which someone has with regard to the relationship and/or the partner. The influence of the continuation of the relationship on a person's self-image also influences personal commitment. One is, after all, a respected customer of a dealer which represents a well-known brand. Moral commitment has the character of self-imposed limitations which arise from a person's value system and a sense of responsibility felt towards the partner. The last type of commitment involves structural commitment; it is created as a result of investments in relationships which may no longer be reversed, barriers to ending a relationship, the availability of acceptable alternatives to the relationship and the reaction from the social environment to putting an end to the relationship.

Interaction exists between the three forms of commitment. An increase or decrease in one of the forms has an influence on one of the other two: a drop in personal commitment does not occur without repercussions for the aspect of structural commitment, for example. If the customer of the operating system concerned is no longer satisfied, he or she will personally grab the first realistic opportunity to get rid of the system and the supplier. Even any existing structural commitment will not be able to prevent the customer from making the switch to another supplier. The history of IBM, among other companies, has proved this concept.

CRM definitions

In another system of classification, which has received both a great deal of attention and a substantial following, three components are identified (Tolboom, 1996):

1 Instrumental or calculative commitment, which is based on a calculation in which costs and revenues are weighed against one another. Through a certain input in the relationship, such as investments, the committed party demonstrates that it plans to remain in the relationship. In many cases, having provided this input would make leaving the relationship too costly because the input is often difficult or even impossible to retrieve completely.

2 Attitudinal or affective commitment, which represents the affective attachment of parties in a relationship and indicates the degree to which goals and values are shared by the parties in the relationship.

3 A temporal component, one that reflects the intention to remain in a valued relationship in the future.

If we compare the two classification types, it appears that there are major similarities to be found between structural and instrumental or calculative commitment. The attitudinal or affective component is furthermore comparable to personal commitment and may even measure moral commitment, dependent on the manner in which it is put into practice. The question remains whether or not it is preferable in conceptual terms to split attitudinal commitment into a personal and a moral component.

Commitment will not have to be determined for only one of the two parties in the relationship, or in this case, the customer. Commitment on the part of the other party, the supplier, also deserves attention. After all, disproportional commitment, which occurs when one individual in the relationship is more committed than the other, can undermine the relationship and make the more committed party vulnerable to opportunism. If a retailer is looking for an advantage in the short term and the brand-product manufacturer operates under the assumption of a long-term horizon, the latter can find itself at a disadvantage. It invests in the retailer and gives it an advantage in the hope of ultimately gaining from this in the future, while the retailer generally cannot and will not think this far ahead.

Commitment, as has been described thus far, is a psychological concept. The pressure that is felt externally to continue or terminate the relationship (see also Johnson's classification) is also psychological in nature. After all, it is the manner in which the individual perceives this influence. Nonetheless, commitment is experienced within a social context (Johnson, 1991). The impact of this context on commitment should not be underestimated. Putting an end to a relationship, such as a marriage for example, can be heavily influenced by the social environment or the norms and values which dominate this environment. A supplier who maintains a relationship with a customer who is engaged in objectionable activities abroad, for example, can also count on being criticised by society.

Trust

Another core element which may be used to describe relationships is trust. Trust is a basic condition necessary in order for a relationship to grow and has been defined by Moorman, Deshpandé and Zaltman (1993) as 'a willingness to rely on an exchange partner in whom one has confidence'. Or, as Morgan and Hunt (1994) describe it: 'it is the perception of confidence in the exchange partner's reliability and integrity'.

One may conclude from these descriptions that trust may be associated with qualities such as honesty, fairness, responsibility, helpfulness and involvement. Of these characteristics, honesty in particular may be seen as one of the foundations of trust. Without honesty, there is no confidence, no integrity. 'The honesty of a partner may be defined as the conviction that the partner is trustworthy, keeps his promises, has the courage to admit to limitations and convey bad news' (Geyskens and Steenkamp, 1997).

Trust also originates in the competency and the courtesy of a person or organisation. One gains competency when the skills and expertise are present and one also has the capability or the opportunity to make use of these. This person or organisation's courtesy must lead to these competencies being employed to protect the customer's interests. The supplier is prepared to provide assistance and places long-term customer interest above its own short-term interests (Geyskens and Steenkamp, 1997).

There are three distinct levels of trust which may be identified. Keeping one's commitments is central to the lowest of these levels (Crosby, Evans and Cowles, 1990). Legal contracts are complied with. One step higher is concerned not with specific behaviour, but with a characteristic of the partner. This person may be motivated and capable, for example. The third level is where one finds general, all-encompassing standards such as integrity.

Trust is, in all likelihood, also a multidimensional concept; evidence that it is a one-dimensional idea is quite scarce. It would also be incorrect to say that suspicion is the opposite of trust.

Trust in someone else generally leads to overcoming feelings of insecurity and doubt. People dare to take more risks; for example, one is prepared to invest more in a relationship. People trust that in the event of problems, the customer will discuss this with the supplier, so that a solution may be found in a constructive manner. Trust also leads to goodwill which causes people to act in a more tolerant manner if a transaction does not live up to their expectations. Trust makes it possible for a higher level of commitment to be attained in a relationship.

Conclusion

In order to realise a close relationship between the customer and the supplier, the trust between both parties will have to grow so that more may be invested in the relationship and more personal 'resources' may be exchanged. The ways in which both parties invest effort in the relationship can have positive consequences for the commitment; the structural as well as the personal and moral commitment may grow.

2.3 The dynamic in relationships

How do relationships begin and grow? Trust and commitment cannot be forced; they must grow. Marketers will have to gain insight into the pattern by which relationships develop and the manner in which they can influence this process.

Following Foa and Foa's insights on 'resources' to be exchanged, we may conclude at any rate that at the start of the relationship, the accent must lie on the exchange of goods and certain services for money. Very few personal resources are exchanged in the beginning. A relationship which is initially characterised by a discretionary aspect and a focus on transactions and cross-selling will have to develop into a long-term partnership in which the supplier functions as a 'total solution provider' for the customer. A service provider who, for example, has the confidence to and is capable of creating an analysis of the transactions completed with the customer in the past can lay the foundation for a consultational relationship: what was the point of the purchase, what did you hope to achieve and how can you gain additional benefits from this supplier? As a result, a bond of trust may be created in which the exchange of personal information becomes something that occurs naturally. The mutual respect (status) can continue to grow. The exchange of more personal and non-concrete resources can cause an increase in the value of the customer–supplier relationship for both parties.

Parties engaged in a relationship should possess certain capabilities necessary to allow the relationship to grow and develop. In order to increase the level of intimacy, the personal exchange of resources, trust and the commitment, both customer and supplier must have a capacity for empathy. Empathy is the ability to see the world through someone else's eyes, from moment to moment. A supplier can place itself within the frame of reference of the customer, and at the same time make the customer aware of the fact that it understands him or her. A condition necessary for this to occur is that both parties must supply information that is open and honest and must dare to 'expose' themselves (self-disclosure).This requires from both parties that they dare to put themselves in a vulnerable position. Customer and supplier will have to accept and have a positive attitude towards one another.

In terms of the negotiations to be conducted and transactions to be completed, empathy is a difficult aspect for marketers and salespeople. The marketer and the salesperson benefit from showing their products and organisation and in putting their best foot forward. They are good at seducing, but less adept at presenting their vulnerable side, listening, and putting themselves in the other person's position.

The development of the relationship may be detailed further on the basis of insights into relationships originating from the field of social psychology. Dwyer, Schurr and Oh (1987) identify five phases in a relationship. During the first phase, both parties *become aware of each other*. Both parties position themselves and take actions designed to demonstrate their appeal to the other party. From the moment that bilateral interactions occur, the second phase begins, that of *exploration* or *sounding out*. This phase begins with attraction. Attraction may develop because both parties think that they aspire to the same goals or it may originate from the perceived personality: he or she is honest or capable. Or it involves a simple attractive appearance! It is acceptable to be seen in public with him or her. The potential of the resources to be exchanged or those already exchanged can increase the appeal of customer and supplier: the supplier's products are good and the customer has a great deal to spend.

The capacity for empathy plays a much larger role during this second phase. More interaction takes place and negotiations will be conducted. The fact that one or both parties are prepared to negotiate indicates that each party is interested in the other. If the relationship is to survive this phase, it is important for information to be exchanged and the reciprocity in the relationship to be monitored: both parties are evaluating the situation on a regular basis and determining whether or not the relationship is satisfying and fair. After all, the future orientation is still limited and the cooperation is still easy enough to terminate at this stage. During these interactions, norms and role and expectation patterns can become complicated for the relationship.

In the *growth phase*, the third phase, the interaction processes from the previous phase are continued. Both parties continue to attract the other, negotiations will continue to take place, norms and expectations will become specified in more detail, and the parties will also evaluate the situation every now and then. However, in comparison with the previous phase, more risks are now taken; activities are performed to try and test out the relationship. The mutual dependency increases and more resources are exchanged.

In the fourth phase of the *commitment* or *saturation*, the relationship reaches its maximum level of commitment, mutual dependency, trust and respect. Many resources are exchanged, including those of a personal and less concrete nature. Potential problems are discussed fairly and openly, and a constructive solution is sought. The social and non-social environments also contribute to the stability of the relationship.

The final phase is that of the *decline*. Directness and a focus on others may indicate that the continuity of the relationship is at issue. The causes of an eventual break may lie with differences in expectations and individual characteristics of the partners, such as differing needs for freedom or renewal. External influences may also make their effects felt.

After introducing adjustments, Peelen (1989) put Dwyer, Schurr and Oh's model, which was based on theory, into practice in consumer markets. A relationship life cycle has been constructed which describes the pattern in which the purchases and the commitment in the relationship change over time under the influence of interactions. Although no explicit focus is placed on trust in the study, the measurement of commitment is not based fully on the insights of Johnson, and the first phase of Dwyer and associates has not been mapped out, the cycle does offer handy pretexts which may be used in interpreting relationship management. At the same time, people will have to bear in mind that the relationship life cycle describes the development of an average relationship (within a segment). Deviations from this outlined path of development will occur; not all consumers will follow the exact same path and changes in the development path will also occur in future. Nonetheless, the cycle offers a practical handle for organisations which would like to develop relationships with customers in a standardised manner. The course of the customer–supplier relationship will first have to be examined before a plan can be devised for the relationship.

In the relationship life cycle (Figure 2.3), the boundaries between the phases indicate moments in the relationship at which a change in the (development) of the

The relationship life cycle

Figure 2.3

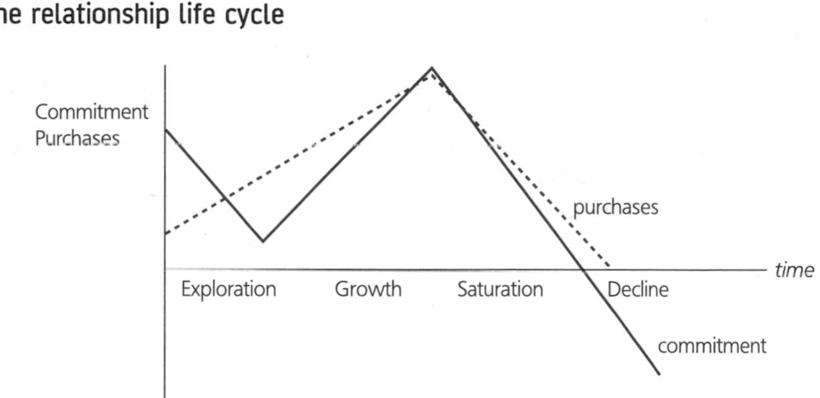

Commitment = *f* (satisfaction, attractiveness, switching costs)

Source: Peelen *et al.* (1996).

behaviour occurs. These key moments exist during the transition from the first to the second phase involved in the first purchase. The growth phase is in turn completed at the moment the increase in purchases changes course, moving from progressive to degressive. Finally, the decline phase begins as the number of purchases begins to drop.

Analysis of the course of the relationship

During the exploratory phase, the customer sees the promises made during communication fulfilled for the first time. The first introduction makes an important impression on the relationship. The level of satisfaction during the exploratory phase is still relatively low; the customers have little to no experience with the products and services of the supplier. The appeal of the supplier depends on the experiences that customers have with alternative suppliers and the differences between the alternative suppliers. The switching costs are still quite low at this stage.

The growth phase (three months to two years) is characterised by a sharp rise in the number of purchases. Customers would like to get to know the supplier's products and services. The advantages of the supplier's offering are now discovered. The satisfaction with the goods and services increases. The supplier is now examined more for its performance than for its reputation or image.

Nonetheless, the commitment in this phase drops slightly, depending on the policy pursued. Doubt and the first confrontation with the actual value-for-money ratio can have a negative impact on commitment. The chance is relatively high that the relationship will be terminated during or just after the growth phase. If a supplier has invested in the relationship, the risk is present that this investment has not yet paid for itself.

The saturation phase (usually after more than two years) is characterised by the highest number of purchases from suppliers and the highest degree of commitment. Not many changes are occurring in either behaviour or purchases at this stage. The relationship has taken shape. During this phase, the supplier's ideal customers are discovered. Satisfaction increases in all respects when compared with the growth phase. Trust grows. During the last two or more years, goodwill has been built up. The appeal of the relationship improves during this phase as well, and the switching costs increase slightly now that the customer has become accustomed to the supplier's methods and offering.

The decline phase begins as soon as the number of transactions starts to drop. Customers may enter the decline phase at any time: after the exploratory, growth or saturation phase. There are various reasons for the deterioration of the relationship. The most common relate to the type of customer and the reduction in the need for the products and services provided by the supplier. There are so-called economy buyers who prefer not to commit and are constantly in search of the supplier with the best value-for-money ratio. Customers who have terminated the relationship after the saturation phase usually no longer have a need for the products.

Challenge for marketers

Marketers who look to develop a long-term mutually profitable relationship with a customer will have to gain insight into the dynamic of the relationship. They will have to recognise when a specific relationship deviates from a desired pattern and they will have to be able to anticipate critical moments in the relationship early. They will have to learn how to influence the relationship in the most effective and efficient manner so that it can develop in the most beneficial way possible. Regardless, every effort will have to be made to prevent customers from ending the relationship as early as the growth phase. This is all the more necessary since the odds are high that the investments which have been made in the customer will not yet have paid for themselves. Chapters 3 and 8 will examine these topics in greater depth.

2.4 Communities

The relationship between two people, also known as the *dyad*, is considered the most elementary form of social relationship. However, in reality, we find more complex relationships between groups of people and the position that each individual occupies with respect to the others. This position is defined within sociology as that individual's social position. In concrete terms, a social position may be defined as *the position which a person occupies in a complex of people interacting with one another.* Some positions are reserved for only one person within society (queen, prime minister). Other positions may be held by several people simultaneously (police officer, teacher, nurse).

Recently, the attention given to these types of social structure has grown substantially. The possibility of forming communities on the Internet is chiefly to blame for this (see the illustration in the next box in which an important reason for forming an online community is provided). The Internet bridges distances and time and brings people together, and thus also customers and suppliers. The term 'communities' is used rather loosely in practice to refer to a group of users or customers and suppliers who interact with one another, without the need to analyse what the connection is within the social structure. Does it involve an open or closed community, in other words: how is the admission of new individuals arranged? Does the supplier represent the centre ('central ego') of the community? Does the supplier have a special position as a result of which he can exercise a high degree of control over what takes place in the network? Or does the community consist of a collection of individuals with a high degree of social cohesion which has developed because the individuals find one another attractive? The supplier may be one of them, he might even stand outside of the community and have very little influence on it. Certain behaviour will probably even be punished because it does not fit within the norms and value patterns or the goals of the community.

CRM illustration

Online communities can provide valuable information to businesses

Businesses continue to make increasing use of community functionalities on their website in order to gather information on their customers' preferences, wishes and needs and to be able to inform these customers about – and to monitor them in their use of – their products and services. The IBM Institute for Knowledge-Based Organizations has conducted research on a number of community sites. There are at least three important sources of information for businesses. During the registration, interesting information may be gathered on new community members (from demographic data to information on their areas of interest). In addition, a great deal of useful information may be gleaned from *discussion boards* – online forums where customers can discuss all sorts of topics with one another and exchange information. Finally, varied *interactive events* set up by the company, and in which a direct contact exists between customers and the company, serve as an important source of information. The most commonly used 'interactivities' are chat sessions with experts (such as *ask-the-expert*-sessions), web seminars (courses on the company's products and services), online opinion polls and e-mail newsletters.

Source: *Marketing Management* (2002).

In essence, communities may be compared with 'normal' communities. In this way communities may be seen as a distinct, geographically separate group of people. A town, a city, and sometimes also districts are referred to as communities. There does not need to be an intimate, direct interaction between the 'residents'. A community may, however, also possess the characteristics of a group. In this case, there is a strong social cohesion within the community and more direct interaction takes place. A community could be called a special type of network.

In principle, there are seven criteria by which to analyse social structures, namely:

1 The number of members.
2 The composition.
3 The degree of interaction and communication.
4 The common goals and interests.

5 The common norms and values.
6 The feeling of solidarity.
7 The permanence.

On the basis of these criteria, groups may be divided into communities. By creating this classification, Merton's famous work from 1957 may be further elaborated upon. He bases his system of classification primarily on the (direct) interaction and the presence of common norms and values and distinguishes between three social structures: *the group*, *the collective* and *the social category*. The intensity of the social relationship also finds its expression here. This is at its highest with the group and at its lowest in the social category.

The group

A group is a small faction within which regular and frequent intensive interaction takes place. Merton's complete definition reads: 'a group is a gathering of individuals who engage mainly in direct communication with one another for a certain amount of time and who develop a more or less common awareness'. With this last concept, Merton means that a system of common norms and values must exist. He also indicates that this involves a permanent whole.

The collective

The collective and the social category distinguish themselves by a lack of direct interaction and communication. Collectives are often large with common norms and values. There is only one position, that of member. It is a long-term yet separate connection that is viewed as a social unit by outsiders. Every now and then, a collective will expand to become a group. Examples of collectives are political parties, religious factions and trade unions.

The social category

The social category involves neither interaction nor communication, nor common norms and values. There is also no solidarity and an internal structure is lacking. In fact, the social category doesn't exist, except for statisticians who use these categories to classify people on the basis of certain qualities. Someone is included in a social category because of his or her age, marital status, hair colour or race. An example of a social category is the 'pensioners' category.

Merton based his classification on extremes: either (direct) interaction exists or it is non-existent, and either common norms or values exist or they do not. Moreover, he overlooks one combination, that in which there are no common norms and values present, yet a direct interaction does in fact occur. De Jager and Mok call this the 'Togetherness situation' (Figure 2.4).

Knowledge of the social structure of the community is indispensable to the marketer and the salesperson in order to:

Figure 2.4

Profile of social structures according to Merton and De Jager and Mok

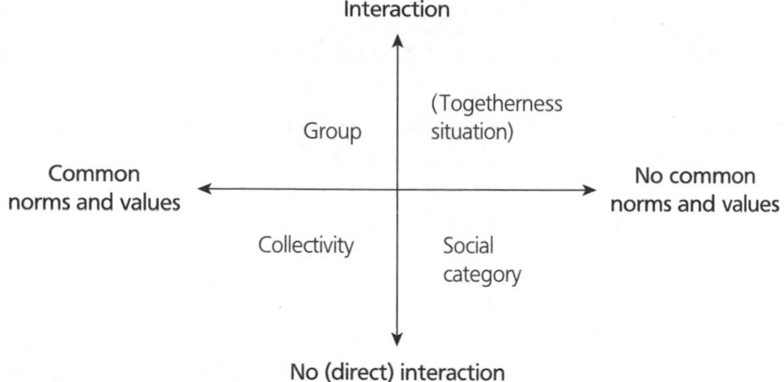

- be able to occupy the proper social position within the community;
- be able to obtain the optimum advantage from the relationships between the individuals in the community.

2.5 Conclusion

Formulating and implementing a CRM strategy without stopping and giving careful thought to the meaning of a relationship between a customer and a supplier is unwise. It might seem like a waste of time to be begin with. Attention is required for issues which are far removed from the task at hand: attracting and keeping customers, developing a new communication infrastructure and individual customer knowledge. However, experience has taught us that to pass over these psychological aspects of relationships can all too often have harmful consequences. If the implications of developing long-term relationships had been examined at greater length, a different strategy and different implementation programme would have been formulated. Issues such as empathy, trust, mutual commitment, relationship development and communities would have been interpreted in a company-specific manner. A discovery would have been made concerning the extent to which the current organisation in all its facets is removed from a relationship strategy and which of the capabilities necessary to apply these are lacking. It should be determined whether this type of strategy would actually lead to a long-term competitive advantage within this organisation's market. A great deal of frustration and many wasted investments could have been avoided.

This is why customer–supplier relationships have been examined in depth from a social-psychological perspective in this chapter. The dyadic relationship between a customer and a supplier was analysed, as was the complex of bilateral relationships existing within a community. An indication was provided of the core elements in relationships and how these develop. Important elements were discussed as a result in order to provide a well-founded interpretation of CRM.

Case study

The relationship between a logistics service provider and its new client

Introduction and assignment

What follows is a description of the relationship between a logistics service provider and its client, a manufacturer of consumer electronics. The subject is the client's outsourcing of the physical distribution activities for all its products and deliveries in northern Europe.

Our question to you is to analyse how the commitment and profitability of the relation evolves in time. Based upon this analysis you are requested to formulate objectives for this relationship and to think of recommendations to realise these targets. You can use the matrix provided.

The development of the relationship

Negotiations

Before the signing of a contract the following subjects have been studied and negotiated:

- The takeover of client's warehouse employees.
- The duration of the contract.
- The way both parties plan to integrate their information systems and the way information will be exchanged.
- The solution for the return logistics (deliveries that have been rejected; damaged products being returned for repair; old products to be used in recycling).
- Which part of the warehouse will be allocated to the client; how many cubic metres will be allocated to the client?
- The choice between a public warehouse (where products of other companies are stored and handled as well) and a dedicated warehouse (only the client's products).
- The selection of the transportation companies that will bring the products to the warehouse and from the warehouse to the customers.
- Service level agreements (reliability percentages, throughput times, minimal order sizes, penalties).
- The transition from the old to the new warehouse.
- The price and tariff structure.

Negotiation outcomes

The ultimate results of the negotiations are:

- A combination of a public and dedicated warehouse (the dedicated area is for the return logistics and the repair department).
- The client will close down and sell her own warehouse; the client's warehouse employees will be employed in the logistics service provider's warehouse as far as possible.
- The information systems of both companies will be connected. So far it seems the logistics service provider's warehousing and transport system can be linked to the order entry, order acceptance, order planning and invoicing module of the client.
- In Germany, the client currently works together with a logistics service provider that competed with this service provider; both companies tried to become the logistics service provider for the client in Germany. The German counterpart however failed; within three months the products have to be brought over from their warehouse to the new site of the logistics service provider; this implies that the logistics service provider's warehouse has to be up and running within three months.
- The initial length of the contract is three years.
- Some 8000 square metres are allocated to the client.
- Transport companies have been selected for distribution (delivery to customers) and for the trunk lines (delivery to warehouse).

- Zero tolerance; rush orders have to be delivered within 12 hours; other orders within 36 hours; there is no minimal order size and there is no penalty.
- Price: there is no open cost calculation; a separate price will be charged for storage, handling-in and handling-out and transportation; investments in handling equipment, rebuilding of the warehouse and information systems will be paid for partly by the client.

The preparation phase (the first three months)

For the first three months until the transition of the stock, all is going well. Only the cooperation with the German competitor can be characterised as time consuming. The consequence, though, is that the German goods cannot be moved on time to the new warehouse in Benelux. Work has started to link the information systems; however, the responsible IT manager at the logistics service provider resigned.

The start-up period (three months after the contract has been signed)

The delivery of the German markets is problematical. The information systems do not exchange data properly. The client is also making some mistakes; it appears they need much more space in the public warehouse than expected and specified in the contract. Furthermore, they could play a more active role in the transition phase; it would help the logistics service provider to move the goods from the competitor's warehouse to their own.

The rescue period (the next six months)

Everything, really everything is being done to solve the problems!

The stabilisation period (until contract renewal)

Finally everything goes smoothly. The perception grows with the client that handling-in, storing and handling-out goods is a rather easy job that actually anybody can do.

Contract renewal

The customer is looking for cheaper solutions. The logistics service provider hopes to extend the contract as part of the investment in this client has not yet been recovered.

	Signing of contract preparations	*Start-up*	*Rescue*	*Stabilisation*	*Contract renewal*
Analyse: commitment (satisfaction attractiveness switching costs long-term orientation), profit contribution					
Conclusion and objectives					
Recommendations: deliver superior value, price, lock-in effect, etc.					

Questions

1 Describe a close customer–supplier relationship in your own words and indicate how this differs from a transactional relationship.

2 What is the relationship between trust and commitment? Give an example to explain your answer.

3 Analyse a relationship you have with a supplier or service provider as a customer. Choose a company with which you have a relatively close relationship. Describe the trust and the commitment on the part of both parties in the relationship, and explain how these have grown.

4 What causes differences to arise in the relationship life cycle between customers of the same company? Explain your answer.

5 What should you know about a customer in order to be capable of and desirous of developing a long-term relationship with him or her?

6 In what ways will a prototype salesperson have to change in order to transform him- or herself into a good relationship manager?

7 Indicate how a marketer would be able to improve the relationship for each phase in the relationship life cycle. Explain your answer.

8 A characteristic of professional services is that an expert, such as a doctor or lawyer, helps customers in exchange for payment.
   (a) How would you typify the balance of power in these relationships?
   (b) What role does the capacity for empathy play in these relationships?
   (c) Under what circumstances can mutual commitment exist in these types of relationships?

9 Describe the social structure in a virtual community of your choice. Under what circumstances would the development of long-term customer–supplier relationships not be advisable? Explain your answer.

References

Arndt, John (1979) Toward a concept of domesticated markets, *Journal of Marketing*, **43**, Autumn, 69–75.

Bagozzi, R.P. (1974) Marketing as an organized behavioral system of exchange, *Journal of Marketing*, **38**, October, 77–81.

Bagozzi, R.P. (1975) Marketing as exchange, *Journal of Marketing*, **39**, 3, 32–39.

Bales, R.F. (1950) *Interaction Process Analysis*, University of Chicago Press, Chicago.

Berry, L.L. (1983) Relationship marketing, in *Emerging Perspectives on Services Marketing*, AMA, Chicago, 25–28.

Berry, L.L. (1995) Relationship Marketing of Services. Growing Interest, Emerging Perspectives, *Journal of the Academy of Marketing Science*, **23**, 4, 236–245.

Boshoff, C. (1997) An experimental study of service recovery options. *International Journal of Service Industry Management*, **8**, 2, 110–130.

Bruhn, Manfred (2003) *Relationship Marketing: Management of customer relationships*, Pearson Education, Harlow.

Crosby, L.A., K.R. Evans and D. Cowles (1990) Relationship quality in services selling: an interpersonal influence perspective, *Journal of Marketing*, **54**, 68–81.

de Jager, H. and A.L. Mok (1994) *Grondbeginselen der Sociologie: gezichtspunten en begrippen*, Stenfert Kroese, Houten.

Dwyer, F. Robert, Paul H. Schurr and Sejo Oh (1987) Developing buyer–seller relationships, *Journal of Marketing*, **51**, April, 11–27.

Fournier, Susan, Susan Dobscha and David Glen Mick (1998) Preventing the premature death of relationship marketing, *Harvard Business Review*, January–February, 42–52.

Garbarino, Ellen and Mark S. Johnson (1999) The different roles of satisfaction, trust, and commitment in customer relationships, *Journal of Marketing*, **63**, April, 70–87.

Geyskens, I. and J.E.B.M. Steenkamp (1997) De rol van vertrouwen bij het opbouwen van langetermijn-relaties in de dienstensector, *MAB*, April, 164–170.

Grönroos, C. (1990) Relationship approach to marketing in service contexts: the marketing and organizational behavior interface, *Journal of Business Research*, **20**, 1, 3–11.

Grönroos, C. (1994) From marketing mix to relationship marketing: towards a paradigm shift in marketing, *Management Decisions*, **32**, 2, 4–20.

Grönroos, C. (2000) *Service Management and Marketing: A customer relationship management approach*, 2nd edn, John Wiley & Sons, Chichester.

Gummesson, E. (1987) The new marketing: developing long-term interactive relationships, *Long Range Planning*, **20**, 4, 10–20.

Gummesson, E. (1994) Making relationship marketing operational, *International Journal of Service Industry Management*, **5**, 5, 5–20.

Gummesson, E. (1996) Relationship marketing and imaginery organizations: a synthesis, *European Journal of Marketing*, **30**, 2, 31–44.

Gummesson, E. (1999) *Total Relationship Marketing. Rethinking marketing management: from 4p's to 30Rs*, Butterworth-Heinemann, Oxford.

Håkansson, Hakan (ed.) (1983) *International Marketing and Purchasing of Industrial Goods: An interaction approach*, John Wiley & Sons, Chichester.

Hinde, R.A. (1979) *Towards Understanding Relationships*, Academic Press, London.

Jackson, Barbara Bund (1985) Build customer relationships that last, *Harvard Business Review*, December.

Johnson, Michael P. (1991) Commitment to personal relations, *Advances in Personal Relationships*, **3**, 117–143.

Levitt, T. (1983) *The Marketing Imagination*, The Free Press, New York.

Marketing Management (2002) On-line communities kunnen ondernemingen veel waardevolle informatie opleveren, *Marketing Management*, November–December.

Merton, Robert King (1957) *Social Theory and Social Structure*, Free Press, Glencoe, IL.

Morgan, Robert M. and Shelby D. Hunt (1994) The commitment–trust theory of relationship marketing, *Journal of Marketing*, **58**, July, 20–38.

Moorman, Christine, Rohit Deshpandé and Gerald Zaltman (1993) Factors affecting trust in market research relationships, *Journal of Marketing*, **57**, January, 81–101.

Oliver, R.L. (1996) *Satisfaction: A behavioral perspective on the consumer*, McGraw-Hill, New York.

Payne, Adrian (ed.) (1995) *Advances in Relationship Marketing*, Kogan Page, London.

Peelen, Ed *et al.* (1996) *Thema dossier Relatiemarketing*, Platform '95, Amsterdam.

Peelen, E. (1989) *Relaties tussen consument en aanbieder, een basis voor herhalingsaankopen*, Haveka, Alblasserdam.

Peelen, E., C.F.W. Ekelmans and P. Vijn (1989) Direct marketing for establishing relationships between buyers and sellers, *Journal of Direct Marketing*, **3**, 1, 7–15.

Poeisz, Th.B.C. and W.F. van Raaij (1993) A psychological approach to relatonship quality in industrial markets, *Papers on Economic Psychology*, 117, Erasmus University, Rotterdam.

Reichheld, Frederick E. (1995) *The Loyalty Effect*, The Free Press, Boston, Massachusetts.

Roos, I. and Strandvik (1997) Diagnosing the termination of a customer relationship, *Proceedings on the New and Evolving Paradigms: The emerging future of marketing*, AMA Conference, Dublin, 12–15 June, 617–631.

Rowe, W. Glenn and James G. Barnes (1998) Relationship marketing and sustained competitive advantage, *Journal of Market Focused Management*, 2.

Schijns, Jos (1998) *Het meten en managen van klant-organisatie relaties*, PhD thesis, University of Maastricht, Maastricht.

Tolboom, Maarten (1996) in Ed Peelen *et al.*, *Thema dossier Relatiemarketing*, Platform '95, Amsterdam.

Webster, Frederick E. Jr (1992) The changing role of marketing in the corporation, *Journal of Marketing*, **56**, October, 1–17.

Williamson, O.E. (1979) Transaction cost economics: the governance of contractual relations, *Journal of Law and Economics*, 2.

Zeithaml, V.A. (1988) Consumer perceptions of price, quality and value: a means–end model and synethesis of evidence, *Journal of Marketing*, **52**, 2, 2–22.

Zeithaml, V.A., A. Parasuraman and L.L. Berry (1990) *Delivering Quality Service: Balancing customer perceptions and expectations*, The Free Press, New York.

3

CRM as an integral business strategy

Strategy is a topic that can be approached in different ways (De Wit and Meyer, 2004). It can imply the discussion of the 'organisational purpose': what is the company's *raison d'être*? Why do we exist; how do we contribute to our stakeholders? But at the same time it can be a coherent, unambiguous and integral pattern of decisions, the outcome of the analysis of opportunities and threats in the business domain and the wider environment and the competencies of the organisation. These decisions address not only *what* the organisation aims for, but also *how* it wants to achieve its goals.

In the context of CRM strategy we will follow Treacy and Wiersema (1996). In their study they identified what they call three value disciplines of the successful market leaders. Each of the value disciplines contains a set of answers to the strategic questions we introduced above; they address how companies can define a value proposition in relation to the customers they choose to serve (*what*) and explain how organisations have to be modelled (*how*) to realise this proposition successfully.

The appropriateness of a value discipline (comprising a logical set of answers to the strategic questions) depends on the context: what type of organisation are we dealing with and what are the characteristics of the environment?

In this chapter we will first discuss the three value disciplines (Section 3.1) and then the context (pages 52–54 and Section 3.2). Attention will also be focused on the results which may be obtained by implementing a CRM strategy (Section 3.3).

In this chapter we will address the following questions

- What are the characteristics of a strategy?
- What are the three value disciplines (strategies) according to Treacy and Wiersema?
- How to formulate the CRM strategy as part of the customer intimacy value discipline?
- How to characterise the CRM strategy (defensive or offensive).
- Which factors influence the applicability and the success of the CRM strategy in both the internal and external environments?
- What may be achieved by implementing a successful CRM strategy?

Practitioner's insight

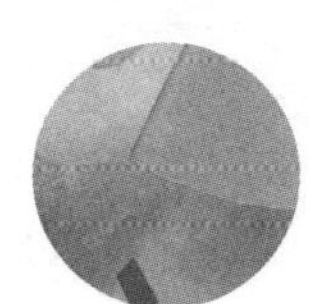

CRM is implemented as a means of lowering costs. Our objective is to lighten the call centre's load by granting customers direct access to the back office so that they may in effect help themselves. Customers have been contacting us with increasing frequency in recent years to ask all sorts of questions about our services. As a result, the pressure on our call centre has grown perceptibly. At the same time, customers are not willing to pay more for our services, making it necessary for us to arrive at less expensive self-service solutions.

This is a situational description which will ring true for many companies. Though each of the organisations involved will, in all likelihood, indicate that they plan to implement a CRM system, the question remains whether or not they will also pursue a CRM strategy. Is the pursuit of accessibility, productivity, reliability and self-service characteristic of a customer intimacy strategy, or is more required?

3.1 The nature of the CRM strategy

In studying successful companies Treacy and Wiersema (1996) discerned three 'value disciplines', namely:

1 Operational excellence.
2 Product leadership.
3 Customer intimacy.

The descriptions of the three 'value disciplines' that follow correspond to those found in Treacy and Wiersema's book. Afterwards (pages 52–54) we will reflect on these disciplines within the context of CRM.

Operational excellence

Companies that employ an operational excellence strategy attempt to find a combination of price, quality and ease of purchase that none of their competitors are capable of matching. They do not spend a great deal of time on innovation or one-to-one relationships with customers. They offer their customers a guaranteed low price and problem-free service. The products are of a good quality. Examples of this type of company are McDonald's, Dell Computers and easyJet, but also Ford at the time that it introduced the classic Model T Ford and the American supermarket chain Wal-Mart.

The business model behind this value proposition focuses on achieving cost leadership. Products are purchased at low prices and in large volumes. The information systems follow the flow of goods closely and remove inefficiencies. Activities within the value chain are closely aligned with one another. Production is standardised and automated, if possible. The staff maintains a high level of productivity and management steers activities tightly and in a centralised manner. Everyone knows the execution plan and the 'commands'. When an order is issued, everyone knows what he or she must do. Strict norms are applied. The accommodation is austere and the overhead costs are low. Characteristic of the company culture are the concepts that efficiency is rewarded and waste is despised. The team is what counts, not the individual. The heroes within this type of organisation are those people who fit in with the group, who climb higher within the company and upon whom one can depend.

Product leadership

Organisations which aim for product leadership constantly work hard to implement innovation and renewal. These companies want to amaze customers, push limits and discover the unknown. Product leaders surprise customers with the newest and best products. Examples of this type of company include Bang & Olufsen, Mercedes, Swatch, Nike, Apple and small tour operators that specialise in a specific country. This type of company must be creative, inspired and must have many ideas. However, as Thomas Edison, the inventor of the electric light bulb once said: 'Genius is 1 per cent inspiration and 99 per cent perspiration.' What is important here is to recognise the good ideas and to expand upon these ideas so that truly new products may be developed as a result. An inspirational vision of a new product is indispensable in order to be able to do this. Apple, for example, set itself the goal of pushing the limits of people's power of creation by developing computers. Clear rules are also helpful. Sony, for example, attached concrete requirements in terms of size and weight in developing its 'Walkman'.

The success achieved by product leaders is dependent upon the success they are able to realise in the market. And this can be risky since it involves new products and services which have not yet been accepted by customers. By managing a portfolio of new ideas, they must be able to counterbalance the failure of certain innovations. In order to maintain the role of innovator continuously, they must be able to foresee the obsolescence of innovations; companies such as Intel are already hard at work on the successor to a product generation before that generation is even launched on the market. New product ideas must be developed quickly, and the products manufactured and introduced to the market.

Decisions are made quickly at companies like this; there is not enough time to analyse situations and determine all of the things that could go wrong. It is permissible to make mistakes. These companies dare to take risks and are in search of new triumphs. It is important to be able to react quickly and to work on shortening design cycles. Product leaders attempt to avoid every type of bureaucracy and to do what they can to allow talent to blossom. The highest form of acknowledgement for talented people is to be chosen for the next, even more challenging project. The product leaders are proud of their inventions, their brainchildren, and will never compromise when it comes to price. In order to maintain this culture, it is more important for new employees to be like-minded than for them to be experienced in the particular industry.

Customer intimacy

The customer intimacy strategy is characterised by the fact that companies build up a relationship with customers. It is not so much the market that becomes the centre of attention, but the individual wishes of customers that count. A great deal of attention is focused on the development of the desired customer base: who do we want and who do we not want as our customers? The company is built up based on the knowledge of the individual customers and their preferences. Products and services are continually adapted to customers' wishes, without asking excessively high prices for doing so. The company positions itself as a partner for its customers, and takes their problems off their hands, offering them total solutions or helping them to perform better, as the case may be ('to help build your customer's business'). The company takes responsibility for the results its customers achieve. Customers do not have to be acquired time and time again via expensive campaigns. Transactions are subordinate in importance to relationships. A company which employs a customer intimacy strategy looks at the 'lifetime value' of a customer, not only at the profit or loss of transactions. Examples of companies that implement this type of strategy are private bankers, or a hotel chain such as Ritz Carlton.

CRM illustration

According to Lester Wunderman, CRM is also an 'unreal specification'. Wunderman: 'The consumer is not interested mainly in relationships with suppliers. He wants a good product for a reasonable price and he wants service. And let's be honest here: suppliers aren't really after a relationship. We want the consumer to buy our products and services. In order to align supply and demand with one another as accurately as possible and to be of optimum service to the consumer, we need information and data from him . . .

The term "relationship" also quickly creates an association with invading someone's private life.'

Source: Lester Wunderman (2003) Dean of Direct Marketing, *Insight*.

The business model for these organisations has been designed to be able to supply products and services from a broader perspective. With their range of products and services, they are sharply attuned to the customer's needs, even if it means that they must act as a middleman between the customer and other suppliers of products and services. They will seldom supply the newest products and services; more often it is the reliable and tried-and-tested solutions that they offer. Customers are seen as the raison d'être for these types of organisations.

A thorough knowledge of the customer as a person, user and buyer is essential in consumer markets. In business-to-business marketing, however, it is the knowledge of the customer's company and the processes involved within it that counts. It involves the insights which must be capitalised on. Account managers or customer managers play an important role in these efforts; these are the lynchpins of the organisation, the people who are in close contact with the customers. These individuals are long-term planners. Sometimes it even seems as though there are hardly any boundaries between them and the customer. They are rewarded for keeping and satisfying customers and increasing the turnover per customer. People who are in direct contact with the customer have a relatively high degree of freedom to capitalise on the customer's wishes. The decision-making authority is delegated to the people who are closest to the customer.

Conclusion

Obviously, the value discipline which fits in best with the CRM strategy is the customer intimacy discipline. The distinctive feature of this discipline is that the company wants to get to know the customer and develop a long-term mutually profitable relationship with the customer. The company wants to provide the customer with customisation. The customer constitutes the most important reason for the organisation's existence, and forms the starting point used in formulating the organisational objectives and the determination of the business model for the organisation.

The business described in the introduction which employs CRM systems to lower costs, increase productivity and make it easier for customers to do business with, is clearly opting for operational excellence. It applies the CRM systems, yet clearly implements a strategy that does not have to be focused on the development of individual customer knowledge and a long-term customer relationship.

It is not recommended to combine the three value disciplines described above. It is difficult to excel in every area, all the more so because excellence in all three of the dimensions would create conflicts among them. The tight organisation and centralisation inherent in operational excellence companies conflict with the 'looser' organisation characteristic of product leaders and companies that strive for customer intimacy. A specific culture corresponds to each of the three strategies, and these cultures are difficult to reconcile with one another. Even a company such as Amazon.com has its critics who feel that it misjudged the situation; combining the individual customer approach with a complete product line and low cost and pricing levels is difficult when company performance is expected to be positive. In order to achieve a 'state of the art' individual customer approach, a great deal of effort will have to be put into the development of technology and the recording and analysis of customer data. Maintaining a full line implies keeping a substantial inventory and incurring high logistics costs. It appears that the investments and the costs involved in customer intimacy and product leadership are difficult to recover. Charging higher prices for the personal service and the options is difficult in a market in which the competition is only one click away. The increase in purchase volume is also insufficient to justify the high level of effort in both areas. Amazon.com has also adjusted its ambitions in this regard.

However, to disregard two of the three value disciplines is no more advisable. Even an organisation that strives for operational excellence will have to maintain a minimum level of innovation and attention to and care for individual customers. The products and services will also have to possess a certain level of quality. Customers of a discounter also expect good quality in the products they purchase there; however, they do not shop there expecting to find the fanciest or trendiest of wares. Likewise, innovators will have to monitor their costs and their connection with customers, and similar remarks may be made with regard to companies employing a customer intimacy discipline. Although the latter experience the safety of a close bond with their customers, it will become apparent that these barriers cannot keep the competition out if aspects of price and quality prove to be an insufficient source of satisfaction in the long run.

Over time, companies can elect to follow a growth path. In the early stage of the implementation of CRM systems, companies tend to work on operational excellence. Their energy is focused on the redesign of the back office. Information on products and services may be retrieved and transactions may be processed online. Information on the completion of the individual transactions may be retrieved. Customers may obtain insight into their transaction and communication history in no time. In short, the back office has become accessible for customers in a problem-free manner. The front office may also be developed further and integrated with the back office, also without problems. The functionality of the Internet may increase further; orders may now also be placed and customers have access to and may view their own personal situation. Within the call centre, this also allows for a better response to individual customer queries.

Companies which pursue this path will first have to justify investments in CRM from a standpoint of aiming to reduce costs. At the same time, a situation is created in which convenience for customers is increased. As was indicated in the example at the beginning of this chapter, an attempt is made to unburden those in the call centre by allowing customers to register their purchases themselves, look up the answers to their questions and so forth.

It is only once the situation of operational excellence is achieved that the time is considered to be ripe for customer intimacy. The opportunities offered by the infrastructure created may be further developed and utilised by expanding knowledge of the individual customer and using it in the contact with the customer. By keeping track of communication and transactions, the supplier increases its insight into the customer. The supplier can truly benefit from the customer knowledge it acquires during its interactions with the customer, and in a relatively inexpensive way; it can supply more customisation, bid farewell to the transaction orientation, and focus on increasing the value of individual customers. The intensity of the relationship with customers may be increased step by step (see the pyramid in Figure 2.1) until the desired level has been reached.

An offensive versus a defensive strategy

Strategies may be typified in numerous ways. Choosing to distinguish between the defensive and the offensive can prove interesting within this framework. An offensive strategy focuses on the conquest of market share, the acquisition of new customers and ridding oneself quickly of any competition. It is a strategy that has been typical in marketing for many years. The defensive strategy, on the other hand, focuses on maintaining and defending one's position. Barriers are thrown up to keep the competition at bay.

CRM illustration

Here are several quotes from a brainstorming session with marketers which illustrate the offensive nature of (consumer) marketing:

- 'Promotions are extremely important. They become a goal in and of themselves. Personally, I set a target for myself to launch five or six promotions per year; this lightens the load on one's conscience. The promotions are extremely short-term oriented. A great deal of importance is attached to efficiency and not enough thought is given to strategy.'
- 'Knowledge of the consumer is insufficient. When a new product is introduced, we are happy if we make it to the trial phase. We do not sufficiently investigate the question: what motivates a consumer to buy?'
- 'We reward disloyalty and punish loyalty.'

Source: Peelen *et al.* (1996).

Figure 3.1 Offensive versus defensive strategies

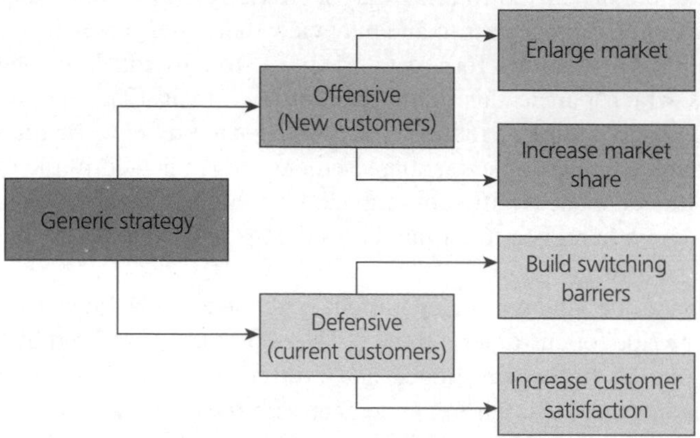

Of the three strategies identified by Treacy and Wiersema, the customer intimacy strategy is the defensive strategy which focuses on customer retention and the other two are viewed as the offensive strategies. In the case of operational excellence as well as that of product leadership, the organisation strives to expand its customer base (see Figure 3.1).

The differences between the strategies have consequences for the standards by which the success of the strategy is measured. In an offensive strategy, the market share represents an important criterion for success, whereas with the defensive strategy, ratios such as customer churn, sales per customer and customer satisfaction play a more important role. In some cases, the value of a customer is calculated in terms of the total number of purchases made in the period they have been buying from the supplier. This is referred to as the 'lifetime value' of a customer (see Chapter 14). Both strategies are set out against one another in Table 3.1 to illustrate a situation of a saturated market with little growth.

Table 3.1 Success criteria for an offensive and a defensive strategy (in a saturated market) (market share vs commitment)

	Market share strategy	*Strategy commitment*
Objective	Customer switching	Customer commitment
Market conditions	Saturated market, little growth	Saturated market, little growth
Primary focus	Competition	Customers
Success measured by	Market share relative to competition	Customer retention Turnover/customer

3.2 The context of the CRM strategy

The applicability of a strategy and its degree of success is determined by the context. Is the organisation more capable than others of implementing the strategy and does this correspond to what is currently happening within the relevant market and the external environment?

Internal

In order to develop a CRM strategy, an organisation must first meet certain preconditions. The situation must be avoided in which a company ultimately chooses to implement a CRM strategy based on negative considerations: for example, if it encounters problems with the quality of its products, their positioning or the logistics, and/or feels the competition breathing down its neck. In effect, the company is not sufficiently capable of translating its customers' wishes into products and services. As a result, customer loyalty is decreasing and switching behaviour develops. The option to implement customer intimacy seems like a solution. In reality, the symptom of customer churn is being treated instead of the actual business problems. The fact that a CRM strategy has the effect of increasing customer expectations is overlooked. By paying attention to individual customers and wanting to develop a relationship with them, those customers will feel special and expect a special delivery performance. However, this is precisely where the company's problems lie. The end result is that now more than ever the company is forced to face facts. The situation described here is not a hypothetical one; whether it involves supermarkets, financial institutions, airlines or car manufacturers, if one looks, one will find examples in a multitude of industry sectors.

Positive arguments will have to be at the heart of the choice to implement a CRM strategy. The consequences of the strategy for the organisation will have to be examined thoroughly (see Chapter 4). Clarification will have to be given of what the company hopes to achieve and the business model behind the strategy will have to be established. The organisation will have to be able to see the reasons for its existence in the customer. The company's success will be dependent on the development of relationships with the right customers. The CRM system will have to be able to be fully developed for the purpose of achieving this goal. The company will have to be built up around the right customers. Those people who work closely with the customer will be the 'heroes' of the organisation and must be allowed a great deal of freedom and authority. Even involving the competition's products is one of the possibilities, if customers specifically request this.

In short, CRM not only involves the marketing or the IT function within a company, but has a way of becoming interwoven in all the departments within the organisation.

External

A CRM strategy must also be in tune with the market and the broader external environment, as described under the next three sub-headings.

Customers

The intended customers will have to appreciate a relationship with the supplier; it is insufficient for the supplier alone to have an interest in a long-term bond with the customer. Certainly not all of the customers will experience this need; there are countless suppliers with whom they do business and at best, it is only a small, select group with whom they would like to build a relationship. To do this, they will have to become involved with the supplier and its solutions.

CRM illustration

A person's 'active' vocabulary consists of 6000 to 7000 words; we have more than 25 000 products. How is the consumer supposed to maintain a relationship with all of those products?

Source: Peelen *et al.* (1996).

Furthermore, the personality of the customer or the culture of the purchasing company will have to be taken into consideration. Some customers do not place any value whatsoever on the development of a relationship with a supplier.

Within the scope of a CRM strategy, customers will also have to accept a differentiated marketing approach. Good customers will be better served and rewarded. As long as the customer refuses to accept this, a CRM system in which a distinction is made between customers cannot be implemented. It appears that this differentiation presents more of a problem in consumer markets than in business-to-business markets, where this is a much more accepted way of doing business (Peelen *et al.*, 1996).

Competition

The success of a CRM strategy also depends on the competition encountered in the market. In essence, a supplier that operates in a market in which it has a monopoly will have to expend less effort to increase customer loyalty than it would if it were active in a market in which it is up against heavy competition. In the United States, the local telephone companies have a monopoly on the regional services they provide; it is only in the long-distance telephone services market that they have competition.

Car manufacturers, on the other hand, must compete with a large number of other producers to win the favour of the customer. A great deal is required before customer satisfaction translates into loyalty (see Figure 3.2). Their expectations will have to be exceeded to a very high degree. Suppliers will have to consider whether this will ultimately be worth their while or whether a more offensive strategy is preferable.

Figure 3.2

The influence of competition on earning customer loyalty

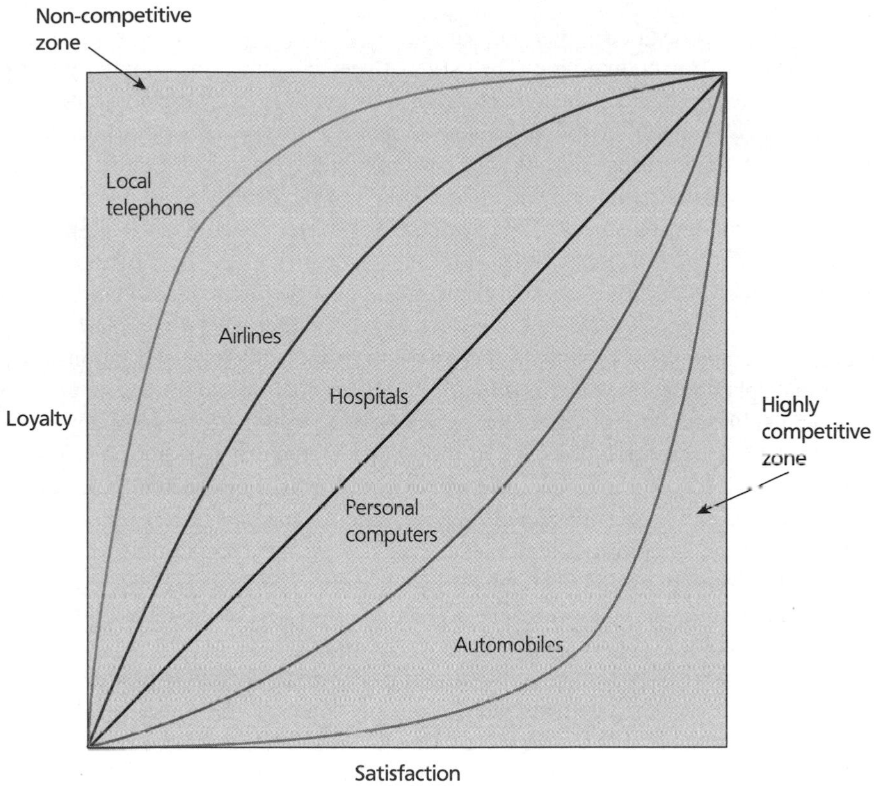

Source: Jones and Sasser (1995). Reprinted by permission of *Harvard Business Review*. From 'Why Satisfied Customers Defect' by Jones, T.O. and Sasser Jr, W., November/December 1995.

Distribution

Companies that employ intermediaries to serve their customers need to find the opportunity within a CRM strategy to strengthen their ties with customers. A certain degree of alienation can occur between the supplier and the final customer, particularly if the intermediaries occupy a powerful position. A CRM system, and usually also a CRM strategy, can offer a solution in this situation. By recording individual customer data and communicating with final customers via the Internet, telephone and perhaps even personal contact, a relationship may be developed. These companies will remain reliant on the intermediary for the initiation and completion of transactions, as the intermediary is better able to perform these tasks.

This is a situation that we encounter in the insurance industry, for example, and also in the automobile industry where importers may contact owners of a particular brand directly. In all of these cases we are confronted with potential channel conflicts because the intermediaries feel threatened by the actions of suppliers. The suppliers approach the final customer directly and could lower the compensation for the middleman or even start selling directly to customers. The final design of the CRM strategy will have to take these risks into account and it will have to be considered whether and how CRM may be employed to the benefit of all the parties involved (see Chapter 4).

3.3 The results of a successful CRM strategy

The relationship between customer and supplier will have to protect the supplier from any action taken by the competition. The bond between customer and supplier will have to lead to a situation in which customers will not succumb to the temptation offered by other suppliers. The supplier should be able to make a mistake without the continuity of the relationship becoming an issue. The customer will be convinced of the supplier's will and ability to satisfy him and will characterise this incident as a one-off and as one without long-term consequences. The customer will even expect that the supplier will adapt to changing circumstances and still be able to qualify as the best partner.

Rowe and Barnes (1998) expect that only close, positive, two-sided relationships in which both partners respect and are committed to one another have the *potential* to lead to a long-term competitive advantage. The development of this type of relationship is a very complex phenomenon which is difficult for the competition to imitate and one that will, in all likelihood, be quite rare (Rowe and Barnes, 1998). If the company utilises its skill to develop these relationships in the proper manner, it will not only have the power to create a long-term competitive advantage, but will also actually accomplish this. In other cases, CRM is expected to contribute to reaching a level equal to that of the competition, obtaining a temporary headstart on the competition, or reducing the distance the company lags behind the competition. These cases also involve an improvement in position which can have a positive effect on the financial performance of the organisation.

The theory that customer–supplier relationships can actually lead to an improvement in financial results has been demonstrated in various studies. The most well-known of these studies is probably that conducted by Reichheld (1996). In his book *The Loyalty Effect*, he provides the results from the study Bains & Co. conducted into the effects of a 5 per cent reduction in customer churn on customer profitability during the course of the customer's relationship with the supplier. The results found for the various industries studied are shown in Figure 3.3. The role of the product appears (still) to play an excessively dominant role in a sector such as the software industry. In a variety of situations, it appears that a good bond cannot compete with the quality of new products or standards. Ultimately we switch *en masse* from WordPerfect to Word or from Netscape to Explorer. The best results in reducing customer churn were observed in those industry sectors in which individual customer knowledge and the creation of trust may be used to strengthen dramatically the value proposition.

The increase in profitability occurs because the acquisition costs decrease with a lower customer churn; fewer new customers are necessary to realise the desired growth in sales. Additionally, serving regular customers is accompanied by fewer costs, regular customers purchase more and may be prepared to pay a price premium. Finally, as 'ambassador' to the supplier, they can introduce new customers (see Figure 3.4).

There are also more scientific studies which have shown that customer–supplier relationships can contribute to a higher amount of sales per customer, repeat purchases or an increase in the customer lifetime value (for example, that of Leuthesser and Kohli, 1995).

Figure 3.3

Influence of a 5% reduction in customer churn on customer profitability

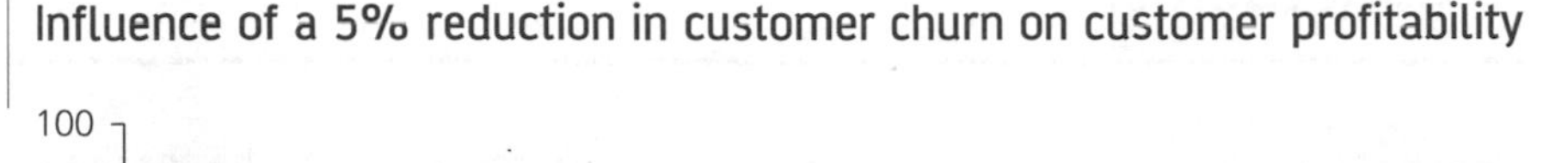

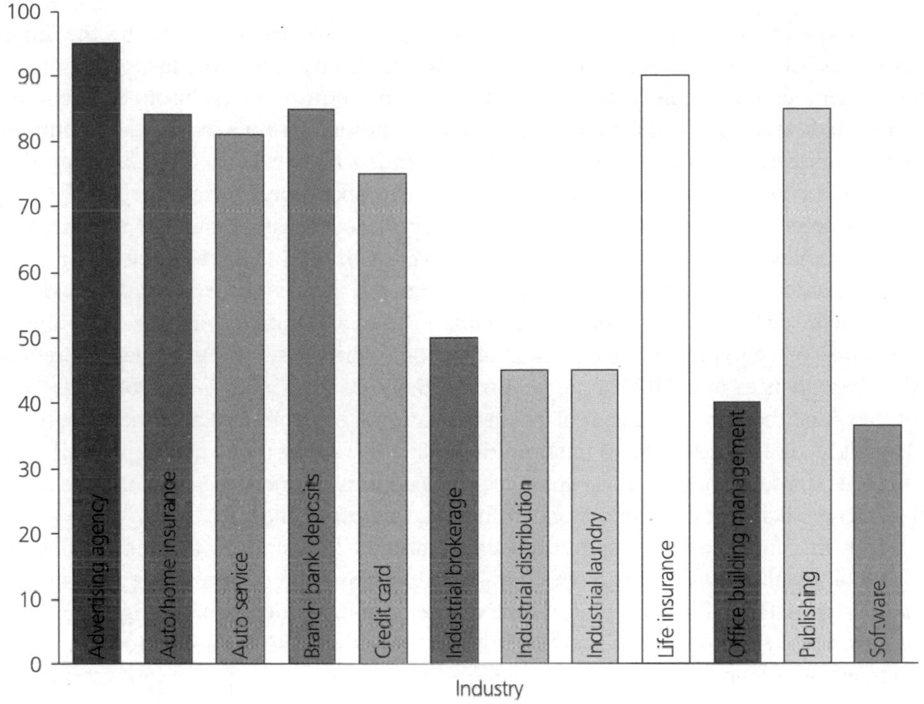

Source: Reichheld (1996). Reprinted by permission of Harvard Business School Press. From *The Loyalty Effect* by F.E. Reichheld. Boston, MA 1996. Copyright © 1996 by the Harvard Business School Publishing Corporation; all rights reserved.

Figure 3.4

Effects of customer loyalty on the profitability of a customer

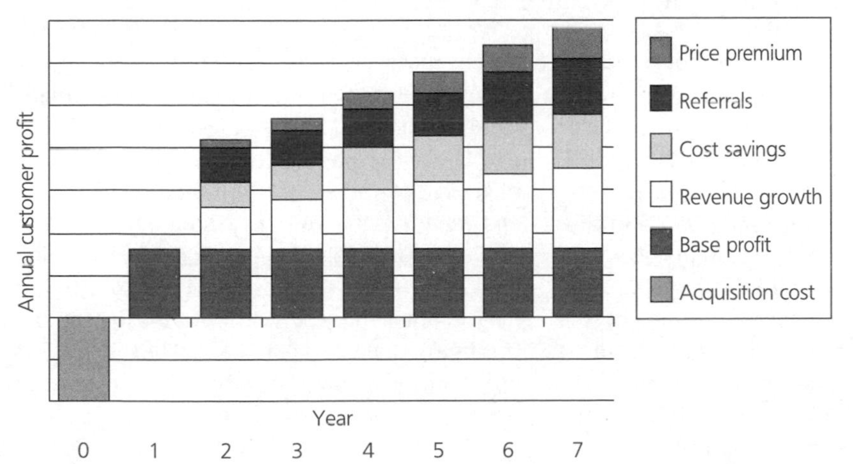

Source: Reichheld (1996). Reprinted by permission of Harvard Business School Press. From *The Loyalty Effect* by F.E. Reichheld. Boston, MA 1996. Copyright © 1996 by the Harvard Business School Publishing Corporation; all rights reserved.

3.4 Conclusion

The introduction of a CRM system on its own is not a sufficient condition for the implementation of a CRM strategy. Organisations which deploy these systems to get to know customers, communicate with them and build long-term mutually profitable relationships with them are implementing a customer intimacy value strategy. A company whose objective in implementing a CRM system is to lower costs or increase productivity and convenience for customers has opted for operational excellence.

Customer intimacy can certainly not be applied successfully in all situations. It places demands on the organisation. The company will need to have its 'house in order' – the brand must be recognisable and distinctive, the quality of the products good, and the system of logistics reliable. There cannot be any negative considerations underlying the choice to implement a CRM strategy, only (primarily) positive ones. Moreover, the consequences of a CRM strategy must be analysed from an organisation-wide point of view and the opportunities it offers in the external environment must be recognised. The right customers value a relationship with the supplier and accept the different methods the supplier uses in its approach to customers. The competition and the distribution are such that they do not undermine the success of the CRM strategy.

It is only in these types of environments that the CRM strategy can lead to positive financial results because customer churn is reduced and the customer lifetime value is increased. After all, it is only in those extreme cases in which actual long-term mutually profitable relationships are allowed to blossom that CRM can lead to a long-term competitive advantage.

Case study

Orange Line

Orange Line is a Scandinavia-based operator of cruise ships and ferries. The organisation owns six cruise ships of varying size and quality. Two are very luxurious, can provide hospitality to over 10 000 guests and are used for one-, two- or three-week trips. The ships travel all over the world and guests embark at different locations all over the world. Sometimes a guest will embark and disembark at the same port, but it frequently occurs that they disembark from a different port from that at which they boarded. Recently the company has started to sell luxurious apartments on these two cruise ships to people who want to spend more time on the ship during the year. Many of these apartments are being sold for the price of a villa (approximately €1 000 000 or more) in addition to which the guests have to pay a yearly service fee. Several of these apartments are being sub-let to family and friends of the owners. Since the start of this initiative, six months ago, more than one hundred of these apartments have been sold.

The other four cruise ships are used for short breaks of three or four days. They depart and arrive in the same port, which is often local to where the guests live. The facilities on board are of lesser quality. Also the prices are much lower for this sort of trip. Again, about 10 000 guests can be accommodated aboard the cruise ship.

The ferries maintain scheduled shipping lines between major Scandinavian ports and ports in the UK, Germany and The Netherlands. The share of private customers (with or without car) as a percentage of the total number of customers is decreasing. Meanwhile the importance of transportation companies is increasing.

The ferries account for 30 per cent of the revenue from the Orange Line; the two luxury cruise ships for another 35 per cent and the other four ships are responsible for the remaining 35 per cent. The ferries generate a small contribution to the operating profit after depreciation and interest (5 per cent), while the cruise ships bring in the majority of the profit. The two luxury ships are contributing very positively.

The future of Orange Line, however, may not necessarily be as prosperous as the recent past. Changes in European tax legislation will impact the tax-free sales of liquor, tobacco, cosmetics, consumer electronics and many other products in the near future. Currently, sales of these products are responsible for about 30 per cent of turnover realised during the three/four-day cruise trips and for an even larger share of the profit (circa 70 per cent). The fee that guests have to pay for the cabin and transport equals 40 per cent of turnover; in most cases the ship itself is, however, not profitable. Only when the occupancy rate exceeds 85 per cent are the costs of the vessel entirely recovered. This occurs only during two months in high season. The remaining share of the turnover comes from food and beverages served to the guests, gambling, health clubs and shows. These additional services are again profitable; the average gross margin is 25–30 per cent.

The one-, two- and three-week cruises on the two luxury ships will not be greatly affected by the change in tax legislation. First of all, they operate to a large extent outside the European Union and, furthermore, tax-free sales only contribute marginally to turnover and profitability. The majority of the sales come from the rental of the cabin (including transport) and additional services on board (food, beverages, shows, health clubs, gambling, etc.). During the year almost all activities contribute to the profit. The break-even point is reached at much lower occupancy rates (50 per cent).

The organisation has a small landside office with 40 employees, responsible for purchasing, human resources, maintenance, marketing, etc. There is one CEO, who chairs the management team (MT). The managers of the functional disciplines are represented in the MT.

Some years ago the organisation started to build a customer database with names, addresses, phone numbers, e-mail addresses, booking behaviour, some demographics (gender and age), satisfaction, complaints and the names of intermediaries where the customers booked their cruise if they did not order directly. One person in the organisation has a small budget for maintaining the database. He facilitates the marketing department by making the prospects lists. People on the prospects lists are approached by mail, phone or e-mail. Marketing is responsible for developing the campaigns. An external contact centre is normally hired for outbound telemarketing activities; inbound telemarketing is done in the in-house call centre. In most cases, outbound calling is done only as follow-up on a mailing. The company refrains from aggressive sales as it always asks for permission to contact the customer.

The current experience with database marketing is promising. The CEO realises the organisation has only made some first steps and many aspects need improvement. However, it is a beginning. It is seen also as a way of exploring what CRM can bring the organisation.

One of the major next steps the CEO of Orange Line is considering is a reorganisation. A consultant told him his organisation is product-oriented rather than customer-centric, which is undesirable for a service provider at the top of the market.

Questions

1. Treacy and Wiersema distinguish between three value disciplines, i.e. operational excellence, customer intimacy and product leadership. Which value discipline/strategy do you advise for Orange Line? Give arguments.
2. Tax legislation will have major implications for Orange Line.
   (a) Formulate five creative tactical recommendations for Orange Line to compensate for the loss of business from tax-free sales and/or to improve business in general.
   (b) Based upon your recommendations, formulate some related requirements for the CRM system.
3. Do you agree with the CEO's intention to reorganise the company into a customer-centric organisation (see also Chapter 4)? If so, what changes in the organisation structure would you recommend for it to become a customer-centric organisation. If not, argue why the current organisation structure is satisfactory.

Questions

1. Under which market circumstances is it unwise to aim for a customer intimacy strategy? Give two examples.
2. Why does the combination of the product leadership, customer intimacy and operational excellence strategies lead to problems? Explain your answer by providing an example.
3. Think of five examples of companies which implement a customer intimacy strategy. Explain your answer.
4. In your opinion, is it possible for the manufacturer of a low-involvement product such as biscuits or crackers to implement a customer intimacy strategy? Explain your answer.
5. Why is a customer intimacy strategy considered to be a defensive strategy? Explain your answer.
6. Is it possible to combine the deployment of a customer intimacy strategy and the maintenance of an indirect system of distribution? Explain your answer. If your answer is yes, provide an example.
7. Reichheld has studied the effects of reducing customer churn on customer profitability in a variety of markets (see Figure 3.3). A substantial difference may be observed between the life insurance market and that for software products. In your opinion, what is a possible explanation for this? Explain your answer.
8. What are the risks associated with Reichheld's calculation method in Figure 3.4? Explain your answer.

References

Jones, T.O. and W. Sasser Jr (1995) Why satisfied customers defect, *Harvard Business Review*, November–December, 88–100.

Leuthesser, Lance and Ajay K. Koli (1995) Long-term manufacturer–supplier relationships: do they pay off for supplier firms?, *Journal of Marketing*, **59**, January, 1–16.

Peelen, Ed *et al.* (1996) *Thema dossier Relatiemarketing*, Platform '95, Amsterdam.

Reichheld, Frederick E. (1996) *The Loyalty Effect*, The Free Press, New York.

Rowe, W. Glenn and James G. Barnes (1998) Relationship marketing and sustained competitive advantage, *Journal of Market Focused Management*, **1**, 2.

Treacy, M. and F. Wiersema (1996) *The Discipline of Market Leaders*, Harper Collins, New York.

Wit, Bob de and Ron Meyer (2004) *Strategy, Process, Content, Context*, rev. edn, West Publishing Company, St Paul, Minneapolis.

Wunderman, Lester (2003) Direct marketing is geen tactiek om een economische dip te overbruggen, *Insight*, **3**, 3, 24–25.

4

The relationship-oriented organisation

The realisation of the customer intimacy value discipline places demands on the organisation. The ultimate goal is that individuals within the organisation derive motivation from their collaboration with customers. Customers should provide inspiration to the organisation to further improve performance. The opposite situation, such as that described in the *Practitioner's Insight* on page 67, should be prevented. Customers with whom providing advice and effort proves to be a waste of time should, in fact, be referred to the competition. Furthermore, the organisation also should invest in its mission, culture, personnel, structure and operating systems in order to create an environment in which striving for customer satisfaction and customer relationships is facilitated and rewarded. Many of the problems mentioned in the *Practitioner's Insight* can arise when people in the front office are rewarded primarily for productivity which in turn results in the idea taking root that customers are preventing them from achieving their goals.

In this chapter, we examine the elements mentioned above, which together help to illustrate an important part of the concept of the relationship-oriented organisation.

In this chapter we will address the following questions

- What type of organisation is necessary to create a CRM strategy?
- What characterises the mission of the relationship-oriented organisation applying a CRM strategy?
- How to spread the mission.
- What is characteristic for the culture of a relationship-oriented organisation?
- What is the structure of a relationship-oriented organisation?
- What is the customer pyramid and how does it relate to the organisation of relationship management?
- What is the role of CRM systems in relationship management?
- What human qualities are required to develop customer–supplier relationships?
- How to communicate within a relationship-oriented organisation.
- What are the service profit chain and the balanced scorecard and how can they, as tools, be used to 'steer' the relationship-oriented organisation?
- To what degree do we appear to be capable of successfully creating relationship-oriented organisations?

Practitioner's insight

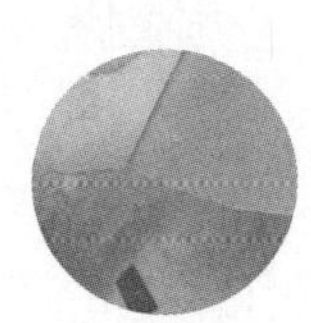

Service Manager John Smith: Customers are great, as long as they don't bother you. They interrupt the business process and keep you from your work. They contact you for every little trifle and expect an immediate solution from you while they're not even capable of remembering their customer number and giving it to you. They've forgotten how to be grateful, yet seem to have become all the more skilled at negotiating. When it comes to doing something in return, they suddenly speak a different language. The arguments they use in the after-sales period contrast sharply with the subjects they offer up during price negotiations. During the sales process, you hear constantly that there are ten other companies out there just like you, but when it comes to service, they remind you of your commitment to the relationship. They remember everything if it works to their advantage, yet when it benefits them to forget something, they will do it in a heartbeat . . .

And you want to set up a relationship-oriented organisation?

4.1 Mission

The starting point of a relationship-oriented organisation is the cultivation and optimisation of commitment between the customer and supplier during their long-term interactions (Peelen *et al.*, 1996). Commitment reflects the intention on the part of both parties to continue the relationship in the future, regardless of changes which may occur in the environment. First and foremost, the foundation for these future plans is the concept of trust. Trust is based on the conviction that the other party will fulfil its promises. It indicates the degree to which the other party strives to meet objectives which are complementary to its own ambitions; or the degree to which the other has a reputation to uphold, meaning it cannot afford to act in an untrustworthy manner; or that it would consider it immoral to operate unreliably. Second, commitment grows along with customer satisfaction; this occurs when expectations are met or exceeded. Third, commitment is influenced by the attractiveness of the relationship; how does the customer perceive the attractiveness of alternatives to this relationship. Finally, 'switching' costs play a role. They indicate how many problems a customer will encounter in ending the current relationship and starting a new one.

Striving for customer commitment is in sharp contrast to the method used by the 'traditional' organisation in which a transaction orientation tends to dominate and the focus is on groups of homogeneous customers rather than on individual relationships. The 'traditional' organisation tends to expend much effort acquiring new and chiefly floating customers. New products, interesting offers and appealing brands are important weapons in the battle to win the customer's favour. The relationship-oriented organisation adopts a longer time horizon. The primary interest does not lie in the profit made on an individual transaction, but on the so-called lifetime value of the customer. The goal is to increase the net present value of the profit contribution made by a

Figure 4.1 The Ashridge mission model

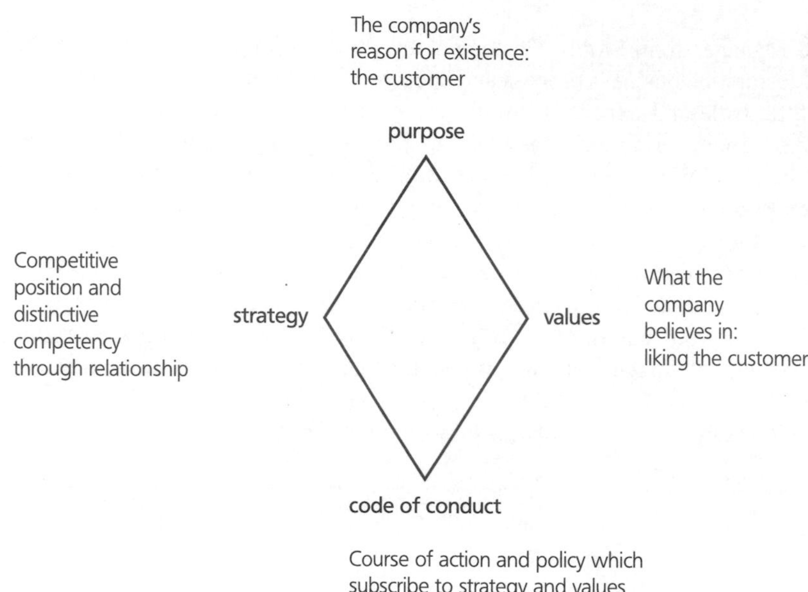

relationship. This may be accompanied by the absorption of an additional loss during the initial transactions. Efforts are made to win the relationship for the company. The company makes a point of learning more about the needs and desires of the individual customers, and examines the uncertainties experienced within the relationship. Knowledge is accumulated in this regard, and actions are taken based upon this knowledge. The preference lies with working with customers to develop and supply customised solutions; either party may take the initiative and there is never only one party that always takes the lead. Communication with customers takes place on an individual level. One-way traffic is kept to a minimum; two-way interaction with customers has clear priority.

Based upon the Ashridge model (see Figure 4.1) the crucial characteristics of the relationship-oriented organisation may be expressed within a mission as follows:

- The objective: the organisation's primary reason for existence is to serve the customer; the idea behind this is that if the relationship with the customer is cultivated, the secondary goals of the organisation will 'automatically' be realised.
- The strategy is that, with an awareness of the company's own identity, the brand image and the group with whom a relationship is desired, the company can work on deepening and broadening the relationship; the primary focus of attention is not the products or transactions but the relationship.
- The code of conduct involves the manner in which relationships are approached; people should be putting themselves in the other person's position (empathy), creating trust, profiling themselves as attractive, open and sincere, lending substance to the relationship and increasing commitment.

- The values involved in relationship marketing may be formulated as: 'the company likes customers', 'the company takes the customer's situation seriously'.

The mission is crucial to the success of the relationship-oriented organisation. The chances of a relationship-oriented company's success are small if top management (Peelen *et al.*, 1996):

- focuses too much attention on the short term and the costs;
- is composed of 'number crunchers';
- does not dare to take enough risks;
- displays too much reactive behaviour;
- does not have enough entrepreneurial spirit;
- does not have enough vision.

In these types of circumstances, marketers will have to demonstrate success in the short term. They are capable of seeing the importance of CRM, but are forced to engage in 'efficiency marketing' or to focus on short-term goals. There is less opportunity to focus on a consistent policy.

A mission in and of itself does not provide enough guidance for the relationship-oriented organisation. First and foremost, there must be what is known as a 'sense of mission' present within the company. It is only after the people within the organisation feel committed to the mission that it will come to underlie their thoughts and actions within the organisation. Everyone is expected to make an effort to cultivate commitment with respect to customers from certain convictions, values and with a specific goal in mind. The customer will recognise the relationship with the people who work for the company. The relationship will not have to be limited to that one contact person with whom the customer often deals and who shields the customer from the rest of the company. He or she prevents the customer from communicating with internal or task-oriented people.

Companies who opt for this solution run the risk that customers will *not* commit to the organisation but will commit instead to the contact person. If this person leaves the company to work for the competition, there is a chance that a number of customers will follow him or her.

Employees will only commit to the mission if their individual values coincide with those of the organisation as a whole. Achieving this type of match is difficult because neither organisations nor people formulate their values and goals explicitly. In most cases, these must be derived from behaviour.

In the mission planning process, the manner in which a 'sense of mission' is obtained must be taken into consideration. In addition to the goals, strategies, values and codes of conduct of those designing the mission plan, focus must also be placed on the values of other involved members of the organisation.

During the mission planning process, strategy formulation, human resources and organisational issues converge. Ultimately a mission will have to be identified which the majority of the people in the organisation feel is worth striving for. Behaviour that is symbolic of the value system and central to the implementation of the strategy will have to be identified.

4.2 Culture

One of the most vital aspects in a relationship-oriented organisation involves the culture. The culture consists of the beliefs, norms and values which are adhered to by the people within an organisation and which have repercussions on their behaviour. In particular, it is behaviour that determines whether an organisation is relationship-oriented or not. The simple fact of whether the personnel in an organisation refer to customers as 'accounts' or 'clients' can provide a fairly good indication of the company's relationship orientation. The way in which employees get along with one another is just as indicative. Usually the customer approach is a reflection of the internal etiquette (Horovitz and Panak, 1992).

The relationship-oriented culture

The culture of a relationship-oriented organisation is characterised by the fact that it understands customers: its employees can place themselves within their world and empathise with them. During brainstorming sessions with marketers, the culture within a relationship-oriented organisation has been further typified based on the following statements:

- 'People dare to show their true selves.' There is openness and insight into who they are. People have the courage to put themselves in a vulnerable position. They dare to show character. They make it clear that they like people.
- People with 'well-developed right brain hemispheres' are deployed. It is not only the rational types who are allowed to decide what will happen within the organisation; they are not equipped with sufficient emotional intelligence to emphathise with others.
- Overtures are made in the proper manner; a sufficient level of empathy is shown in the other; he or she is creative and displays unique and surprising behaviour.
- People come across as sincere, otherwise customers could get the impression that they are being manipulated in a relationship by a marketer. They prevent the customer from perceiving attention from the supplier as something being done purely for show or, even worse, from thinking that the company is using false intentions to play upon their personal feelings, that the only goal of the approach was to bring a transaction to fruition. Customers are left with a feeling that they have been abused and the supplier can forget any hopes it might have had for a relationship.

Interest

Employees who subscribe to the norms and values which apply within the company may become emotionally involved in the organisation and are prepared to make extra efforts in the interest of the relationships (Horovitz and Panak, 1992). In addition to employees, customers may also become involved in the corporate culture.

Thanks to a uniform and strong culture, a company may also adapt more quickly. The employees within an organisation have the same beliefs. They are similar in certain respects. For certain challenges and problems, they will have a preference for similar actions and solutions, independent of one another. As a result, procedures may be relaxed and responsibilities and decision-making authority may be delegated. The organisation may become 'flatter' and in a position to make decisions and take action more quickly. A strong culture influences the behaviour within organisations. A situation arises where: 'That is just the way things are done here, there is no other possibility.'

Creating a corporate culture

It has been firmly established that a corporate culture influences actions and therefore the company's relationship orientation. However, there are often still question marks over the 'makability' of the corporate culture. After all, it is extremely difficult to force employees within a company to accept fundamental norms and values. Moreover, these tenets are not often described in precise terms or it is unclear how they may serve as a guideline to actions taken in a variety of concrete situations. Additionally, we often encounter more than one group culture within organisations. The norms and values of the managers, for example, differ from those of the factory employees; the two have many areas that overlap, but there will be others that conflict with one another.

It appears that the corporate culture is more impressionable than we had thought a number of years ago. However, this requires a thorough approach and a long-term horizon. According to Horovitz and Panak (1992), it is important to:

- Describe the common values and norms.
- Position those persons who spread the culture and who are seen as an example by others, in the appropriate positions within the organisation.
- Communicate more intensely internally regarding the values and norms, and translate these into concrete actions.
- Deploy symbols and other information carriers in the dissemination of the philosophy; examples include clothing, a mascot, a pin, a mirror in which the personnel can see themselves before they meet with customers, or a card on which the philosophy is printed.
- Apply this to human resource management: which persons will be appointed or fired? How does the company advertise to acquire new employees? How are they trained and educated further? How is behaviour that fits within the culture rewarded and other behaviour discouraged?
- Take measurements. It is highly advisable to measure concrete performance with regard to relationship orientation so that no ambiguity arises with respect to the improvements which must still be made.

4.3 Structure

Organising around customer contacts

The creation of space necessary to cultivate relationships with customers requires company activities to be organised around customer contacts. Organising activities based on functions or products leads to a situation in which customers' needs are not met quickly and accurately enough. After all, a customer's request will have to be submitted to persons other than the contact person for approval. And to fulfil the request, assistance will have to be obtained from other departments. It is typical of these other departments that their objectives do not run exactly parallel with the interests of the individual customer concerned at that particular moment.

Often quoted is the example (IBM) of providing supplier's credit to customers. When the company was still functionally organised, this process took several days. The application had to go from one department to the next before the final answer could be given. Now that a so-called process organisation has been set up, the processing speed has been accelerated significantly. One person who has all of the relevant information at his or her disposal and who works at one location is responsible for making the decision regarding the application. The possibilities of interacting with the customer and to supply customisation have now increased as well. In the former situation, this would have led to an unacceptable extension of the processing period and to reduced efficiency.

This example involving IBM concerns a partial process, one which is part of a larger whole, namely that of the approval and completion of a transaction. Or, even more all-encompassing: the relationship with the customer. In a relationship-oriented organisation, it is desirable for activities which ensue from the management of a relationship to be classified in succession under an organisational unit which bears the responsibility for the relationship. Here lies what is known as 'customer ownership'.

Organising 'customer ownership' is a source of serious conflicts and is a major reason for the failure of several CRM implementations. In many organisations, functional, product or area managers occupy senior positions in the hierarchy while people in direct contact with customers have operational tasks and have to execute the decisions of these seniors. The transition towards a customer-oriented organisation implies the rise of customer managers in the hierarchy at the costs of others. They have to give up part of their 'kingdom'. Product managers, for example, that dominated the marketing approach will have to recognise that customer managers will become the captains of the value chain: they decide which customers will be addressed, when and with which proposition. It is no longer the exclusive privilege of the product manager to set objectives, to allocate budgets and direct marketing activities. Of course, they will not give up their position in the organisational hierarchy without resistance. Effective change management is needed to realise this turnaround (see also Chapter 19).

Organisational forms

Customer management may be organised in a variety of ways. In many consumer markets, this is even 'outsourced' to retailers who are responsible for the sale and

The customer pyramid

Figure 4.2

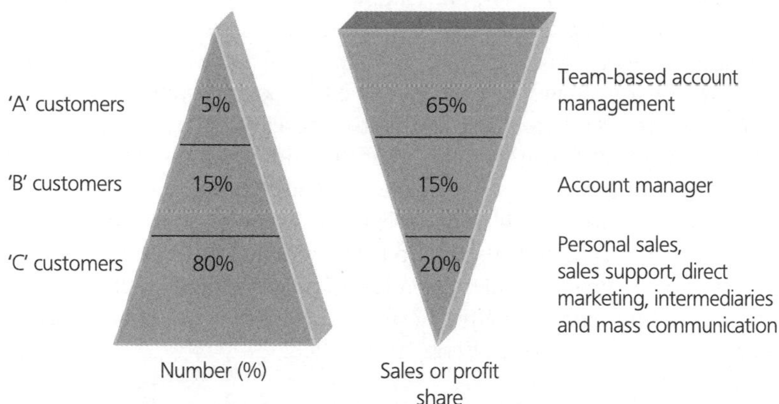

delivery of products. Direct contact with the supplier is minimised. The margin on the product does not allow for extensive communication and the supplier does not have the capacity required to be able to handle the amount of customer contact involved. The question also remains whether the consumers consider this type of contact desirable with these sorts of 'low involvement' products. It is only in those situations in which the consumers' involvement with suppliers is high, where the 'lifetime value' of the customers (see Chapter 14) permits this and opportunities arise which lend the relationship meaning, that it is useful to facilitate direct contact between consumer and producer.

Organisations which take customer management into their own hands often find the customer pyramid useful (see Figure 4.2). The pyramid makes a distinction between larger and smaller customers. At the top of the pyramid, we find a small number of large customers, the 'A' customers, who represent a substantial portion of sales. At the bottom, we find the small 'C' customers, who, separately and collectively, contribute relatively little to sales. The intermediate group may be designated the 'B' customers.

The group of 'A' customers may have reached proportions so large that they go beyond the capacities of an individual account manager. The sales from this type of customer are so high that contact must be maintained with too many people at too many different locations, and customisation must be provided as well. The decision may be made to set up an account team that manages the relationship with these customers. Some team members may originate from the business units which must develop and/or supply parts of the products for the customer, others may handle logistics or service, for example.

One person may even have to assume the responsibility for the coordination of the entire relationship (Workman *et al.*, 1998). The choice of the person with final responsibility represents a complex issue for many organisations. If we hire someone from the 'business' to bear the responsibility for a product line, then we can guarantee that we are hiring someone who can 'get things done' within the company. This is particularly the case when the person comes from the organisational unit which must supply the largest portion of the products to the customer. At the same time, there is a risk that the interests of the other supplying departments will not receive their fair share of attention and will thus no longer be asked to provide the best integrated solution to customer problems. If, however, an account manager is appointed who is not from within the supplying organisational units, then the risk exists that he or she will not be able to count on enough support from these units. He or she will be too demanding and will thus represent a customer who is perceived as being unattractive. It seems that there is no single optimum solution and that in all cases, the success of the chosen configuration depends upon the willingness of those involved to do their best to ensure the overall success of the customer as well as of their own organisation.

In putting together the account team, it is also advisable to take the qualities of the individual team members into consideration. The individuals collectively form a team which has the competency to develop the relevant relationship with the 'A' customer to ensure that it is a long-term mutually profitable one. There must be sufficient qualities present within the team to ensure (Verra, 1994):

- the relations within one's own organisation as well as those with the customer;
- the acquisition of new orders;
- the negotiation of the deal;
- entrepreneurship;
- control over the quality of delivery;
- management of the project.

The team composition may also be modified at a later stage of the relationship. A subject such as project management can be much more important in the beginning than it is at a later stage; after all, the order has yet to be received. The products or services must be supplied or provided in accordance with the pre-determined specifications. Later, once everything is running more or less smoothly, it can be worthwhile to dedicate more attention to entrepreneurship and relationship management. The best new sales opportunities are to be found in existing customers with whom good relationships are maintained.

In many cases, 'B' customers, those characterised by smaller proportions and complexity than 'A' customers, may be managed by an individual account or customer manager. This individual has one or a limited number of customers for which he or she is responsible.

The numerous 'C' customers with small sales potential who spend very little on their purchases from the supplier may, for example, be assigned to a customer group manager, customer service or a help desk. The possibilities for supplying customisation to this type of customer are few; the development of new products and services is usually geared towards the top customers. It is, however, essential to develop a customer-oriented approach within the relevant department and to motivate and develop the 'front-line' employees so that the relationship with these customers may also be developed in an appropriate manner. The employees will have to identify with the mission and the norms and values of the relationship organisation. They will have to feel a bond with the company and must be able to take pride in their contribution to the organisation's success. Investments will have to be made in their skills and attitude so that they are both *willing* and *able* to meet the challenges offered by the customer. They will have to be stimulated to present themselves as a leader in performing their tasks so that the customer's interests may be promoted properly. They will have to be offered prospects for future growth in the organisation.

The role of CRM systems in the various organisational forms

The role of the CRM system will vary for each of the three types of customer. The largest will be that designed to serve the 'C' customers. This category involves a large number of customers for whom a large portion of the customer history and profile will be maintained exclusively in databases. There are very few people who know the customers on an individual basis and who can form a mental picture of these people. To a great extent, communication with the customers will also take place through IT-supported channels. Suggestions will be made by computer systems to indicate the course which the development of the relationship may follow. CRM systems will play a less prominent role with larger customers. They assist the account team primarily in the efficient and timely identification of the players on both the customer's as well as the supplier's side, and the communication between the two. A network of communication channels may also be developed which can ensure a more efficient and simple exchange of messages than that which was possible previously. A larger portion of the customer profile will also have to be developed outside of the automated CRM system, in people's minds. Decisions involving the relationship development will also be automated to a lesser degree; it remains largely a human task.

4.4 People

It is people who develop relationships, not the IT applications. People with social skills are indispensable in relationship-oriented organisations. Anyone who must maintain contact with customers every now and then will have to be sufficiently competent in this area. This involves the *agents* in the call centre, the representatives, the service staff as well as the people in the administration department. All of these individuals are capable of communicating with customers on product information, invoices, purchases, complaints, etc., and must be able to gain a proper feel for the relationship. It goes without saying that it is expecting too much to require that everyone should have the same level of competency in this area in addition to proficiency in their 'own area of expertise'; however, the all-too-familiar situation must be prevented in which non-commercial personnel communicate too much from their own point of view and their corresponding tasks with customers who are experiencing a problem with the supplier.

Important aspects of the social competencies are (Peelen *et al.*, 1996):

- the capacity for empathy;
- the ability to create congruence;
- the ability to use an unconditionally positive approach to the other person.

Empathy may be described as the ability to see the world from the customer's eyes, from moment to moment. The person capable of empathy is thus able to place him- or herself within the customer's frame of reference and can also make it clear to the other person that he or she is aware of what is involved when they find themselves in a similar situation. This person demonstrates to the customer that he or she is sympathetic to the customer's problems.

Empathy requires first and foremost that time is invested in the other person. In addition, people must possess certain skills, some of which may be learned during so-called sensitivity training courses, listening campaigns, role-playing exercises and in-depth debriefings at meetings with customers. During these types of session, an evaluation is performed, together with the customer, on the manner in which people have behaved during a project. One of the goals is to increase the sensitivity of the people involved to the customers' needs.

Congruence is related to openness, transparency and sincerity. It means that one party will profile itself as being realistic with respect to the other party. In other words, a professional façade is not what is wanted here. Adopting an open attitude often serves as an example to the other party: openness encourages openness.

Congruence tends to benefit from an honest and open exchange of information without politics and hidden agendas. Investing in the exchange of information leads to the creation of trust and commitment and makes it possible for partners to gain a better idea of one another's needs and expectations.

By communicating more frequently, being open to positive as well as negative assessment, being prepared to express both positive and negative aspects, and being honest about limitations and capabilities, congruence is given the room it needs to grow.

From a social-psychological standpoint, it has been posited that it is important to be able to maintain an unconditionally positive attitude towards someone because it indicates that one accepts the other person. Within a commercial setting, this implies that one is supposed to value the customer, regardless of his or her behaviour and value to the organisation. This can mean that an unequal situation is temporarily accepted. If the other person underperforms temporarily, it is advisable to accept this. That person has either encountered problems along the way or has been compelled to do so.

Social competencies will not only be of use in the relationship with customers, but will also prove useful internally. On an internal level, relationships between people and departments often fall short of the mark. There is room for improvement in the collegial atmosphere between people, there is insufficient goodwill between colleagues, and the communication between departments does not flow smoothly. And it is precisely in those organisations with limited job descriptions and decision-making hierarchies that the teamwork between departments and people is essential in order to be able to cultivate any type of relationship at all.

In general, there is also a great deal of room for improvement in this area when it comes to customers. The quotation in the box below, which was taken from brainstorming sessions with marketers, illustrates this.

CRM illustration

Even commercially oriented people within companies have a *fear of investing in the relationship* from time to time: 'We get cold feet. We are actively engaged in the pursuit of new customers. Only, every now and then we take a blunderbuss approach, and we don't know what will be left over if we take closer aim.' Improving communication will require many modifications including:

- Product specialists will have to become customer specialists. They will have to offer an emotional product. In order to be successful, you will have to possess other qualities.
- Emotion and intuition will have to play a larger role. Hitting the right nerve will also become more of a question of experimenting and 'learning by doing'.

Source: Peelen *et al.* (1996).

4.5 Communication and information

From the illustration above, it appears that the quality of a relationship-oriented organisation depends to a large extent on the quality of mutual communication. Are we capable of conducting a dialogue with one another? Do people have the social skills (see Section 4.4) to 'carry on a good conversation' content-wise, or will it end at a well-intended attempt to tempt (a boost to sales)?

And, are we sharing with one another the information that we need in order to be able to cultivate relationships – both internally and externally? Does the service employee communicate the information he has just gleaned during customer contact to the customer manager so that she can take past events into consideration during subsequent contact with the customer? Does the call centre agent know what type of question the customer once asked the organisation in an e-mail?

The quality of the communication between the parties is influenced by the structure and division of labour. If duties and positions are organised on the basis of contact with customers (see Section 4.2), then there is a better chance of conducting a meaningful dialogue with customers. The areas common to both parties seem relatively large. If the front-office employee is exclusively responsible for creating invoices, however, then this would not be the case to such a great extent.

Nonetheless, in many situations the contact between a customer and the organisation will not go via one person. IT systems can play a role in this, but will never be able to take the place of a person. People will have to relinquish the information so that the system can retain and distribute it. They will have to invest time and effort in doing this and will have to get past certain barriers. People will have to abandon the idea that sharing information can potentially detract from their headstart on their colleagues and thus damage their own career.

Investments in IT and data will have to be organised so that they make a real contribution to customer information. Many databases are filled with enormous amounts of data, yet are capable of producing only a limited amount of useful customer information. Many of the actions of people who have contact with customers are not even based on these data. Substantial investments in systems and data are thus not always completely justifiable.

CRM illustration

Brainstorming sessions with marketers have shown the following to be desirable:

1 To redesign the marketing information function within the organisation, this time from the customer's point of view.
2 To attach more importance to qualitative information so that we can learn more about the customer's social world.
3 To attach more importance to other sources of information:
   - Spending more time with the customers.
   - Communicating more with employees who are in contact with customers.
   - Conducting more qualitative market research.
4 Approaching and using quantitative data more intelligently: a number of people hold the belief that by looking at the data from a different angle, more information may be extracted from the data files. It has been proposed that 20 per cent of the consumers who may represent 80 per cent of sales are the most sympathetic towards you. The trick is to pick up on the signals these customers are transmitting. The customer database will also have to be segmented much further.

Source: Peelen *et al.* (1996).

This topic will be discussed in depth in Chapter 5.

4.6 Systems

Even organisations with a relationship-oriented mission and culture, a customer-oriented method of organising, and people with social skills communicating expert information can fail during the development of relationships. A great deal depends on the manner in which these employees are steered. Are they rewarded for increasing turnover and achieving short-term results or do they also receive incentives as the customer lifetime value (see Chapter 14) increases? Theoretically, the customer's value, both current and potential, is established and serves as a starting point in measuring, guiding and evaluating employee performance.

An organisation in which, for example, account managers are assessed primarily on the basis of the quarterly turnover they achieve will encounter problems in the development of long-term mutually profitable relationships. The account manager is driven by 'the system' to exhibit sales-oriented behaviour; he or she will focus on products and customers with whom sales success may be achieved in a relatively short period of time and with relatively little effort. His or her interest in customers who have just made a purchase will be low, while these are precisely the types of customers that are in urgent need of attention. Completing the transaction can be a rather risky event for these customers; they may be in doubt about whether their decision to purchase was the right one. They need affirmation of their purchase decision and would probably like support in putting the product into use. An account manager who is not available to assist the customer at that point can arouse the suspicion in customers that the manager has lost interest in them now that he or she has 'hauled in the loot' (Levitt, 1983).

Service-profit chain

Although the customer lifetime value is the ultimate standard by which 'customer owners' must be steered, it is also advisable to measure and evaluate their activities using other criteria as well. After all, an airplane is not only steered on the basis of altitude. Several other gauges are welcome on the dashboard to chart the course and determine whether or not the pilot is on course. The 'service–profit chain' (Heskett *et al.*, 1994), originating from analyses of successful service organisations, connects 'hard' values with 'soft' performance indicators (Figure 4.3). The hard criteria, financial in nature, are related to the profit that is earned on customers. The soft criteria indicate which factors influence the results: how satisfied and committed are the customers? What is the employee satisfaction level? What is the quality of the internal service; a specific example would be the information systems with which the front-office personnel must work. The level of satisfaction with the system can influence not only the rate of personnel turnover but also employee productivity. Experienced staff are more efficient and produce higher quality service which in turn results in an increased level of customer satisfaction and customer retention. Ultimately, this will lead to the achievement of better financial results.

Figure 4.3 The service–profit chain

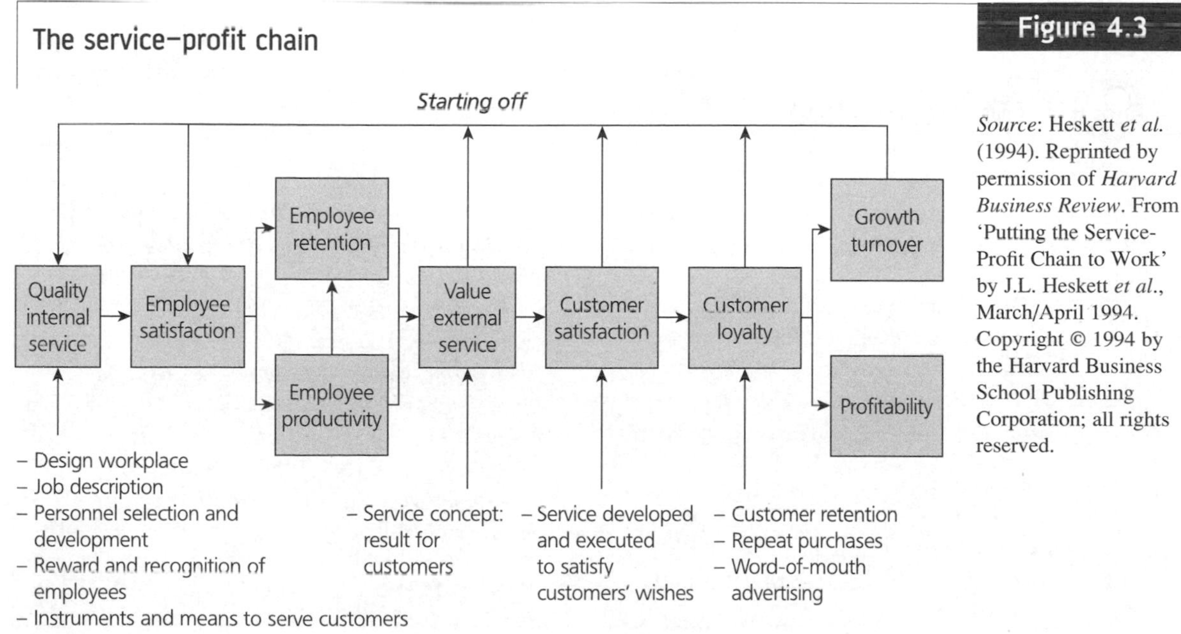

Source: Heskett *et al.* (1994). Reprinted by permission of *Harvard Business Review*. From 'Putting the Service-Profit Chain to Work' by J.L. Heskett *et al.*, March/April 1994. Copyright © 1994 by the Harvard Business School Publishing Corporation; all rights reserved.

There is also an interaction at work between the factors mentioned; satisfied employees are in a better position to satisfy customers and vice versa: an employee is more easily cheered by a happy than by a complaining customer. The 'service–profit chain' model helps managers to make sound decisions on investments so that a higher level of service (and thus customer commitment and satisfaction) will be achieved (Waalewijn, Peelen and Wijnia, 1999). The investments in the work environment and the competencies of the people have an effect on the level of employee satisfaction and can provide a positive impulse to the manner in which customer and employee can influence one another. Someone who is equipped to perform his or her duties will derive more satisfaction from this than someone who must continuously improvise. He or she has the knowledge and the skills and can use professional tools to satisfy the customer and develop a relationship with him or her. The employee can rely on the organisation; he or she knows that it will fulfil the promises it makes to its customers.

Balanced scorecard

The model of the service–profit chain may be adapted to fit that of the balanced scorecard, which originated from the criticism of the traditional financial systems within companies (Kaplan and Norton, 1996). The conclusion Kaplan and Norton drew is that financial reports often focus too much on the past and not enough on the future. In budgets, which *are* focused on the future, too much emphasis is placed on the short term and risk avoidance. Very little attention is given to the question of whether or not strategic objectives are being met as a result of the expenditures involved. There is also a lack of awareness for the 'soft' factors (see above), which ultimately determine the organisation's success. The result is that the financial management system of the organisation is treated separately from the strategic planning system. If people are not

CRM illustration

The situation sketched by Kaplan and Norton is not foreign to marketers, as is evidenced by the following quotations:

> *If you have a budget, you often tend to invest that to 'boost volume', when you actually should try to use it to make a long-term sale.*

> *The concept of thinking in terms of 'lifetime value' has not yet met with broad acceptance. The transaction value is still the centre of attention. A customer is still evaluated based on the one car he may buy, not on the three or four cars of the same brand he may buy over the course of time.*
>
> *Even though we try to speak the 'bookkeeper's' language with a term such as 'lifetime values', it appears as though he disapproves of the outcome of the calculations. There seems to be an aversion to the time horizon ('lifetime') and the insecurity which exists on the level of the future yield.*

Source: Peelen *et al.* (1996).

prepared for it, the risk exists that strategic plans will inadvertently suffer if they are included in the financial system.

Since its introduction in 1996, the balanced scorecard has been received very positively within the business community; by 2004, it had been applied within a substantial portion of businesses worldwide. The balanced scorecard offers the possibility of fitting the service–profit chain model within the organisation's management system. Strategic objectives direct the formulation and target setting of hard and soft criteria. Within the balanced scorecard, four different perspectives are identified, namely (Kaplan and Norton, 1996):

1 Satisfaction of the shareholder, to be measured in financial terms. An indication will have to be given to show how the current and potential customer value ultimately contributes to an increased satisfaction on the part of shareholders.
2 Customer satisfaction and loyalty.
3 Internal processes. The performance indicaters for the internal perspective measure how (in terms of results and quality) the organisation identifies, serves and retains the right customers.
4 Learning and growing. By learning and growing, the organisation's areas for improvement come up for discussion. An indication is provided on how the organisation and its employees may improve their competencies.

In comparison with the profit chain, the shareholder's satisfaction is measured as well as the customer's, but explicit determination of the employee's satisfaction is lacking. However, the quality of the processes is addressed. In the model, the performance of the internal processes aimed at identifying, attracting, serving and retaining customers is measured. As such, activities are defined and measured that have to result in the satisfaction and loyalty of the customers. Within the perspective of 'learning and growing', the competencies to be developed are examined in more depth as are the aspects of personnel and the information system.

To decide which indicators to include in the balanced scorecard we need to derive the critical success factors from the strategy. The criteria which are crucial to the success of the strategy need to be identified and measured. Concrete indicators and norm scores are to be formulated for these criteria on the basis of the four perspectives (see Figure 4.4; Kaplan and Norton, 1996).

It is extremely important to involve the employees concerned in the completion of the balanced scorecard. After all, one of the most important objectives of the card is to communicate the strategic plans and translate these into actions by those involved in the organisation. It is a challenge to describe the vague, abstract terms which are used to formulate the strategies in words which are relevant to the daily tasks of people in the company. In this way, an attempt is made to prevent strategic ambitions from 'getting any further than the boardroom'.

Being able to determine the optimum scores and the relationship between indicators from the different perspectives is a learning process. The influence of a certain marketing activity on customer satisfaction and financial results will have to be established by trial and error. Lessons learned from practice will have to be remembered, disseminated and utilised in the process of perfecting the system of measurement and policy in the future.

Figure 4.4 From strategy to critical success factors

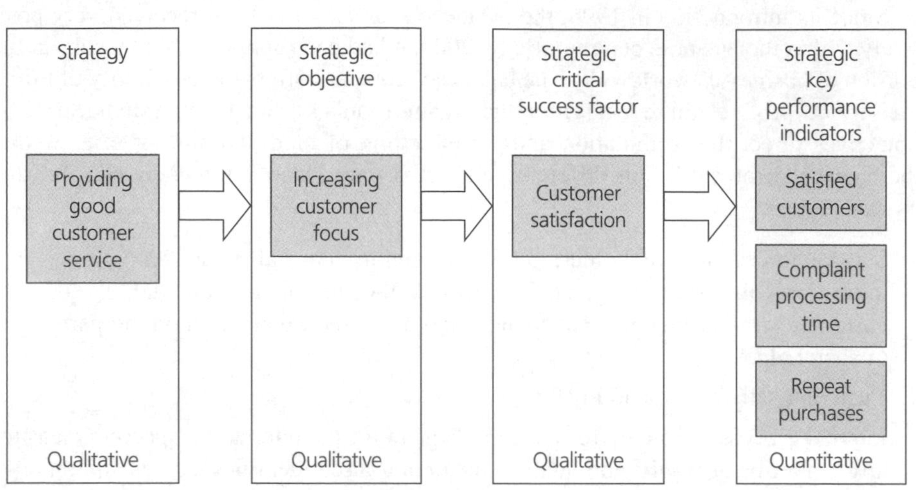

CRM illustration

A Japanese restaurant whose strategy is to get non-Asian people, who regularly dine out interested in and committed to Japanese cuisine will have to fill out its balanced scorecard through a process of experimentation (John Klug, 1998). Many people from this target group dine at restaurants serving foreign food; however, they seem to avoid the Japanese restaurant because its prices are too high and the level of familiarity and appeal of this type of Asian cuisine is still too low. The restaurant implements the marketing strategy of serving a Japanese meal which is well-enough adapted to the local taste preferences for an average price and in oriental, comfortable surroundings. Regular customers are recognised and receive a hospitable welcome. Aspects which determine the success of this type of restaurant from the perspective of the process include accessibility, average table occupancy and use of space, guest turnover time, drink consumption per guest, productivity of the kitchen and the serving staff, the optimum bar capacity, customer satisfaction with price, the meal and the staging, sales and profitability. The restaurant will have to achieve a certain score for each of these aspects in order not only to acquire and bind customers but also to be able to satisfy shareholders. A solution will have to be found for the eternal field of tension that exists between increasing profits, managing costs and customer management. The restaurant's success actually depends on two factors: the maintenance of an average price level as well as cost level, and the development of a steadily growing, regular clientèle.

If one of the aspects on the balanced scorecard receives a score that is too low, then it has unavoidable consequences for the other aspects; the success of the formula depends on the quality of the balance achieved. A turnover time which is too short has consequences for the aspect of customer satisfaction, but at the same time, the maintenance of a competitive price level will be at risk if one group of guests keeps a table occupied the entire evening. This is certainly the case when the restaurant with an average price level has chosen an expensive top

Balanced scorecard for a Japanese restaurant

Figure 4.5

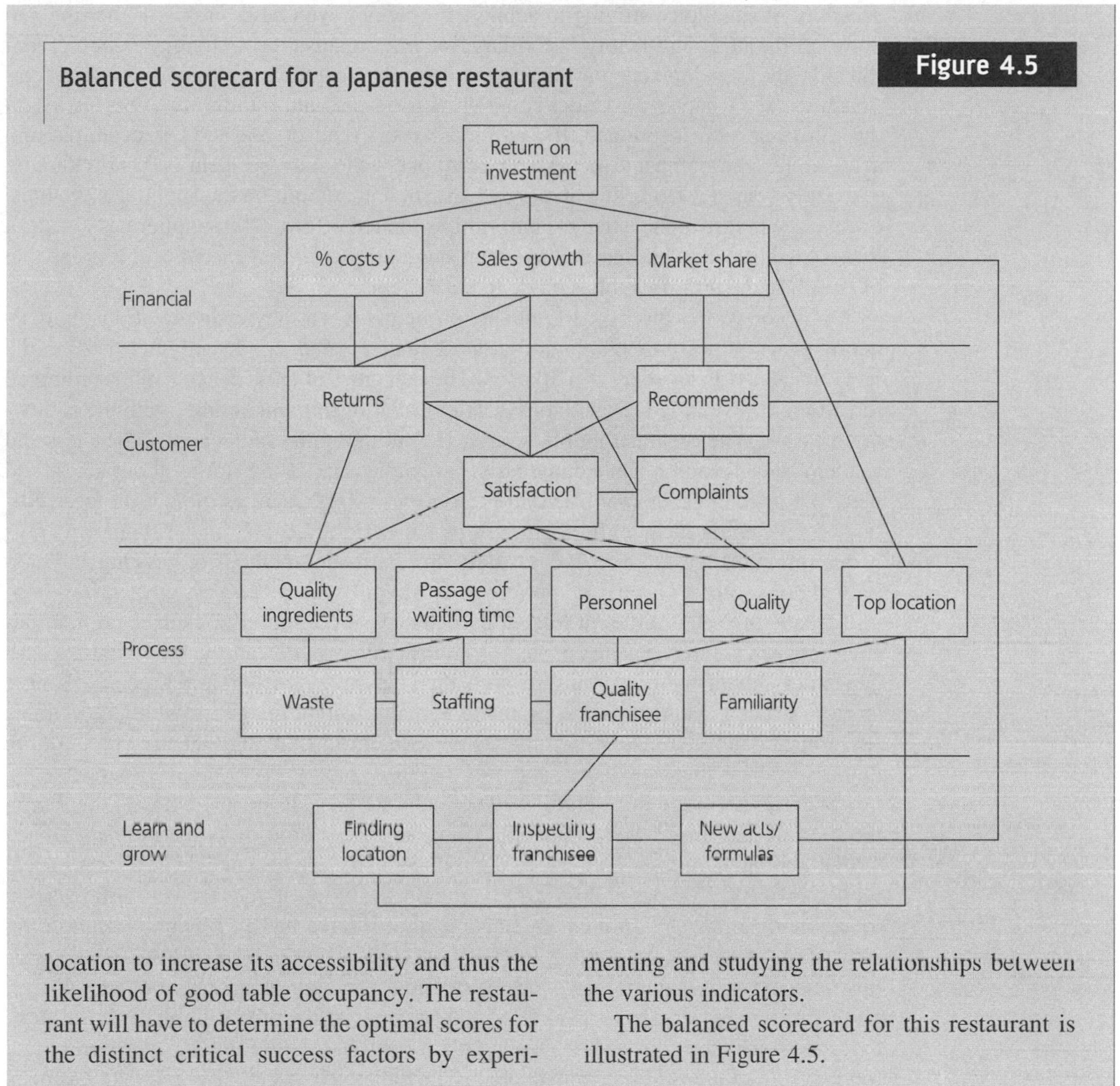

location to increase its accessibility and thus the likelihood of good table occupancy. The restaurant will have to determine the optimal scores for the distinct critical success factors by experimenting and studying the relationships between the various indicators.

The balanced scorecard for this restaurant is illustrated in Figure 4.5.

4.7 Where do we stand?

Where do we stand with the development of a relationship-oriented organisation? Is it a utopia which cannot be gained in practice? Or is it an ideal, which, if recognised as such, can provide guidance and direction to the organisational development? Or is it the type of organisation that, in the right situation, must grow? The answer to all three of these questions is yes, depending on the situation. It seems that many organisations are far removed from the relationship-oriented type of company we have sketched here. In a variety of situations, striving to achieve it may not even be desirable. Either the gap between the ideal and reality is too large or the organisation's strategy is not geared towards the development of long-term mutually profitable customer–supplier relationships (see Chapter 3). Under some circumstances, and by this we are referring to the third question mentioned, the relationship-oriented organisation is desirable and achievable. The company focuses on customers who may be identified individually, who truly want a relationship and spend a sufficient amount on the supplier's products or services to justify the latter's relationship-oriented efforts. The supplier has also 'got its act together', and has reached a certain stage of *operational excellence*. It is capable of fulfilling the promises it has made to customers.

Many companies discover formidable problems when they create relationship marketing programmes. In 1998, Fournier, Dobscha and Mick conducted interviews in the United States with a variety of marketers. The outcomes of these conversations prompted the article 'Preventing the premature death of relationship marketing', with the following message. The customer intimacy strategy is at the centre of attention. Managers and academics believe in it. On a daily basis, companies are telling stories about a new and better approach to customer orientation. It does, in fact, seem as though the possibilities of developing meaningful relationships with customers are greater than ever. This is due not in the least to new, increasingly more efficient methods of gauging and capitalising on customer needs and preferences. Anyone who looks a bit further, however, will frequently see a different image, particularly in consumer markets. The relationship between companies and consumers is difficult, to put it mildly. Anyone who asks consumers about their relationship with their so-called corporate partners will hear stories of a confusing, stressful, insensitive, manipulative market in which consumers feel trapped and victimised. Companies are content in thinking that they know more than ever about their customers and can therefore satisfy every demand. Consumers, however, do not share this optimism. They tolerate the salespeople who are there with their list of questions for consumers in hand, no matter how small the purchase. They struggle through the over-abundance of products in the range. They do their best to deal with the overkill of possibilities. They juggle the flow of requests to participate in loyalty programmes. Customer satisfaction figures have hardly reached a high point; if anything, they are just starting to climb back up from an all-time low. Complaints, boycotts and other expressions of dissatisfaction from consumers are abundant.

In short, it appears that organisations are unable sufficiently to implement the strategies to which they adhere. They do not place enough focus on the customer and think too much from a position of self-interest. The balance between give and take has been disturbed. They come across as insincere. They have yet to give customers enough friendship, loyalty and respect. There is too much one-way traffic, too much is being sent and there is a shortage of competency for empathy. Companies and the people who work there do not possess sufficient social skills.

Although the conclusion reached by Fournier and colleagues leaves little room for uncertainty and offers very little hope, it does, however, paint a realistic picture.

4.8 Conclusion

The design and implementation of the customer intimacy strategy places demands on the organisation. It places demands on the mission and the way in which it holds people's interest, on the culture, the organisational structure, the communication and the management systems. It goes without saying that these demands are dependent upon the intensity with which people hope to build customer–supplier relationships (see Chapter 2, Figure 2.1), and the type of product that will be developed and supplied. Even then, it seems that the challenge remains too great for many companies. The gap between reality and the ideal can be so large that a sober view and approach is the most appropriate. A plan in which people grow and move towards a relationship-oriented organisation is preferable. A situation in which we aim for a strategy that is not yet practicable should be averted in order to prevent the 'premature death' of relationship marketing.

Case study

Telecom Italia Mobile cuts churn and increases value

Background

'Telecom Italia Mobile (TIM) won Gartner's first European Excellence Award for customer relationship management.' In Italy, TIM is the market leader serving more than 25 million subscribers. 'In 2002, at a group level (including international operations), TIM generated revenue of more than €10.9 billion from its services portfolio – including voice communications, SMS, Multimedia Messaging Service and value-added services, such as info SMS, Wireless Application Protocol Push, general packet radio service and voice portal.

'In Italy, mobile telecommunications is a mature market with strong competition and downward pressure on prices. In such a competitive market, TIM had to understand its customers' needs and expectations, as well as their value and likely behavior. It could then use that insight to drive customer interactions to increase customer loyalty and satisfaction.

'The CRM effort was led by the marketing department, closely supported by the customer services organization.'

Approach

TIM's CRM programme focused on high-value customers. Customer insight has helped the company to tailor new offerings to customers' requirements and in that way create more customised, relevant and valued new services. Channels have been integrated and applied in a consistent way and helped to personalise each customer contact. Several processes have been re-engineered. A Siebel eService system has been implemented to support seven call centres with more than 5000 agents. Point-of-sale locations for retail customers were linked to the system and Oracle's online marketing campaign management system was launched.

Change management in particular

'However, key to TIM's success was its change management. TIM had to create the right culture internally, so that employees and partners understood that the company's relationship with the customer had to be treated like a personal relationship. The wants and needs of both parties have to be met to create an enduring relationship.

'Change management is always a major issue in creating a more customer-centric enterprise. TIM has tackled cultural issues in an innovative, creative and particularly Italian way. As part of an ongoing program of education and change, it created an internal training video that draws comparisons between the relationship with the customer and romantic relationships in the real world. Customer churn is likened to divorce and buying from multiple vendors is depicted as unfaithfulness. The video stresses the importance of attraction and value for both sides in an enduring love affair. This video has been used very successfully in Italy and aligns very well with the local culture.

'TIM has not reorganized sales, customer service and marketing by segment, except in call centers. Objectives and incentives for customer service, sales and marketing staff have been aligned and given a much stronger customer-centric focus, helping to create a much closer working relationship between marketing, customer service and sales.'

Results

TIM realised a 40 per cent reduction in churn within postpaid high-value customer segments and an 80 per cent reduction among customers that joined the Milleuna TIM loyalty programme. Traffic for high-value customers was increased by 3.5 per cent, while the margin rose by 3 per cent. The costs of retaining subscribers decreased by 16 per cent.

Source: *Case studies*, J. Radcliffe and B. Wood, CS-17-6919, Research Note (22 April 2003) Gartner Inc.

Questions

1 What are the pros and cons of a CRM initiative that is led by the marketing department?

2 According to one of the managers, change management was key to TIM's success. Which conditions were met within the market and organisation that made it possible for change management to make the difference between success and failure?

Questions

1 What types of demand does the customer intimacy strategy place on the organisation? Provide a description of the relationship-oriented organisation.

2 Gather the mission statements of a number of companies and evaluate to what degree these do justice to the objective of creating a relationship-oriented organisation. Substantiate your answer.

3 Drawing up a mission statement is simple compared with implementing one. Think of a number of concrete measures to promote the internalisation of the mission statement. The internalisation indicates to what degree the employees in the company identify with the aspects included in the mission.

4 In practice, CRM is cited as having the following important advantage: 'thanks to CRM, we are able to institutionalise the relationship with customers'. What do you suppose is meant by this? Explain your answer by providing an example.

5 To what extent is the organisation of a supermarket equipped to implement a customer intimacy strategy? Explain your answer.

6 Formerly state-owned companies are sometimes characterised by an insufficiently customer-oriented culture.

(a) Name an example of this type of company and describe how this is the case.

(b) Formulate two recommendations for the short term and two for the long term necessary in order to stimulate a more customer-oriented culture.

7 What is your opinion of the idea of a customer 'taking a seat' on the supplier's account team? Name three aspects on which your opinion depends and explain them further.

8 Within a relationship-oriented organisation, everyone must have a current, correct, complete and consistent image of the individual customers. Reality often tends to deviate from this ideal, in spite of the implementation of supportive CRM systems. Name four possible causes of this and explain your answers.

9 In this chapter, an example was provided of a Japanese restaurant which hoped to win and bind customers to its formula.

(a) Formulate the specific critical success factors for this company from the four perspectives of the balanced scorecard.

(b) Specify which indicators you would like to include in the balanced scorecard for each perspective.

10 In the article 'Preventing the premature death of relationship marketing', the premature demise of the customer intimacy strategy is portrayed. What will have to be done to prevent this from happening?

References

Fournier, Susan, Susan Dobscha and David Glen Mick (1998) Preventing the premature death of relationship marketing, *Harvard Business Review*, January–February, 42–52.

Heskett, J.L., T.O. Jones, G.W. Loveman, W.E. Sasser Jr and L.A. Schlesinger (1994) Putting the service–profit chain to work, *Harvard Business Review*, March–April, 164–174.

Horovitz, Jacques and Michele Jurgens Panak (1992) *Total Customer Satisfaction: Lessons from 50 European companies with top quality service*, Pitman Publishing, London.

Jones, Thomas O. and W. Earl Sasser, Jr (1995) Why satisfied customers defect, *Harvard Business Review*, November–December, 88–99.

Kaplan, Robert S. and David P. Norton (1996) *The Balanced Score Card: Translating strategy into action*, Harvard Business School Press, Boston, Massachusetts.

Klug, John (1998) *Benhana of Tokyo*, Harvard Business School, Boston, Massachusetts.

Levitt, T. (1983) *The Marketing Imagination*, The Free Press, New York.

Peelen, Ed *et al.* (1996) *Thema dossier Relatiemarketing*, Platform '95, Amsterdam.

Verra, G.J. (1994) *Account management: filosofie, instrumenten en implementatie*, Kluwer: Deventer.

Waalewijn, P., E. Peelen and S. Wijnia (1999) *De Marketing Balanced Scorecard*, Kluwer, Deventer.

Workman, John P. Jr, Christian Homburg and Kjell Gruner (1998) Marketing organisation: an integrative framework of dimensions and determinants, *Journal of Marketing*, **68**, July, 21–41.

Part II

CRM Marketing Aspects

The second part of this book examines the marketing aspects of CRM. We will discuss the four sub-areas, namely:

1 *Customer knowledge*. How can data from databases be used to help us create customer knowledge? How can we derive a return on our investments in customer knowledge? How can we avoid violating customers' privacy?
2 *Customisation*. How can we use this customer knowledge to provide our customers with a customised offer? How can we meet their specific needs and how can we gear pricing to their individual situations?
3 *Communication*. How can we improve accessibility for our customers? How can we conduct a useful dialogue with them?
4 *Relationship policy*. How do we develop a high quality customer database with customers with whom it is worthwhile developing a relationship? How do we develop a mutually profitable relationship with these customers?

5

Customer knowledge

Within the field of information management, a distinction has always been made between data, information and knowledge. *Data* are details; the date on which a prospect became a customer, the value of the last purchase, the term within which payment was made and the customer's address. Data become *information* as soon as a user assigns a meaning to them. The data say something about the identity and profile of the customer; as a result, it becomes possible to create an image of who the customer is. Information becomes *knowledge* as soon as action is taken on the basis of this information; because the customer's profile is known, we know when we should offer him which products or services.

The pitfall should be avoided in which the attention becomes too singularly focused on the collection, maintenance and analysis of the data. This should include the objective of developing a new 'crystal ball' for which many costs must be incurred and investments made yet the results fail to materialise. What is important is to keep the ultimate goal in sight: knowledge. This involves using the information in developing a relationship with customers and this requires people to utilise sources of information creatively.

This chapter will first examine the definition and financial aspects of data quality: how many costs and how much income are related to investments in data quality (Section 5.1)? We then approach customer data as an important asset for which we must see a return (Section 5.2). Next, the focus will shift to the actual development of the customer profile (Section 5.3): how can we identify the customer? What do we want to know about him or her? Finally, the important issue of privacy will be discussed (Section 5.4): the expansion of customer knowledge is only possible as long as the customer agrees to it!

In this chapter we will address the following questions

- What is the value of customer knowledge?
- How to utilise data: taking action based on customer data.
- What demands are placed on the use of customer data that represent an important asset for the organisation?
- How to organise for data management (various stages of professionalisation).
- How to transform data into customer knowledge (developing the desired customer profile).
- How to combine data from various sources to develop the customer image.
- How to respect privacy.
- What is in the Personal Data Protection Act?
- How to formulate an information policy: how can you honour customers' privacy and at the same time use customer data to create value for the customer as well as for the company supplying the products or services?

Practitioner's insight

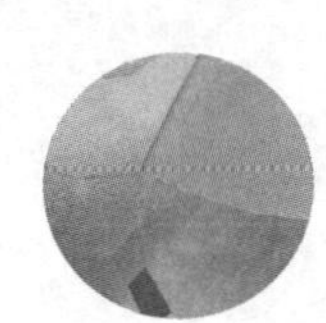

Has the computer become the modern-day version of the gypsy fortune-teller's crystal ball from the nineteenth century? Might the consumer's true make-up be found in the computer and seen on our screen? Can we, thanks to the information we find there, somehow shine a light into our customers' heads and gain an understanding of how, individually, they value their relationship with us? Can we tap into their thinking processes and see how they arrive at decisions and adopt certain behaviour? If this were the case, we would never have to leave our offices again. Personal contact with customers would then no longer be necessary. The non-explicit knowledge found in the heads of employees from the front office would not add anything of importance to the information which may be gleaned from the computer system. The technology appears to be perfect and can, to a great extent, replace people. It may seem to be a story of the future, for it is certainly not a portrait of the present-day reality; it is not even an illustration of the reality at companies with an exemplary database management department.

Rather, the challenge today is to combine information on customers which originates from different sources. Market research, databases and experiences of front-office personnel must be compiled in order to create an accurate, up-to-date and consistent image of the customer. An image whose value is recognised and cherished by everyone within the company; it is the source of success.

5.1 The value of customer knowledge

Data quality defined

Customer knowledge relies on the quality of the customer data. Incomplete, inaccurate, outdated data will not help us to understand the customer. If we talk about quality in general terms, it may be defined as something which gives us a good feeling (Mergen, 2003). However, this feeling is difficult to define in concrete terms since it concerns so many different aspects. A feeling offers few solid bases on which to measure and manage quality.

In order to gain a better understanding of quality, it may be defined from different points of view. We will mention several here under the following sub-headings.

From a technical point of view

In general, quality is specified from a technical point of view through the use of standards and norms which must be satisfied by a production process and the product to be manufactured. Examples related to data would be specifications for the number of positions that the name may contain, the number of fields in the database being filled, etc.

Practical value: from the point of view of the customer

Value perception and needs are criteria that the customer applies to determine quality. What does the customer want the other to know and what is it worth to him or her that he or she is recognised and known by the supplier?

Practical value: from the point of view of the supplier

The quality of relationship data becomes apparent to the supplier from the response it receives to a marketing campaign. Does it involve a person or an organisation that is doing the buying, are they profitable and do they wish to develop a relationship with the supplier? In other words, what is the commercial value of the name, address, city, etc.?

Intrinsic quality

The intrinsic quality of the data depends on the characteristics and features of the data items themselves. Quality may be approached in the most objective manner from this angle. The customer database is of good quality if it corresponds to *current* reality; no data are missing – they are *complete*; the data have been stored *correctly*; and every customer appears only once – each customer is *unique*.

$$\text{Quality customer database} = \text{Current} \times \text{Complete} \times \text{Correct} \times \text{Unique}$$

- Current: to what extent does the database depict a representation of the current reality?
- Complete: the completeness of data concerns the availability of a value as well as the completeness thereof. When the customer database is designed, each item of data must be examined to determine to what extent it is necessary, strongly desired, or just 'nice to have'. The last category is not essential for the business process especially if it later appears that this field is hardly ever filled in or maintained.
- Correct: the data are correct and, if applicable meet the standard or are valid within a collection of possible values. Correct means not making keying errors, and exercising caution by not guessing that 'Carl Donaldson' spells his first name with a 'K' and by not assuming that the customer's name is 'John Maclaughl**a**n'.
- Unique: in principle, each customer should only appear once in the customer database.

In some studies, the aspect of the accessibility of data is added to this list. In doing so, we indicate to what extent those using the customer data are able to retrieve it within the time span allowed for this. It is particularly important for agents in the contact centre to be able to access the database quickly so that they may conclude the customer contact in a satisfactory manner.

Spending money on data quality

To improve data quality one has to spend money.

Relevant customer data need to be gathered and their quality needs to be managed. Information on the identity and profile of the customers, ex-customers and prospects has to be collected and registered. Data have to be compiled from different sources and, if necessary, bought from external data suppliers who will supply single-use data. Data need to be retrieved from one's own back-office systems on transactions, payment history and identity, for example. We have to keep track of which topics were discussed, when and with whom, during front-office communication with customers. Investment is needed in software designed to compile these data and to manage them. We have to make sure that data do not become obsolete. Mistakes, which occur automatically when data come together from so many sources, have to be identified and corrected. Hardware and networks must be adapted to meet the demands of these database applications, while ensuring that the safety and speed of the other operational applications are not jeopardised. Call centre agents, for example, must still be able to input an order quickly and to verify the delivery of an order.

One may conclude from this description that the set-up and maintenance of a database with customer data require spending and investment. In deciding whether or not to set up this type of database, there is a significant risk that a number of the activities mentioned above will be overlooked and thus the costs of the necessary investments will be underestimated. When it comes to CRM programmes, which also include the development of the 'multichannel' environment and the integration of the front and back offices, there is a particular tendency to underestimate investment in data with respect to that found in hard systems. During the realisation of the project, the company will then be faced with budget overruns and/or concessions to be made in quality, which ultimately endanger the financial success of the entire CRM programme. There are cases known of companies with millions of customers that found they had to reserve as much budget for the hardware as for the database.

If we become aware of which expenses must be incurred in order to collect, register and keep data up to date, it will also become clear that we only have to invest in those data which ultimately contribute to the customer profile that we would like to create and which will come to form the basis of our actions. It is too easy to register 'everything we run across', only to have to determine ultimately that most of it has very little meaning. Keeping these types of files up to date involves a great deal of work and expense.

The waste resulting from poor quality

In order to convince those members of management charged with making decisions on investments in data of the importance of data quality, it can be interesting to present them with the expenses that result from the *lack* of quality in data. These costs are easier to demonstrate with a higher degree of certainty than the future profits which may be earned from 'good quality data' and can thus be used as an argument while convincing managers of the importance of quality.

Identification errors

In creating an estimate of the waste, we limit ourselves initially to the quality of *identification*: are we capable of addressing or writing to the person or organisation using the correct name, address, telephone and e-mail address? Incorrect identification can lead to the following waste (Mergen, 2003):

- Returned mail items; in addition to the fact that production and mailing expenses have been wasted, the postroom must incur expenses to 'handle' the returns and the database manager will have to correct errors in the database.
- Double mail items which have been sent to the same address because certain customers are registered more than once in the database.
- E-mail that is returned or sent twice. Although the waste is less substantial than that experienced with physical mail items, corrections will also have to be carried out in the database.
- Incoming telephone calls which cannot be processed sufficiently. The data necessary to be of service to the customer either cannot be found quickly enough or are missing entirely. The caller must wait a long time or will only get an answer to his or her question in a subsequent conversation which must be effected at his, her or the supplier's own initiative. This requires the *agent* to spend additional time on the telephone and can even lead to additional expense for the telephone call.
- Salespersons, account managers and service engineers who visit the customer at the wrong time, at the wrong location or after having made preparations from inaccurate data. Their time and travel expenses have been wasted.
- Errors in invoicing. Customers either do not receive an invoice or have received an incorrect invoice for the services provided to them. Errors are either not reported, for example if they are to the customer's advantage, or require rectification. Sales are lost and/or corrective expenses are the result.

The consequences of errors can extend even further than the direct waste mentioned above. In the long run, the effectiveness of communication and the level of service are affected. The likelihood increases that the customer's perception of post and e-mail will deteriorate to the level of junk mail, and the telephone will be reduced to a bureaucratic 'pillar-to-post' facility. Opportunities to use the wasted time effectively are missed; the salesperson, the service engineer and the account manager could have gained a customer or even please another one during that lost time. Customer satisfaction and commitment suffer. Errors can provoke irritation on the customer's part. In general, the most damage is done when errors are made in the gender or name of a customer (AGB Interact, 1995).

CRM illustration

Research commissioned by Human Inference which was conducted by AGB Interact has provided insight into the seriousness of the errors made in addressing companies and people in the business market. The top five errors made by suppliers at which customers take the most offence are:

1. Mistaken gender designation.
2. Incorrect company name.
3. Error in company name.
4. Not addressed to the proper person.
5. Last name spelled incorrectly.

Source: AGB Interact (1995).

Profile errors

In addition to identification, errors may also be made in the *profile*. These will result in similar waste, but will be smaller in scope. The communication will be less focused; we will be less capable of forming a full or accurate image of the customer and, as a result, will be less capable of effective communication. The message will be less powerful or will ultimately reach people and businesses which do not belong to the central target group.

Calculations of this waste represent a key argument in favour of investing in data quality. After all, these amounts can be quite substantial. Preventive investments to correct errors in identification and develop better profiles suddenly seem to produce returns. In this way, procedures geared towards improving quality stand a better chance of being implemented. Investments in tools are within reach so that the database can be de-duplicated[1] and comparisons may be made with other databases in which up-to-date data on identities and profiles may be maintained.

The earnings stemming from data quality

Influence on the effectiveness of acquisition activities

First of all, data quality increases the effectiveness of acquisition. The response rate to efforts increases: the right customer is approached with the right offer at the right time. Not only does the likelihood of completing a transaction increase, but also that of attracting the right customer. For example, an investment fund capable of identifying customers who are willing to run an above-average risk is more likely to be successful by issuing communication on a new emerging market fund. The response rate rises and customers are acquired who are satisfied with the product. A sudden fluctuation in the rate of the fund will not lead to dissatisfaction and customer churn. The clientèle is prepared for this.

Direct marketing (DM) experiences have shown that the quality of the database – the so-called list – has the most influence on the response achieved by a certain DM campaign (Roberts and Berger, 1989). The effect of this is nearly as substantial as that of the offer, the message and the incentive combined (see Figure 5.1). The quality of the offer, its communicative packaging and the promotion's allure to incite the prospect to take action have collectively just as much influence on the response as the composition of the list.

Influence on the customer value

Data quality will have repercussions not only on customer acquisition but also on customer retention and relationship development. The development of a relationship depends on the data that companies have about the customer. Besides, it is difficult to build a bond with a stranger. It is, however, hard to demonstrate a direct connection between the data quality and a customer's lifetime value (see Figure 3.4). The question

[1] People and companies which appear more often than once in the database are identified; steps are taken to make sure that the proper description is maintained for these subjects.

Figure 5.1 Impact of the list, the offer, the communication and the incentive on the response

is whether or not data can offer prospects for future success in changing markets. The retention and development of the relationship are dependent on many more factors than data quality.

At the same time, in performing calculations, people will find themselves confronted with the situation in which investments in data will produce a future rather than an immediate return. As a result, management's approval for investments in data quality will depend not only on the outcome of rate of return calculations in many cases, but also in the 'faith' that they have acquired in the value of data and customer knowledge. This can require 'evangelising' on the part of the people who are involved in the development and management of databases. They must be able to spread the word on the importance of the data quality, even if it involves an activity with which they have less affinity.

5.2 The utilisation of data as an asset

Utilising data

Data are resources in which a great many investments are made and must continue to be made by relationship-oriented organisations. They are assets which must be exploited. First, it is important for organisations to make the right investments, or in other words, record the proper data. Second, the value of these resources only becomes apparent at the moment they are put to use. It is only then that data are converted to information and knowledge. Handling data improperly leads to only a portion of data's potential value being realised or, even worse, a situation in which the data value is nullified. Given the fact that the value and purpose of investments in customer databases are frequently discussed topics, the management and exploitation of these data deserve a great deal of attention. Historically, organisations are accustomed to managing physical resources. Data possess entirely different qualities and their management differs considerably from that of physical resources such as machines. Typical problems faced by organisations that invest in and utilise data are shown in the following box.

Typical problems within organisations involving investments in and utilisation of data

Strategy

- There is no connection between the company's and strategic business unit's strategy and the data and information strategy.
- The company does not know which data are the most important.
- The data necessary to implement the strategy are not available.
- The influence of new sources of information or data are not incorporated into the formulation of the strategy.

Knowledge of data resources

- Insufficient knowledge within the company of available data and the manner in which they may be converted into useful information.
- Employees cannot find the information they are looking for.
- Information chains, which run from data creation to use, are not being sufficiently identified and managed.

Access

- Employees do not have access to the data they are looking for, even if they are aware of their existence.
- Data are not being shared.

Quantity

- There are too many data that have little or no value.
- There is a great deal of redundancy in the data and it is not being managed.
- Superfluous data are not deleted but continue to require attention.
- Everyday terms, such as customer or profit, have many different meanings.

▶

Quality

- Data values are inaccurate, not updated or inconsistent which leads to additional expenses being incurred, the decision-making process becoming complicated, and the quality of operational management declining.

Need for new data

- New data are not gathered at the speed desired by the organisation.
- Reliable sources of data appear to be difficult to find.
- Data structures are difficult to adapt.

Use

- The use of the data is ineffective.
- Decision-making is insufficiently based on facts.
- New market opportunities are not adequately identified.

Security

- Data are exposed to unauthorised use, theft, viruses, loss and unintentional destruction.

Privacy

- The concept within businesses of handling data in a confidential manner is poorly understood.
- Poor understanding of legitimate and illegitimate use of customer and employee data.

Organisation

- Management responsibilities with regard to data are poorly defined.
- Organisations' bases for policy with regard to data and information are 'brutal'.
- There are no procedures in place for dealing with data issues within the organisations.

Source: Levitin and Redman (1998).

The organisation of data management

Organisations normally proceed along a path of growth. A professional database organisation is not created in a day. It is a learning process, characterised by success one day and crisis the next. The following evolutionary path was constructed on the basis of brainstorming sessions held with database managers (see Figure 5.2).

Stage 1: the pioneering phase

The first steps onto the database management terrain usually consist of the creation of the first address file. This is done by a marketer, who does this as a 'hobby' in addition to his or her normal tasks as the result of an idea or marketing campaign.

Stage 2: the specialisation phase

The successes that are achieved as a result of the first step form the justification for further investment in database management. A separate staff department is created. People begin to focus specifically on file management and acquire additional skills in the preparation of analyses of the data. More information is gathered and recorded, in many situations without people having a clear idea of the marketing analyses that they hope to perform and the customer profile that they would like to create. The developments are such that those involved are heading for a crisis.

Figure 5.2

Growth stages in database management

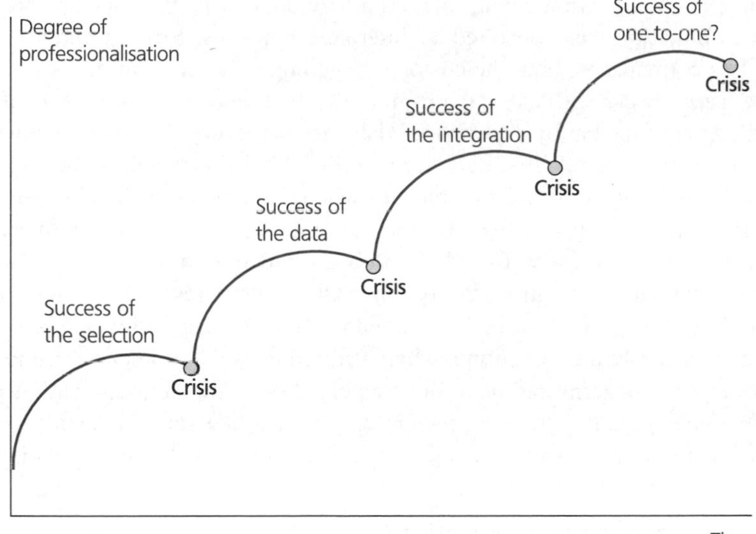

Stage 3: the multifunctional teams

Investments in this staff department of database specialists appear to fail to produce the desired return and become a topic of discussion. A period of review starts in which the organisation of the database management is modified. People realise that close teamwork must exist between the marketers, database specialists and the front-office staff who actually make contact with customers. The situation must be prevented in which database specialists retreat too often to their 'island'. At the same time, marketers must become more involved in database management. They should discover the possibilities it offers and provide guidance to the collection, registration and analysis of the data. Contact employees must also experience the benefits of the data in their own work so that they are prepared to put forth extra effort to record contact history.

The multifunctional teams to be formed are held responsible for the results they achieve with customers. Database management moves from being a cost centre to a section of a profit centre. Data and information are evaluated on how they are acted upon in the market.

The staff department with database specialists which was set up at that time can continue to exist as a development centre with the responsibility to further develop customer knowledge as a profitable aspect. The department can indicate the path to be taken for further development of customer knowledge in a more distanced manner, without becoming engrossed in daily operations. What are the useful aspects to know about customers? How do these fit into the marketing approach? Which sources may be consulted to obtain these data? How do we ensure that these data are also utilised in marketing?

Stage 4: system integration

Once companies provide prospects and customers with the opportunity to contact them via multiple communication channels, then a new crisis usually crops up. Previously, customer information was consulted by internal employees. Errors remained internal and could be corrected without the customer catching wind of them. Data which were difficult to access were still 'extracted from the system' and disseminated thanks to the tricks pulled out of the hat by experienced database managers. The multichannel environment, however, demands that data are recorded 'real time' and are accessible, not only for the benefit of front-office employees who should be immediately apprised of a discussion conducted between the customer and the organisation via another channel, but also for the customer, who would like to be provided with a solution via the Internet. Without human intervention, the system will have to supply customisation where and when the customer asks for it. There are no options for correcting any errors made. This stage of the system integration is often referred to as the moment of truth. Hidden mistakes become apparent and also immediately disrupt the communication process. They inflict damage and irritate marketers and front-office staff. Investments in data quality will not tolerate postponement during this phase and are implemented urgently.

Stage 5: one-to-one communication?

Ultimately a multichannel environment becomes linked to the customer data and the processes in the back office (such as order entry, delivery, etc.) and a situation arises in which people can perhaps work slowly, step by step, towards the ideal of one-to-one communication (Peppers, Rogers and Dorf, 1999). Independent of time and place, communication is facilitated between customers and the company. The systems are designed so that they can support and initiate many types of incoming and outgoing contacts. Companies that are overzealous in aiming for this ideal often find themselves in a crisis. The organisation cannot handle the complexity and lacks the information it needs to provide useful answers to its customers' questions. Reality must be allowed to take precedence over the vision at this point. A more differentiated communication process will have to develop incrementally through different channels. Those parts of the process which pay off and are capable of being implemented must take priority.

5.3 From data to customer knowledge

What data would we ultimately want from the customer? What profile would we like to see from the customer. How do we want to profile the customer and use this information in marketing? These are the questions we must ask in order to design the policy that is geared towards the development and utilisation of data as an important asset of the organisation.

In answering these questions, the data are frequently used as a basis for reasoning. Different data are examined to determine if they are useful for marketing purposes, while the other point of view, whereby the desired customer profile and relationship marketing policy are used as a basis for reasoning, can lead to acting in a more goal-oriented fashion. There is an ultimate goal which functions as a guideline in defining the data which are gathered through a variety of sources. Pursuing this approach requires that database managers and marketers are able to formulate their ultimate goal (see development stage 4 in the previous section).

CRM illustration

Customer knowledge: the story behind the data

Interview with Gerard Wolfs after he won the title of Direct Marketing Man of the Year 2001

'It is still the old direct marketing, the way I learned it while working for my first employer, Reader's Digest. Those old principles are still adhered to. Even if we adorn new systems with multichannels, data warehouses and campaign management systems, we still continue to work according to the old traditions. With cross-selling, we try to find those customers whom we have the best chance of convincing to purchase a new product. Apparently we are not interested in why they would be interested in doing this. Quite simply, they now have a few characteristics in common with people who also bought this combination of products in the past. And the implicit thought is that this will apparently also be the case in the present. The best part is that we feel that this procedure fits in with customer relationship management; aiming to create long-term relationships between customer and service provider.

'We will have to listen to customers much more. Listening begins with registration, and we do, in fact, do this. However, what we neglect to do is interpret that which we have heard. What is the story behind the event? We explain so little. We take action immediately. From the data, it appears that the "member get member" campaign has resulted in the acquisition of high-quality customers. Therefore, we should start stimulating more people to acquire customers via an incentive. We overlook what the motive was for the customer to introduce another one; was it someone he knew that he wanted to help by putting him in contact with you? We are not aware that the ambassador then later asked his friend if he was satisfied with you as service provider and that he saw to it that his "customer" had the proper expectations of you. We are not fully aware of how this behind-the-scenes process is disrupted by sending incentives, and that there is a risk that the customer will lose the quality stamp that he has earned as canvasser.

'If we were to examine the story behind the event more often, we would start to see things differently. Other things become important. Is it now ultimately the customer's purchase that is important or the time he is willing to spend on you? Time indicates whether or not the customer considers you to be important and is involved with you. Whether he likes you or not. You have more interest in the person behind the event, and this is ultimately what it's all about, right?

'If you would like to develop a bond with a customer, you must be interested in the story behind the event and/or the person! How can you achieve customer intimacy otherwise? Subjective aspects will have to play a more important role; not only hard data! More emotional intelligence will have to be involved; an optimum balance will have to be created between EQ and IQ.'

Source: *Tijdschrift voor Marketing* (*Magazine for Marketing*) (2001).

Organisations which would like to implement the customer intimacy strategy and develop intensive relationships with customers will not only have to form an image of the customer as a *buyer*, but also one of the customer as a *user* and as a *person* or an *organisation*. If we only focus on the collection of data about the buyer, we are implicitly implementing a product leadership or operational excellence strategy (see box on page 103: Customer knowledge: the story behind the data). It seems to us that it is the transactions and not the relationships that count. At the same time, we must realise that the collection of data about the customer as user and person and/or organisation is associated with higher costs. This normally involves not those data which are made available by the financial back-office systems, but those which are collected separately or which must be gleaned via third parties. Data which are less objectively measurable are also involved to a certain degree; the personality and the values of a person are abstract and imperceptible. Although they have stable characteristics, measuring and keeping track of these types of data represent quite a challenge.

We will also have to realise that these types of data have less to do with behaviour and more to do with the characteristics of the customer. It is difficult to demonstrate that a connection exists between these data and the response to communication. Nonetheless, communication may make a contribution to the 'customisation' of the customer contact and relationship management. It provides us with a better customer profile that can assist us in being of better service to the customer.

A practical solution to the problem which has arisen is to combine data from different sources. Traditionally, databases' strength lies in their ability to supply behavioural data about the buyer and, in terms of market research, their suitability is to provide data on the customer as user, person and/or organisation. The information obtained during personal contact with the customers serves to further improve the profile.

One important point which must be considered in the merging of different sources of information is that market research, as opposed to databases and customer contact, usually produces anonymous and aggregated customer information. A method must be devised to link customer profiles reliably from both quantitative and qualitative market research to individual customers. A number of hard behavioural criteria must provide insight into the qualitative profile that corresponds to an individual customer. A technique such as cluster analysis may be employed for this purpose. Robeco Direct (Wolfs, 2003), for example, a financial services company based in the Netherlands, successfully applied this method to describe the profile of its customers in the various segments in greater detail. Within the database, a cluster analysis was used to identify different segments on the basis of hard (behavioural) criteria. Through qualitative research, extensive profiles of prospects, customers and former customers were created as person, investor and buyer of Robeco services for each segment.[2] Using disposable cameras, respondents recorded photographs of images that were important to them. They then provided an explanation of these images during extensive sessions; they indicated what was important to them and the roles played by money and investment in their lives. Particular attention was placed on long-term characteristics which are not very susceptible to change. The customer profiles proved very useful in the creation and implementation of marketing strategies for each customer segment. For example, it is now known what motivates the so-called *dignitary*: which values he pursues. His investment

[2] Comparative research showed that the database and the qualitative study both led to the same segmentation.

profile and corresponding investment and communication behaviour are known and may be capitalised on. The company does not bother him with product introductions which do not interest him, and he is addressed with a tone of voice and with communications that appeal to him.

Creating a meaningful customer profile complete with matching relationship marketing policy is a learning process and requires a learning culture that is typical to direct marketing and that should also be typical of CRM. The purpose of new data that fit conceptually into the customer profile the company would like to develop will have to be determined through experimentation. Tests will have to be used to study which campaigns are or are not effective within the framework of the marketing policy. Experimentation with different communications to ultimately determine what does or does not work in certain situations is also deserving of attention. Efforts must be taken to develop, produce and send certain types of messages to carefully selected people and organisations. Discipline is required in order to retain the lessons learned from previous tests so that they may be benefited from in future. Assessments of marketing campaigns must be prepared before new ones are initiated in the course of hectic day-to-day activities.

Which data?

To sum up, as may be concluded from Figure 5.3, it appears that on an individual level data are usually collected in databases on the following topics (Peelen, 1999; Hoekstra, 2001; Tapp, 2001; among others):

Figure 5.3 The use of different sources of information to create a complete customer profile

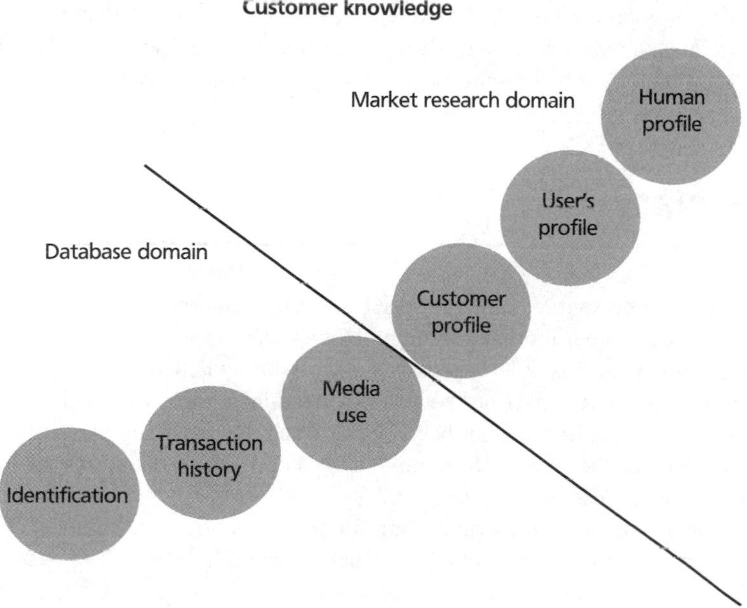

- Identification of the customer or prospect: the most basic data include the name, address, city, telephone number and e-mail address.
- Segment: to which segment does the customer belong? Being able to categorise a customer in a certain sub-group is crucial in order to be able to provide him or her with a differentiated offering.
- Communication channel preferences: it is also important at an early stage to determine the nature of the customer's communication channel preference. What is his or her opinion on certain channels? In which situations and at which times will he or she have a preference for a certain channel?
- Transaction history and customer value: which products or services has the customer purchased from the organisation in the past? How may the customer's payment behaviour be characterised? There are additional summarising criteria which may be used to describe the transaction history, examples include the Recency Frequency Monetary Value scores (see Chapter 11), lifetime values, share of wallets, and customer contribution margins (see Chapter 14). Direct marketing practice has taught us that historical buying behaviour is one of the best predictors of future purchase behaviour.
- Communication history: recording communication which has taken place is important in order to be able to conduct an ongoing dialogue in which repetition can be avoided. A communication summary can offer points of reference in determining the method which may be used to achieve increased depth in the conversation so that more personal data may be exchanged.

Events are a subject for which it can prove interesting to collect data on an individual level. Events are incidents which occur in the environment and lives of customers which induce them to perform a transaction. A birth, a marriage, reaching a certain age, the purchase of a car, a pay rise, termination of employment and moving house are all examples of events which lie at the foundation of the purchase of a number of insurance policies. Being able to obtain data on these events can open up new possibilities: an offer may be made to the prospect at precisely the right time. Some of this type of data may be procured from third party organisations.

5.4 Privacy

Customer data represent a valuable asset for organisations that are interested in implementing a customer intimacy strategy. However, it must be realised that this value is dependent upon the customer's permission; to what extent will he or she allow the supplier to get to know him or her better? Once the information is used in an undesirable manner, the value of the asset becomes an issue. By invoking privacy legislation, customers can force the supplier to remove their data from its databases and prohibit it from making further use of the data.

This privacy issue is an important point for consideration in database management. Now that more and more customer data are being recorded in suppliers' databases, the fear continues to grow that customers will resist this activity on the basis of privacy considerations. It may be said that suppliers who collect and record personal data on their customers without prior permission have thus entered the 'physical and mental space' of their customers. The risk exists that customers will not recognise the purpose and necessity of this interference in their personal environment: why does someone have to have insight into his or her personal situation in order to supply a product? There will certainly also be customers who are worried about the abuse of personal data by this, or even another organisation to which the data might be sold or rented. Owing to the rapid expansion of the 'electronic highway', it is extremely easy to distribute data rapidly; physical or geographical distances have little or no impact any more. Customers can also see the suppliers' 'hunger for information' as an unwelcome invasion of their personal environment by a relative stranger with deviant objectives and interests.

Examples of situations of public opposition to certain suppliers' practices

- The Netscape browser automatically created a record of the number of visited websites and pages on the user's PC. This record was automatically made available to the owner of the websites that the user visits. The customers' objections led to the creation of the present Netscape browser option to 'turn off' the cookies function.
- Microsoft was also subjected to a similar protest from customers. The first time that Microsoft went online, it took advantage of the opportunity to record its subscribers' PC configuration. Public protest resulted in Microsoft abandoning this practice.

Source: Hagel III and Rayport (1997).

Hagel III and Rayport (1997) believe that the objection to recording personal customer data is less related to the fundamental need to protect one's privacy. In their eyes, customers are generally prepared to act pragmatically. Situations have been known to exist in which customers are prepared to pay premium prices to suppliers who exercise caution in using their personal information and who use it to their customers' benefit. Customers provide this information voluntarily and willingly. There are also cases in which customers receive payment for information they provide.

In their analysis of the privacy issue, Hagel and Rayport make little distinction between individuals. Privacy, on the other hand, is a personal topic; everyone can have different notions of privacy. The boundary between what is and what is not acceptable is different for every customer (Woudstra, 1999). Some will operate pragmatically, but others may approach it purely as a matter of principle. For a supplier, it is important that it takes the different views of its customers into consideration.

5.5 Personal Data Protection Act (Singewald, 2004)

In determining the method to use with regard to the collection, recording, updating, distributing and use of data on customers, a company needs to be aware of the European Personal Data Protection Act, a consequence of the guidelines of the European Commission on this subject. It replaces old legislation which was perceived as being too rigid and bureaucratic to be able to offer a satisfactory answer to the issues central to the information society. In today's society, physical borders fade and it is difficult to determine who is registering data. In the new legislation, it is the *processing*, rather than the *registration* of personal data that is central. Each action or each group of actions involving an item of data on an identified or identifiable natural person, apart from certain exceptions, requires the unambiguous permission of the person involved.

CRM illustration

Before we can accept your request and execute the contract, XXX Inc. will require your personal data. We will also be able to use these data to inform you about relevant services provided by XXX Inc. and its subsidiaries. If you are not interested in receiving this information, you may send written notification of this to XXX Inc., PO Box . . .

In this example, the obligation to provide information has been satisfied. The company responsible for the data has been named, as well as the purposes for which it would like to use the data. Finally, there is a reference to the right of objection.

If data are not obtained from the data subject, the person responsible will inform the data subject of the following (unless he or she is already aware of this information):

- The identity of the person responsible.
- The purpose(s) of the data handling.
- Circumstances under which further approval is necessary to guarantee the data subject of proper and careful processing.
- The rights of objection.

The time of the notification is the moment that the data was (initially) recorded by or provided by a third party to the person responsible. The *obligation to provide information* lapses if this requires a disproportionate effort on the part of the person responsible.

The person responsible undertakes to process the data *properly and carefully* as well as *honestly and legitimately* in order to prevent errors being made. Appropriate organisational and technical security measures must protect the personal data from loss, theft or any form of illegitimate processing. They must also prevent excessive and irrelevant use of the data. Those gathering the data have the task of monitoring the accuracy and precision of the data. Data shall not be kept in a form that makes it possible to identify the data subject for longer than is deemed necessary for the realisation of the objectives.

Modifications or updates to the data may only be performed *by order of and under the authority of* the person responsible for the personal data.[3] Processors are bound to preserve the confidentiality of the personal data of which they have become knowledgeable, except to the extent that any statutory provision obligates them to provide notification of this or the necessity to provide notification arises from their duties. External service firms such as call centres, database managers, data-entry firms and fulfilment houses which perform activities involving data and which defer to the responsible party and save data under that person's responsibility are processors. (Consultancy) firms over which the client does not exercise any authority are not processors by this definition and are themselves responsible. The responsibility for the data will normally have to be precisely provided for in contracts entered into with third parties.

The registered data subject has *right of inspection* with regard to his or her data. The data subject must be notified within four weeks. For this inspection, the data subject may be charged a small fee. Upon request, the person may also obtain information regarding the underlying logic of the processing of the personal data.[4]

In cases where data are being processed in connection with the creation or maintenance of a direct relationship between the responsible party and the data subject with a view to acquisition for commercial or charitable purposes, the data subject may submit an objection to such processing at all times at no cost to him- or herself.

CRM illustration

If you are not interested in receiving this information, you may send written notification of this to XXX Inc., PO Box . . .

In the case of an objection, the responsible party must take the steps required to terminate processing of the data immediately. The responsible party must notify the data subject of his or her *right of objection* at least once a year, through promotional material or advertisements, for example. In the event of violation, the data subject is entitled to compensation for damages and to commence proceedings with a 'registration board' which is charged with, among other responsibilities, the supervision of the processing of the personal data and compliance with the law.

[3] Formally speaking, it is advisable to include this task description in employees' job descriptions.

[4] A data subject can thus in essence demand inspection into the cross-sell or retention models which the responsible party uses in his or her work.

The right of objection and the various channels of communication

• Addressed e-mail	opt-out
• Telephone (voice)	opt-out
• Fax	opt-in
• Automatic telephone calls without human intervention	opt-in
• Unaddressed e-mail	opt-out
• E-mail: customers	'soft-opt-in'
prospects	opt-in

opt-out = right to block by data subject him/herself
opt-in = prior permission needed from data subject to send messages

In most EU countries the old legislation does not include a section on the processing of *special personal data* such as that involving religion or philosophy of life, race, political persuasion, health and the like. *Explicit permission* is required for the processing of these types of data. Tacit or implicit consent is in any case insufficient; the data subject must have expressed his or her will to grant permission for the data processing in question orally, in writing or by virtue of his or her behaviour. It must be clear that the data subject has been sufficiently informed to be capable of comprehending the significance of his or her consent. The subject may not be caught by surprise in this regard.

A *notification requirement* applies to companies which process personal data. To this end, the names of the responsible party, the processor, the purposes of the data processing, a description of the data and their application, the recipients, the security and cross-border data traffic are all to be specified on a notification form. Companies are exempt from this requirement if:

- Many common, standard processing activities are involved; simple personnel, wage administration or bookkeeping activities.
- Short periods of data retention apply.

The maximum administrative fine for failure to notify is €5450 in the Netherlands. With regard to criminal law, it can also lead to the imposition of a fine and even a prison sentence.

Self-regulation

In spite of the impression some of the descriptions in the law may give, governments in many European countries strive to increase citizens' own awareness of privacy so that they may protect themselves more (see Woudstra, 1999). Consumers must increase their awareness of registrations and must be in a position to exercise control over the processing of personal data themselves. In order to achieve better transparency, national governments hope to inform citizens of their rights, companies' obligations and options available to citizens to protect themselves within an electronic environment.

Companies are also encouraged to regulate this issue independently. Self-regulation is considered to be an important tool. The legal system is not considered capable of responding quickly enough to abuse occurring in the electronic environment. Ethics play an important role in self-regulation. The word 'ethics' has its origin in the Greek word 'ethos', which may be translated as habit, custom or disposition. In Latin, the word 'ethos' was translated from the Greek as *mos, moris*, also meaning 'custom' and giving us our word 'mores'. Therefore, in terms of origins, ethics and morality mean exactly the same thing: that which concerns normalised behaviour (i.e. custom). Over the centuries, the word 'morality' has, however, come to take on the meaning of the set of rules of conduct accepted (by the group or culture), while the word 'ethics' has come to be defined as the (critical) way of thinking about morality.

5.6 Information policy

In the information society, the possibilities for collecting, recording, processing, distributing and utilising data continue to increase. It is becoming important for companies to formulate a vision on these topics in which consumers, the competition, legislation, the value of data as a resource, morality and the possibilities offered by IT are all taken into consideration. According to Godin (1998), translating this vision into a marketing concept leads to the formulation of 'permission marketing'. A central theme within permission marketing is the asking of permission from the consumer: permission to ask them to focus attention on a commercial message and to disclose more about themself so that the supplier can supply customisation (Godin, 1998). Although the name accentuates a topic that merits a great deal of attention within marketing, it would be exaggerated to refer to this as a new form of marketing. Within marketing, which focuses on the exchange of resources, information is actually recognised as one of the potential resources for exchange. According to the existing marketing concept, a supplier must exchange information with customers on a voluntary basis and during these exchange processes, must strive for customer satisfaction and the perpetuation and development of the relationship. The fact is that the two-sided exchange of information is, in many cases, a subject which receives insufficient attention within the (relationship) marketing policy which focuses primarily on the exchange of goods and services for money. Information ends up in a 'no-man's land' where somewhat 'brutal' views are held. As a result, data are not always obtained in exchange on a voluntary basis; it almost seems as if they are stolen and used without permission being granted. These are methods which do not even fit within the existing marketing concept.

The recording of data on the quality of the customer–supplier relationship and the stage in which it is located is a point of particular interest for database managers. Commitment and trust, which grow as more personal and less concrete resources are exchanged (see Chapter 2), are abstract concepts, the measurement of which requires a great deal of work. More questions will have to be asked of customers in order to be able to make a 'rough' estimate. Customers could perceive this measurement as a nuisance. At the same time, many costs will have to be incurred in order to be able to gather the data. If people realise that measurements must be repeated on a regular basis in order to be able to keep the information up to date, then they will become increasingly aware of the aspect of cost.

The challenge for database managers consists in devising a way to gather regular, reliable information on the quality of the customer–supplier relationship at a relatively low cost and in an accessible manner. A model that is capable of translating currently available behavioural data that comes in on a frequent basis into measures of commitment and trust on the part of the customer would be an excellent solution.

5.7 Conclusion

Customer data which are developed into customer information which may be acted upon form one of the most important building blocks of CRM. Without customer knowledge, the relationship policy will lack substance and focused communication based on customer profiles cannot occur. Investments in this type of data are usually a lot higher than management expects beforehand. Increasing the ability to gain insight into these investments and the consequences of a lack of data quality is effective for making management aware of the scope and relevance of data quality. Making the business case for the importance of data quality is probably better served by this type of argument than one which sings the praises of the future profits to be earned from data quality.

As a first point, developing customer information requires a professional organisation. Database management is not an activity which may be done on the side. Nor is it a function which is the exclusive preserve of specialists in a cost centre. In order to guarantee that marketers and those working in the front office will act upon the customer information which has been made available, it is recommended that database management is organised through the use of a multifunctional team. With the support of a professional staff, these teams can further enrich the customer information and utilise it profitably. It is possible within a learning organisation to work on the construction of the desired customer profile and matching marketing policy. Various information sources may be combined in order to complete this picture.

Furthermore, the utilisation of data requires a well-devised privacy policy. Customers will have to consent to the supplier getting to know them; they will have to see the benefit of this as well. *If they cannot see the advantage in this, then the value of this extremely important business asset will shrink rapidly.*

Case study

Customer knowledge at Center Parcs: a life-long holiday!

Introduction

Center Parcs is a holiday resort with locations in several European countries, for example Germany, France and the Netherlands. Customer relationship management is one of its successes. The secret: 'it is not about the value the customer represents to us but about the value he or she wants.'

Richard Verhoeff, director of e-commerce at Center Parcs: 'None of our customers is equal. *The* market and *the* customer do not exist for us. All that our guests have in common is the money and the time they spent with us. It is our challenge to get to know them better. . . . It was the objective of our yield management system to optimise cottage rental, but nowadays we also want to actively offer services at different contact moments. Experience tells us that guests who participate in more activities are more likely to return. But before you can do this, you will have to answer questions such as: who are our guests? When do they come? What do they want? In other words: we need customer profiles. Of course, segmentation is nothing new. In most cases customer groups are distinct and differ in the value they represent for the organisation (customer value). Customer relationship management then simply means retaining the good customers and stimulating them to increase their expenditure, while in the meantime the bad customers can leave.

Profiling customers

BPK Acxiom, a database and CRM consulting firm, approached it from a different perspective and began by analysing the *emotional and instrumental values* of a stay at Center Parcs. These values change with the life cycle of a customer. He comes as a little child with his parents, when he is older he brings his girlfriend, and again later his family. Each of these roles asks for a different approach. Also, the value of the attractions differs for each customer, depending on his life cycle, the time of his stay and the people that accompany him. Verhoeff: 'The swimming pool on a Saturday morning has a completely different function from that on a Sunday afternoon, when there are a lot of small children around.'

To clarify this, BPK Acxiom developed life scenarios. Peter Severens, director at BPK Acxiom: 'We write *life stories*. What are the motives that drive people? Where do they come from? What are the events in their life and in specific situations? And what goods and services are consumed during these events? We map people's life cycles and store them in the database.' The scenarios have been tested and refined in panel research together with a market research agency, named Signicom. It resulted in the definition of a number of customer groups and a customer-value pyramid per customer group. The value pyramid contains suggestions for product development and communication. The tone-of-voice, the actual proposition and the sales arguments match the values and preferences of the segment.

CRM software

CRM software plays an important role during the implementation of this customer group project. Center Parcs uses the forecasting software developed by DataDistilleries (now owned by SPSS) during direct and telemarketing actions. Relations are selected that have the best chance of booking during a specific period. But also, ►

salespersons benefit from the software. Marcel Holsheimer, founder of DataDistilleries: 'Our software helps to predict the interests of a person during a contact moment.' Specific phone scripts and offerings can be formulated. Verhoeff: 'Some customer groups appreciate it if you give them a discount right from the start, others first ask for an explanation of your products and services and only let you know at the end if a discount is demanded.' Although the customer groups and formats help, one should never forget that it remains people's business.

To predict what Center Parcs' customers are interested in, DataDistilleries can benefit from an enormous database with customer data that have been collected over the years. As early as 1984, Center Parcs started to store relationship and transaction data. However, through the years the organisation has been reactive in its use of these data. Erna ter Weele from BPK Acxiom: 'Currently, changes are focusing on improving customer insight and exploiting this information in actions.' Since DataDistilleries' software is user friendly, marketers no longer have to rely on IT specialists and can act faster. Verhoeff: 'Time to market is very important. If you notice the occupancy rate of your park is not optimal for a particular weekend, you only have a few days to do something about it.'

Results

Although Center Parcs is pleased with the results to date, Verhoeff is convinced the potential of the system is larger. 'An additional positive result of €3 million is a beginning. We have 3.2 million customers a year and if they spend an additional 2 per cent, revenue will increase by several tens of millions. By making more active use of the call centre in outbound actions, by stimulating cross-selling in the call centre, via the Internet and during contact moments in the park itself, revenues have to grow.'

Source: Theo Loth (2003) Een leven lang er tussen uit, *Adformatie*, March, **11**, 13, 36–37.

Questions

1. Consider the way Center Parcs and its consulting and research firms profile its customers. Apply the method, described by Peter Severijns, to yourself or someone who visited a holiday park once before. What kind of customer profile can you construct?
2. What are two advantages and two disadvantages of applying this customer profiling approach?
3. In what ways can Center Parcs differentiate its marketing for different customer groups?

Questions

1. You are a database manager and would like the approval of senior management for investment in the improvement of data quality. You have ten minutes to present your argument to the board. Outline the essence of this argument.
2. Specify the wastes that occur as a result of a lack of data quality.
3. Why is it so difficult to base the value of data quality on the transactions to be gained from certain customers in the future?
4. The data which are received by companies via e-mail and the Internet on the identity of customers apparently have a relatively low level of reliability.
   (a) What could be the underlying reasons for this? Name three and explain your answers.
   (b) What can a company do to guarantee the quality of these data?

5 Choose an organisation of which you are a customer.

(a) Describe yourself as a customer and provide concrete information on which data must be registered in order to be able to describe you as a customer.

(b) Indicate which data may best be obtained from market research and which may best be registered on an individual level. Explain your answer.

6 The professionalisation of database management is characterised by an evolutionary path. Every success appears to be followed by a crisis. If one has knowledge relating to this path of development, it should be possible to avoid the crisis. However, this appears to be difficult in practice. What is a possible explanation for this, in your opinion?

7 According to the European privacy legislation, you, as customer, are permitted to ask a company which details of your data it is retaining in its database. Approach a company of which you are a customer and ask for these registered data. Describe the mechanics of this process and provide your reaction to the data that had been recorded.

8 Why does the nature of the privacy issue change in the knowledge and network economy? Support your answer by providing two examples.

References

AGB Interact (1995) *De kwaliteit van de tenaamstelling*, AGB Interact, Dongen.

Godin, S. (1998) *Permission Marketing*, The Free Press, New York.

Hagel III, John and Jeffrey F. Rayport (1997) The coming battle for customer information, *Harvard Business Review*, January–February, 53–65.

Hoekstra, Janny C. (2001) *Direct Marketing*, 2nd edn, Wolters-Noordhoff, Groningen.

Levitin, Anany V. and Thomas C. Redman (1998) Daa as Resurce: Properties, Implications and Prescriptions, *Sloan Management Review*, Autumn, 89–101.

Mergen, Norbert (2003) Het beste systeem faalt als de kwaliteit van de relatiegegevens niet deugt, de ROI van goede relatiegegevens, *De Kern van uw zaak*, Human Inference.

Peelen, Ed and Norbert Mergen (2003) Klantendata: de resources van de 21ste eeuw, *Customer Base*, **9** (Yearbook), 12–15.

Peelen, Ed (1999) *The Relation Oriented Organization*, Nyenrode University, Beukelen.

Peppers, Don, Martha Rogers and Bob Dorf (1999) Is your company ready for one-to-one marketing?, *Harvard Business Review*, January–February, 151–160.

Roberts, Mary Lou and Paul D. Berger (1989) *Direct Marketing*, Prentice-Hall, Englewood Cliffs, New Jersey.

Singewald, A. (2003) Personal communication, Nyenrode University/Human Inference, Breukelen.

Singewald, A. (2004) Personal communication, Nyenrode University/Human Inference, Breukelen.

Tapp, Alan (2001) *Principles of Direct and Database Marketing*, 2nd edn, Pearson Education, Harlow.

Wolfs, Gerard (2003) Kwaliteit van data en het kennen van de klant, *Masterclass Relationship Dataquality*, Nyenrode University/Human Inference, Breukelen.

Woudstra, B. (1999) *Interactieve marketing, hoe verken je de grenzen van wat je van de consument mag weten?*, University of Amsterdam.

6

Communication and multichannels

The development of various communication channels, such as the Internet, telephone and the mass media, through which supplier and customer can communicate, requires substantial investment and effort. Suppliers will have to learn how customers make use of these channels and how they may combine this knowledge with their marketing goals. These channels will also have to be integrated with one another as well as with the personal contact points between customer and supplier. These topics are all examined in this chapter. We will first provide the definition of multichannels that we use for the integrated communication methods. Next, we will focus attention on the individual channels from which the multichannels are composed and the developments these undergo. Discussion will then turn to the customers and how they use the channels in their communication process. Finally, on the basis of these insights, policy recommendations will be provided with regard to the development and deployment of multichannels.

In this chapter we will address the following questions

- What is the significance of multichannels?
- What are the communicative characteristics of multichannels?
- How will the integration of communication channels result in a network of contact points?
- What are the developments in the different communication channels?
- How to use the channels for different types of customers in a variety of situations.
- What is the influence of multichannels on price setting?
- How to deploy multichannels; how to realise that the channels support the communication process in the different phases with different customers and prospects in an efficient and effective way.

Practitioner's insight

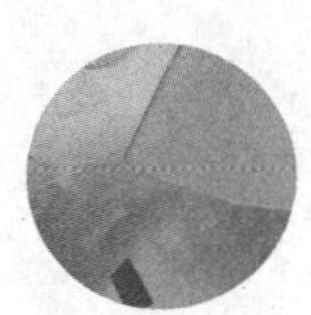

When everything was still small scale, personal contact was considered normal. However, due to industrialisation, the distance between customer and supplier has grown larger. In situations in which the supplier was faced with large groups of customers, mass media were utilised to send messages. These messages quickly took on a seductive and persuasive tone. Market research was conducted to determine whether or not the message had got through and/or if there were still any special requests. With increasing communication pressure and the fragmentation of the mass media, the efficiency and effectiveness of this one-way communication decreases. Moreover, thanks to the emergence of IT, the possibility of a two-way exchange of information on a more individual basis exists which is not necessarily accompanied by an inordinate amount of additional effort and expense. Customers can contact the supplier regardless of the time or their location, and vice versa. Communication in the true sense of the word seems to be coming within easy reach once again in markets with many customers. It is no longer reserved for markets with few customers and suppliers and large transaction sums. It brings customer relationship management within reach of a larger group of companies which gather, enrich and distribute the information they have on their individual customers.

6.1 Multichannels defined

With the emergence and widespread use of the telephone and the Internet among business customers and suppliers, the possibilities for customers and companies to get in touch only seems to increase. The term 'multichannels' is used to refer to this growth in the number of channels available.

Confusion of concepts

'Multichannels' is a term that inherently leads to confusion. After all, are we talking about communication or about distribution channels? Or perhaps both?

We propose that it involves the channels through which information is exchanged in contact; in other words, multichannels involve communication channels. If they were channels of distribution, then it would involve participants in one or more channels. The reason is that a distribution channel (marketing channel) is defined as: 'the succession of channel participants who perform a function in the distribution or marketing of a certain product from the (raw materials) producer to the end user' (Waarts *et al.*, 2004).

It is not entirely unexpected that a confusion of concepts would arise. Interactive communication channels such as the telephone and Internet (which, literally speaking, is a network and not a channel) are actually utilised nowadays for typical distribution functions such as closing transactions, executing payments and delivering information products.

Description of the concept

We therefore also describe multichannelling as the contact processes between a customer and a channel participant (producer or retailer) in all of the phases of the relationship. Currently the word 'touchpoint' is also quite popular to refer to these contact moments.

CRM definitions

'Multichannel management is not very different from managing all sorts of channels leading to various target groups. If, in this case, channels were to be described as being solely communication channels, then the concept of multichannel management would not really involve anything new and could be described in terms of the age-old concept of integrated marketing communication.

'By using various new channels, customers are actually infiltrating the organisation; it becomes transparent. The front office shifts from the store to all of the areas within the organisation where the customers may make contact. In addition to the many outlets, these also include the call centres, the homepages and the possibility to ask questions by e-mail. The interaction between organisation and consumers during these various contact moments is substantial. Questions must lead to concise advice and the contact follow-up also deserves attention. The ease, speed and service during each contact moment determine the added value for the consumers.'

Source: Interview with Van der Plas, Macintosh Retail Group.

6.2 The channels

How may the various channels be described in more detail? What is implied by the fact that channels may be used independently of place and time? How do they differ from one another in terms of 'communication power'? How may they be integrated with one another to form a network of contact or touchpoints?

Independent of time and place

First of all, we can construct a continuum that runs from 'one-to-many' to 'one-to-one' communication; websites, e-mail and the telephone may then be placed in the middle (see Figure 6.1). These channels, supported by IT, make it possible to interact with a large group of people at a relatively low cost. These channels are fairly independent of time and place; they may be utilised at the most varied locations and at any given time.

Figure 6.1

Communication continuum

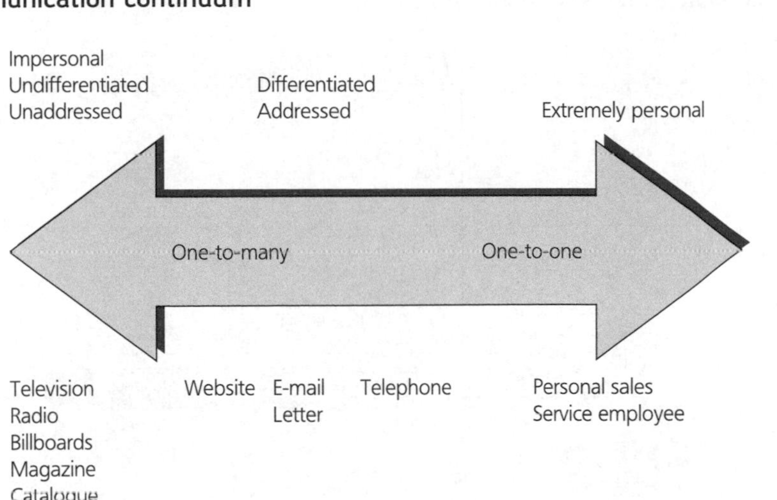

Thanks to this independence with regard to time and place, the importance of context increases. Communication can occur any time, any place. The environment and time in which communication takes place can lend a different meaning to the contact. In addition to the content, it is also important to focus on the context.

Communication power

As a result of technological developments, we have seen the communication power of the channels grow both independently of one another and in connection with one another. Owing to the emergence of technologies such as digiscents (sense of smell) and force-based technology (sense of taste), it has become possible to create the illusion of a reality for users by stimulating nearly all of the human senses. This contrasts sharply with channels in which exclusively static information is still being used and only a small number of senses are being stimulated. An example of the latter would be a newspaper.

Although the channels supported by IT do very well, the mass media and personal contacts continue to play a vital role. The fact remains that mass media may be used to convey a certain message to a large group of people at a low cost, whereas in terms of the social dimension, face-to-face conversations continue to score higher than contact in which machines function as the interface between two people.

We can gain more insight into the communication power of the various channels if we look at the following dimensions (based on Lombard and Ditton, 1997):

- The degree of interactivity (y-axis in Figure 6.2):

  Questions which might be examined within the scope of interactivity include:

  - To what degree does the communication from someone else receive a direct or delayed response or no response whatsoever?

Figure 6.2 Dimensions in which channels may be scored

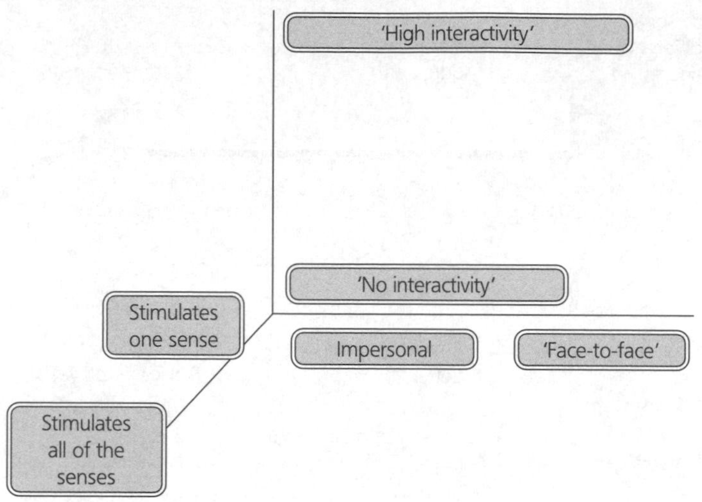

  - Who 'must go to whom' in order to achieve contact?
  - Who dictates the speed at which the information is transferred (pacing)?
- The degree of personality (the *x*-axis):
  - Is there face-to-face contact or is a medium used to reach a large target group ('one-to-many'). It is possible to make a channel more 'personalised' by using a personality medium to allow the viewer or listener to experience a sort of parasocial conversation in which he or she participates. A channel may also become 'more personal' by ascribing certain human characteristics to it; a good example of this is the first pay terminals which had a sort of 'human face' to speed up the adoption process.
- The number of senses stimulated by a channel (*z*-axis):
  - To what extent is the medium capable of providing an accurate representation of objects, events and people that corresponds to 'reality'? The possibilities to imitate this reality are becoming increasingly available. In this case, we refer to this as immersion: the degree to which a virtual environment is created which coincides with the user's experience in reality (virtual reality).

With regard to sensory aspects, the challenge is to make the transition as it were from a two- to a three-dimensional world. We have to think up creative solutions to compensate for the technical limitations. For example, it is possible to stimulate the senses for a commodity pizza by adding the theme of the wood ovens of Tuscany. Introducing the theme of Tuscany to a theme park on the Internet enriches the brand experience even more. Visuals and music from Italy further reinforce this. And, digiscents (digiscents.com), basil in this case, would bring Italy that much closer (Van der Schans, 2001).

'In order to convey the concept of the icy coolness of Mount Everest, we could display a dynamic image of mountains and snow complete with flash text (words such as icy, cold, frigid, pure, and invigorating) and sound (energetic music, intense winter wind).' In future this brand experience could be intensified even further with the scents of eucalyptus, for example, and the tactile sensation of mountain climbing, thereby stimulating four of the five senses (Van der Schans, 2001).

Now that we have modelled our insight into the communication power of channels, we can return to the challenge offered by multichannels. In doing so, we should not lose sight of the fact that customers do need channels that receive high scores for all of the criteria in every situation: each customer brings different information needs and channel preferences to every situation.

It must also be noted that the challenge does not lie in substituting mass media and the face-to-face channel with IT-supported channels, but in fitting these channels into the entire contact process between customers and suppliers. In this way, the use of multiple channels contributes to the construction of a network of touchpoints equipped with sufficient sensory aspects, interactivity, accessibility, reality and efficiency. The quality and efficiency of the contact are distributed along the three dimensions: the limitations of the individual channels are overcome by the coherent application of different channels. Consumer and supplier are connected.

In the situation most worth striving for, the successive contacts fit together seamlessly so that an uninterrupted dialogue can arise. The initiative originates from both parties, and both react promptly to one another's communication. They listen and respond to one another. In terms of substance, there is no unnecessary repetition, and diverse subjects are raised for discussion. The conversation is captivating and binding.

Interweaving of channels

One of the most important developments in the multichannel field is the manner in which channels interweave with one another to form a network of touchpoints. This integration is not limited to the IT-supported channels alone; it extends to mass media and direct mail (printing on demand). And besides people, objects (microwave ovens, refrigerators, central heating units, security equipment for homes, etc.) also get connected. The following sections discuss a number of current types of integration.

Integration with a mass medium such as television: interactive television

Interactive television involves television and employing the underlying cable network in the use of the Internet.

Integration of mobile telephone and Internet: WAP

At the end of the twentieth century, the expectations for WAP were high. 'Wapping' is the verb that derives from Wireless Application Protocol and this is a standard used to receive information via one's mobile telephone; the mobile phone can be used as an Internet browser. These days, however, many people dare not utter the word. The lack of sufficient bandwidth and an insufficient amount of thought being put into useful, feasible applications for mobile Internet have not done the WAP cause any good.

The telecom industry seems to have learned its lesson; the introduction of WAP's successor, GPRS, is being kept low profile.

CRM illustration

The future of interactive television

Are viewers really interested in interactive television (iTV)?

Countless studies have been conducted worldwide on the attitudes on iTV services and applications held by viewers. These studies have shown that television remains primarily an entertainment medium; the interest in iTV services is limited. One reason for this seems to be a lack of knowledge and awareness of what the services have to offer viewers. Two popular iTV applications, video on demand and electronic television guides, suggest, however, that the right products will ultimately be well accepted. At present, the popular interactive services include (interactive) advertising, games, weather reports and sports.

The important reasons to subscribe to iTV include the need for more/better channels and programmes, and improved (digital) image and sound quality. Interactive services (Internet access, home shopping) are seen as added advantages. The primary reasons to use interactive features while watching television are immediate involvement and participation. In spite of several successful applications, the consumption of and income earned from iTV continue to lag behind expectations. It is likely that the fact that television is already a firmly rooted entertainment medium acts more as an impediment than an advantage in the distribution of iTV. Another barrier is that many new viewers initially investigate the possibilities of iTV with a great deal of enthusiasm, yet ultimately abandon it out of disappointment with the unreliability, slowness and lack of depth. This, combined with high expectations of the 'interactive television experience', probably makes it difficult to win back disillusioned viewers. For this reason, the most likely future scenario would be that of passive and interactive content co-existing in order to be able to alternately meet the passive and interactive needs of television consumers.

Source: *Admap* (2003).

CRM illustration

GPRS is finally here, but who wants it?

GPRS, the 'mobile Internet' that is the packet-switched successor to WAP and the precursor of UMTS, has arrived. A British research firm expects that by 2003, there will be some 5.9 million GPRS users in Europe. This means that 35 per cent of the GSM subscribers will have a GPRS subscription.

Whether or not GPRS will be a success remains the question. There is certainly no shortage of equipment available to access GPRS; this is no longer an impeding factor. The availability of services, however, is a hindrance. Those interested in having access to GPRS will always have to want to be online as well as be willing to pay for it.

Source: Klaver (2002).

CRM illustration

Forrester: penetration speed of UMTS overestimated

Only 10 per cent of the European mobile callers will use UMTS by 2007, the wireless technique which allows not only sound but also images to be sent.

Operators in most European countries will not reach a break-even point until 2014. Companies in Finland, France, Italy and Switzerland, will be the first to achieve this point, probably somewhere between 2010 and 2012. The reason for this is that there is the least amount of competition in these countries, even though the market is quite large. Providers in England, Germany, Spain and Portugal are not expected to be in the black before the year 2015.

Forrester foresees additional problems with the technology and the networks. Entering into partnerships and concluding service-level agreements will also contribute to the delay in the breakthrough of UMTS.

Source: Forrester (2002).

SMS or text messaging, on the other hand, has, almost unintentionally, experienced an extremely high level of acceptance and continues to grow. Consumers even pay for this service. It is a technically much simpler solution that was discovered and picked up on primarily by customers.

SMS text messaging allows users to send short messages to the memory of the mobile phone where they are stored, and they may then be read offline. With WAP, a direct connection is made and you browse through your information as you would normally do on the Internet.

CRM illustration

Content by the cubic metre

'With mobile communication, you pay for each bit that you send. SMS owes its bizarre success to this pay-per-packet principle. Entire schoolyards appear to be full of children who are willing to pay twenty-five cents to send no more than 160 characters of text by mobile phone. No one saw the success of this dopey technology coming.'

This is not the case with the Internet, however. No one is willing to pay twenty-five cents to send an e-mail message. 'The difference quite simply lies in people's perceptions. It is sheer madness. Ultimately, it is something that people will pay for. According to recent estimates, SMS accounted for turnover of €10 billion this year (2001) alone.'

Source: Verkooijen (2001).

Integration of fax, telephone, SMS, e-mail and Internet thanks to the contact centre

Important developments in the call, or perhaps even better, contact centre relate to the integration of voice technology, fax, SMS, e-mail, web and IP telephone services. These all-in-one solutions make it possible to manage the call flow within the call or contact centre for the entire organisation (with one or more locations). Extensive management information is made available to call centre managers and capacity utilisation is displayed real-time.

These new technologies provide customers with the opportunity to contact the supplier via a website, telephone (voice), e-mail or fax. The customer is recognised regardless of the channel used to enter, and switching to another form of contact is simplified. For online website visitors for example, it is easy to contact a live agent by simply clicking a button thanks to the implementation of real-time text-chat applications and/or voice-over Internet protocol. Another possibility is that customers may be called back at a time of their choosing. A hotel reservation company in the United States that implemented this application was able to call consumers back within fifteen minutes and saw its online reservations increase by 30 per cent.

In particular, the ability to handle incoming e-mails in call or contact centres becomes important; customers prefer this. They expect an answer within a timeframe of 24 to 48 hours. Using intelligent software, e-mails may be answered using standard responses. Some 80 per cent of e-mailed questions are those asked most frequently. There are sufficient possibilities to automate the response system either partially or completely (for example, E-serve from the Swiss company AAA-sim, www.aaa-sim.ch, and Q-mail from Emailco in the Netherlands, www.emailco.nl).

CRM illustration

Q-mail from Emailco allows e-mail interaction via the Internet. Customers ask their questions on an Internet page dedicated to this purpose by filling in a screen; they also receive an answer via an Internet page. The use of Internet pages offers various advantages. Customers may be asked to provide additional information and during the response, illustrations and buttons may be used to start subsequent operations. Internet pages are also easier to protect from unauthorised 'onlookers' than e-mails.

Source: Peelen *et al.* (2000).

Fax messages sent to an e-mail address

A service-free application – which is offered by eFax.com, for example, in the United States, is the receipt of fax messages via one's e-mail address. Users simply surf to the sign-up page, fill in the required information, and receive a free 'e-fax' number. Customers, employees, friends or family members can send a message to this e-fax number from their computer or fax machine. E-faxing works in the same way as e-mails with attachments.

6.3 Customers and the use of the channels

In technical and creative terms, the IT-supported channels offer good opportunities to conduct a dialogue and create an experience, if so desired. However, before the use of multichannels can grow to become a success, it will have to be ascertained whether customers are actually using these channels. And this is not limited to whether or not they are surfing the Internet from time to time, but specifically concerns the application of these media by a variety of customers to certain purchase and use situations. Customers differ from one another in the manner in which they use the different channels. Having knowledge of this behaviour and these preferences is essential to being able to create a dialogue and/or the desired effect.

Consumer markets

In research conducted by IPM and Peelen and associates (2000) for KPN Telecommerce, the issue of channel use was examined further with respect to consumer markets. On the basis of the stable personality traits (these are traits which may change only slightly over time, if at all), consumers were divided into eight types:

1 Conservative / Passive / Social
2 Conservative / Passive / Instrumental
3 Conservative / Active / Social
4 Conservative / Active / Instrumental
5 Open / Passive / Social
6 Open / Passive / Instrumental
7 Open / Active / Social
8 Open / Active / Instrumental

Conservative consumers are focused on security and familiar forms and frameworks. They view new media somewhat sceptically. Open consumers are the opposite of conservative consumers and are eager to experiment with new things, such as new media. They have more knowledge of media, relatively speaking.

There are many more differences between conservative and open consumers. First, some of them are passive and have a strong tendency to focus on judgement cast upon them by others or to attach a great deal of importance to these opinions. They are more likely to trust others and are very relationship oriented. Others, however, are active and have a need for control, prefer to follow their own lead and ignore 'true' advice from others.

Second, consumers may be instrumentally or socially oriented. With the instrumentals, it is the result that counts; they are efficient and purposeful and are more individually oriented. They do not derive security from a 'good feeling', but from more 'objective aspects'. Social consumers 'just' find contact with others pleasant, they prefer face-to-face contact to the telephone, and most certainly prefer it to the Internet. Efficiency is not the highest goal; it is considered important to get a 'good feeling' from the things that are done.

The eight types of consumer differ from one another in the degree to which they would like to have control and are prepared to make use of IT-supported channels. Consumer type 1 is the least open to new channels and is not after control; type 8 is the opposite in this regard.

Goal-oriented consumer behaviour

The use of and the appreciation of the various channels in goal-oriented consumer behaviour also differs with regard to the phase in which the relationship is located (see top of Figure 6.3). In general, the most positive opinion is that on the shop channel. The shop is the most trustworthy, flexible, offers personal contact, can be pleasant, offers the most 'security' and 'safety', permits problem-free two-way traffic in communication, and is the natural point of reference for other channels. It is a channel that is always used by most consumers in addition to other channels: complementary and irreplaceable.

Although stable personality traits determine the extent to which a person is innately inclined to have a positive or negative attitude towards certain channels, it should not be forgotten that a coincidental, situational experience with a channel is capable of overruling any personality-determined negative attitude. Various other factors may also – and often to an even greater extent – determine the choice of a channel, such as:

- The 'top of mind awareness' of a channel, dependent on situational factors such as availability, knowledge of and experience with channels.
- Risk perception of the product/service (high risk perception leads to more extensive information-search behaviour which can in turn lead to the use of more channels and thus more intensive use of one or more channels and more personal contact during phases 3 to 6).
- Intrinsic interest on the part of the consumer in the product or service (this too can lead to more intensive information-search behaviour, resulting in more intensive use of one or more channels and sometimes in the use of multiple channels).
- Subjective experience of time. Consumers who feel they have little time available will act instrumentally and in a goal-oriented manner and devote a relatively large amount of time to 'efficient' channels.
- The attitude about a channel that is particularly dependent upon consumer-related factors such as familiarity and experience with and knowledge of a channel.
- The product. For typical feel/see/smell products, the Internet will be less important than it is for catalogue products (which you can choose on the basis of the product specifications) and certain types of services (which are intangible). Consumers prefer to smell perfume, see and try on clothing, and test drive a car. The Internet can only provide information about locations where the products may be seen, felt or smelled or is suitable for the completion of unchanged repeat purchases. The Internet can also lend support after the purchase in the provision of services; examples would be providing information about service outlets, obtaining product information and scheduling appointments.

Figure 6.3

Use of the channels by various consumer types in different phases of the relationship

	phase 1	phase 2	phase 3	phase 4	phase 5	phase 6
The telephone		8, 6, 7 / 1, 2, 3	1–8	8, 6, 7 / 1, 2, 3	8, 6, 7 / 1, 2, 3	8, 6, 7 / 1, 2, 3
Internet	8, 6, 7 (2–5)	8, 6, 7 (2–5)	8, 6, 7 (2–5)		8, 6, 7	
The shop	1–8 / 8, 6, 7	1–8 / 8, 6, 7	1–8 / 8, 6, 7	1–8 / 8, 6, 7	1–8 / 8, 6, 7	1–8 / 8, 6, 7
Free local paper	1–8	1–8				
Direct mail	2, 4, 6, 8				2, 4, 6, 8	
Television	1–8	1–8	1–8			
Radio	1–8					
Paper, spec. mag.	1–8 / 8, 1, 3	1–8 / 8, 1, 3	1–8 / 8, 1, 3			
Billboards	1–8	1–8				
Social environment	1, 3, 2, 4	1, 3, 2, 4	1, 3, 2, 4			
Advisers	5, 7, 6, 8	5, 7, 6, 8	5, 7, 6, 8	5, 7, 6, 8		
Consumer guide			2, 4, 6, 8 / 5, 7	2, 4, 6, 8 / 5, 7		

1	2	3	4	5	6	7	8
conservative passive social	conservative passive instrumental	conservative active social	conservative active instrumental	open passive social	open passive instrumental	open active social	open active instrumental

Phase 1: observation; phase 2: general information; phase 3: targeted information processing; phase 4: choice of supplier or brand; phase 5: transaction; phase 6: after-sales period.
The numbers shown in the cells relate to consumer type. The interest in a medium during a certain phase is indicated by the background colour of the cell. The darker the background, the more important the medium for the consumer types specified in the cell.

Source: Peelen *et al.* (2000).

Business-to-business markets

The type of research which has been conducted for the consumer market has, as far as is presently known, not yet been performed for the business-to-business market. The acceptance of PCs and the Internet has, however, made more progress here than in consumer markets and the use of these IT-supported channels is also further advanced.

Nonetheless, as in consumer markets, personal contact remains extremely important in business-to-business markets. Face-to-face meetings are without doubt considered vital to obtaining trust and commitment.

6.4 Influence of the channels on pricing and the formation of relationships

Thanks to multichannels and the Internet in particular, prices will drop and the formation of relationships will be placed under pressure. This is a fear that seizes many a supplier and one which may be substantiated. After all, the Internet can potentially lead to (Peelen, 2002):

- More transparency. The Internet and the World Wide Web bring parties together. Distances and times are bridged. Thanks to handy indexing and search systems, it is possible to create a summary, in a simple manner, of alternative suppliers and the prices and conditions under which they deliver. An idea of the quality of the suppliers may also be gained.
- Lower transaction costs. In theory, IT-supported channels and networks simplify the completion of transactions. Search costs may decrease and the deal may be closed more easily.
- More customer power. The Internet makes it possible for customers to employ transaction mechanisms which were previously non-existent in the particular market or purchase situation. This usually involves mechanisms which give the customer more advantages than the supplier. The customer is placed in a position to play suppliers off against one another thanks to, for example, an auction situation.

This fear is partly unjustified. Research results show that the drop in prices on the Internet is not as severe as was once thought. Moreover, it appears that customer behaviour has not been changed by the arrival of the Internet: customers who choose suppliers on the basis of quality will continue to do so.

Consumer markets

The hype is over and we now know that the effects of the Internet (for the time being) are less far-reaching than we had expected a few years ago. *First,* it appears to be more difficult to develop certain functionalities. A price comparison site seems to be something that may be created quickly; however, it is obvious that setting up and maintaining a reasonably complete database is no easy matter. This is certainly the case if we would like to provide consumers with the option of using their mobile phones to determine whether or not a certain durable consumer good is priced competitively in a certain shop. In this case, we must be able to inform the consumer about the current prices in shops in the neighbourhood. The first question is whether these retailers would be willing to divulge this information, with the knowledge of its intended purpose on the

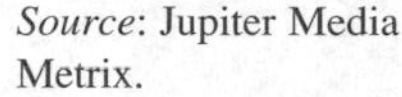

One-stop shopping

Figure 6.4

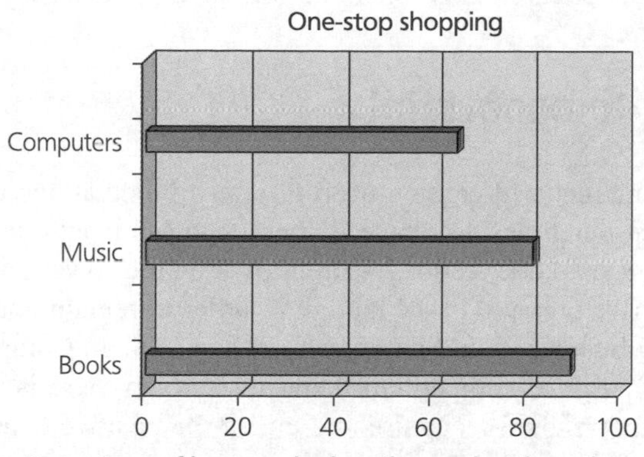

Source: Jupiter Media Metrix.

site. Furthermore, there is the problem of applying a unique identity code to the articles. This technology is not at all well developed in most industries, although the food sector is an exception. And, finally, it remains to be seen whether or not the critical mass necessary to make this market information profitable in the operation of a company can be realised quickly enough.

Various comparative websites – in so far as these still exist – limit themselves in consumer markets to providing insight into the pricing levels maintained by Internet suppliers and provide this service as part of a larger package of services that they offer via the Internet.

Second, we have passed over consumer behaviour to a certain extent. Consumers do not determine their preference for a brand and supplier on the basis of price alone; other factors influence their purchasing decisions. Additionally, research has shown that consumers continue to make their purchases, just as they did before, in the first 'shop' in which they come across an interesting offer (see Figure 6.4). In the United States, apparently only 10 per cent of those searching on the Internet are actually looking for bargains; in all likelihood, this was probably the case in the past as well.

Business-to-business

In the business-to-business market, the situation is not much better. A study conducted by McKinsey showed that for 30 per cent of the purchase managers surveyed, the cost benefit was the motivation to purchase online. These managers expect fewer search costs and lower transaction costs because a great deal of paperwork can be completed more efficiently. Most purchase managers believe that the benefits are not gained at the expense of the supplier's margin.

In reverse auctions, half of the buying organisations surveyed do not appear to choose the suppliers with the lowest prices.[1] Some 87 per cent of the buyers who did

[1] Reverse auctions are auctions which are organised by buyers and not by suppliers and where it is the suppliers who may bid instead of the buyers.

not opt for the organisation with the lowest price ultimately remained with their current supplier. Of the organisations which did their purchasing on the Internet, only 15 per cent of them tried the price-sensitive model of the reverse auction.

From threat to opportunity

The fear that the Internet will cause a drop in prices in situations in which online as well as face-to-face purchases are made is thus invalid for both consumer as well as business-to-business markets. Actions geared towards the lowering of prices and the intensification of price pressure in the market in order to remain one step ahead of the competition on the Internet should be viewed with suspicion. Companies will have to be careful not to fuel price competition themselves when there is no obvious reason to do so. Instead, they should recognise and utilise the positive benefits that IT has to offer. The power of the communication channels will have to be employed in order to take advantage of the individual customer situations. Knowledge of individual customers will have to be developed and used appropriately in order to be able to be of better service to these customers.

Multichannel environment

The number of transactions that are completed online is limited in both consumer as well as business-to-business markets. In many situations, there is no single communication network or channel which supports all of the stages of customer behaviour. Customers will usually make use of a mix of channels. The Internet will more likely function as a network from which simple information may be collected. The call centre of companies will usually be approached for short, simple questions for which a direct answer is desired. Personal contact with the seller is particularly appreciated if this party can provide value as an adviser, can make things tangible or can provide buyers with emotional confirmation of their choices.

6.5 Recommendations on multichannel communication

Now that the channels have been identified and defined, the trends have been described and the behaviour of customers with regard to multichannels has been analysed, an indication may be provided of what we would like to achieve with multichannel communication.

The maximum performance?

Getting the most out of the new IT-supported channels is a challenge for many. The goals are to:

- surpass the shop experience;
- increase the efficiency of company processes and reduce costs;
- enlarge the market and customer range; and
- improve the organisation's flexibility and versatility.

To achieve all four of these goals using a multichannel network would yield the optimum result, and this is the overarching goal which should be pursued.

CRM illustration

The multichannels of Merrill Lynch

Traditionally serving a small target group, Merrill Lynch several years ago decided also to trade stocks and options via the Internet. This new low-cost service is a response to several competitors which had begun to generate many new customers and increased turnover via the Internet. However, Merrill Lynch offers its customers something extra via the Internet. Customers can purchase a consultancy subscription and thereby gain access to the knowledge of Merrill Lynch's investment advisers. The traditional method will continue to exist for customised advice.

The customer can choose how he or she would like to use Merrill Lynch's service. As a result, a channel mix is created which consists of the traditional channel as well as the service method of online investing by which many new users worldwide are able to complete transactions with Merrill Lynch via the Internet.

Merrill Lynch has elected to group all of these activities under one brand. Initially this resulted in a decrease in the stock price. Investors were fearful of channel conflicts and a deterioration of the company's image.

Source: de Beus (1999).

The objective of the integration of channels is to develop a dynamic network in which contact processes between customers and suppliers may take place with a limited degree of dependence on time and place, in the desired form (communication power; see Figure 6.2), with the desired content and minimal (acceptable) costs and efforts for both parties. In addition, there must be considerable navigation possibilities for the customer. This interweaving of channels leads to the often-quoted flow concept of Hoffman and Novak (1996).[2] The communication progresses smoothly as a flow without many shocks, repetitions or delays.

In order to achieve this, the use of the IT-supported channels should not be limited to one phase or individual phases in the customer–supplier relationship, but instead should extend across different phases (see Figure 6.5).

[2] It should, however, be noted here that the flow described by Hoffman and Novak indicates an extremely ideal situation in which consumers become engrossed in the communication, forget the world around them and navigate fluidly from one contact point to the next.

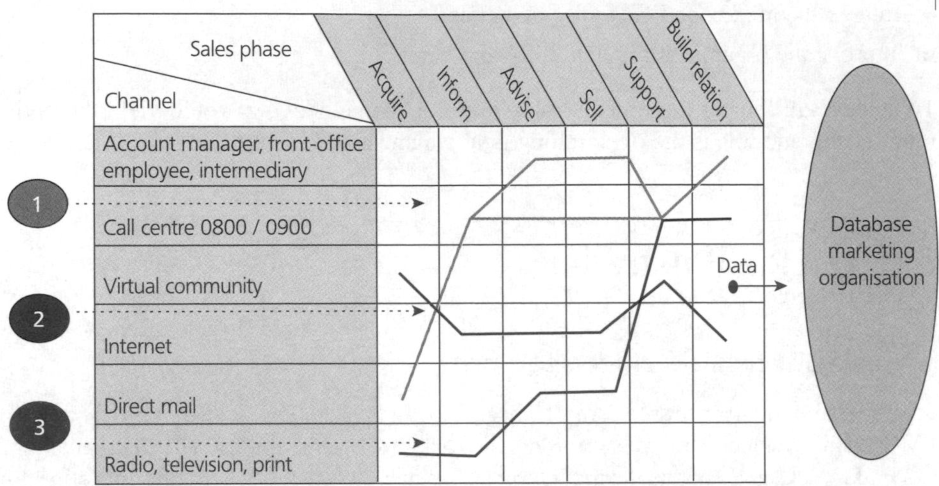

An environment in which personal, time- and location-independent, (non) face-to-face interactions may take place at a low cost

With IT-supported channels, contacts must be linked together; the channels are equipped with the necessary memory capacity for databases and interactivity necessary to be able to achieve this. Linking contacts to one another can take place in different stages of the relationship:

1 In the beginning, during the orientation and selection phase.
2 Just before and during the transaction.
3 During delivery and after-sales service.

1. In the beginning, during the orientation and selection phase

Fitting the IT-supported channels in at the beginning of the relationship is quite difficult. As was mentioned in Section 6.3, the Internet actually plays a limited role in the first phase of the customer–supplier relationship (general orientation). The telephone also gains in strength during the later phases of the relationship; the medium is often found to be too invasive if a relationship does not yet exist.

It is particularly during phase 2 that a suitable role is reserved for the Internet. There is a good chance during this phase that the Internet will produce a substitution effect with regard to direct mail (for various services and catalogue products). The costs of an Internet contact will potentially be lower than those of a direct mail contact and furthermore, the Internet offers more possibilities for interaction and customisation of the content. Internet contact may be followed up by telephone (live agent, call-me-back service), or by e-mail (or post). At present, the experience in call centres is that after having visited a website, customers tend to ask more complex questions. Agents must have sufficient expertise to be able to serve the customer satisfactorily; outsourcing these call centre contacts is difficult (Plasmeijer, 1999).

In order to stimulate or attract traffic to a site, references to the site will have to be included in classic media (see the CRM illustration box below), sites will have to be registered with search engines (these account for the largest portion of visits to websites), the method of the search engines will have to be taken into account when designing the site and pages, and a network of reciprocal links will have to be created (which keeps consumers connected to the Internet and continues to intrigue them within the relevant field of interest), and possibilities will have to be explored to set up an automatic 'site' connection (for example, an infrared scanner on the GPRS device reads the URL from a billboard and makes the connection).

In achieving interactive contact in this phase of the relationship, it is important to employ the principles of permission marketing. The concept of permission marketing is not new, but thanks to the Internet, and e-mail in particular, it has taken on a new life (Van Bel, 1999). By asking the customer if he or she objects to being approached with commercial messages, the chance of conversion and purchase is increased.

CRM illustration

Direct mail versus permission e-mail

Personalised permission e-mails (happypoints, EuroClix) in which recipients, in addition to receiving the correct information, are given the option of saving for free products or discounts, produce higher rates of conversion than traditional direct mail, according to Forrester Research. An average click-through rate of 18 per cent applies to e-mails, and a conversion to sales rate ranges from 4 to 56 per cent. With standard direct mail, the response percentage varies from 0.01 to 2 per cent and the conversion percentage (to sales) from 0.05 to 1 per cent.

Source: Van Bel (1999).

2. Just before and during the transaction

The role of the IT-supported channels before and during the transaction can vary. The entire transaction can be completed via IT-supported channels which, as was previously discussed, is particularly suited to catalogue products and services with a high information content and indirect distribution (for example, the travel industry). This way of doing business offers prospects for lowering costs and improving the level of convenience, while at the same time satisfying the customers' information needs.

The IT-supported channels may also be integrated with physical outlets such as a shop. This appears to be particularly interesting with convenience goods which may be ordered via the Internet or telephone and picked up at the counter in the shop where they are then wrapped. A functionality may be introduced into the IT-supported channels which is helpful for consumers in the preparation of their order list and encourages them to make certain purchases (automatic replenishment of kitchen cupboards and refrigerators fitted with scanning equipment, a stored standard shopping list, promotional offers tailored to the customer profile, savings- or loyalty programmes). In this type of situation, the shop can fulfil the role of assisting customers in 'fun shopping' for see/feel/taste/smell products, impulse and luxury products and in giving customers a warm welcome. Savings can likely be found in terms of physical store area.

However, it is also in buying situations in which consumers have a heavy involvement (speciality and shopping goods) that IT-supported channels can play a role when it comes to the store. With the aid of online POIs (points of information) in the store or using SMS text messaging, consumers may be provided with 'objective' product information. The *high tech* component of electronic contact can be supplemented with the *high touch* service of a store employee.

3. During delivery and after-sales service

IT-supported channels can play a crucial role in the customer–supplier relationship after the purchase, with the goals of:

- lowering costs;
- improving service and image;
- utilising options available to obtain new business and extra sales.

Lowering costs Opportunities to lower costs with the aid of IT-supported channels are extremely important in many situations in order to be able to justify investments in multichannels to top management. Cost reductions may in general be realised with less risk and more quickly than increases in sales. A decrease in costs may occur because substitution of the e-mail or telephone (with live operator) channels with the Internet has taken place (self-service); the *personal touch* component is reduced and the *high tech* component increases. Consumers consider this desirable or acceptable because at this stage of the relationship (after-sales and delivery), communication often involves brief questions and standardised communication.

Improving service and image Providing service via IT-supported channels is referred to as e-service. E-service works according to the principle of self-service, yet nevertheless usually leads to an improvement in service and/or image for customers. For example, e-service provides consumers with the opportunity to trace the delivery of an order. By visiting a site and typing in the customer- and order number, the customer can see where his or her shipment is located at that particular moment. Questions about the operation of a machine may be answered via e-mail or by consulting the FAQ (frequently asked questions) section on a website without the need for a front-office employee to be called in.

Generating new business The opportunity to generate new business and increase sales is available to organisations which use their physical outlet as a location from which e-commerce or telephone orders may be collected. BP can utilise its petrol stations more and more for these purposes. Petrol stations are locations where consumers need to go to fill up their cars. While there, they might as well buy their convenience goods as well, or if they have ordered them in advance, collect these orders and make any impulse purchases as well. This situation prevents consumers from having to go to a separate location to buy their convenience goods; after all, this would require an effort from consumers which does not exactly fit into the era in which the mottos 'any place, any time' and the 'connected consumer' are so prevalent.

6.6 Conclusion

The range of IT-supported communication channels which suppliers may use is experiencing considerable growth and offers possibilities to conduct a dialogue and create a sensory impression both efficiently and at a minimum expense. Independent, in part, of time and place, large groups of customers may interact with the supplier. The creation of this type of 'remote' interaction continues to increase as the communication power of these media grows.

In order to develop and utilise these channels successfully, suppliers are required to obtain insight into customers' preferences for and use of these channels. If knowledge is lacking in this regard, then a customer-oriented communication process cannot be facilitated. Moreover, the opinion may mistakenly take root that IT-supported channels, and the Internet in particular, encourage market transparency, growing customer power, switching behaviour and price pressure.

On the basis of insight into the use of multichannels, and taking strategy, finances and other aspects into account, we can determine what we hope to achieve with multichannels in communication processes.

Case study

Secrets of success for going mobile

The mobile Internet has been a huge success in Japan, but can it spread as explosively in the west? I believe that it can in fact it can spread as fast as the fixed Internet in the 1990s and the GSM mobile standard has done in the past ten years. Achieving this will require mobile operators, equipment suppliers and content providers to learn from – but also to adapt from – the Japanese business model. The power of the fixed Internet derives from its ability to create highly connected 'nodes' – take, for example, the Amazon website, which links millions of prospective purchasers with the items they are seeking. In mobile telephony, by contrast, the core secret to success is in the way agreement is sought between the various players involved to ensure they all get their 'cut' from the value chain. This 'agreement' force was present in building NMT, the first generation mobile standard, and has been present in different mobile initiatives ever since. As I see it, these two forces are clashing in the mobile Internet. I argue that the force of 'agreement' is losing power while the force of 'highly connected nodes' is still very much underused, at least in the west.

To explain, let's have a look at how the Japanese mobile Internet has developed. In 1999 – in contrast to the situation in the west – most Japanese did not have fixed (PC) Internet access in their homes, so the concept of the mobile Internet fell on to fertile ground. The Japanese emphasised open access to the Internet, but also wanted to standardise the quality of access for the user, and this led to the practice known as 'cut in five seconds', in which the connection would be lost if the site failed to download in five seconds.

This virtually closed access to the existing World Wide Web of 1999, but the Japanese consumer did not notice, since the web at that time ►

was a non-Japanese medium. NTT DoCoMo, the Japanese mobile operator best known for its i-mode mobile Internet service, and its competitors focused on creating Japanese content. In the beginning this was free (or almost free), which meant high access rates and the emergence of the type of highly connected nodes I mentioned above.

This explains why the mobile Internet has become so popular in Japan. But can we do the same in the west – that is, create super-connected mobile nodes and introduce some form of quality criteria which in practice denies access to (or makes accessing) the 'traditional' web, less interesting?

I believe this can be done and already there are some initiatives (such as the 'dotmob' domain name that identifies specific Internet content for mobile devices, and price reductions of content) which are following this path. Free and highly interesting mobile content is one necessity along this path, which emphasises the importance of creating 'highly connected super nodes' and disagrees with, or downplays, the traditional 'Nordic agreement' model.

Another reason for the success of the mobile Internet in Japan was the 'orchestration' business model, which went beyond the traditional agreement model. NTT DoCoMo used its competence and market power to design and procure the handsets it wanted from Japanese suppliers and it also set the rules and price levels to content producers and suppliers.

This model, which I refer to as 'orchestration', has proved successful in Japan, where it was pioneered. But it has taken a long time for the west to understand the power of the Japanese model. Western players have learnt its value through a step-by-step approach of trial and error. Presently Vodafone live! and also the Nokia Ngage device might be regarded as attempts to orchestrate in the west. However, I do not believe that the 'orchestration' business model can be successful in the west. The next business model in the west might be based on some type of 'cultivation' of the market.

What is, however, very clear is that the 'Nordic force of agreement' is losing ground. This is evident also by looking at the implication of Moore's law on mobile business. Moore's law implies that phones will increasingly become more like computers. This brings a completely new set of players into the market and thus simply because of the number of players in the value chain, agreement cannot be reached in the Nordic sense.

So, to spread with explosive speed the mobile Internet needs super-connected nodes and a 'cultivating' business model. But one can also ask if there is something that is presently slowing down the speed of introduction of the mobile Internet in the west? I would argue that SMS (text messaging) is doing this. This might sound a radical thought, but look, for example, at how the Minitel slowed down the introduction of the Internet in France.

SMS is a barrier to the growth of the mobile Internet for several reasons. 'Super-nodes' are difficult and in some cases impossible to create with SMS. SMS value-added services are based on remembering numbers and people remember numbers rather poorly. SMS value-added services work on a national level only – it is a limit of the technology and no market (single country) in Europe, for example, is bigger than Japan, i.e. the individual size of the SMS markets limit the maximum size of the super-nodes. Third, SMS value-added services always have a price (transaction based) and thus would restrict the experimentation with free content that the creation of super-nodes would encourage.

I would like to emphasise, however, that not everything in the mobile Internet has to be super-connected or free. In fact, a lot of the content in Europe will be language-specific and thus limited in market size. The present content industry is focused on personalising the user's phone for a price – a lot of this industry might remain. A lot of the content will be peer-to peer in character (therefore free), but limited and unable to create highly connected nodes. But, I am arguing that super-connected nodes – as big as possible – are worth striving for and their existence is the catalyst of the fixed Internet, as it should be for the mobile Internet, too.

Interestingly the barrier SMS presents to the growth of the mobile Internet derives not only from value-added services, but might also reside in the SMS message itself. In Japan SMS has lost ground to e-mail via mobile phones for several reasons. I recognise that the Japanese did have some initial difficulties with e-mail, e.g. junk mail. However, the price of a single message bit in Japan is far below our current price level, and according to studies on communication patterns made in Japan, the way the Japanese use e-mail does not differ from the way SMS is used in the west.

It is actually also interesting to study how SMS is at the very core of the present western business models; so the barrier to a more Internet-based messaging and content culture is not necessarily a choice of the user, but something that is thoroughly embedded in western mobile operators' business structures.

Source: Ville Saarikoski, FT.com site (9 June 2004).

Questions

1 Analyse why the mobile Internet has become a huge success in Japan. Where do you agree or disagree with the author of this article?

2 How do you think the mobile Internet can become a success in your country? What can you learn from the Japanese best practice case?

Questions

1 Upon which aspects does the communication power of an IT-supported channel depend?

2 How can a creative solution be found to the technological limitations of digital channels for stimulating all of the senses? Explain your answer by providing an example.

3 Interactive television is seen as the solution for getting the late majority to use the Internet. Why should this be so?

4 How would you estimate the potential use of interactive television among the conservative, social, closed consumers (see consumer typology in Section 6.3)? Substantiate your answer.

5 Upon which factors does the penetration of GPRS depend?

6 What explanation can you provide for the popularity of the shop among the consumers when compared with the Internet, telephone, television, newspapers and the like?

7 What allows someone with certain personality traits to use IT-supporting channels differently from other people with similar traits? Illustrate your answer by providing three examples.

8 In your opinion, what is the influence of the Internet on price setting in markets?

9 Why does the telephone play an unimportant role in the first phase of the contact process between customer and supplier? Explain your answer.

10 In what way does a mail-order house attempt to generate new business through the utilisation of multichannels? Conduct a small-scale study and describe and evaluate which new IT-supported channels a certain mail-order house has chosen to develop over the past five to ten years.

References

Admap (2003) De toekomst van interactieve tv, *Admap*, January.

Bel, E.J. van (1999) Permission marketing op Internet, www.vodw.com/making waves

Beus, J. de (1999) De multichannels van Merrill Lynch, *Emerce*, November.

Forrester Research (2002) Penetratiesnelheid UMTS overschat, *ITCommercie*, 5/6, 7.

Hoffman, D.L. and T.P. Novak (1996) Marketing in hypermedia computer mediated environments: conceptual foundations, *Journal of Marketing*, **60**, 3.

Klaver, Leo (2002) GPRS is er eindelijk, maar wie wil het?, *Emerce*, February, 41–43.

Klootwijk Emis, Jasper and Esther Maatje (2001) *Channel Preferences in Europe*, Berens Business Press, Woerden.

Lombard, Matthew and Teresa Ditton (1997) At the heart of it all: the concept of telepresence, *JCMC*, **3**, 2, September, 35.

Peelen, Ed, Arnout van der Swaluw, Wilfried Hutten, Frank Slisser and Erik de Vries (2000) *Multichannels, de inpassing van ICT ondersteunde kanalen in het contactproces met consumenten*, KPN Telecommerce, The Hague.

Peelen, Ed (2002) Prijsbeleid in een transparante wereld?, *Sales Management*, **16**, November.

Plasmeijer, Pauline (1999) *Zoekgedrag op internet*, PhD dissertation, Erasmus University, Rotterdam.

Schans, W.M. van der (2001) *Conumentengoederen en merkcommunicatie op internet, theoretische verkenningen en praktijk*, Erasmus University, Rotterdam.

Verkooijen (2001) Content per kubieke meter, *Emerce*, September.

Waarts, Eric, Ed Peelen, Nico Lamperjee and John M.D. Koster (eds) (2004) *Marketing Lexicon*, 4th edn, Kluwer/NIMA.

7

The individualised customer proposition

This chapter examines supplying customisation to customers. The first section defines customisation and the ways in which this may be achieved. We then deal with the question: to what degree do we want to approach customers in an individualised manner? The supplier's offering will be examined as well as the customer's contribution: the price to be paid.

In this chapter we will address the following questions

- What is the significance of an individualised customer proposition?
- How to arrive at an individualised offering (following Pine and Gilmore, and Van Asseldonk).
- How to achieve customisation in the supply chain.
- What is the proper form of a customised offering?
- How to formulate and implement an individualised pricing policy.
  - Price structures.
  - Price sensitivity.
  - Revenue management.

Practitioner's insight

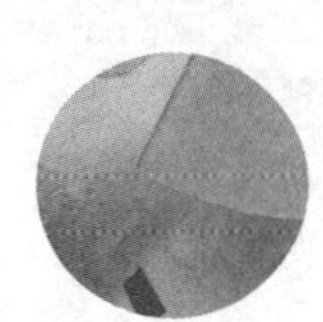

You are the customer of a company that speaks very highly of you and would like to develop a relationship with you because you are the 'right customer' and have indicated that you appreciate the supplier's approach. Your expectations rise . . . you feel special . . . you expect customisation in products and/or price and you are disappointed if it appears that the company treats you according to the standard method. Or you allow yourself to choose from an enormous series of variants, between which there is barely a discernible difference. You expect that you will be able to determine the ideal solution for yourself, together with the supplier . . .

Companies that arrive at a stage in which the relationship with the customer intensifies are confronted with these customer expectations for which they will have to formulate an appropriate solution. Situations must be avoided where the individualised customer approach leads to too much complexity in company processes and thus also to unreliability and inefficiency. A method will have to be found for combining economies of scale with flexibility. Or we will have to grow towards a new economic order geared towards control of, and reduction in, complexity. Individualisation is desirable where it is valuable for the customer and feasible for the supplier.

7.1 Customisation

In many CRM projects, the subject of customisation is hardly ever addressed. The focus is usually on the realisation of the CRM system and the development of customer knowledge. The formulation of the relationship strategy is delayed, and it is no wonder that the individualisation of the customer approach is at times not even on the agenda. If there is any interest in this aspect, it originates from product, production and logistics specialists.

Nonetheless, customisation is one of the building blocks of CRM which must be further described and interpreted. The customer's perspective must play a central role and product-oriented thinking will have to be shifted to the background. The main question is: what value can we supply to the relationship? And not: how can we further differentiate the product so that individual customers can find something to their liking? Or as Peppers, Rogers and Dorf (1999) put it:

> ***Customers . . . do not want more choices. They want exactly what they want – when, where, and how they want it . . .***

Within this framework, it is undesirable and even too easy to place the burden of choice on the customer. The best solution will need to be determined jointly, in interaction with the customer. This has far-reaching consequences for many companies because it requires reasoning from the standpoint of the customer instead of from that of the product. How does a customer behave, or in other words, which activities does he or

Figure 7.1 Delivering value to the customer

Source: Based on Bügel (2002).

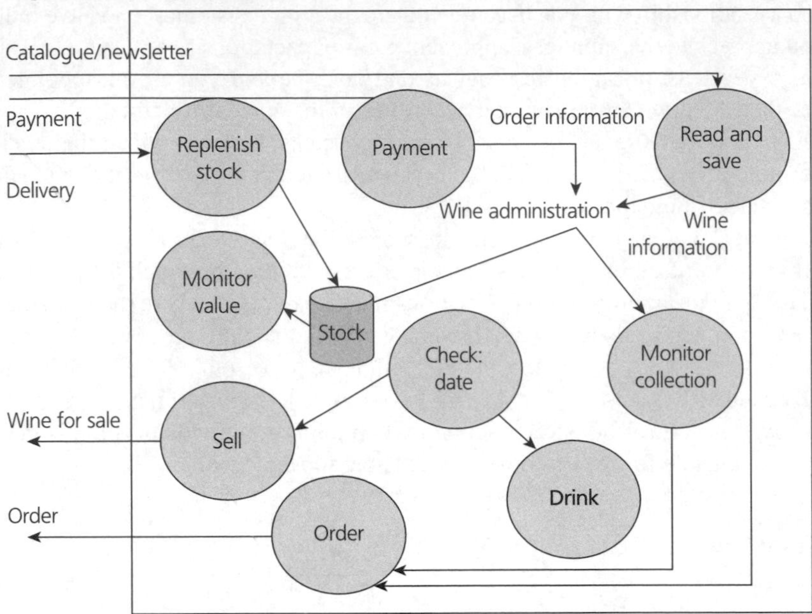

she perform? Can we make it easier on the customer or can we make him or her more successful? Are there activities that we perform better than the customer? Is there a product or service we can offer him or her which will result in the achievement of this success?

Figure 7.1 (based on Bügel, 2002) shows how a wine house (Le Caveau) can supply value to its best customers who have a wine cellar with a valuable collection. The wine house can support the purchase and sale decisions, keep the inventory system up to date, provide alerts for when the wine is suitable for consumption or sale, and provide assistance in the development of a file with background information. This service may be realised with the aid of software packages which can be installed locally in customers' systems which can be networked to the wine house's central system. In essence, the supplier is gaining more in-depth knowledge in the value processes of the customer and examines them to find out whether he can make them more effective or efficient or can perform these better than the customer. Instead of simply recommending or selling products, it takes the wine management over from the customer. In interactions with the customer, it will have to learn what his or her preferences are so that the appropriate purchase, sale and consumption decisions may be made.

A comparable example is Peabody, an online supermarket in the United States which is part of the Ahold group (Van Asseldonk, 1998). This company has advanced interactive search programs at its disposal to help customers create the virtual supermarket that is best suited to them. The shelf space plans, the depth and breadth of the ranges may all be adapted to the customer's individual preferences. Shopping lists may be created and saved. Peabody learns from each and every interaction with a customer. At the end of the store visit, the shopkeeper asks for a valuation of the shop experience. This positive feedback can represent input necessary to provide additional service, either free of charge or for a fee. An example would be providing additional nutritional information free of charge. In this way, Peabody is integrated in the customer's 'shopping process' and helps the customer simplify and better manage this process.

7.2 Individualisation of the product offering

Supplying customisation places high demands on our production systems. Characteristic of our economic society is that a great many products are manufactured by large-scale production systems. Typical aspects of these production facilities are that they are expensive to purchase and are inflexible, yet the variable production costs are low. Supplying customisation places pressure on these systems. In order to be able to provide the customer with a heterogeneous offering, many series must be run and high management costs are incurred. Extensive planning is indispensable and stocks of final products are necessary in order to be able to satisfy customer demand quickly and reliably. The result is that the economies of scale decrease perceptibly due to the smaller size of each production run and the fact that the management costs are increasing. Not only does a less desirable financial situation arise, but, in operational terms, the complexity will result in a decrease in the system's reliability as well.

In order to overcome this impasse, Gilmore and Pine first proposed the solution of mass customisation and mass individualisation in the 1990s. Their solution is still positioned in the Industrial Age since they search for possibilities to supply customisation within the borders of the existing production systems. In his thesis, Van Asseldonk goes one step further by offering recommendations for a different order than that found within the Industrial Age.

The insights offered by both solutions are examined in the following two sub-sections.

Mass customisation according to Gilmore and Pine[1]

The basic idea behind mass customisation is the same as that behind the production of variants within a mass production system; however, there are important differences. Instead of the customer choosing one product variant, each customer provides unique information so that the product may be tailored to his or her specific needs. The production process must be very flexible in order to satisfy these needs. There is no stock kept of finished product, nor is this possible if the product must be truly individualised. It requires the organisation quickly and immediately to react to or anticipate customer wishes. The lack of inventory has advantages (low stock costs) and disadvantages (customers must wait).

[1] Based on the adaptation of the original article from Gilmore and Pine (1997) published in the *Harvard Business Review* by Marion de Graaf for the Marketing Guide 'De Klant centraal'.

Figure 7.2 Forms of mass customisation

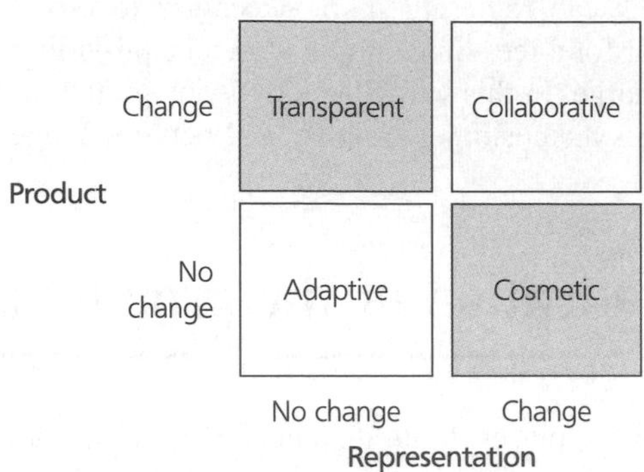

The technological differences between mass series production and mass customisation are considerable, yet gradual: mass customisation brings with it richer flows of information and places stricter demands on process flexibility.

There are four separate approaches to supplying customisation which are named cosmetic, transparent, collaborative and adaptive (see Figure 7.2). The categorisation is based on the manner in which customers make their wishes explicit to suppliers. It is not often that one of these approaches will always be the only correct one for every similar situation; the trick is to compile the right mix under the right circumstances, whether it involves a product, process or business unit.

Cosmetic customisation

The first way to implement mass customisation is by making a simple adjustment in the product's exterior (representation). This is also referred to as cosmetic customisation, and requires no further adaptation of the product itself, only the product's representation. The company presents a standard product in a variety of ways to different customers. This approach is suitable if customers use the product in the same way and the only differences that exist involve the way in which the product is presented. The packaging and the display of the product may be different, and the promotion may also differ. Planters packages its peanuts in different sizes for different retailers. Representation includes packaging, sales materials, terms and conditions, the product's name, the prescribed usage and the location.

Transparent customisation

When the company adapts the product but not the representation, it is practising transparent customisation. In this case, the product's adaptation is made invisible by giving all of the different customised products the same appearance. Transparent customisation is supplied by companies who provide individual customers with unique products and services, without explicitly informing them that these products and services have been produced especially for them. This approach is suitable when the customer's wishes are predictable or easily inferred, or when customers do not wish to repeat their preferences every time. Companies observe customers' behaviour without getting directly involved and then gear their range of variations on a standard product inconspicuously yet precisely to customers' needs. Take ChemStation, for example, which, after a long period of observation, is able to supply customers with precisely the right soap at the right time. Customers thus never have to remember what it was that they used and when they needed to order it.

Collaborative customisation

When the product as well as its representation are adapted, collaborative customisation is involved. Each adapted product may be recognised in this case by differences in its external features. Companies that focus on the collaborative variant maintain a dialogue with individual customers in order to assist them in formulating their needs. A product offering is then created that fulfils these needs and then the products are made to order. This approach is suitable for companies whose customers are not capable of easily conveying what they want. Paris Miki, a retailer of spectacles, developed a digital system that advises customers in their choice of a frame. The costs are lower because fewer complete products need to be kept in stock.

Adaptive customisation

The opposite of this last approach is adaptive customisation in which neither the product nor the representation is adapted. A company with an adaptive customisation strategy offers one standard product that is designed such that users themselves may adapt it to suit their own needs. The adaptive approach is applicable in companies with customers who are looking for a product that serves different purposes under different circumstances. An example of this is the lighting system designed by the Lutron Electronics Company. Customers may choose pre-programmed types of lighting. For example, you would require one type of light for reading and another for a romantic dinner. The customer has the option of adapting the functionality and capacity of the product during use.

Choice of the right strategy

Which of the four strategies should be chosen? Companies that are forced to further adapt a product to individual customer preferences can opt for the collaborative approach. This avoids having to make adaptations after production. Moreover, inventory costs are minimised because it is no longer necessary to keep finished product in stock.

With an adaptive approach to customisation, companies are not supplying a tailored product offering, but instead create standard products which may easily be tailored or adapted by the customer him- or herself. Take, for example, Lutron's customers. The situation for every one of them will be different. The form, the layout and the location of the windows is different in every room. Additionally, weather and the seasons mean that the light coming from outside varies. People who spend time in the room and use the room influence the light available and place their demands in terms of this light. After the one-time programming of Lutron's lighting system, customers may choose one of the settings quickly and effortlessly and at any given moment. In this way, the suppliers are transferring the control over products or services to the customers.

The cosmetic approach to mass customisation is suitable when the standard products are satisfactory to the majority of customers and it is only the form of the product that must be adapted to their individual wishes. This takes place towards the end of the value chain. Well-executed cosmetic mass customisation replaces the non-cohesive and inefficient responses to questions from customers with a cost-effective competency by which every customer is offered precisely that product that he or she desires.

In the transparent approach, companies satisfy the needs of separate customers unbeknownst to them. The product is changed, but in such a way that the customers are not even aware that the product they are buying is a customised one. The company follows the behaviour of individual customers over time and observes predictable preferences. This method requires that the company has the luxury of time at its disposal in order to expand its customer knowledge and be able to supply individual preferences in an increasingly more precise manner.

Sometimes a combination of strategies is desirable. One example is Datavision Technologies Corporation, a San Francisco-based producer of sales material.[2] It effectively combines three of the approaches, namely the collaborative, the cosmetic and the transparent approaches. The company gathers data from all sorts of different sources in order to produce its customised image materials for the sale of different products. The videotapes that each customer receives are based on a detailed profile of their desires and previous purchase behaviour. The system links every element of the customer profile to a specific video, voice-over, melody, image form, graphics and other image segments. It then automatically compiles the script and presentation modules. In this way, customised videotapes are produced which are then packaged in customised packaging. The interaction of Datavision with customers to discover the aspects of the product which are the most important to them results in a form of collaborative customisation. The production of the videotapes is a form of transparent customisation. Datavision uses the cosmetic approach when the customer's name appears on the videotape label and during the introduction on the tape. The combination of the three approaches results in an effective and relevant marketing message.

Customisation in the supply chain

Lampel and Mintzberg (1996) partially supplement this classification created by Gilmore and Pine. Their categorisation indicates to what degree the supply chain provides customisation. In a fully customer-oriented value chain, the individual customer desire is integrated forward to the level of the design (see Figure 7.3). In a chain in which exclusively standard products are supplied, the individual customer desire is not even integrated as far as the lowest layer in the chain.

Postponement occurs if certain customer-specific activities in the value chain are postponed until the last possible point in the process. In the kitchen of a restaurant, bouillon is kept in stock. The preparation of certain soups on the menu is postponed

[2] The company is no longer active.

Figure 7.3

How far is the individual customer order integrated in the supply chain?

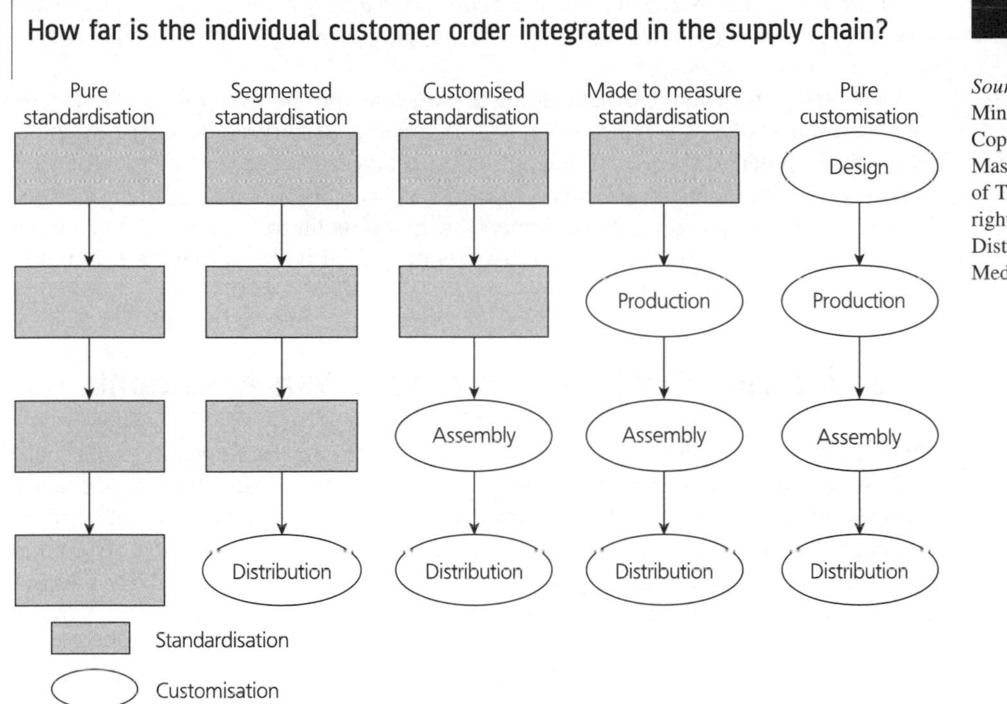

Source: Lampel and Mintzberg (1996). Distributed by Tribune Media Services.

until the customer order comes in. As soon as the customer makes his or her selection known, the semi-finished bouillon product will be used to make the final soup within an acceptable period of time. The advantage is that the stock level may be kept limited and that the size of the series and the degree of predictability of the demand in the non-customer-driven portion of the value chain remain relatively large. At the same time, reliable customisation may be supplied for relatively low costs.

To evaluate the potential for mass customisation in the customer-driven part of the chain, a useful starting point is the determination of the number of (spatial) dimensions. Processes that involve only a single dimension are by nature easier to customise than three-dimensional processes. Let's start by examining an arbitrary one-dimensional process. If we want to manufacture the shaft of a golf club, we saw a metal rod off at the right point – a simple task which requires a simple tool, namely a saw. For the proper length (this is a dimension), we place a guide that holds the rod in place. We then slide the rod along the saw blade. The instrument is very flexible in this one relevant dimension and may be easily adapted for digital control. *Voilà*! Individualised golf clubs.

More complex, however, are the two-dimensional printing and print-related technologies. Paper is a flat, two-dimensional medium. The printer creates a pattern on the paper that consists of zero-dimensional (points), one-dimensional (lines), and two-dimensional (planes) objects. We know that Johann Gutenberg made the printing process considerably more flexible, and in recent years laser and digital technologies have served to enhance this flexibility even further. Gone are the days when we had to think about the set-up time necessary in order to print two totally different pages next to one another. The computer takes care of everything and the processes seem almost to take place simultaneously.

Most three-dimensional manufacturing processes are not very flexible, and if they do work, the dimensions are typically limited. A numerically driven lathe, for example, makes three-dimensional objects, but only if the rotation proceeds symmetrically, such as is the case with baseball bats and decorative table legs. Robots are flexible in all three dimensions; however, they are expensive, slow and difficult to control. For this reason it is not likely that we will see customised sections of car bodywork in the near future as these are three-dimensional objects.

Mass individualisation according to Van Asseldonk

Although mass customisation is an important first step in the direction of the individualisation of the customer proposition, it is not the final destination, according to Van Asseldonk. It is limited to products and services that may be individualised by introducing adaptations during the final phases of the production process. Examples include PCs, pizza, soup, car accessories and the like. In situations in which customisation is desired at all of the levels in the value chain, we are confronted with flaws in the current industrial order. In addition to a loss of the effects of economies of scale and an increase in the production costs, the coordination costs rise as well. Consultation and agreement are necessary too often and with regard to too many different issues: what are we going to produce? When? In what quantities? And so on.

The example from Chapter 1 (page 10) has already illustrated this. In that example, the situation was examined in which a retail trade concern was planning its transport activities from the distribution centre to the branches. In order to ensure a reliable delivery from the extremely wide range of products while maintaining the minimum inventory in the shops, an extensive planning system was necessary to be able to arrange the movements of goods and vehicles. Ultimately it appeared that there were just as many lorries needed as there were branches, and the question arose why the control of the logistics system could not be decentralised to the branches: give each branch its own lorry and have it arrange its own supplies.

In other words, another method is necessary to be able to manage the complexity and changeability involved. The principle of the planning type of business in which instructions are given and followed must be abandoned. A less technocratic and more organisational business is desired, one which bears more likeness to living organisms in a society. Through self-organisation, networks or groups form which display coherent, orderly and meaningful behaviour. They appear to materialise from 'thin air'. Coalitions are formed in which the interests of the group and the individual go together harmoniously. Adjustments to this occur without too much friction. Hierarchical control is lacking, as is the hand of the leader that applies structure. There is no longer an elite group that is all-knowing and decides what is best for the collective whole.

We are therefore seeking ways of reducing complexity on a local level. Patterns are hiding behind the almost seemingly infinite series of product and service variants which may be helpful in reducing the diversity. The example in the following CRM illustration box clarifies this.

CRM illustration

An infinite number of options

Supplying customisation to consumers can lead to an explosion in alternative solutions that we have to be able to offer customers. An illustrative situation is that of supermarkets which have expanded their selection in recent years with the addition of all sorts of products and varieties in order to meet the individual consumer needs. The result is that a supermarket easily offers a customer 10 120 different purchase combinations. A so-called basket analysis to determine which product customers are actually placing in their shopping carts has shown that the diversity may be reduced considerably. Some 32 000 shopping carts filled differently only covered 6 500 routes. If we imagine the distances between the products purchased in the shop space and try to arrive at clusters, we can cut back the diversity even further. It implies that there are structures and routines at work in the underlying behaviour. It is thus not necessary to offer an infinite number of combinations to customers in order to be able to supply customisation. It is sufficient to know the 'path' that the consumer will follow *at a certain time and during a certain opportunity* or the cluster in which he or she will be doing the shopping. The supplier must find this out in its interaction with the customer and use this information in real-time situations.

Source: Van Asseldonk (1998).

Recognising patterns amid the chaos requires a different type of interaction with customers. In a conventional approach, an architect, for example, would determine in advance where the paths in the space between two office buildings should be placed. Based on interviews with groups of people, routes would be identified and calculated using computer algorithms to determine where the footpaths should be constructed. The problem is that afterwards, respondents felt slightly uncomfortable with the proposed solution and in practice, it will appear that they will walk next to the paths. A more effective solution for identifying a pattern is to refrain from constructing footpaths between the office buildings in the first year after construction, and instead to make a decision where the paths should be constructed at the end of the year on the basis of the observed walking patterns of the occupants (Van Asseldonk, 1998).

A similar approach is also seen with the adaptive products in Gilmore and Pine's model and the so-called smart products such as Tivo.

Counterbalancing the solution prescribed previously of reducing the complexity on a local level is the idea that the system as a whole, the organisation, for example, can handle a larger complexity and dynamic. Each of the cells operates relatively independently and adapts itself to the changing circumstances; the relationships between them are also adjusted continuously. An intersection where the traffic lights have been removed and replaced by a roundabout will experience an increase in capacity, in many cases; more vehicles and pedestrians can cross the intersection within an hour, for example, faster than they were previously capable of doing.

CRM illustration

Smart products

Many products are becoming more intelligent thanks to the application of information and communication technology (ICT). The Tivo digital video recorder incorporates this technology to learn what its users' individual programme preferences are. During a certain period of time, the recorder can record a large number of programmes, basing its decision on which programmes to record on the viewer's preferences. Tivo infers these preferences from the individual valuation numbers it has gathered.

There are also electronic publishers in existence that register the interests and valuations of their individual customers and based on this information, arrive at the composition of a customised magazine or newspaper.

A note in the margin

Customisation fans are of the unjustified opinion that everyone, everywhere and at all times wants customisation. The demand for customisation is limited and this is likely to remain the case. Though it is true that the current technology can support large-scale customisation for reasonable prices with reasonable action times, this can only happen if it involves only a few features of a couple of products. If mass customisation is to supply true value, it must involve features for which the people's preferences vary greatly. In addition, the preferences will have to be easy to observe. We see applications of this in particular with:

- purchases of durable goods such as cars;
- digital products and services such as music, software, literature;
- online services, such as entertainment, news services;
- luxury items which accommodate complex individual tastes such as cosmetics and clothing;
- retail trade – because retailers are in closer contact with consumers, they are in a position to develop a learning relationship with them sooner than producers.

Many custom products that we currently see on the market are novelties. Their attraction is their entertainment value or element of surprise. Examples of these types of products include soap with your name in it or cakes with your photo in the icing. The value of these products is by nature only fleeting.

7.3 Individualised pricing policy

Distinct from supplying a customised product, whether or not in the form of an experience, is the individualising of the pricing policy.

Customers differ from one another in the value that they assign to a supplier's products. Dependent on the time and the situation, even individual customers will not always have the same valuation for the proposition. Nonetheless, should a company decide always to charge everyone the same average price, this implies it accepts a lower profitability. It would then seem that individual customers do experience the advantages of customer relationship management, yet the supplier does not quite dare to derive the maximum profit from it, and allows a price premium (see Figure 3.4, page 59) to be lost.

In order to prevent this, exploration of the possibilities for an individualised pricing policy is recommended. Experience has been acquired in this regard on the Internet and in multichannel environments, and in yield and revenue management. These are discussed in the sub-sections below.

Possibilities to implement a precision pricing policy thanks to e-commerce

E-commerce stimulates experimentation with other pricing models and the Internet brings pricing models within reach, which was previously not the case. For example, a customer used to have to pay prior to gaining *possession* of the product, whereas the Internet, on the other hand, charges customers for *the use* of the product. A publisher no longer has to ask for payment for the sale of the book, but instead can charge the customer for the pages he or she reads. It used to be customary for the price to remain the same for a certain period of time, now this may be varied with more ease. Furthermore, it was the supplier who set the price, not the customer. It was also not the custom to give certain products or services away free of charge in order to 'lock in the customer' as a paying user of the follow-up services.

Although many of these price setting methods are presented as innovations, it often appears that they have already been tried out in another market situation or in the past. An example of this may be seen with Stephen King, who tried to sell one of his books on the Internet, chapter by chapter, and gave the first chapter away free. It seems he was preceded by Charles Dickens who had been forced by poverty to sell his work in instalments – if he had waited until it was finished, he would have risked starvation. In the commodity markets, auctions have proven successful for years in bringing groups of customers and suppliers together, and thanks to the emergence of standards (such as uniform product codes), this has also been made possible in other markets. Without sensory perception, the appropriate quality for a specific product on the Internet can be determined on the basis of a uniform product code.

Whether the alternative price structures are new or not does not detract from the potential that they hold to lend substance to a precision pricing policy in which the price is adjusted to that which individual customers or segments are prepared to pay at a certain point in time. By implementing a precision pricing policy, the current system of pricing with all sorts of possibilities for offering discounts requires adjustment. The suspicion that a precision pricing policy will lead to an even less manageable jumble of price agreements than that which we currently encounter in any given company is also unjustified. On the contrary, the precision pricing policy will have to be computerised to a great extent, and for this reason must be described fully using explicit

CRM definitions

Pricing structures

Bundling and unbundling:

- a subscription as a form of bundling: a decision is made to purchase multiple products over time;
- combining various products in one package in order to stimulate cross-selling or deep selling as a form of bundling;
- pay-per-view and payment per transaction as a form of unbundling; payment is made for each component.

Discounts and additional compensation:

- order size, ordering method (via the Internet, the store, the representative), payment method (cash, by cheque or credit card), delivery (urgent, collection, home delivery), quality of the customer (new customer, gold, silver, bronze customer) set the supplemental price or the discount.

Fixed versus dynamic pricing:

- bids during auctions as an example of dynamic pricing;
- pricing for which the level is determined by the availability (yield management or revenue management).

Accepting pricing or setting pricing:

- does the client accept the price or is he or she determining it?

Price tailoring:

- one-by-one price setting (in bilateral negotiations) versus a price that applies to many (the market price).

rules. In addition, the policy will have to be able to be explained to customers in a transparent environment.

Within the framework of the adjustments to be implemented in the pricing structure, it will have to be determined which elements of the value proposition will be grouped together and for which a price will be requested, and which will be broken down into their constituent parts. At the same time, it can be interesting to consider once again which prices or discounts will be linked to the times of purchase or delivery. Prices for the possession of products may be replaced by rates for their use. Payment may be asked for complementary services involving product use. Volume discounts may be made dependent on the product or service package that customers purchase. In many cases, it will not be the completely new pricing structures or models that count, but an enrichment of the existing system that is important, one with a view to 'what the individual customer is prepared to pay in a specific situation'.

Possibilities for precision pricing are available (thanks to IT) because:

- We have better means of testing at our disposal. On the Internet, it is relatively simple to adjust prices to certain times and/or for certain visitors to the websites. The response to the modified prices is also measurable using electronic means, so that the effects of price changes on demand may be determined. As a result, the price elasticity of certain customer groups at certain times may be measured more accurately than was previously the case. This knowledge can be useful in the further design of the pricing policy.

- We are easily able to adjust prices on the Internet. There is no longer any need to publish and distribute price lists, or brochures and catalogues with price indications. In the ideal situation, a simple adjustment of the relevant detail in the database will suffice.
- We can create customer profiles. We can determine for individual customers or customer segments what their preferences and wishes are and which price they are prepared to pay.
- We are able to tailor the price determination to the available capacity and goods in stock. The price setting may therefore be linked to an objective of optimising the capacity utilisation.

Factors that influence price sensitivity

- Who will foot the bill for the purchase costs?
- What is the purchase price as a component of the total costs to be incurred?
- Is the buyer the end user?
- To what extent does the price function as an indicator of quality and can the quality be determined separately from the price?
- How easy is it for people to shop?
- Is there a time constraint?
- Does the product lend itself easily to comparison?
- Can customers switch easily between suppliers?
- Are the product differences marginal?
- Is the long-term relationship with the customer important?

Source: Nagle and Holden (2001).

It goes without saying that there are risks associated with the implementation of a precision pricing policy. With pay-per-view pricing, the supplier must be prepared for a considerable drop in turnover. The purchase volume will decrease, the readiness of customers to pay a high unit price is usually lacking, while their price sensitivity will increase because they are charged for the duration of the usage time. And charging a higher price to loyal customers does not always lead to better financial results, as Amazon.com was able to experience at first-hand. The idea behind it was that loyal customers would be treated to more service by Amazon.com than other customers and would be charged a price premium for this; the organisation had an extensive profile of these customers at its disposal and could use this to offer them even more valuable customised offerings. Once these 'good' customers of Amazon.com got wind of this, they were quite displeased, not surprisingly. As a loyal customer, one expects a price advantage, not a disadvantage.

In short, suppliers must never lose sight of customers' acceptance of a differentiated or discriminating pricing policy. The price differences will have to be considered understandable and even desirable from the customers' standpoint. Someone pays a higher price because he or she is being helped at the last minute and is being given priority over others. Someone may also experience a price advantage, but in exchange for this, he or she is excluded from certain additional services, is provided with less certainty in terms of the time of delivery, or receives lower quality.

Revenue management

Revenue management is the skill of maximising yield by differentiating the price and by allocating parts of the available production capacity across the various price classes. It has its origins in the US airline industry of the 1980s. Owing to privatisation and mounting competition, companies saw prices and margins shrinking time and time again. In order to emerge from the downward spiral of falling prices, the system of revenue management (still named yield management at the time) was developed.

The development of a revenue management system requires a great deal of information. In order to be able to determine the maximum feasible price at a certain point in time, data are necessary on the historical booking patterns, current booking information and accurate predictions on the bookings to be expected per price class for a specific flight. For an airline company with an average of 1500 flights per day and 220 seats distributed among eight booking classes for each flight, 330 000 seats must be divided among 12 000 price classes (buckets). The planning for these seats begins 330 days before departure and is monitored and adjusted at different times. In total, this amounts to optimising 3.96 million price classes and 110 million seats.

Nevertheless, through the application of revenue management, different North American airline companies were able to achieve an increase in revenues of 5 to 10 per cent (Peelen and Smelt, 1994).

Outside of the airline industry, revenue management has since been applied to the service sector in which companies are confronted with similar capacity problems; examples include (container) shipping companies, car rental companies and hotels. Of relevance here is the fact that the service sector cannot create inventory: production and consumption of the service take place simultaneously. In general, it holds true that revenue management may be applied effectively if:

- the supplier works with a relatively fixed capacity that may not be increased in the very short term;
- the inventory is transient; unused units will be lost permanently during production;
- the fixed costs are high;
- the cost of modifying capacity is high;
- the sale and service costs for customers are minimal;
- the demand may be segmented into groups with homogeneous preferences in terms of price and level of quality;
- customers accept price differentiation;
- the service may be sold in advance or reserved and/or the demand fluctuates sharply.

The principle of revenue management

The effects of revenue management may be clarified through the use of the Marshallian demand curve from micro-economic theory which shows the relationship between sales and price. When companies implement an equilibrium price, they miss out on income that customers were prepared to pay. There are those customers for whom the product or service represents more value than the price paid for them. This consumer surplus can, to a great extent, be skimmed off through the introduction of multiple price classes.

Figure 7.4

Revenue management with a fixed capacity

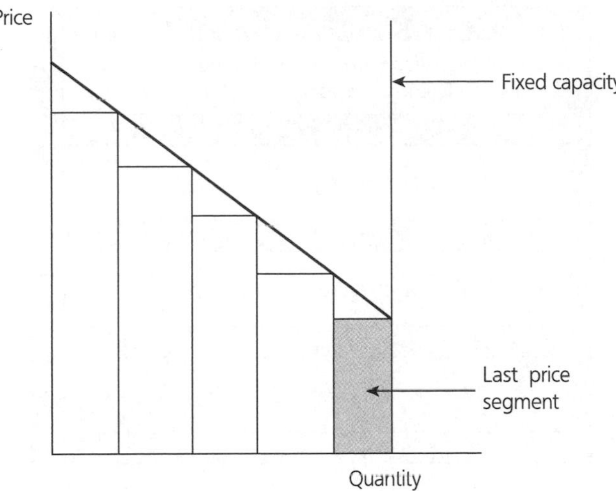

Instead of working with an average price, a differentiated pricing policy is implemented (see Figure 7.4). Additionally, by offering discounts, the price-sensitive segment of the market may be addressed, one which would otherwise be unreachable, and thus a higher capacity utilisation is realised. The result is that by introducing a differentiated pricing policy, a company is capable of generating higher turnover, capacity utilisation and revenue. The achievement of this is dependent upon the manner in which the stocks or capacity are sold during this time.

Formulating a revenue policy

The revenue policy (allocating capacity to segments and determining prices per segment) is designed in a process involving a number of steps (Figure 7.5).

The first step involves dividing the market up into homogeneous submarkets which have differing preferences regarding service *and* price. During this process of segmentation, special attention must be paid to avoiding what is referred to as 'dilution'. Dilution occurs when the segments are not separated by distinct boundaries, and customers who are in fact prepared to pay more, nonetheless find a way to pay lower prices. In the airline industry, for example, there is a condition imposed that in order to qualify for a low price, the traveller must stay over a minimum of a weekend.

A price will have to be set for each segment taking into consideration the service package offered, the cost structure, the prices set by the competition, and the perceived value. The range within which the price may be allowed to vary may also be indicated. In determining the number of prices, it must not be forgotten that the degree of complexity increases rapidly. The airline example has already illustrated this.

In predicting the demand for each price class and for the total market, standard statistical techniques such as time series analysis and regression analysis may be used. On the basis of historical data, these techniques are used to estimate the demand for the

Figure 7.5 Step-by-step plan for revenue management

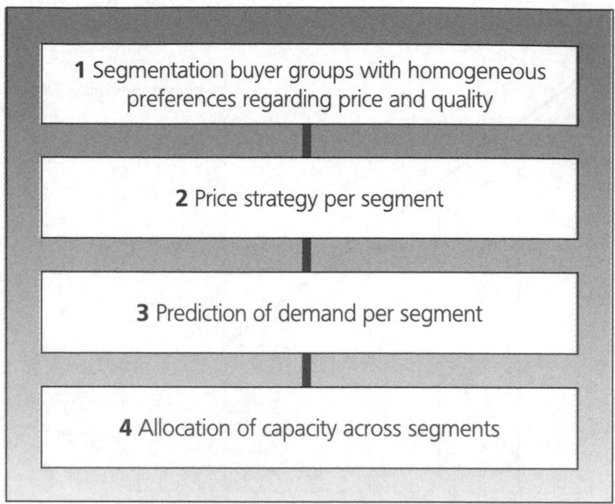

service at a specific time and in a specific situation. Predictions may be made of the demand in various price classes or segments.

In all likelihood, the most important step in the process is the allocation of capacity to the different price classes. The demand predictions serve here as a starting point. Various allocation algorithms are used to distribute the capacity among the price classes. The most commonly applied method is the threshold curve method. Using this technique, the minimum and maximum booking curves are constructed with the aid of historical data. The minimum booking curve determines the threshold under which the number of reservations or transactions (preferably) may not fall. In order to prevent this lower limit from being reached, the price must be lowered. An example of this is the last-minute flights. The progress of the maximum bookings curve is determined by the maximum capacity that we are willing to assign to a certain price class. Customers who are interested in qualifying for the service will fall under a higher price class.

Airlines told to end price discrimination

Europe's airlines have been forced to end price differences of up to 300 per cent offered on the same flights in different countries, after a six-month inquiry into their ticketing policies.

The announcement came at the end of an investigation by the European Commission into the fares charged by 18 European airlines including British Airways, Air France, Lufthansa, SAS, British Midland, and Virgin Atlantic. BA and SAS admitted having different ticket charges but Giles Gantelet, spokesman for Loyola de Palacio, the EU transport commissioner, said all airlines had now ended the practice. 'A little bit of naming and shaming has achieved results,' he added.

One example was a return flight from Frankfurt to Berlin which cost €88 (£59) when purchased in Germany but €268 in Belgium. A 50 per cent differential was found in a flight between the UK and Germany.

Although the Internet has revolutionised airline ticket sales, many companies still structure their systems so that travellers have to use a website geared to their country of residence. As personal information and credit card addresses have to be provided, and tickets often have to be mailed out, there is no opportunity to circumvent the system by using a site belonging to the same company in another country. Similar factors have applied to purchases made via travel agents or direct from airlines' sales offices. However, EU law means that companies are not allowed to discriminate between European customers on the grounds of their place of residence.

Of the 18 airlines contacted by the Commission, 16 responded, with most saying that they did not operate in this way, and others saying they had stopped the practice. Italy's Alitalia said that, due to its current financial crisis, it was unable to give a proper response, and Olympic Airlines of Greece failed to reply.

However, a test by the Commission confirmed that all airlines had ended the practice. Mr Gantelet said: 'In rare cases some restrictions may still exist for certain paper-based tickets, but all electronic tickets are now available throughout the EU without discrimination, except – in some cases – for differences in handling fees. As a result, price levels are now similar for all EU residents.' He added that the Commission would continue to monitor the airlines to make sure the problem does not return.

Steve Double, head of news at BA, said: 'It is an issue which we were always comfortable with and we were always confident of the outcome.' Yesterday's announcement also marks a successful outcome for the Commission, which might have had difficulty making a legal case stick.

The Commission's powers over airline prices are limited, although it could take action if it judged that there had been a breach of EU treaty provisions, which lay down a level playing field for business within the internal market.

Source: Stephen Castle, *The Independent*, (8 June 2004).

7.4 Conclusion

Supplying customisation implies a different interface with customers. Supply-driven value chains will have to be transformed into demand-driven ones. The supplier will have to learn what the customer wants from its interaction with him or her. The supplier will have to avoid leaving this choice entirely to the customer by presenting him or her with an oversupply of alternatives, and instead provide guidance to the customer in creating the desired solution. This requires different interactions between customer and supplier than we are accustomed to in many markets. Information technology plays an important role in the support of this process with large groups of customers. Next, a feasible and manageable solution will have to be found in order to be able to supply this customisation. The realisation of an individualised customer proposition can lead to a great deal of complexity and can endanger the manageability and efficiency of the value chain. This also means that it must be determined when and where a standard solution will suffice, and where actual adaptations are desirable. For example, will a cosmetic solution suffice or will adjustments have to be made in the physical product? Can a standard product be constructed with flexible performance or is customisation unavoidable? Will the representation of the product have to be adapted or can this remain standardised? In order to realise customisation, adjustments in the value chain can be necessary, which results in individual customer orders surfacing further along the value chain. In this case, it is wise to shift customer-specific activities as far as possible towards the end of the process (postponement), in order to allow the demand-driven portion of the value chain to remain as small as possible with respect to the supply-driven portion. Should the complexity ultimately appear to be unmanageable, then study of the possibilities proposed by Van Asseldonk is recommended. Is there an order conceivable in which small cells organise their activities in cohesion with one another? The complexity is reduced within the cells, while it is the whole that is capable of surviving in a complex and dynamic environment.

A customised product offering requires individualised pricing that is tailored to how much a customer is prepared to pay for this offering. Thanks to e-commerce, there has been renewed interest in pricing policies. The fear that the Internet would lead to market transparency and price reduction has proven to be unfounded. The Internet should be seen instead as offering opportunities for pricing policies, considering it opens the door to creating precision pricing which may be implemented thanks to a knowledge of individual customers, the market and available capacity. Adapting existing pricing structures and pricing policies to values that individual customers experience in the supplier's offering provides better prospects for good financial results. In doing so, however, we must not lose sight of the risks involved in a precision pricing policy.

Case study

Fokker Services: total integrated solutions

Fokker Services BV is the service organisation that partners owners and operators of its aircraft. Although Fokker, the manufacturer of the Fokker airplanes, is bankrupt, the service organisation, which was taken over by Stork, is highly successful. In the early years after the bankruptcy, many airlines were not too pleased with their Fokker aircraft, but currently they are quite positive. KLM in 2003 even said it wished it had more Fokker 100s and Fokker 70s.

The achieved customer satisfaction level is the result of the approach of Fokker Services. Since the organisation operates separately from an airline manufacturer it has been able to become a customer-centric instead of a product and technology dominated organisation. The main objective is no longer to sell more planes and parts, but to solve customer problems and to take care of customers. Parts sales and lease, maintenance service and technical expertise have been combined in one offering to customers. It is a combination of products and services that is unique for the industry and allows Fokker Services to provide integrated maintenance solutions.

A major reorganisation of the service organisation stands at the basis of this new approach. Currently, account managers form the top of the organisation and make it truly customer oriented. They represent all parts and services the organisation can deliver and do not represent one of the business units (Component & Material Services, Technical Services and Aircraft Services). They are rewarded for the contribution they make to the success of their clients. Extensive investments have been made in training of the account managers to improve their knowledge and customer orientation. New departments have been created that support the account managers with logistical and technical knowledge, during sales processes and during the delivery of the services.

Fokker Services distinguishes between customers that want modular services (parts, technical expertise and maintenance) and customers that prefer a total solution. Customers are also segmented in terms of price sensitivity. In total it serves more than 250 clients, among them commercial airlines and military organisations.

Several creative dedicated solutions have been invented by Fokker for its total solution customers. Abacus, for example, is a win–win–win concept: on a worldwide scale, customers and Fokker Services share their spare parts stock. Fokker Services takes care of the lease stock, forward exchange and component reconditioning services. The result is a significant reduction in costs and an increase in efficiency. Furthermore, airlines can lease the parts they store on their site and do not have to buy them. Parts that are removed during repair work are sent back to the Fokker Services repair shop for repair or remanufacturing. Fokker also helps its customers by organising an online parts trading market where they can buy and sell pre-owned serviceable parts.

Recently the organisation also invested in an extranet, named MyFokkerfleet.com, for major clients – mainly Fokker aircraft operators and owners. To be able to offer this service, the organisation had to define customer processes and to align its processes with them. The richness of the MyFokkerfleet.com information assists operators in their daily work.

The extranet also allows operators to place orders for spare parts and to give feedback. Tracking and tracing functionalities help customers monitor the processing and the delivery of their order. Information can be exchanged with the repair shop and other departments. Further, the knowledge base with technical expertise is made available to customers on the extranet. All technical expertise, a major competitive resource of the organisation, is readily accessible to key clients to solve their specific in-service problems. Each customer finds fully customised information related to their aircraft modification status. The extranet is there to assist the customer at the critical moments in the relation. Since the account managers are connected to the extranet as well and receive specified e-mail alerts when their clients are considering a purchase, they have real-time information to act on. They know the 'critical incidents' in the relationship and can be there to assist at vital moments – not in the role of parts salesman, but primarily with the aim of supplying care.

To serve the migration of aircraft from one airline to another, Fokker Services invested in remarketing programmes, named Future100© and Future50©. These programmes aim to increase the marketability of the Fokker airplanes and to give new buying airlines confidence in the quality and reliability of the planes in operations. The Future programmes provide customers with a full service package and have supported, amongst others, Germania Airlines, Helvetic Airways and Austrian Airlines in their choice of Fokker planes. Giving new and switching customers specific attention is commercially attractive, but does not completely match with

a CRM orientation. Fokker Services, therefore, also launched a MyfirstFokker.com website to offer a Future full service package to existing customers that show interest in a total solution.

Source: Fokker won the CRM Excellence Award 2004; the case is based upon interviews and the jury report.

Questions

1 How does Fokker Services segment its market?

2 In what way does Fokker Services customise its offerings to specific customers?

3 Can you think of other applications of the win–win–win concept outside Fokker?

Questions

1 Supplying customisation requires companies to transform themselves from product- to customer-oriented companies that recognise the methods that must be used to make their customers happier or more successful. Insight into the value chain is required in order to accomplish this. The supplier must be able to identify how to facilitate or take over the activities from the value chain. Give an example demonstrating this; do not repeat the illustration from this chapter but devise your own.

2 What are the different forms of mass customisation identified by Gilmore and Pine? Think of your own example for each form.

3 Mass customisation is associated with postponement.
   (a) How is postponement defined? Provide an example.
   (b) Why is it a goal to postpone customisation and to perform as much as possible 'at the bottom' of the value chain (see Figure 7.3)?
4 What limits the applicability of mass customisation?
5 Van Asseldonk proposes that Gilmore and Pine's solution is typical of the Industrial Age, which is nearing its end. He outlines a solution that is typical of the Knowledge and Network Economy. Describe in your own words his approach to the individualisation issue.
6 What has demonstrated that the initial fear that the Internet and e-commerce would lead to growing price competition and falling prices (see Chapter 6) was unjustified?
7 How does IT make it possible to implement a precision pricing policy?
8 Formulate the outlines of a precision pricing policy for a four-star hotel in your country's capital designed to accommodate business guests as well as tourists from all over the world. Explain your answer.
9 Which recommendations would you give to Amazon.com to help it realise a price premium programme for loyal customers?
10 Create a pricing structure for a publisher of loose-leaf magazines which has chosen to offer its content via various channels. Keep in mind that the publisher previously sold its magazines exclusively on a subscription basis.

References

Asseldonk, Ton G.M. van (1998) *Mass Individualisation: Business strategies applying networked order to create economic value in heterogeneous and unpredictable markets*, TVA Management, Veldhoven.

Bügel, Marnix (2002) *Klantenloyaliteit, over ongelijke behandeling in het digitale tijdperk*, Pearson Education, Amsterdam.

Gilmore, J.H. and B.J. Pine II (1997) The four faces of mass customization, *Harvard Business Review*, January–February, 91–101.

Lampel, J. and H. Mintzberg (1996) Customizing customization, *Sloan Management Review*, Autumn, 21–29.

Nagle, Thomas and Reed K. Holden (2001) *The Stategy and Tactics of Pricing*, 3rd edn, Prentice Hall, Englewood Cliffs, New Jersey.

Peelen, Ed (2002) Experience marketing, *HEO-ICT*, Amsterdam.

Peelen, Ed and Patrick A.W. Smelt (1994) Als produktie en consumptie samenvallen: yield management, *Tijdschrift voor Marketing*, May, 30–34.

Peppers, Don, Martha Rogers and Bob Dorf (1999) Is your company ready for one-to-one marketing?, *Harvard Business Review*, January–February, 151–160.

Pine, B. Joseph, James H. Gilmore and B. Joseph Pine II (1999) *The Experience Economy: work is theatre and every business a stage*, Harvard Business School Press, Boston, Massachusetts.

Schmitt, Bernd H. (1999) *Experiential Marketing: How to get customers to sense, feel, think, act and relate to your company and brands*, The Free Press, New York.

8

The relationship policy

The relationship policy is the last of the four building blocks of CRM. Now that we have discussed customer knowledge, the channels and the value proposition, we can examine the relationship policy in further detail: the manner in which the supplier's relationship with the right customers and prospects may be further developed.

Step by step, this chapter will explore how this policy may be designed and implemented. We will begin on the aggregated level of the customer database, and move to the more planning-based development of the relationship with the individual customers over time. Along these lines, the first section will deal with the improvement in the quality and size of the customer database (Section 8.1). We will describe the relationship policy for the different segments within the database (Sections 8.2 and 8.3), and indicate how this may be translated into a contact strategy (Section 8.4). Section 8.5 focuses on loyalty programmes and the role these play in the further development of the quality of the relationship.

In this chapter we will address the following questions

- How can we improve the size and the quality of the customer database; how to acquire the right customers?
- How can we segment the customer database?
- How can we formulate the relationship policy for each segment; how to develop a product and service package for the different segments?
- How to formulate the relationship policy for each phase in the relationship; how can we develop the relationship with customers over time?
- How to derive the contact strategy from the relationship policy; how are we going to communicate with customers within the framework of the relationship policy to be implemented?
- Loyalty programmes: what does the term mean, what are their representations and what is their role in the relationship policy?

Practitioner's insight

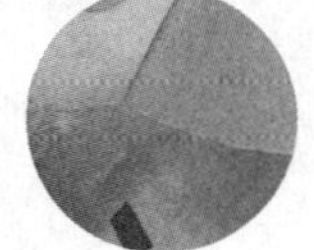

Hello John! How's your golf game coming along? Hi Miriam, how are the children? I think it's truly amazing how you've been able to combine your career with raising a family. Hi Jenny! Has your cat fully recovered from his operation? Hi there, Frank! Happy belated birthday! When were you planning on taking your early retirement?

Hello, Europe! How are you doing?

Thanks to CRM, the number of friendships in Europe has increased a thousandfold. Doubts seem to have disappeared. Supplying organisations are capable to maintaining relationships with over 300 million residents of the European Union – and without ever having spoken to them personally or having given them the name of a regular contact person. And without even taking a minute to stop and consider whether or not these customers would even want to have a relationship with the supplier.

8.1 Improvement of the size and quality of the customer database

Who do I want as a customer? What are the differences between relationships and what does this imply for my relationship policy? These are questions that are related to the customer database and lie at the basis of the development of a relationship marketing policy. For a supplier, it is important to create a plan whose objective is to increase the quality and quantity of the customer database. In relation to the customer pyramid (see Figure 2.1), a policy will have to be developed that aims to increase the number of top customers. Non-profitable customers will have to be discouraged from making purchases from the supplier in the future or will have to be approached on a transaction basis: each order placed must ultimately produce a positive result. At the same time, a balance must be found between customer acquisition and relationship development. After all, without growth in the number of new customers, the future of the organisation is hardly certain.

In order to reduce the non-committal aspect of acquisition and relationship management, it is recommended that the supplier formulate concrete objectives and allocate part of the budget for various activities (see Figure 8.1). Which results does the organisation hope to achieve with existing customers in segment A, B, C or D? Does it want to maintain the relationship, develop it further or possibly even end it? What is the return on investment (ROI) or lifetime value (LTV) that the supplier expects to see as a result of its activities?

How does it then plan to acquire customers in a targeted manner? Companies segment within the customer database on the bases of the characteristics and the behaviour of the customers. It is harder to make these distinctions with non-customers. It is perhaps possible to link indicators which are available externally to the different customer groups, by which prospects may also be grouped into segments. In this way insight may also be gained into the potential profitability of the different non-customers. The different acquisition methods and the intended conversion results may be specified for the

Figure 8.1 Relationship planning and customer profitability

	Total market 100%									
	Existing customers 40%				Non-customers 40%					20% *
	Segments 40%				Look-alike segments 20%				P 20%	
	A 5%	B 10%	C 20%	D 5%	a 2.5%	b 5%	c 10%	d 2.5%	*Do not contact P = prospect	
10 20 . . . 100	Cultivate 50%	Retention 40%	Migrate 30%	Recover 20%	Referral 20%	Acquire 40%	Acquire 30%	Reactivate 20%	Qualify 30%	
Lifetime value Return on investment	5000 20%	2500 15%	1750 10%	1250 5%	1000 10%	850 −10%	750 −15%	650 −5%	500 −20%	−1500 −50%

Source: Wang (1998).

different categories of prospects based upon previous experience. An indication may also be given of whether or not active efforts will be made to acquire customers within the relevant segment or whether the company will simply rely on the autonomous growth which arises from customers who 'report' to the company, whether or not this is the result of a recommendation from a customer of the organisation.

It will certainly not be possible to segment all of the non-customers according to a method employed by the supplier. However, there may be interesting future customers to be found among these prospects. A good qualification for the potential value represented by this group is just as desirable in order to be able to formulate an appropriate and profitable acquisition policy.

8.2 Relationship policy per segment

The relationship policy will then have to be elaborated further for each of the customer segments. A somewhat paltry relationship policy in terms of content is to be expected if the profitability and profit potential for a customer is an all-determining factor for the design of this policy. This is a factor of which companies are often forewarned. In order to develop a mutually profitable relationship, it is necessary to focus attention on the current and potential economic and non-economic value that each of the parties represents for the other.

Nevertheless, it is good practice to build a framework on the basis of financial arguments, within which the relationship policy may be determined for each segment. A distinction is often made between A, B, C and D or gold, silver and bronze customers and is utilised quite widely. On the basis of the current and potential customer value of the three customer groups, it is then determined how much latitude is available to satisfy customers and to develop the relationship further. Additional details may be incorporated such as how the supplier would like to be available for its customers, what level of service it would like to offer its customers, and through which channels and with what frequency it would like to communicate with them. Figure 8.2 contains a further specification of the service and communication profile per segment.

Relationship planning: communication and service profile per segment

Figure 8.2

Source: Bügel (2002).

Availability and service level

		Gold	Silver	Bronze
Access	Telephone Face to face E-mail Internet	Free calls Personal Account manager Newsletter Personal page	Regular call rate None Newsletter Personal page	0800/0900 no. None None Standard
Service levels	Telephone Response time 1st/2nd line	24 hours 20 seconds 90%/10%	24 hours 30 seconds 80%/20%	Office hours
	Account manager Back-up	Experienced and trained Yes	Young None	None
	E-mail Response time	 1 hour	 4 hours	 24 hours
	Internet personalisation	 High	 High	 Less
Communication	Newsletter Transaction status Education Activities/campaigns	+ hardcopy Internet + mail Seminar Face to face	ID Internet + mail Internet Tel./mail	E-mail Internet Internet E-mail
Service levels	Newsletter Frequency Personalisation	 12/yr Yes	 4/yr Yes	 3/yr No
	Transaction Frequency Costs	 12/yr Free	 6/yr Free	 3/yr Fee
	Education Frequency Costs	 2 seminars/yr Free	 2 seminars/yr Contribution costs	 None
	Activities Incentives Personalisation Cross-selling	 Max. 25% Yes $p > 50\%$	 Max. 15% Yes $p > 35\%$	 Max. 5% By name $p > 5\%$

Naturally there are other categories which are possible in which the focus lies on the value that both parties represent or will represent for one another. Should both parties be important to one another, then they can work on a 'true partnership'. In situations in which the friendship originates from the supplier but not from the customer, then it remains to be seen whether the customer may still be won over to the relationship within the financial restrictions. The policy is different in the reverse situation, in which suppliers are confronted with loyal customers whom they do not consider important. The question is then whether the customer will have the opportunity to win the supplier's friendship. There is a better chance that he or she will have to pay a high price or that his or her custom will be discouraged. Exchange situations in which customer and supplier consider one another fairly unimportant will most likely not outlive the transaction stage. Neither will invest very much in the other; the customer's satisfaction with the transaction will be considered important as long as the supplier can earn a margin on it (Schijns, 1998).

These types of categories that are more difficult to put into operation are found even less frequently in practice. The most important reason for this is that the financial interest of the supplier tends to dominate.

8.3 Relationship policy by relationship phase

In the implementation of the relationship policy per segment, the relationship life cycle will have to be taken into consideration; this indicates the pattern the relationship will follow in its further development under the influence of the internal interactions. Figure 2.3 (page 37) illustrates an average relationship life cycle which is encountered in many markets. The corresponding policy is outlined in Figure 8.3 (Peelen, 1989).

During the exploratory phase, the relationship starts out positively. The supplier has positioned itself as an attractive company in order to acquire the customer, and this has raised certain expectations. The relationship is still quite fragile; a common

Figure 8.3 Relationship policy per phase

Source: Peelen (1989).

	Exploratory	Growth	Maturity	Decline
Transaction	Low	Growing	Stable	Declining
Commitment	Average high	Decreasing	Maximum	Low
Objective	Both higher	Both higher	Retain	Prevent, departure
Policy	Inform Differentiate Measure satisfaction	Interact Appeal Cross-selling Customisation Exceed expectations	Change routines	Determine cause, suggest solution

history has not yet been created which they may fall back upon. The goal of the relationship policy in this phase is to reinforce the relationship and to increase commitment. Customers must be led as quickly as possible from the exploratory to the saturation phase. It is also desirable to increase the volume of transactions so as to produce a return on the investments which have been made in the relationship.

During this exploratory phase, the two-way exchange of information is an indispensable element to a policy whose priority is the development of a long-lasting relationship. This involves information that is necessary to stimulate follow-up transactions and the purchase of products and services which have not previously been purchased (cross-selling). At the same time, the customer's satisfaction with the supplier will have to be followed closely; it is precisely in this early stage of the relationship that it is important to be able to spot negative developments quickly and to take action.

Typical of the growth phase is that the commitment aspect can sometimes undergo negative development which can endanger the continuity of the relationship. Analysis of a great many customer databases has shown that customer churn is high among customers who have not yet developed a long-term relationship with the supplier. Those customers for whom the costs of acquisition have not yet been covered display a heightened risk of leaving before they have even become profitable. Besides, the ability to identify with the supplier loses some of its value. Doubts may arise regarding the appeal and uniqueness of this supplier. Barriers which stand in the way of the termination of this relationship and the start of a new one are perceived to be lower than they were previously.

The goal of the relationship policy during the growth phase is thus to increase the commitment and to continue the positive growth trend seen in the turnover. Those activities that demonstrate and emphasise the uniqueness and appeal of the supplier are valuable. The same applies to cross-selling activities; experience teaches us, in fact, that customers who purchase more than one type of product or service from a supplier are less likely to show signs of terminating the relationship. The customer experiences the advantages the other party has to offer and, besides, the switching costs can increase; after all, a replacement will have to be found for the supplier that fulfils several needs.

Opportunities to exceed the expectations of the customer will have to be seized. By leaving an unforgettable impression, the relationship can suddenly find itself sailing on smooth seas. The service system generally offers good prospects. A characteristic of services is that it is difficult for customers to accurately evaluate the level of quality that they may expect from the competition with which they have no experience. After all, service is intangible and quality may only be assessed on the basis of experience. Furthermore, it appears that many customers have a conservative attitude on average because they estimate the level of service of the organisation with which they have experience to be higher than that of an unknown competitor.

However, perhaps service alone is insufficient and an experience will also have to be created. This can, in fact, be the case in markets in which all of the suppliers compete on the basis of service. In order to leave a lasting, personal impression on the customer, the supplier will have to expend even more effort. It will have to orchestrate the consumption situation, stimulate the customer's senses and arouse emotions (see Chapter 7).

It is in the saturation or maturity phase that a supplier encounters its most profitable and loyal customers. The investments in the customer have already been recovered, the chance of the relationship being terminated is low, and the level of spending by the customer is relatively high. Each party knows what it may expect from the other. Trust has been built up; in the past, both have proven to be reliable. If one of the two makes a mistake, this does not lead to an immediate end of the collaboration. The belief exists that the other party has not knowingly or intentionally 'dropped the ball' and is prepared to repair the damage. The challenge in this phase consists in breaking out of routines or preventing similar habit patterns from forming in an early stage. At the same time, the parties must continue to express their mutual appreciation for the relationship.

The decline phase signifies a possible end to the relationship. It may begin shortly after the beginning of the relationship or later on. Turnover decreases and commitment lessens. The objective of the relationship policy in this phase is to determine the causes of the change. To the extent that it is desirable and possible, a solution may be suggested. However, in many situations, the cause may be external; the need for the supplier's services has disappeared. A person may no longer have their car, and for this reason no longer requires his or her membership to the auto club. It is an accomplished fact, and there is not much that may be done to change it. This may also occur when the quality of the service is the cause for the deterioration of the relationship. By getting in contact with the customer and 'righting the wrong', the supplier may, in many cases, steer the development of the relationship back in a positive direction once again. Research has even shown that these customers can ultimately become the most loyal ambassadors. The personal attention and the involvement on the part of the supplier in this situation have surpassed the customer's initial expectations.

During this phase, the supplier must exercise care in dealing with price shoppers who place many demands on the organisation, are difficult to please, and who do not strive for any type of long-term relationship whatsoever. Efforts and the investments that go along with them will rarely prove to be profitable with this type of customer. One finds this type of customer less frequently among the customers that only threaten to leave the supplier after having been customers for many years.

8.4 Translating the relationship policy into contact moments

In order to realise relationship management, a communication plan must be outlined. An ad hoc communication policy or a product-driven communication policy is useless. The situation in which product introductions or promotional activities prompted by the competition determine the timing of contact is undesirable. A great deal of thought must be given to communication, and events organised by the supplier, the customer and the market will have to be assigned a position within the framework of the planned relationship development (Peelen, 1989).

During the exploratory phase, both parties will have to feel one another out (Dwyer, Schurr and Oh, 1987). The supplier does not yet know what type of potential the customer represents, and in which segment he or she must be categorised. A differentiated approach is thus still difficult in this phase. It is also undesirable to invest too much in communication efforts because it is unclear what the ultimate value of the relationship will be. Companies that offer a welcome packet or make a welcome 'call' have positive experiences. A portion of this type of activity may be a questionnaire or interview during which questions are asked about the other wishes and/or purchase plans of the customer, in addition to inquiries about his or her satisfaction with the product or service. In general, these types of initiatives meet with positive response, and a substantial portion of the customer base lends its cooperation in their execution. The result is that important information is gathered which allows the customer to be placed in a segment and indications are obtained about the ways in which the customer may be encouraged to make follow-up purchases.

Communication geared towards the realisation of the subsequent transactions is a crucial component of the relationship. It is recommended that communication calendars are developed which may be used to note when the customer will be approached and with what particular information. Concrete goals may then be linked to the achievement of a specific result during a certain period.

In addition to the cross-selling possibilities which arise during customer contact in the exploratory phase, the outcomes of the cross-selling analyses may also be used to companies' advantage. These may indicate what the chances are of the customer considering the purchase of the product concerned within a certain period, and whether or not approaching him or her is worth the effort.

Customers who have made more transactions in later phases of the relationship prove their value to the supplier. It is financially justifiable to bend and shape the relationship from a transactional one into a relational one. A policy focused on cross-selling can make room for a policy that targets the creation of a partnership. Suppliers may open the dialogue to accomplish this; in order to 'break the ice', it may be beneficial for them to take the lead and provide customer-specific information. Robeco Direct, a Dutch financial services company, sends its valuable customers a personal annual report, for example. In this report, the customer will find information on the stock market and his or her investment portfolio in particular, and if possible, his or her risk profile. In effect, the organisation is surprising its customers with this information service, but in a positive way. The information provided actually raises new questions, which will induce some of the customers to contact Robeco Direct. An open and substantial dialogue is thus started with these customers that marks the point that a transaction-oriented relationship is shaped into a relationship-oriented one. The customer discloses confidential information and allows the other to provide advice. The level of trust grows; each dares to place more of their fate in the other's hands.

It is important to seek contact with customers who threaten to end the relationship or those who have already done this. Simply demonstrating interest can provide an important reason for customers to adjust their image of the supplier. Even a portion of the customers who have already left may be persuaded during an exit interview to give the supplier another chance.

It goes without saying that an organisation cannot succeed in developing an efficient and meaningful dialogue with all of its customers in each of the different segments. Repeated efforts to start up communication can fail to produce results. The supplier remains the one who takes the initiative. In order to prevent this from becoming a source of irritation, it might be a good idea to 'park' these customers and leave them alone (Figure 8.4). After all, communication efforts with this group do not lead to conversion and increased profits.

Figure 8.4 **Relationship policy by segment: from cross-selling to total solution provider**

Source: Peelen (1999).

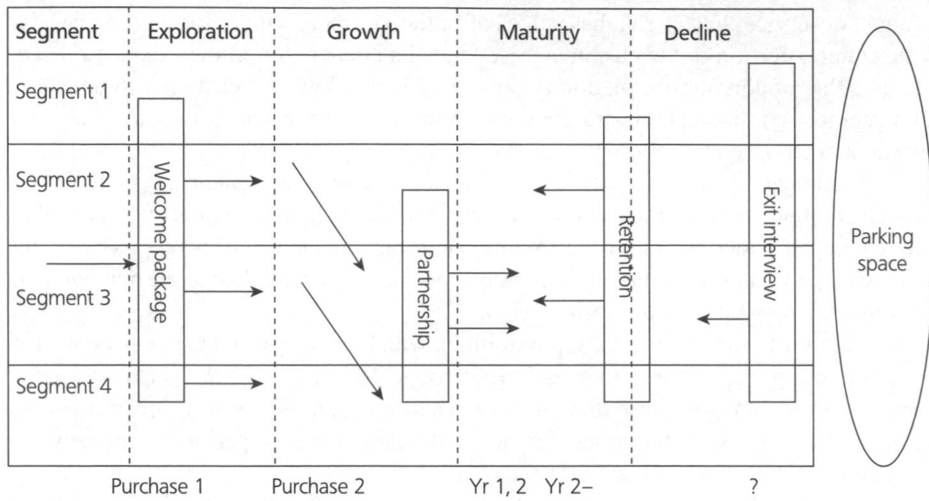

Communication pressure and initiative

Reasons to communicate with customers can originate from a variety of sources. The company may be introducing new products, or might have created a special promotion, or perhaps it would like to inform the customer about specific developments in the industry. An insurance company has a new form of savings account, or would like to provide customers who are insured via their employer with an extra special offer, or inform them about the consequences of upcoming legislative changes for their pension fund. Events may also occur involving the customer which may make it interesting to establish contact. Returning to the insurance company example, perhaps there is a new addition to the family, the customer is planning to move, change jobs and/or there has been an incident involving damage. Insight into events involving the customer which are either imminent or have already taken place is important for the relationship policy. These are the moments during which purchase opportunities occur.

In creating the contact plan, the supplier, depending on the stage in the relationship, will have to determine which occasions may or should be acted upon and which should not. Situations will have to be prevented in which good customers are approached too often or customers in the 'car park' remain spared from information completely while there are, in fact, customers among them who are profitable on a transaction basis. Companies will also have to aim for a situation in which the initiative for contact does not lie solely with the customer or the supplier; a certain degree of equilibrium is preferable.

Finally, the company will often find that it is difficult to obtain reliable information on imminent events involving its customers. It is difficult to make contact at exactly the right time with the customer; we are often too early or too late. The challenge facing the marketer is to increase his or her familiarity with the supplier so that the marketer's company is automatically the one the customer approaches at the time the need arises.

Influence of marketing communication on relationship development

Although a communication plan is a requirement in the design and implementation of the relationship policy, care must be taken to ensure that the importance of this plan is not overestimated. The commercial communication between customer and supplier often constitutes only a small part of the total communication regarding the purchase, use and ultimate discarding of the product by the customer. To a certain extent, contact occurs via the company; however, information may also be obtained in other ways such as via the press, independent experts, and family and friends in the customer's environment. Policies incorporating the positive influences inherent in these independent flows of communication are not employed often enough and can be very efficient. Studies (Verbeke, Peelen and Brand, 1995) have shown, for instance, that customers who are acquired via a 'member-get-member' promotion can represent a relatively high value to the company. The chance that they will stay and develop into profitable customers is above average. Communities in which customers help one another and the supplier may have just as substantial an impact on customer retention and relationship development.

8.5 Loyalty programmes

In order to further develop the commitment of their customers, various companies also implement loyalty programmes (Broekhuizen and Peelen, 1997). Within this context, the term 'loyalty' is associated with, *among other things*, (collective) savings schemes which are linked to a database containing information on the name, address, city, certain behaviour and background information for individual customers. The success of the programme lies in providing customers with specific rewards. The intention is to reward loyal, frequent buyers more often. The distinction is made between good and bad customers with the aid of behaviour registration. With Esso, for example, we see that a distinction is made between customers who buy more and those who buy less. Motorists who buy fuel from Esso more often can qualify for double points. In reality, companies are careful about discriminating between bad, good, better and best customers. Worries exist that if the company applies this distinction, it will encounter resistance from certain consumers.

This way of rewarding customers fits in with operant conditioning, a theory describing ways in which individuals learn from the rewards and the punishments that they receive for certain behaviour. It describes a method of learning for which very few mental processes are necessary. People learn from certain types of conduct. Actions are not preceded by information-seeking behaviour outside of the internal memory, and evaluation of alternatives for different aspects (attributes) is lacking. The mental processes take place on a very limited basis and the preference for the supplier or brand is mentally embedded to a limited degree. The future is not explicitly involved in the consideration, and the underlying values and goals held by the other party are not examined.

An additional aspect is that in collective savings programmes the effect of selective rewards is weakened by the fact that the supplier or the brand is associated with the programme to a lesser, and certainly not exclusive, degree. The question arises whether customers become loyal to the various organisations awarding points or to organisers of programmes such as Airmiles (UK and Netherlands), Thrumf (Norway), Smiles (France), Happy Days (Belgium).

True loyalty will therefore not come from this type of 'selective reward behaviour'. An additional dimension is necessary and it appears that airlines have been successful in this respect or have at least made a concerted effort to be so. Airlines are an old and well-known example of organisations which set up frequent flyer clubs. Apart from rewarding 'loyal behaviour', they also aim to increase the preference for the organisation through image- and service-related activities. In addition to rewarding certain flying behaviour, all major airlines, for example, look for possibilities to accommodate the customer, in particular with services that go further than the simple offer of 'transport via the skies'. Through the use of lounges, express check-in counters and facilitating partners, and by sending out a magazine, they attempt to empathise with their customers and to obtain a commitment in return.

If this strengthens the involvement with the supplier, mental processes are activated; efforts are made to improve the intrinsic satisfaction (with the services of the supplying organisation). The probability increases that choices are made for the future and that the underlying values and goals of the organisation evoke positive associations.

The possibility also exists that the selective way of rewarding customers should be seen as an extension of the organisation's other activities, such as general service, thematic advertising and product quality. The loyalty programme is then the added bonus, the surprise added to the products or services the company offers. But even so, it would be even 'purer' if the term was not exclusively linked to the long-term savings programme, but instead was connected to all of the supplier's relationship-oriented efforts.

In summary, we may say that within 'real' loyalty programmes:

- The individual relationship between supplier and customer comes into play as the company discriminates between good and bad customers; the database makes it possible to do this.
- A psychological as well as a behavioural basis exists; the parties empathise with one another, accommodate one another, surprise one another and commit to one another; they have every intention of continuing the relationship and to continue making transactions.

Categories of loyalty programmes

The examples quoted above (Esso, collective loyalty programmes and the airlines) have already made it clear that there is great variety among loyalty and savings programmes. The differences lie primarily in the objectives of each programme, the manner in which and times behaviour is rewarded, the accessibility of the programme, the nature of the reward and the interaction, and the party or parties involved in the programme.

On the basis of these differences, we would like to distinguish between three groups (see Table 8.1). First, there are the *savings programmes* for which it must be said straight away that these are not true loyalty programmes in the sense described above. The focus here is on encouraging the customer to make transactions by rewarding him or her for certain behaviour: purchasing. Within this group, a distinction may be made between short- and long-term savings programmes. The *short-term savings programmes*

Table 8.1 Categories of loyalty programmes

Type	*Threshold*	*Communication*	*Objective*	*Incentive*	*Operant conditioning*
Savings programme	Performing a purchase transaction	Geared towards points and gifts	Increase spending behaviour of customers; retention of customers	Free or with additional payment (product-related) reward	Yes
Club programme	Customers must register; the conditions under which members are accepted vary (buying history, payment of contribution, etc.)	Geared towards product and brand, or points	Increase customer involvement with brand/supplier Long-term commitment with the customer and thus more purchases	Information (magazine), possible discounts, insurance, credit, guarantees, etc.	No, cognitive processes also take place
Relationship marketing programme	Minimum number of transactions	Geared towards customer usage patterns, product/brand, points and gifts	Increase *mutual* involvement between customer and supplier; long-term commitment with the customer and thus more purchases	Complementary products and services, including customer magazine, advice, service, discounts, credit, etc.	No, cognitive processes also take place

Source: Broekhuizen and Peelen (1997).

primarily aim to stimulate behaviour. Within a relatively short period of time, the consumer, for an additional charge or free of charge, may be eligible to receive a gift. In the event that they are successful, it becomes apparent how difficult it is to cancel this type of programme. Shell, for example, several years ago found it difficult to stop the green stamp programme. The *long-term savings programmes* are the more well-known: the Airmiles points programme being perhaps the most well-known. These days, we often see combinations of long- and short-term savings programmes. In order to prevent consumers from having to wait too long for their rewards, and the chance that the desired customer behaviour will decrease, customers receive promotional stamps in addition to Airmiles.

Second, there are the so-called *club programmes*. People are offered the opportunity to become members of a club either free or for a very small fee. Upon registration, customers receive a card with which they may identify themselves as participants. There is a great variety to be found in these cards: from private label cards offering credit facilities to co-branded credit cards. The advantage for consumer members lies in the company magazines, discounts, payment facilities and insurance that they receive. Provision of these benefits is made dependent on the actual purchase behaviour either to a limited degree or not at all. A striking example of a club involves Felix or Pedigree

Pal pet foods. Thanks to nutritional guidance, birthday cards and other small tokens of appreciation from the supplier, members are able to take better care of their animals. The Fox Kids club, with its large number of members, is a good example. Or within the educational sphere: former students of the Erasmus University in Rotterdam are given the opportunity to perpetuate their bond with the university as alumni and as such, qualify for discounts for conference registration fees, lectures, events in Rotterdam and a free library card.

Finally, there are the *relationship marketing programmes* or the 'real' loyalty programmes. The starting point for these programmes is that their goal is to improve the involvement suppliers and customers have with one another. Suppliers capitalise on the customer's situation and, through the structured use of various marketing tools, work on enhancing commitment and purchasing behaviour in the long run. Participants in these types of programmes may often identify themselves with a card so that the interactions in the relationship may be registered on an individual level. Thanks to the database, focused communication and customised services are possible and the programme is capable of zeroing in on various events which are relevant to the customer. Furthermore, the goal of the reward structure for every participant is to be capable of obtaining a reward of his or her choice within a foreseeable period and within certain margins. Moreover, the company discriminates between good and bad customers. This phenomenon becomes readily apparent in the frequent flyer programmes created by the various airline companies in which passengers can save to obtain product-related rewards within the not-too-distant future, such as flights and upgrades, or for rewards related to the participant's interest, such as enrolment in a Burgundian cuisine cooking class. The size of the reward is also linked to the number of kilometres the customer has flown per year in a certain class.

Effectiveness of loyalty programmes

The effectiveness of this third type of loyalty programme also depends on the degree to which the company is in a position to surprise, appreciate, activate and inform the customer (see Figure 8.5) (Alberts and Buitendijk, 1995). Has the supplier been successful in venturing off the beaten track every now and then and *surprising* the customer in a unique manner befitting his or her identity? Is it capable of showing its *appreciation* for the customer by inviting him or her to a customer day or similar event? Or has the customer been invited to participate in a workshop, the theme of which is the valued opinion of customers? Or has the supplier been particularly successful in *informing* and *activating* the customer? Successful relationship management concentrates on all four of these dimensions. As Figure 8.5 illustrates, an imbalance may be prevented when there is insufficient focus on the elements of surprise and appreciation.

8.6 Conclusion

A thorough relationship policy starts with a plan for the improvement of the size and quality of the customer database. By indicating in which direction the organisation

Relationship management

Figure 8.5

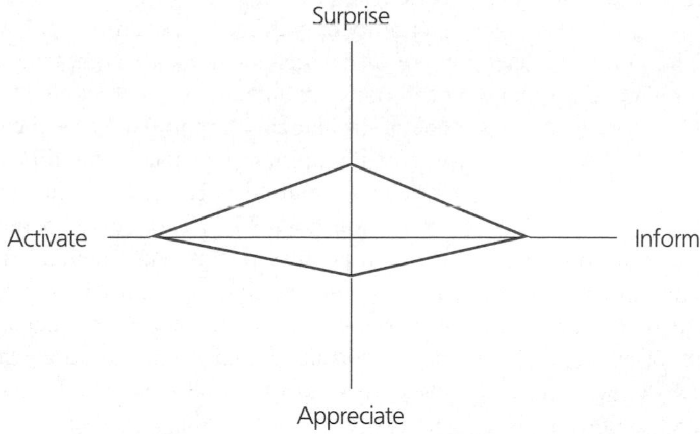

Source: Alberts and Buitendijk (1995).

wishes to steer its development, the company demonstrates that it has a good idea of the type of customers with whom it would like to develop a relationship. Next, the outlines of the relationship policy may be formulated for the segments and/or target groups from this database. On the basis of the current and potential value of the customers in a group, the decision may be made as to which level of service will be offered and how intensive the communication will be with the customers. A framework may be created within which the policy focusing on the relationship development of customers or customer groups may be designed. This policy will then have to be translated into a contact 'strategy'.

Finally, at the end of the chapter we discussed loyalty programmes. A distinction was made between the savings and club programmes and the 'real' relationship marketing programmes which provide suppliers and customers with an extra incentive on all fronts to do business with one another.

Case study

Idefix's patrons need to exhibit increased loyalty

Introduction

Idefix is one of the largest food retail chains in Europe; it is positioned at the upper end of the market. As a result of current developments in the market, the number of Idefix customers that shop at more than one supermarket has increased by 20 per cent during the past five years. Although other chains are also confronted with this development it will nevertheless be necessary for Idefix to reverse this trend. The increase in customer loyalty will need to result in a greater turnover and profitability per customer. Loyalty will need to result in more purchases (increased volume), the acceptance of a premium price (more luxurious products), lower operating costs (lower recruitment costs and costs of shop-floor staff) and new customers (as a result of recommendations).

You are asked to participate in a project team that formulates a plan to stimulate customer loyalty.

The supermarket

Idefix with its 600 stores employs six different supermarket formats, based on the differences in their floor area. The magnitude of the product range depends on the available floor area. The product range offered by the two largest supermarket formats can be ranked amongst the most comprehensive to be found anywhere in the country.

Within the various formats, Idefix's head offices tailor the composition of the product ranges to the local circumstances of each branch.

Supermarkets are characterised by the need for operational excellence; they have not been designed for a customer-intimacy strategy.

Rewards for loyal customers

Idefix has introduced two cards: their own and the Air Miles card. The Idefix customer card can be regarded as a means of identification and a loyalty card. The chip on the customer card provides the concern with the ability to maintain records of the number of points and, to a certain level of detail, the customer's history of purchases at the company's stores.

At the time of the introduction of the Idefix customer card the savings facilities were complementary to those of the Air Miles system. The Idefix card offered customers an opportunity to become eligible for an incentive within a short period of time; the Air Miles card offered this eligibility only in the longer term[1]. The two cards were also considered to be complementary to each other in other fields. Although Idefix was one of the shareholders in Air Miles the concern was of the opinion that the probability that this card could be used to create 'real' ties with customers was not great. The company believed that the card possessed a greater potential to attract new customers, since the card was – and is – accepted by the market leaders in other segments of the consumer market. In addition, the company also saw possibilities in a link between the two customer databases, in so far as this is permitted by law.

At present the Idefix customer card is used to provide selective discounts to customers; their profile is used to select the incentives they are to receive.

Idefix is still seeking the ideal formula for the deployment of the customer card to create and encourage customer loyalty. The company is giving thought to the optimum mix of loyalty tools. In the compilation of this mix, attention will need to be given to short-term special offers, existing savings-stamps schemes, and a competitor's ideas to invite customers to become a shareholder or open a savings account with the supermarket.

Questions

1 What is the potential contribution a customer loyalty card can make to Idefix's expansion and profitability?

2 Describe the outline of a strategy designed to increase customer loyalty.

[1] The Air Miles gift range has since been expanded such that it is now possible to exchange points for gifts within a short period of time after becoming a member.

Questions

1 Why is it so important for the first requirement in designing the relationship policy to be the improvement of the size and quality of the customer database? Explain your answer.

2 In Figure 8.1 a distinction is made between customers and non-customers. It is suggested that certain indicators can be used to segment non-customers in the same way as customers for whom an extensive profile has been developed.

(a) Provide an example to illustrate this method.

(b) Indicate which risks are associated with this method.

3 What criticism can you offer for categorising customers into groups according to their current and/or potential profit contribution?

4 Some companies do not categorise into customer groups but instead make a distinction between groups on the basis of the effects which may be achieved within them. In this way, the potential profitable non-customers (see Figure 8.1) will be identified as a target group where the penetration and 'share of wallet' must be increased. According to these companies, the advantage of this method lies in the fact that a more accurate indication is provided of what one hopes to achieve within a certain target group, and which means are necessary to achieve this. How would you evaluate this method? Explain your answer.

5 Chapter 3 examines customer knowledge. Distinctions are made in that chapter among the customer as buyer, user, and person or organisation. Can you see the possibilities of dividing the customer database into type of person or organisation? Can this categorisation replace one that focuses on profit contribution? Explain your answer.

6 Creating a distinction between the communication and service levels of so-called gold, silver and bronze customers can lead to irritation among customers. How can this irritation be prevented? In your opinion, how should a company handle this situation?

7 What type of possible relationship exists between the quality of the customer database and the existence of a low point in the relationship during the growth phase?

8 What is an easy method for determining what stage a specific relationship is in?

9 What role do loyalty programmes play in the relationship policy?

10 Devise methods that a specific organisation may use to surprise, appreciate, inform and activate customers within the framework of the relationship policy.

References

Alberts, Paul and Nico Buitendijk (1995) *Relationship Management: Tips*, REM, Amsterdam.

Broekhuizen, Ilya and Ed Peelen (1997) Het belonen van trouwe klanten, *Tijdschrift voor Marketing*, July–August, 52–56.

Bügel, Marnix (2002) *Klantenloyaliteit, over ongelijke behandeling in het digitale tijdperk*, Pearson Education, Amsterdam.

Dwyer, F. Robert, Paul H. Schurr and Sejo Oh (1987) Developing buyer–seller relationships, *Journal of Marketing*, **51**, April, 11–27.

Peelen, Ed (1989) *Relaties tussen consument en aanbieder, een basis voor herhalingsaankopen*, Haveka, Alblasserdam.

Peelen, Ed (1999) *The Relation Oriented Organization*, Nyenrode University, Beukelen.

Schijns, Jos (1998) Het meten en managen van klant-organisatie relaties, PhD thesis, University of Maastricht, Maastricht.

Verbeke, Willem, Ed Peelen and Rene Brand (1995) Consumers engaged in a member-gets-member campaign: an agency perspective, *Journal of Marketing Communications*, Winter, 175–192.

Wang, Paul (1998) *Database Marketing and Customer Connections*, Achmea workshop, Zeist.

Yim, Chi Kin (Bennett) and P.K. Kannan (1998) Consumer behavior loyalty: a segmentation model and analysis, *Journal of Business Research*, **44**, 75–92.

Part III

Analytical CRM

This section of the book focuses on analytical CRM which is that area of CRM that involves the expansion of customer knowledge and its application in customer contacts. An important foundation of analytical CRM is created by the relationship data. Making sure the proper data are recorded with the desired intrinsic quality makes it possible to implement the desired relationship policy. The relationship data are used in statistical and datamining analyses to make selections: who will and who will not be approached with a certain offer at a certain time? The selection analyses which lie at the foundation of the relationship policy (see Figure III.1) will be examined and include: segmentation analysis, cross-sell and retention analysis. Although the result of the marketing activities is determined to a great extent by the selection, knowledge must also be developed on the effectiveness and the efficiency of the marketing activities. Are the proper channels being used? Is a dialogue being conducted effectively and efficiently? Are customers being encouraged to purchase in the manner desired? Do the marketing activities lead to an improvement in the customer–supplier relationship? Have the activities produced the desired financial results?

Finally, attention will be focused on the aspect of management reporting. Management information is necessary to further finalise the policy, to communicate and to evaluate. Lifetime value is an important piece of information; however, supplemental information must also be provided. The balanced scorecard appropriate to the CRM strategy will supply this control information.

This part, in particular Chapters 10, 11, 12 and 13, examines analytical CRM issues in a fairly in-depth manner and is intended for readers with knowledge of data analysis.

Figure III.1 Sub-aspects of analytical CRM

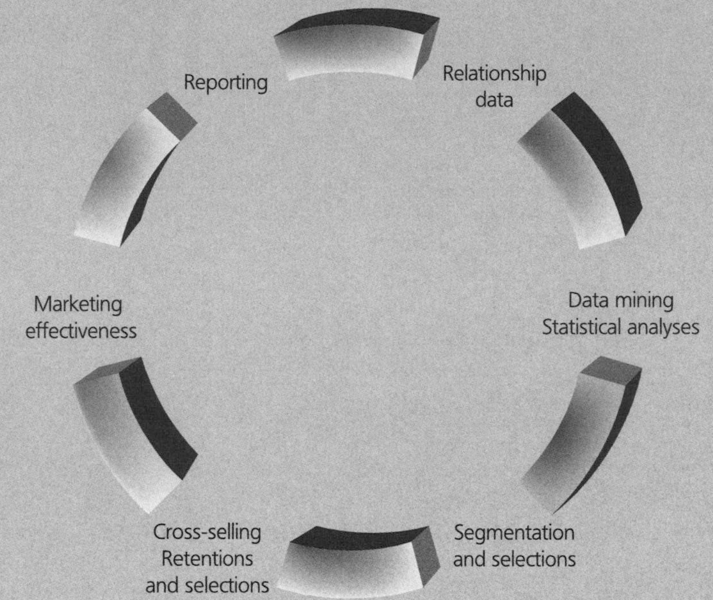

9

Relationship data management

This chapter describes how an accurate, complete, current and unique customer profile may be developed in databases. We will first discuss the identification of customers in the customer databases and will then focus attention on the manner in which the customer profiles may be further enriched to benefit the relationship policy.

In this chapter we will address the following questions

- How to measure and control for the quality of relationship data used to identify customers.
- How can we profile customers?
  - What types of databases are there (structured and relational)?
  - Which characteristics may be used to describe customers?
  - How can we measure these characteristics?
  - How can we maintain the customer profile?
- What types of external and internal sources (lists) are there to expand the database qualitatively and quantitatively?

Practitioner's insight

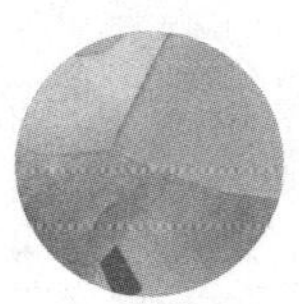

Sometimes one must look at the databases and data warehouses of suppliers in amazement. Even if you have never bought or ordered something from some of them, your name still appears in their databases and they know a thing or two about you. For others, you are a regular customer, yet it appears that your information is not registered properly. You cannot even identify yourself with certainty. They know your account number or invoice number, but have not yet discovered the person behind the numbers. However, with the truly professional companies, you will find a real and complete customer profile for yourself. They have succeeded in harvesting all of the relevant data from all sorts of databases, both inside and outside the company, and have compiled them all into one data warehouse. They are successful in building this database and keeping it up to date. It is easily and quickly accessible so that front-office employees at different locations and in different employment positions can be of real assistance to you.

9.1 Customer identification

(Peelen and Mergen, 2003)

Relationship data used to identify a customer include:

(a) the basic data consisting of name, address, sex and company name;

(b) supplementary data on the date of birth or incorporation date, nationality or industry, telephone number, legal form, company registration number.

Typical of these customer data is that they are used by the entire organisation and therefore form part of the *infrastructure* of the company. The exchange of customer

CRM definitions

Within consumer markets it will have to be determined whether a customer is an individual or the household in which he or she lives.

In business-to-business markets information for the customer – to the extent this is relevant – will have to be recorded with regard to the holding company, the division, the business unit or the department, and the contact people.

data takes place between nearly every one of the processes in the value chain. Data may develop in a process or change when:

- the service department determines that the customer has moved;
- the accounts department announces that the customer is on stop and may not receive any further shipments;
- the distribution department receives a returned package due to a correct yet improper address;
- the marketing department receives mailings returned with the notification 'person no longer works here';
- the invoice does not arrive;
- a customer is also a supplier.

Data are input into the system from a coupon that comes in as a result of a direct response advertisement, a mailing or a telephone call from a customer to the call centre or via the Internet. Transactions take place and the data are used for commercial purposes (mailings, call centre, by account managers, analyses), service (the service engineer) and in production systems (insurance policy documents, account statements, order confirmations, invoices, etc.). Data for existing customers may be completed using external sources or large groups of new customers may be imported. Sometimes databases are merged to form an entirely new database. Different departments and different people use the database in their own way and with their own goal in mind. In this type of environment, the quality of the customer data must be monitored to prevent deterioration, thereby lowering the company's profitability.

For these reasons, it is advisable to set up a central database. From the outset, the priority may lie with the preservation and monitoring of quality. People will not be able to make changes on their own initiative and time will be reserved to update the identification data. One person or a number of people within the organisation will be dedicated to managing the quality of this data in a professional way. Using access codes and other facilities, others will only experience the advantages of this system.

Operationalising data quality

Since these customer identification data are used all over the organisation, managing their quality is an even more serious challenge. From a practical point of view the *intrinsic quality perspective* (see Chapter 5) offers the best opportunities to measure and manage the quality, although it remains difficult. Quantitative indicators can be developed to estimate the accuracy, correctness, uniqueness and completeness of data. The quality indicators offer the possibility of setting concrete standards to guide the degree and the direction of improvement. Despite the practical value of the intrinsic perspective, quality needs to be managed from the different viewpoints.

Technically the OCR equipment has to be able to read the written names and addresses, and the number of positions in the database has to allow for the complete registration of the data.

Furthermore, the *receiver*, for example Mrs X, has to be recognised and addressed in the way she prefers. In principle, every customer desires and expects his or her data to be used, written and pronounced correctly. Correctly identifying and addressing the customer requires the correct combination of customer data such as name, address, sex and date of birth. Nonetheless, this identity deserves some degree of differentiation. For example, we accept addresses printed only in capitals on an invoice, or a shortened name on a credit card. Provided this is done correctly and the name, say, 'J.P.T. COLLINGWOOD-HEATHERTON' is not shortened to 'J.P.T. COL-HEATHERTON'. However, if we are invited to attend a customer day via a mailing addressed to us personally, or when we are called by an account manager to make an appointment – 'Good afternoon, Mr HEATHERTON . . .' – then we are clearly placing higher demands on the quality. Even the smallest of mistakes can arouse negative emotions.

The medium for which the processing of the customer data occurs is characterised by limitations and/or technical standards. The receiver obviously accepts this. The need for quality is directly related to the expectation to which the processing is being subjected. This applies even more to internal use: for an ad hoc overview of the outstanding debtors, it is acceptable to limit names to 25 characters, use capital letters and print using the least expensive printer available. It is important only that the amount is correct and the telephone number is included.

The quality of relationship data becomes apparent to *the supplier* if he or she is able to identify and address the relations in the appropriate way. In some studies, the aspect of the accessibility of data is added to this list. In doing so, we indicate to what extent those using the customer data within the time span allowed for this are able to retrieve the data. It is particularly important for agents in the contact centre to be able to obtain access to these data quickly enough that they may conclude the customer contact in a satisfactory manner.

With databases maintained in a normal manner, duplication of entries may be expected to lie between 10 per cent and 20 per cent. The cause of duplication is that there are several sources of customer data that are recorded independently without proper matching with current data. With databases involving natural persons, the household can be a disruptive factor. On the one hand, several people in the same household can have the same initials and last name; in this situation, data such as date of birth and sex can have a high distinguishing value. However, the chance is just as great that parents and children with different surnames comprise one household. It is then difficult to estimate whether or not there is one family or more at that address. With organisations (companies, government bodies and so forth), not only does the name create complexity, but the addresses do this as well. Companies often have more than one branch and maintain separate postal, delivery and invoice addresses.

The name is perhaps the most important piece of data for a customer, yet this bit of information is not validated in most customer management systems in which typographical errors may be found and unknown names are ignored. A Dutch study on the perception of errors in the ascription used on commercial post showed that 6 per cent of recipients threw the post unopened into the bin if an error appeared in his or her name or that of the company; 32 per cent of those surveyed found it extremely annoying (AGB Interact, 1995). Although the research is now some years old, there is no reason to assume that a great deal has changed in this regard since that time.

Control addresses assist in preventing fraud

Control addresses were previously used primarily to determine whether or not a mailing had arrived at its intended destination. These days, control addresses play a major role in the detection of fraudulent use of databases.

Almost every company has valuable databases at its disposal and should treat these with extreme care. Many companies feel it will suffice to include a selection of its own staff to conduct a check. However, if legal steps are taken due to improper use, the court is not really interested in 'internal inspectors'. For this reason, direct mail experts emphasise that it is also important to include external control addresses.

Source: *Direct Marketing* (2002).

Measures geared towards improving the quality of identification data (based on the experience of Human Inference)

Several measures can be taken to manage the quality of relationship data and to overcome situations where Mrs Fortmann is addressed as Mrs Voortman or where her name one day is spelled Fortmann, and the next Voortman.

Reference databases play an important role in this. In many countries, postcode tables are normally quite complete, up-to-date, accurate and contain unique descriptions of relations. Also, several governmental databases – if accessible – can be helpful. Suppliers can compare their customer data with these reference databases and

Multiple identities of Dutch addresses

Many postal services in Europe make postcode tables available that include street and city names, among other information. The question here is, what is, in fact, correct in this table since there might be three standards: the standard of the postal services; the Dutch NEN standard; and the council decree (the name given to the street by the local council).

Further, the postcode table is never completely up to date: the street names in the new housing developments lag behind for a variety of reasons. The address should also include the house number and any suffix added to this number. This last element in particular is actually not possible to check; there is no standard for this and by tomorrow there could be a letterbox placed next to the door complete with house number suffix. And what is the correct city name in Dutch for The Hague? 's-Gravenhage or The Hague? Years ago, the 's-Gravenhage council decided that from that point on, Den Haag was the preferred name for the city. City names in local dialect were not included in the postal code tables for many years.

Not all of the addresses appear in the postcode tables: delivery addresses, for example, such as a pumping station in the dunes in the north of Holland. Gas, water and electricity will have to be supplied to this address.

Source: Mergen (2003).

formulate rules about handling discrepancies. Understanding the quality of these external sources is very important in the process of formulating these rules.

To further resolve the identification problem, a customer is 'designated' a customer number, key words, matchcodes or a combination of postcode and house number. By assigning a unique *customer number*, it seems that the problem of identifying customers is solved. However, these data are error-sensitive, not always available and usually not customer friendly due to their length. Customers cannot normally remember them and are difficult to identify if they call, for example. *Key words* may provide a solution if there are many customers with the same name and are therefore difficult to differentiate from one another. The problem with this is that the person who chooses the key word is a different person from the one who later looks up the customer. *Matchcodes* may be used for the same purpose. In order to pick out the correct Jones from the other six hundred in the database, a matchcode may be used which consists of a combination of a number of letters from the name, the street name and city name, for example. However, the method is impractical to use, does not have a search code and is error-sensitive. A building may be identified in the Netherlands and UK by the *postcode and the house number*; however, this does not necessarily apply to the household and/or the individual customer who may even reside at several addresses. Problems also occur with this type of code if the customers relocate.

In order to find a solution to the identification problem, there is something to be learned from the ways in which people tend to search and compare. For example, how do the police describe a fugitive? It is well-known that they use people's physical features that distinguish them from others and together make a person unique: height, sex, hair colour, moustache, glasses, etc. Some of these features may change, and are therefore not reliable as identifiers; nevertheless, their misallocation does not prevent a correct identification. Even if the moustache has been shaved off, the suspect can still be identified among the masses.

The challenge now is to develop an intelligent system that makes it possible to identify our customer in databases on the basis of administrative instead of physical features. They must be able to deal with the fact that there are many Joneses and they have to be able to determine whether Philips refers to the name of the holding company, the surname of the family or the name of the company divisions or branches. Companies may develop these types of system themselves, but there are also standard applications available in the market.

The demands that are placed on the system vary from one application to another. Speed plays a larger role with the contact centre, whereas for speech technology applications (voice processing), the aspect of reliability will have more immediate priority.

In addition to being used for finding customer data, these types of intelligent systems are also useful in verifying new customer data which has been entered. For example, it may be verified online whether or not someone who has logged on as a new customer is truly a new customer and not someone who already appears in the database. The quality of the filling-in of customer data is also monitored; has the person placed his or her postcode in the right box on the Internet form and is the prefix in the right place? In this way, duplication and errors may be prevented beforehand. These systems can also play a role in comparing databases. Potential and certain duplications are pointed out. By the time the databases are merged, this will already have been taken into consideration. The application possibilities mentioned here are preventive in nature; they prevent database pollution at source. When the system is deployed to de-duplicate a database, the quality check takes place later, and it is the remedying of errors that is key.

9.2 Expanding the size of the customer database

The database containing customer data may be expanded in different ways to allow for the inclusion of more people and/or organisations. In evaluating the quality of the alternatives, we can examine the intrinsic relationship data quality as well as the commercial value represented by these customers: are they good buyers-to-be?

Response to external lists

The growth may come from the responses to lists (with names, addresses, cities, e-mail addresses and/or telephone numbers) which have been rented or purchased from third parties. A common construction is one in which these external lists may only be used once for a marketing action and that the response to this may be incorporated into one's own database. These lists are designed with another objective in mind than that for which the organisation plans to use them. The quality of the data has never before proven itself in this situation so that the response which will be produced by a marketing action is as yet unknown. In general, this quality will be lower than that of the internal database, the so-called house list.

These types of external list may be sold or rented directly by the company that has created them, but there are also intermediaries – 'list brokers' – which may be contracted for this purpose. The price of a name–address–city list depends on the degree of selectiveness involved: how many characteristics were used to select the name–address–city list? Another factor which plays a role is the results achieved by others in marketing activities using these lists and its influence is based on the scarcity of addresses in a certain market.

Response via own channels

As the number of channels through which direct communication with prospects and customers may take place increases, the importance of external lists tends to decrease. A period in which customer data was scarce seems to have come to an end. A new era has begun in which the challenge is more one of dealing with information overload and growth.

People are asked to identify themselves before they may be assisted via the Internet or telephone. The quality of the data that come in through these channels varies. A relatively high number of people do not fill Internet forms in correctly. Prefixes end up in the wrong field, errors in dates of birth and telephone numbers go uncorrected. The likelihood that inaccuracies occur is often high in situations which require that certain fields be filled in because the registration will otherwise be rejected.

In call centres, the name, address, city and the like will be filled in by the agent who bases this information on what he hears. In the event of doubt, he will have to ask how something is spelled. He will have to prevent a situation from occurring in which certain fields are either not filled in or are filled in incorrectly because he considers it time consuming, or he feels the question is too intimate, too likely to annoy the customer and/or risks lowering the chance of a sale.

Coupons and forms to be filled in that are returned as a result of a direct response advertisement display errors. Among these registrations there is sure to be a form filled in by a Mr Bear who lives on Zoo Lane in Animal City.

The commercial value of these customer data is influenced by the marketing action that lies at the basis of the registration. Does a prospect or customer provide his or her data because he or she registered spontaneously or because an acquaintance recommended doing business with the supplier? Or is he or she responding to an interesting offer seen in Newspaper A, B, C or Magazine X, Y, Z? Or is there a risk that a 'surfing adventure' on the Internet ends with the filling in of the supplier's registration form? In general, the commercial value of the name–address–city lists in the last two examples is lower than in the first two. Also, those who become customers through a member-get-member campaign appear to represent a high above-average value. For one reason or another, those people who are doing the recommending, feel responsible for their friend's or acquaintance's satisfaction with the supplier. He or she does not want to be blamed, or have to hear 'What have you done to me this time?'

It is important to keep track of what the quality and commercial value are of the customer data that come in through the various channels. In future, the organisation will benefit on the basis of this experience by making use of those channels and campaigns that have already proven their worth.

9.3 Customer profiling

In order to be able to identify customers, there are a variety of relationship data necessary with regard to name, address, city, year of birth, incorporation date, registration number in the commercial register and the like. This information involves a description that is made up of the customer's fixed characteristics. Within the scope of analytical CRM, a further profiling of the customer is desirable. For a more complete customer profile, it is necessary to be able to describe the customer as 'buyer', 'user' and 'person' or 'organisation' (see Chapter 5).

If a relational database is being used, data from two or more different databases may be linked thanks to one or more common characteristics such as the customer or order number. The data are recorded in tables. Each row represents a customer, and information may be found in the columns regarding how this customer scores in terms of characteristics such as last purchase date, amount spent, method of payment, expressed complaints, product ownership, response to messages from the supplier, etc. Two or more tables may be partially or completely merged and/or adapted, thanks to the common elements. The suitable combination may be found in an interactive manner so that characteristics from various tables may be merged and presented in the desired sequence. Each new combination is evaluated on its own merits; if the solution is satisfactory, the process stops or a decision is made about how a better profile may be developed in a subsequent step. The process is comparable to finding one's way. Once you arrive at a new junction, you assess which way you will go in order ultimately to arrive at your destination. In structured databases these possibilities are lacking. The creation of a record is fixed; an indication is provided of the sequence in which the customer's characteristics or order will be described and how many positions the description of each characteristic may have (see Chapter 17).

The degree to which we aim for completeness in creating profiles is an economic issue, one that was discussed in Chapter 5. In this chapter, we are limiting ourselves to a description of the available sources and methods used to expand the customer profile. The risk for which companies must remain prepared is that of too much data being recorded. A marketing action has been carried out and has produced a database, a survey has been held and has resulted in data, the clickstream has been kept track of in an extremely large log file and so forth. Each of these elements of the database seems to contribute to the completion of the customer profile. However, it is probably not feasible to compile these for each or all of the important customers in the database, let alone maintain these data.

Which characteristics?

Decisions about which data will or will not have to be gathered and maintained should not be made on an ad hoc basis. An ideal customer profile (for each segment) will have to form the foundation, one which is indispensable to being able to implement the planned relationship policy (see Chapter 8). Table 9.1 is an overview of the characteristics which may be measured, registered and maintained in order to complete the customer profile.

Measuring the characteristics

There are various ways to keep track of and measure the characteristics in the database. We usually choose not to keep all of the 'raw' data, but instead to revise them so that a better and more easily maintained customer profile develops.

Some measurements of characteristics are the result of extensive analyses and calculations. The assignment of a customer to a segment may be based on a complicated segmentation model (see Chapter 11). For the calculation of the current or potential customer value, costs will have to be allocated to a customer and a lifetime value model will have to be used (see Chapter 14).

As far as the transaction data are concerned, the turnover for each transaction may be recorded separately. The cumulative turnover for one year and the data for which the transactions took place may be registered at the same time. In order to arrive at a handy summary, data are classified into one of three types in marketing:

- Recency data, which indicate the date of the customer's last purchase.
- Frequency data, which relate to the number of transactions and payments customers have made since a certain time within a certain period.
- Monetary data on the value of all of the orders and payments within a certain period.

Table 9.1 Customer profile

Aspect	*Characteristic*
Segment	In which segment should the customer be placed?
Customer value	Annual turnover. Contribution to profit on an annual basis. Share of wallet: the portion of the total expenditures in a certain product category that a customer spends with us during a certain period of time. Lifetime value: the value of a customer for the total expected period that he or she is a customer of ours. Calculations may be made for the turnover value or the contribution to profit. Discounting may take place to take the time value of money into consideration.
Transactions	Turnover and profit contributions of purchases. Description of the purchase. Payment behaviour: have payments been made within the allotted time or should the customer be considered to be dubious? Method of payment.
Products	Which products has the customer purchased, in which quantities and at which time? When does the warranty period expire? Have repairs been performed? Which ones?
Communication through the Internet	Which address was used to log in? Which page did the customer use to enter the site? What was the clickstream? Via which page did the customer exit the website? What was the duration of the visit? Which banners were responded to?
Communication by telephone	When, about which topics and on whose initiative has contact been made by telephone? Who was/were the contact person(s) within the organisation?
Other communication	Which mailings did the customer receive and when did he or she receive them? How did he or she respond to these? When and to which direct response advertising did the customer respond? What is the customer's preference for certain communication channels (in specific situations)? Has the customer notified the organisation that he or she prefers to be excluded from (certain) marketing communication activities?
Satisfaction	Customer's satisfaction with products, services, communication. General satisfaction with the supplier.
Customer characteristiscs	Identification data; see Section 9.1 of this chapter. Type of residence, type of city. Composition of household, income, education, socio-economic class. Lifestyle or end values to which the customer aspires. Industry code; nature of company activities. Size of company. Type of legal entity. Etc.

The measurement of the product purchases and ownership is relatively clear. Which product does someone use or own and when was it purchased? Has the warranty period expired? Has damage already been repaired? Insight into the ownership of products made by the competition is also welcome.

Telephone contacts are generally kept track of quite extensively. A record is kept of the times and subjects of each conversation, who the supplier's contact person was, which agreements were made on the possible continuation of the contact, and on whose initiative the contact originated. These data are indispensable to maintaining the dialogue. The data may be reduced, for example as is done with transaction data, for the development of the customer profile.

Communication via the Internet presents a new challenge. Logfiles containing clickstream data can take on enormous proportions and place a huge burden on the storage and computer processing capacity. It is recommended to distil several relevant data from these raw files. The quick availability of this data can have positive effects on turnover and customer development. It provides the supplier with the opportunity to profit from the specific demand and opportunities that arise. The time that is allotted for this is shorter on the Internet than in a mailing programme, for example. The data may also be used to make the websites perform more effectively.

In comparison with many of the data mentioned above, satisfaction data do not measure behaviour but instead gauge an attitude which may not be observed visually. We must often infer how the customer feels about the supplier from the evaluation he or she gives. The degree of satisfaction is often expressed in a score on an interval scale. Characteristics of this scale are that it contains a minimum and a maximum value, for example zero and seven, and that the space between the two scores does not provide information on the differences in the level of satisfaction.

The result is that data on satisfaction, which are difficult enough to obtain, are less reliable than transaction data, for example. It is therefore not surprising that behavioural characteristics appear to be a better predictor of future behaviour than similar attitude data (see also Chapter 3). It is only extremely low or high scores that appear to possess a predictive value. In cases where the supplier fails to take action, complaints and dissatisfaction point to the imminent departure of the customer, and a very high degree of satisfaction corresponds to the continuation of the relationship.

The nature of the additional customer characteristics from Table 9.1 is heterogeneous. Some of them vary very little or are easy to measure whereas others are not. In making decisions regarding the measurement and recording, these factors will have to be taken into consideration. The efforts that must be made to acquire the data in a reliable manner will have to be in proportion to the commercial value that they represent for the relationship policy.

Maintenance

Data become outdated and lose their value. It is not always easy to indicate when this occurs. Some data never change, such as date of birth. For other types of data, this is more difficult. For example, should a customer who had indicated his or her desire to no longer receive commercial messages from the supplier five years ago still receive no e-mails? Is someone who has not made any purchases for 13 months still to be considered a customer? And will a buyer be refused if he paid a bill too late 15 years ago and was labelled a delinquent payer? Is an address still correct that was input into the system 12 years ago?

Standards will have to be set. The demands which are placed on the currency of the identification data will naturally be higher than those which are applied to the additional customer characteristics. In some cases, the 'sell-by date' is linked to a fixed period of time; in other cases, this may be flexible. If it is necessary to the continuation of a relationship that the customer gives his or her current address details to the supplier, then it is not necessary for a fixed time interval to be applied. This is the case, for instance, with a bank where a person maintains a current account. The method used in the event of obsolescence will also have to be determined: will action be taken to gather the data once again or will an 'empty field' be accepted?

Data sources

Various sources are available in order to further enrich the customer profile, such as:

- Internal:
  - the contact database (or datamart) of the contact centre in which the communication history is maintained;
  - the product databases in which the product ownership is registered;
  - the transaction database in which the purchase, delivery, invoicing and payment information is recorded;
  - the sales information system;
  - the marketing database which keeps track of the mailings which have been sent, customers' potential product interests, customers' preparedness to receive information from the supplier, and answers to questions which have been asked in questionnaires.
- External:
  - there are service providers that set up databases containing characteristics of natural persons and legal entities; data from these databases may be rented or purchased for the purposes of enriching one's own customer database.

Internal sources

Companies that have developed a complete and extensive CRM system are usually able to draw from a variety of sources in order to supplement customer profiles in a so-called marketing data warehouse (see Chapter 17). Various operational systems are active for the processing of transactions and for production. Databases are linked to these systems from which data may be retrieved for the data warehouse. An extensive database will have to be maintained separately in the contact centre which contains data on the contact history. Sales staff will also have to work regularly with the company's own sales information system. Data will be able to be retrieved from these files and processed for recording in a marketing data warehouse.

In general, the value of these internal data is much higher than that of data that have been obtained externally.

External sources

A variety of companies can provide assistance in the enrichment of the customer profile. Without going into all of them in-depth, we can discuss a number of them which differ from one another in the manner in which they can make a contribution.

Customer values Initiatives from marketing research firms are known (such as those made by Claritas and GfK) which, through large-scale random sampling surveys, take measurements among consumers to determine which brands and products they own, or which purchases they expect to make. This provides perspective not only when it comes to attracting new customers, but also in the calculation of penetration percentages and even 'shares of wallet'. If, for example, it is known which insurance an individual has with different companies, a calculation may be performed to show what the share of wallet is for a specific organisation. The same may be done for the coffee makers that different catering companies have installed or the CRM software which has been implemented by certain companies. And, with the aid of a 'charibarometer' which indicates the amount and types of charity organisations to which someone donates money, potential and share-of-wallet calculations may be performed.

Postcode segmentation Experian and Acxiom are examples of organisations that are capable of creating a profile sketch of the household living at a certain address on the sole basis of the postcode. An indication may be given of:

- The type of house involved: flat, terraced house, semi-detached home, villa, farm; whether it is owned or rented by its inhabitants; what was the construction date; quality of the neighbourhood, etc.
- The location: city or countryside.
- The composition of the household: young or old single person, two-person household, household with children.
- The household income.
- The possible employment situation: who is currently employed in the household, still works or has reached the age of retirement?

The data involve the profile that is measured within a certain postcode area in a number of observations. If a varied profile is encountered within a zone, the reliability of the measurement may decrease. This may be the case in the centres of large cities. By performing additional measurements and applying adjustments in the area zones, an attempt is made to improve the quality.

End value segmentation Obtaining insight into the customer as a person (see top right of Figure 5.3) and not only as a buyer and user, seems to be a challenge that is hard to meet. One market research firm that attempts to provide insight into this field is Motivaction. A tool known as a socioconsult compass is used to measure stable

CRM illustration

Geographic information systems: How does GIS work with internal and external databases?

An example . . . Banks usually maintain a database that is composed of POS (point-of-sale) data obtained from payments, PIN transactions, private label credit cards, CRM applications and postcode information, among other sources. These data are also referred to as internal data sets. Next, sales transactions can be linked to the branch number where the purchase was made, for example. With the aid of GIS software, this information is coded. The customers are also localised, which provides insight into customer profiles and spending patterns, among other things, per branch and on the basis of postcodes and regions (external data sets).

By using geographic information, a marketer may obtain information on the current situation faster and in a more organised manner enabling targeted campaigns to be initiated. A picture of the aspect of time and the yield of each activity may be obtained straight away, which allows the result to be adjusted. Customer profiles may also be linked to external data sets with lifestyle information, for example, and clusters to determine the purchase behaviour of a specific target group on the basis of demography, the so-called search for lookalikes. Every department of a bank or company may learn a great deal about its customers through the use of database queries.

Once the purchase behaviour of customers has been mapped out, their addresses and income levels can be determined. The locations where the highest concentration of customers live must be where a company aims its marketing activities. At the same time, the company may determine how prepared a customer is to drive to a certain branch.

Source: Zoeten (2002).

characteristics that lie at the basis of individual behaviour (see Figure 9.1). The score shown on the compass determines the course someone will follow.

On the basis of the answers from respondents in surveys conducted by Motivaction, a number of segments were identified. These are shown in Figure 9.2.

Recently, a new group was identified: the hedonistic post-materialists. Their social environments differ in terms of the answers they provide to the questions which lie at the basis of the socioconsult compass. Significant differences between the consumption behaviours displayed by the various groups have also been observed. These not only involve magazine and newspaper subscriptions and insurance behaviour, but also the purchase of products such as rice.

The use of external databases

In order to make a decision about whether to rent or purchase an external database, the following aspects must first be considered:

- To what extent may data be used in consumer markets to enrich suppliers' individual customer profiles, helping these companies in their marketing efforts to the individual? Within the framework of the new European Personal Data Protection Act, permission will have to be obtained from the consumer to do this.

Figure 9.1 Socioconsult compass

Source: Motivaction. © Motivation International B.V. 1999 www.motivaction.nl

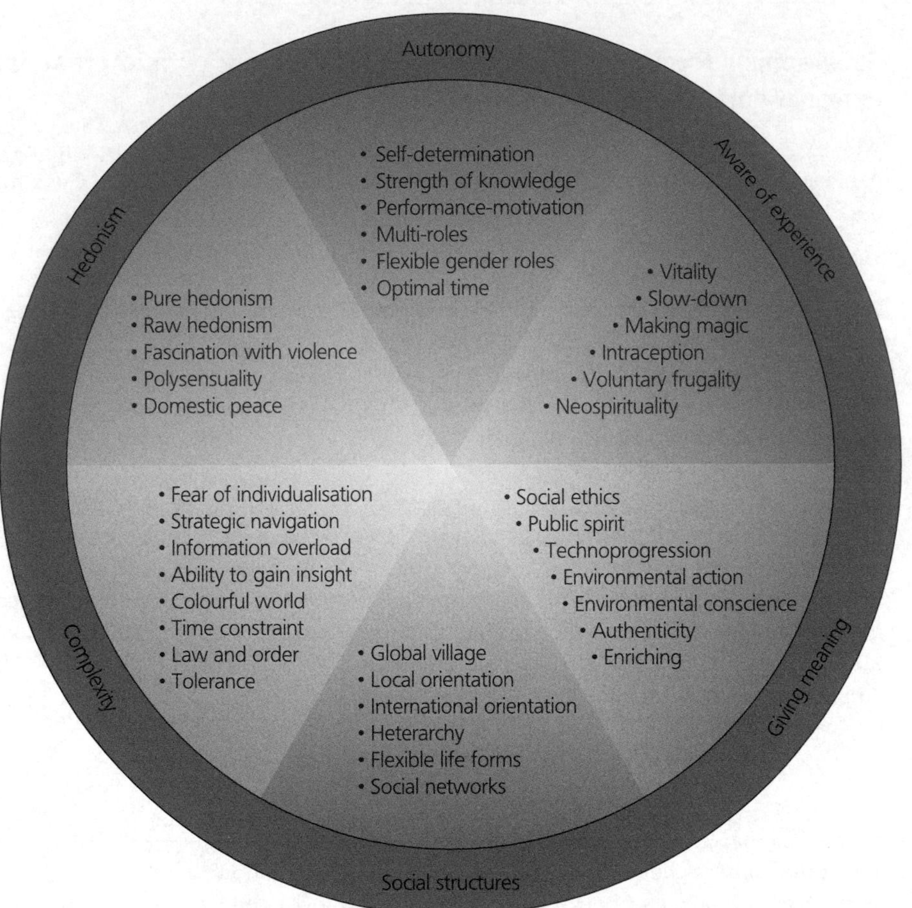

- What is the intrinsic quality of the data involved? In other words, how current, complete, correct and accurate are the data?
- For which persons and companies are the data available? If, for example, the external data are based on a random sampling, there is the chance that these have been gathered for only a (small) portion of the customers. Models will have to be developed in order to estimate how other customers score with regard to the characteristics. It goes without saying that inaccuracies occur as a result.
- To what extent can the databases be linked? Can the identity of the people and organisations be determined unambiguously in both databases so that proper matching is achieved? Postcode databases do not allow unambiguous identification, which can lead to a certain loss of quality.
- What price will be charged for the databases and what conditions are placed on the use or possession of the data?

It is advisable to test the commercial value of these databases in marketing activities. On the basis of the (increase in the) response that is realised as a result of the databases,

Figure 9.2

Social environments in Europe

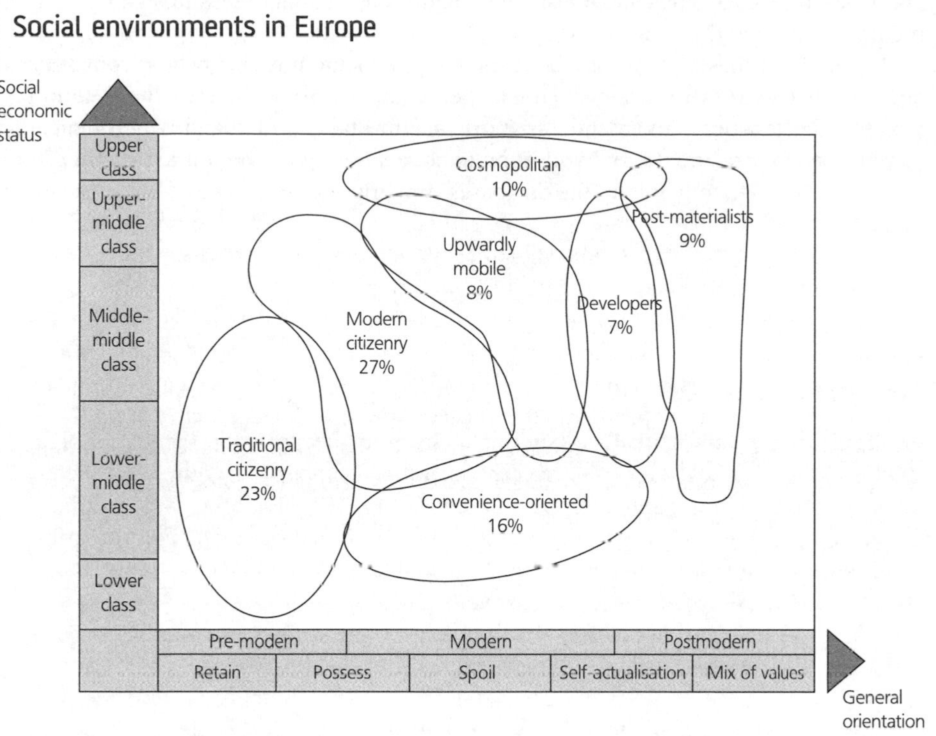

Source: Motivaction. © Motivation International B.V. 1999 www.motivaction.nl

it may be determined whether or not it is worth incurring the expenses that are associated with the use of the external data.

It is worth mentioning that the data from these external databases may also be used in the acquisition of new customers. If the profile for the current customer database is determined on the basis of the external data, then a search may be performed within that database for so-called lookalikes. These are people or organisations that possess the same characteristics, appear in the third party's database, yet are not current customers. Based on their profile, an above-average chance of response to acquisition efforts may be expected.

By combining data, interesting opportunities may present themselves. By relating local data to data on income and ownership, for example, prospects or suspects may be identified. Someone who runs a household alone in the centre of a city in a rented residence and has a high income level will probably spend a great deal on cultural activities (visits to museums and the theatre, etc.).

9.4 Conclusion

The foundation of the customer data is formed by the data which may be used to identify customers. It is the description, expressed in administrative characteristics with which the customers may be picked out in a crowd, as it were. The quality of these data must be controlled: are they current, complete, correct and unique? Various methods and (intelligent) systems can be employed and organisational measures can be implemented to manage the quality.

The relevant master data may be further supplemented by other data from internal and external sources in order to enrich the customer profile. It must be determined which characteristics – fixed and variable – need to be recorded and which indicators can be used to measure these. In addition to concentrating on the initial design, efforts must also be made to maintain the databases properly.

Case study

Optimisation of addresses for EURO 2000

The organisation of the EURO 2000 Football Championship applied strict guidelines during the sale of tickets to the international public. Each individual was allowed to buy only one ticket for him- or herself and one for a guest, and the personal data of both were to be registered. To avoid tickets falling into the hands of hooligans and unofficial traders, EURO 2000 asked Human Inference for assistance.

'Beforehand, we knew people would try to get hold of more than one ticket,' said Jos de Kruif, EURO 2000's ticketing sales manager. The simple de-duplication tool the organisation used to identify those people in the database produced a list of suspicious cases. Customer service, however, kept on facing weird requests.

What EURO 2000 wanted then was first of all a validation and standardisation of the names and addresses in the database. The tickets would be sent to customers shortly before the start of the game. Therefore it was of utmost importance for the personalised tickets to be distributed to the right addresses and the right persons.

Names were set in a standard format with a program named HIquality Name and it was the function of HIquality Name to apply capitals in the proper way. Around 21 000 Dutch and 2600 Belgian names were corrected; 2200 names were rejected because the family name was missing or replaced by a company name. Controlling and standardising the *addresses* was done with the help of HIquality Address. HIquality Address compared the filled-in address with the most similar address in the postcode databases of a specific country. An error margin was incorporated and all prevented addresses with minor differences were printed on a list. For countries without available postcode databases other solutions were invented.

More than 60 per cent of the addresses were standardised in the format the organisation desired. There were numerous reasons for adjusting the addresses – see Table 9.2.

To de-duplicate the database, EURO 2000 applied HIquality Identify. Experience teaches that most fraudulent people only make minor adjustments in their personal data; the system HIquality Identify assesses this similarity between records.

The database with sold tickets contained, before analysis, approximately 400 000 records. The de-duplication exercise produced 9 per cent potential double names and addresses. From the perspective of safety control this is a significant filtering outcome. The same names with different first letters were found many times. First and last names were exchanged or the names were represented with and without the maiden name, apart from their own house number that of a neighbour was used and their own slightly adjusted birth date was given.

To prevent organised fraud, not only individual records were compared but also groups of records. In case person 1 resembles person 4, person 2 matches person 4 and person 5 shows similarities with person 1, the group relations

Table 9.2 Errors during standardisation and validation of names and addresses

Name errors	*Address errors*
Name is not the name of a private person	Address can be standardised, but was abbreviated
Name and sex are conflicting	Alpha section of postcode was incorrect or missing
Two persons having the same name	Foreign address
Part of the name is left out	Incorrect address
Unknown double last name	Incorrect street name
Unclear interpretation which results in different ways of writing a name	Incorrect or missing street number
Family name missing	Industry park
Maiden name was left out; sex unknown	Unique address missing
Unknown element	No unique standardisation possible
	Address does not make sense
	City and postcode do not match

were presented. In this way a street in Reykjavik was identified where several persons together requested 60 tickets.

There were three sources of personal data: the Internet, a data-entry agency and the EURO 2000 office itself. Since all three sources had their own database characters, diacritics were presented in varying ways. After importing the data in an SQL file the ö became a ™ or "" and Å became a ±. Although this complicated data comparison, it turned out that several persons ordered tickets through multiple channels.

Hooligans formed a special risk category during the analysis. The German, English, Belgium and Dutch football associations provided databases with names of hooligans who were no longer allowed to enter a stadium. Fifty hooligans were identified this way. De Kruif: 'to avoid critics afterwards we had to do everything to get these people out of our databases!' Each of these 50 hooligans had ordered one or more tickets and all of them were cancelled.

The resulting data set was used by EURO 2000 for accepting and fulfilling orders. The list with minor errors was processed manually. This also holds for people who potentially ordered more than two tickets for a match. Many of them probably would not have known they were only allowed to book two tickets or made an unintended error. They do not necessarily have to be cheats. EURO 2000 in total refused 1100 orders. In the end, only actual knowledge of those people in Reykjavik can tell you if they acted in bad faith or not. This is also the case for the 48-year-old man from a little village in the country who lives with his 47-year-old brother at the same address . . .'

Source: *Memo* (2000) **13**, 3, September, 3–5.

Questions

1 Identify the data quality issues in this case.

2 How do you evaluate the way EURO 2000 addressed these quality issues?

3 How can you estimate the financial value of (a lack of) data quality in this case?

Questions

1 Why are the data used to identify the customer considered to fall under the infrastructure of a company? What consequences does this have for the manner in which this database is maintained?

2 The quality of the customer data may be approached from a variety of angles. It is said that the intrinsic quality approach offers the most practical pretexts. Can you explain this in more detail?

3 Unjustifiably, efforts to improve the intrinsic data quality are sometimes equated with de-duplication. What is the difference between the two?

4 Which measures would you recommend a company such as a holiday park to use to manage the intrinsic quality of the data which allows it to identify its customers?

5 The experience in direct marketing is that behavioural traits better predict the response to a direct marketing campaign than characteristics which are related to attitudes (including satisfaction), lifestyles and end values. What is your explanation for this? Suggest four reasons.

6 The commercial value (quality from the point of view of the supplier as user) of external lists (name–address–city lists) is usually lower than that of internal lists. What explanation would you offer for this phenomenon?

7 It is a challenge for marketers to construct a customer profile with a minimum of indicators and/or criteria which nonetheless sketch a rich profile.

   (a) Formulate 15 criteria for a company of your choosing with which the customer profile may be developed within the framework of the relationship policy.

   (b) Indicate the source from which these data are likely to be collected.

8 Logfiles with data on clickstreams and Internet behaviour bring new challenges with them. Describe these challenges and indicate how a company may best deal with them.

9 Motivaction is a market research firm that provides data with which the customer may be further profiled as a person, instead of as a buyer and user. Name three advantages and three disadvantages which are associated with these data. Answer the question from the point of view of a company of your choosing.

10 How does the European Personal Data Protection Act influence how external data may be used (see also Chapter 5)?

References

AGB Interact (1995) *De kwaliteit van de tenaamstelling*, AGB Interact, Dongen.

Direct Marketing (2002) Controle-adressen helpen tegen fraude, *Direct Marketing*, **9**, 5.

Garvin, David (1984) What does product quality really mean?, *Sloan Management Review*, January.

Memo (2000) Optimalisatie adressen EURO 2000, *Memo, tijdschrift over de kwaliteit van relatiegegevens*, **13**, 3, September, 3–5.

Mergen, Norbert (2003) Het beste systeem faalt als de kwaliteit van de relatiegegevens niet deugt, de ROI van goede relatiegegevens, *De Kern van uw zaak*, Human Inference.

Peelen, Ed and Norbert Mergen (2003) Klantendata: de resources van de 21ste eeuw, *Customer base*, **9**, Yearbook, 12–15.

Redman, Thomas C. (2001) *Data Quality: The field guide*, Digital Press, Boston.

Zoeten, Frank de (2002) Gebruik van geodata en kaarten maken complexe bedrijfsomgeving inzichtelijk, *Beyond, Mapping, Marketing and Datawarehousing*, September, 11–13.

10

Data analyses and datamining

We have not yet achieved sufficient success in our role as a superior competitor in integrating the explicit customer knowledge obtained from data analyses with the implicit customer knowledge obtained from the human brain of contact persons. In order to improve this situation, the goal of this chapter and this book are to familiarise users of data analyses with:

- the possibilities offered by (statistical and) datamining techniques, so that they learn how to derive the maximum amount of profit from this resource; and
- to initiate them into the analysis process in which a role is set aside for them as well.

Before going into data analysis in depth, Section 10.1 will examine the experiences others have had with data analysis. The analysis process will then be discussed further in Section 10.2. Section 10.3 focuses on datamining, describing current techniques with certain potential from the artificial intelligence sector.

The next two chapters will focus on the application of the techniques involved in the analysis of segmentation (Chapter 11), retention and cross-sell issues (Chapter 12).

In this chapter we will address the following questions

- How may datamining (and statistical) techniques be used to enrich the customer profile?
  - What are the experiences with data analyses?
- How should the analysis process be designed? A thorough formulation of the problem, careful preparation of the analysis question, how the data are prepared in the database for analysis, the analysis itself, the report.
- What is the significance of datamining?
- What are datamining techniques?

Practitioner's insight

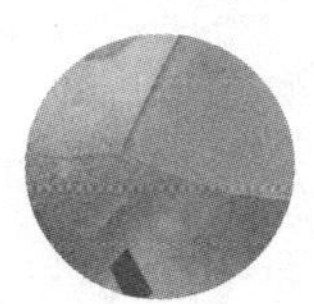

The number of analysis questions a marketer may formulate in the design of his or her marketing policy proves time and again to be inexhaustive. One group of questions relates to the effectiveness of campaigns. Do customers become more price-sensitive if they are regularly enticed by promotions to purchase a product? What is the effect of excessively high communication pressure on the effectiveness of campaigns? What is the effect of the personalisation of the offer?

A second group has to do with making selections: which people will receive a certain offer? Will someone approaching the agent in the call centre be referred by him to another interesting product? To whom should we offer the new product? Can we keep this customer if we set his or her complaint right? Which events taking place in the external or internal environment are the ones that determine that someone has a certain need for the product at a specific time?

It is essential to handle the scarce analysis capacity within companies with care. The most crucial of the questions available from the series must be chosen and used. This requires an active contribution from marketers; they are not only spectators standing on the sidelines, but are party to the formulation of the research questions, the preparation of the analysis and the interpretation and implementation of the results.

10.1 Experiences with data analysis

Many organisations are quite pleased when their operational CRM systems work. One may deduce from this that the expectations with regard to the quality of the data analysis should not be set too high. The focus is on the implementation of the systems; satisfaction reigns once the system is stable and operational. The time is simply not available to set up a data warehouse for marketing objectives. Ideas must still take shape with regard to the analyses to be performed for this purpose and it is only those organisations that have a history with direct marketing or database marketing that have gained the necessary experience with the recording and analysis of customer data. However, every leap forward brings with it disadvantages; data analyses for a transaction-oriented organisation operating in a single-channel environment differ from those for a company with a CRM strategy already in place. It is no longer just the prediction of a response or conversion to an individual mailing or outbound telemarketing campaign that matters. The campaign will have to be looked at within the context of the entire relationship marketing policy. Research is needed into the effects of both incoming as well as outbound communication through different channels on transactions and customer values. More in-depth knowledge of the customer behind the buyer should be developed.

It seems that opportunities to benefit from this increased need for information exist in abundance. The growth in data within many companies is, after all, quite substantial. Data become available via the Internet, call centre, sales information systems, surveys and back-office systems (see Chapter 1 in particular). As the databases grow in size, so do the possibilities for analysis. Using datamining techniques, purposeful, visible connections may be sought between selected variables in an exploratory manner. It is not necessary to indicate beforehand which relationships are expected between which variables. Patterns in data are recognised which are unrecognisable to the naked eye.

Several years ago, datamining seemed to be a magic word. If we no longer have to specify beforehand which relationships are expected between variables, and no demands are placed – such as with a normal distribution – on the application of the techniques, modelling seems to become a simple and not very time-consuming activity. The promise of exposing hidden patterns has caused dollar signs to flash before many an eye.

Reality, however, seems to have caught up with the ideals and dreams. The results achieved with datamining have turned out to be disappointing. In various tests in which datamining was compared with classical statistical techniques, early datamining techniques did not score better than the classical, older yet more trustworthy techniques. In themselves, these first experiences were positive in the 1990s and did not give cause to renounce datamining entirely. On the contrary: it proved that datamining is not as simple as was originally thought. The impression that the data could be entered into the computer without too much bother and that the results would just be there for the taking, appeared to be incorrect. The old maxim 'rubbish in – rubbish out' also appears to hold true with respect to datamining. Careful data management and thorough preparation of the analysis question remain indispensable. Professional experience with the techniques is a condition for turning quality input into quality output. This way, datamining does not have to be implemented in situations in which statistical techniques may also be sufficient and insight and experience with the extensive palette of datamining techniques is desirable in order to obtain good results. Finally, the interpretation of the end results requires a skilled eye.

Over the course of the analysis project, different disciplines make contributions. To leave the entire project in the hands of a data analyst will not lead to the desired results. An optimum degree of teamwork is necessary between the database manager, the data analyst and the marketer. Those who gather the data or use them will have to assist those who enrich them. Language barriers and differences in interests between the three specialists will have to be overcome. The cooperation between them should not be thought of as a waste of time. On the contrary, acting as a team should give them energy and represent a reason to give priority to their collaboration.

10.2 The analysis process

Successful data analysis requires progressing through the different stages in the analysis process in a responsible manner (see Figure 10.1 for a description of the phases which come after the formulation of the problem).

Problem formulation

The first and most important phase involves the formulation of the research question. It has already been indicated in the introduction that an extensive range of questions is

Figure 10.1

Phases in the analysis process

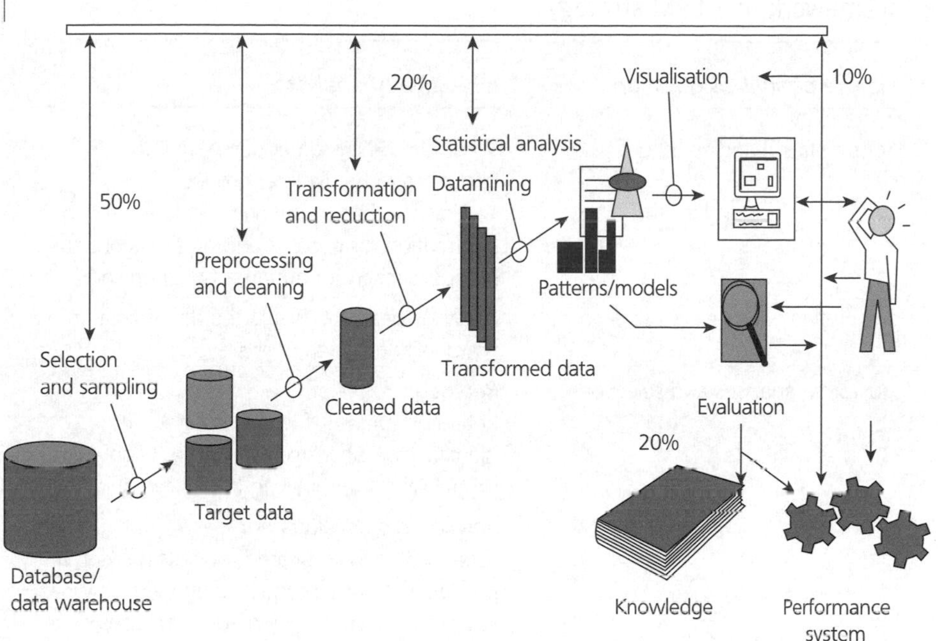

Source: Slisser (2000).

available. Given the fact that the analysis capacity is very limited in many organisations, it is only the essential and feasible questions which should be addressed. It should come as no surprise that a marketer is primarily interested in a model that points out customers at the time that they are going to start familiarising themselves with the market in order to purchase products and services that the company supplies. When is a certain person going to move and thus be 'in the market' for a mortgage? When will the car need to be replaced? Discussion about the relevance of this question is not necessary; however, the feasibility of this analysis problem does deserve attention. Should current data on relevant events such as a move and the maintenance costs of cars become available from external sources, then creating a stable model with high prediction power is promising. Should these data be lacking, creating such a model will become more difficult. It must be determined whether or not the data may still be obtained elsewhere or whether it is wiser to reserve the analysis capacity for other problems.

The types of formulations of questions which are relevant within the CRM strategy framework are summarised in Table 10.1. The ultimate goal of the analysis questions in the first three rows is to make selections from among the organisations and/or people to whom an offer will be made. This is represented by the four main areas of focus which lie at the foundation of the relationship policy, as is illustrated in Figure 8.4 (page 174). In the final row, the effectiveness of the marketing action or campaign is the central theme. Which approach and which lists may be used to encourage prospects to make the most profitable (on a long-term basis) purchases?

In order to arrive at the actual creation of a model, a further description of the question is desirable. An exploratory analysis of the problem area can be enlightening. Descriptive statistical techniques, such as frequency and cross-tables, and the graphic

Table 10.1 Summary of the types of analysis questions within the framework of a CRM strategy

Nature of analysis question	*Objective of analysis*
Segmentation and selections	To divide the customer database into homogeneous customer groups To draw up lists of the name–address–city information for persons and organisations to be approached for a marketing campaign
Acquisition analyses and selections	Analyses geared towards the determination of the quality of different lists
Customer analyses and selections	*Retention* Retention analysis, focused on the early identification of customers with a heightened probability of terminating the relationship *Relationship development* Cross-sell analysis, geared towards offering a product(s) from a product category from which customers have not yet made purchases Deep-selling analysis whose goal is to increase the sales in a certain product category Up-selling analysis by which more premium products are sold
Analyses to determine the effectiveness of the customer approach	Response-analyses of marketing campaigns, databases/lists: which campaigns or databases/lists score the highest?

illustrations derived from these, usually provide helpful solutions. They provide insight into the economic importance of a retention analysis, for example, or provide insight into the turnover and profit share of single customers in proportion to that of customers who have purchased more than one product. The exploration helps in the formulation of the final research question within which framework the dependent variable(s) and independent variables will ultimately have to be defined. It will be determined how, for example, cross-selling and retention are measured and which independent variables must be included in the model (see also Chapter 12).

Preparations

Before performing the final analysis, a random sample may be pulled from the database. The advantage of taking a random sample is that less of the system's storage and analysis capacity is used. The random sampling provides insight into the quality of the intended data. How may data be cleaned up so that erroneous data may be corrected and duplication eliminated? Are metadata available? A simple definition of metadata is structured data about data; metadata ensure consistency in the data, that variables in the database are defined in the same way. For example, when a product is referred to within an organisation, everyone is talking about the same thing.

The way to measure specific features may also be examined. For example, the purchases made by a member of a book club may be quantified in a number of ways. Is the most recent purchase the one that is to be studied, or the total number of orders per year; the amount involved in the last or all of the purchases; the changes in the purchase patterns as compared with a previous period; the purchases made by an individual or the household, etc.? In exploratory analyses, the most relevant variables may be selected. In classifying models, these are the variables that distinguish the best; in other words, they make a distinction between groups. Variables which have the greatest power of prediction are those which are preferred in probabilistic models.

Cases may be collected from the data set with measurements of the relevant variables in order to compile the final analysis database. Particular attention should be paid to the distribution among the scores for the independent variable. A random representative sampling, in which each case has the same probability of being included in the final database, is not automatically the preferred one. In order to be able to model the exit behaviour of customers, for example, a 'substantial number of ex-customers' must be included in the final database. A segmentation analysis also requires representatives from the different segments which are encountered. Stratified random sampling may be chosen to perform this, so that for each stratum or layer (segment), a fixed number of observations are collected at random. In some situations, the final conclusion will be that it is not possible to compile a high quality analysis database. A cross-sell analysis performed on a database of an organisation which had not taken any cross selling initiatives in the past will obviously offer very little to go on. Continuing the analysis process in this case will be pointless.

The final analysis database may be divided up into a training and a validation set. The first training (or validation) set may be used to develop the model. The validation set is used to test the reliability of the developed model. To do this, the data from the validation set are plugged into the model. The outcomes from the model are compared with the actual scores for the independent variable, which are also available in the validation set.

The compilation of the final analysis database is a time-consuming activity and one which can easily occupy half of the total time spent on the complete analysis project. If this preliminary segment must be run through for each selection or effectiveness analysis, a large portion of the analysis capacity would then be 'lost'. There is a great deal to be gained if a final data set can be constructed which may be used for different types of analyses. Financial institutions, for example, have this type of final data set at their disposal which includes some 60 to 100 variables used in the compilation of lists. This aids them in making quick selections of people and organisations which are approached with a certain offering, which may vary from product A through to product Z. In principle, they are capable of responding quickly to the market and providing input to the campaign management system that is responsible for the operational management of the promotions and campaigns (see Chapter 18).

Final analysis using statistical techniques or datamining techniques

There are a variety of techniques available for performing the final analysis. Within the category of statistical as well as datamining techniques, there are many alternatives available. They vary from regression, cluster and discriminant analyses to neural networks, genetic algorithms, decision trees and case-based reasoning. Different variations exist for each of the techniques separately. Experience and insight into the techniques is desirable in order to arrive at a reasoned choice and application of this choice.

The most experience has been gained using statistical techniques. Insight exists regarding their reliability and applicability. Their disadvantage is that the dependent and independent variables must be specified beforehand as well as the relationships between them. Linear relationships and an independent result variable such as the response or the segment are usually assumed. Additionally, various techniques assume a certain distribution among the scores for the variables. Skewed distributions with many non-respondents and few respondents may hinder the application of these types of techniques, or require a (logistical) calculation of the raw data materials. In situations in which it is possible to satisfy these conditions, the statistical techniques are still preferable to datamining techniques.

Datamining techniques may prove their worth in situations in which:

- it is not known beforehand what relationships exist between the variables;
- non-linear relationships exist between the variables.

Section 10.3 discusses several of these techniques in more detail.

Visualisation

The final step in the analysis process involves the reporting and visualisation of the outcomes. Setting aside time for this last step in the project requires discipline, but is definitely rewarding. After all, research outcomes that are not easy to communicate will never be accepted by management. The outcomes of some datamining techniques, such as neural networks, provide very little insight. It is those results that must be visualised. Simple figures must specify what the effect changes in several relevant variables have on the ultimate dependent variable. What is the effect on the response of lowering the introductory price, for example? What is the effect on the response of expanding the mailing list by an extra 10 per cent of the prospects from the data set?

10.3 Datamining

The increase in the quantity of data and the decrease in the available analysis time have led to a growing need for an inductive method which will assist in finding useful relationships between (selected) data. Datamining is just such a method. Narrowly defined, datamining is 'the automated discovery of interesting, non-obvious patterns hidden in a database that have a high potential for contributing to the bottom line' (Peacock, 1998). Those relationships which exercise influence on the strategy and operations of the organisation and are ultimately capable of contributing to the realisation of their objectives are interesting ones. In datamining, one makes use primarily of so-called machine learning and adaptive techniques which require less involvement from people than do static techniques. The origin of many of these techniques lies in artificial intelligence. These include neural networks, association rules, evolutionary computation and decision trees. The box below contains a description of the techniques.

Datamining techniques

Neural networks

Artificial neural networks attempt to imitate biological neural systems. These biological systems consist of neurons simply linked closely together. If a neuron receives a number of stimuli and the sum of these stimulations exceeds a certain threshold value, the neuron fires off a stimulus to the connected neurons. These neurons will in turn supply input to other neurons so that a network is created consisting of several layers of interconnected neurons. For example, if a person places his hand on a hot furnace, he will receive many stimuli that exceed these threshold values and fire off stimuli to the related neurons. Pain is felt, the hand is removed, an exclamation of pain is expressed, and so forth.

The simplest artificial neural network is characterised by one input and one output layer. However, it is possible to apply additional layers. The layers between the input and the output are referred to as hidden levels; unlike the input and output layers, there are no values given from which the scores of these intermediate neurons or nodes may be derived.

In order to determine the final model, the weights and values of the nodes at the hidden levels will have to be calculated. This occurs during the training of the model. During the training or learning, the weights in the model will be adjusted so that the input values correspond with the desired output values. In an iterative process, which is executed entirely by the 'machine', or which is performed under human supervision, a model is formulated that fits. Different methods are available to run through this adaptive exercise. This adaptive nature of neural networks is one of the advantages of datamining techniques. When statistical techniques are used and the outcomes are unsatisfactory, a new model will have to be developed; a neural network model adjusts itself. Another advantage of neural networks is that no knowledge is required beforehand of the expected relationships between variables.

Evolutionary computation

Evolutionary computation (EC) is a collection of algorithms based on biological evolutionary processes: how do people and animals choose a partner, reproduce, evolve and increase their chances of survival (survival of the fittest)? EC is really optimisation program routines, guided by the principles of natural evolution. They are search procedures based on the concepts of natural selection and genetics. EC is used for the optimisation, prediction, classification and design of decision rules. For an electronic retailer, for example, EC represents a technology for optimising the design and arrangement of how its website positions and communicates with visitors. ►

The algorithms are particularly useful in the analysis of problems into which very little insight may be gained. As long as the number of variables and the size of the data collection remain limited, the analyses may be relatively easily performed on a PC, although the expertise of an analyst may be necessary in order to obtain an appropriate model final.

Association rules

With association rules, pronouncements may be made on the relationships between the characteristics of a group of known individuals and one or more aspects of their behaviour. An example of a rule is: household with three or more people, living within a five-minute walking range of the store are frequent customers of the store. Normally, data are provided as support for the validity of the rule. Rules can be helpful in cross-sell analyses (see Chapter 13).

One reason why rules are popular is that each rule seems to represent an independent insight into the database. New rules can be added to an existing rule set without disturbing existing ones already there.

Decision trees

Decision trees are popular in many areas of marketing and can also be used to analyse web-based data. The advantages of decision trees are found in their ability to generate understandable business rules. Decision trees split a database into classes that differ as much as possible in their relation to a selected output. They indicate, for instance, what the probability is that a household will terminate the relationship if no transactions have taken place for six months and the household's income falls within the range from A to B. See, for example, CHAID and CART in Chapter 13.

Case-based reasoning

With case-based reasoning, a new problem situation is sought among previously occurring cases with similar characteristics with a positive or beneficial outcome. Case-based reasoning maintains an institutional memory of prior problems so that when a new one comes in, old solutions are retrieved and matched to answer similar new problems. It is a simple, yet powerful method of indexing, which is more akin to remembering than to learning. To determine the location for a new store, successful stores will be sought along with the characteristics of their location. The decor, composition of the product range, service, pricing and promotion of these stores will all be adopted by the new store. The basic concept is that of association.

The advantage of case-based reasoning is that abstract concepts may be made concrete. The method is intuitive and simple for managers to understand. Additionally, it may work with qualitative and discontinuous variables, and the calculations it makes are simple. One disadvantage may be that the outcomes are based on the past, when an optimal solution for the problem had not yet been found.

Source: Peacock (1998); Venugopal and Baets (1994); Mena (1999).

In addition to the narrow definition of datamining given above, broader descriptions are also found in the literature (Peacock, 1998). As well as exploration, various broad descriptions include the confirmation and testing of relationships found among datamining techniques. Classical and Bayesian statistical techniques may be used here as well. In the broadest sense of the word, datamining is described as the discovery of knowledge in databases (Peacock, 1998).

Several datamining tools have been introduced on the market by, for example, SAS (Enterprise Minter), SPSS (Clementine), MATLAB, etc. Each one has different options, and some are built for specific applications and as a result prices vary greatly. An overview can be found on www.softwaremag.com. Although the tools assist the user through all steps of the data analysis, their application requires familiarity with the techniques. They guide the user through the data preparation phase, the sampling (training and validation sets), the modelling and the presentation of the results, but . . . 'It is not a magic box into which raw customer data can be fed and out comes the solution' (Drozdenko and Drake, 2002).

Neural networks are a popular technique within datamining. The results that are achieved with them within CRM are not all positive, however. Zahavi and Levin did not achieve encouraging results in 1997, having arrived at similar outcomes using a logistical regression model. Bejou, Wray and Ingram (1996), on the other hand, did encounter positive results in a study on the influence of sales representatives on the quality of the customer–supplier relationship. The same applies to the DMSA which commissioned an exploratory study on adaptive techniques in 1997. The evaluation on the use of neural networks in selections and target group definitions was positive. In their summary article in which they compare neural networks with statistical techniques, Venugopal and Baets (1994) cite various studies in which the superior performance of neural networks is demonstrated. When compared with static techniques, the best results are achieved when non-linear relationships occur between variables. Moreover, neural networks appear to be benefited by the occurrence of multicollinearity, if more than one dependent variable is present or if there are many missing values. The quality of the solution is also heavily dependent on the data preparation and the analyst's knowledge of the different models. The degree of insight provided by the ultimate solution may qualify as another disadvantage of neural networks. Usually, supplementary sensitivity analyses are desirable in order to be able to gain insight into the important relationships between the input and output variables.

10.4 Conclusion

One of the challenges presented by CRM is to make the implicit customer knowledge found in the minds of the contact persons explicit, so that it may be recorded, distributed and used for a larger group of customers. The current experiences with data analysis are still somewhat pathetic. The datamining techniques which have been launched have not yet produced the kinds of results which were originally expected of them, and statistical techniques are laborious, place many demands on the data material and cannot handle all of the issues. On the other hand, it is encouraging that a portion of the results achieved may be explained as being a result of the unskilled and careless use of the techniques. If the data analyst, database manager and the marketer, acting in a constructive collaborative group, carefully run through the analysis process, some of the potential disappointment may be avoided. The topic may be formulated properly, the final data set may be compiled in a well thought-out way, there are suitable and advanced techniques which may be employed, and the outcomes may be clearly reported. The analysis contributes to the expansion of the explicit knowledge about customers and the knowledge may be capitalised upon in the relationship policy.

Case study

FT

Reaping the benefits of customer insight

During the late 1990s, companies invested millions in customer relationship management (CRM) systems such as sales force automation, campaign management and call centre systems. Given the importance to any business of establishing and building relationships with customers, this is not surprising. But despite this rush, many companies have been disappointed by the low return on investment from CRM. Being able to handle more calls per agent or run more marketing campaigns has been of limited value.

The real returns come when *business intelligence software* is used to drive these operational systems. This software opens up opportunities such as up- or cross-selling in the call centre, targeting campaigns at specific customer segments and increasing the relevance of the offer made and its value to the customer, thereby increasing response rates.

The ultimate aim is to combine CRM with business intelligence to produce a 'closed loop' system in which business intelligence analyses customer behaviour and produces a list of targets for a specific product or service. The campaign is managed using the CRM software and the business intelligence systems then assess the results to produce a more refined campaign.

However, few organisations have reached this level of sophistication. As Colin Shearer, vice-president of customer analytics at SPSS, a supplier of predictive analytics software, says: 'Most companies have always dealt with their customers en masse.'

According to Mr Shearer, business intelligence software is ideal for assessing the profitability of individual customers by matching the cost of serving each one against the revenue he or she generates. The organisation can then develop marketing campaigns that target its more profitable customers. At the same time, unprofitable customers can be diverted towards lower cost channels, such as automated voice systems or a website.

'You need to identify the small percentage of very high-value customers that are generating 80 to 90 per cent of value in the company,' he says. 'You are also interested in the trends, such as customers who are dropping out of the top to become less valuable and take their business elsewhere.'

The final stage of the process is to use data mining software to predict how individual customers behave. This software uses advanced mathematical algorithms to reveal hidden patterns and relationships in sales data. The results can be used in a number of ways: to group customers into different segments according to similar behaviour and characteristics; to determine which products or services a customer is likely to buy; to identify which customers are most likely to defect to another company; or to assess how much of a credit risk a potential customer poses.

David Bradshaw, a senior analyst at Ovum, explains that such assessments once required advanced mathematical knowledge to build and run data mining models. 'You still need people with expertise to set up the business intelligence system,' he says, 'but business users are increasingly being trained to build, analyse and exploit segments. You are "handing over the toys" to the business people to do the analysis themselves.'

Vodafone, the mobile network operator, has a single contact number for its call centre and routes each caller to the appropriate team of agents for his or her segment. According to Julian Moss, UK development manager: 'Business intelligence enables our touch points to target the right groups of customers, to understand them and to have a close relationship with them.'

Spaarbeleg, a Dutch subsidiary of Aegon, the life insurer, has a growth strategy based on expanding sales to its existing customer base, rather than on acquiring new clients. It uses SPSS real-time predictive software to suggest cross-sell opportunities to agents in its inbound call centre, which handles 1m calls a year from 1.6m customers. To avoid pestering them, its agents gathered enough information in just 180 000 calls to develop a targeted recommendation. In a third of these calls, the agent determined that the customer was receptive enough to make the offer and of these, a further 22 000 were converted into sales worth €30m.

Business intelligence reporting is also ideal for managing performance in contact centres. It can help set and track targets and spot trends, and it can provide management dashboards that display key performance indicators, such as how many calls agents are handling and how many are closed within agreed service levels. The use of business intelligence is becoming increasingly important in the face of new legislation introduced to guard against unwanted e-mail and to allow individuals to bar cold telephone calling. Mr Shearer points out that with fewer opportunities for outbound marketing, organisations must take advantage of cross-selling at service call centres.

As Mr Bradshaw explains: 'You may only have one chance of approaching a customer. This is pushing people into micro-segmentation of their customers. Rather than having five or six major segments, they may have many thousands, each with 100 to 1000 customers. You analyse the behaviour of the micro-segments so that you know what they want to buy, how they want to buy it and how to approach them.' 'The problem with the business intelligence vendors', he adds, 'is that they have targeted the technical experts. They haven't yet really got to the point where business people are able to use their marketing analytics. They are trying to do better, but [the CRM vendors, such as Unica Corporation, Siebel and E.piphany] have targeted people who actually do the marketing.'

It is clear that business intelligence is needed to drive CRM activities. However, the trick is to create a closed loop system that combines customer profitability with data mining. Only then will an organisation be able to concentrate on giving profitable customers the best and most relevant products and services.

Source: Rod Newing, FT.com site (8 June 2004).

Questions

1 What is the difference between business intelligence (BI) and (analytical) CRM?

2 Do you agree with the following statement in the text: 'The ultimate aim is to combine CRM with business intelligence'? Give detailed arguments why you do or do not agree.

Questions

1 The traditional shopkeeper who still maintains personal contact with his customers is considered to have more (implicit) knowledge of his customers than the CRM manager with expensive software and databases at his disposal.

(a) Do you agree with this statement? Substantiate your answer.

(b) In what areas does the (implicit) customer knowledge fall short? Give an explanation.

(c) Why is it that the CRM manager appears to lag behind the classic shopkeeper?

2 How may the collaboration between data analysts, database managers (in so far as these do not also take on the task of analysis themselves), and marketers be improved? Suggest a number of creative measures.
3 Name four typical analysis topics within the framework of the CRM policy to be implemented.
4 Describe the analysis process involved in the setting up of a retention analysis.
5 Which phases in the analysis process in particular require the marketer's contribution?
6 Indicate in which way a tour operator may measure the booking behaviour of its customers.
7 What is the purpose of the distinction made between a training and a validation set?
8 What is the difference between statistical and datamining techniques? When may the latter be advantageous?
9 Explain how neural networks work.
10 Which limitations will the marketer continue to run into, even in an organisation with professional analysis capacity, in the expansion of the customer knowledge through data analysis? Explain your answer.

References

Bejou, David, Barry Wray and Thomas N. Ingram (1996) Determinants of relationship quality: an artifical neural network analysis, *Journal of Business Research*, **36**, 137–143.

Drozdenko, Ronald G. and Perry D. Drake (2002) *Optimal Database Marketing: Strategy, development and data mining*, Sage Publications, Thousand Oaks, California.

Eiben, G., F. Slisser, E. Peelen, *et al.* (1995), Modeling customer satisfaction in the market for mutual funds investment companies with neural networks and genetic programming, *Proceedings ESOMAR Conference*, The Hague, 17–20 September.

Mena, Jesus (1999) *Data Mining Your Website*, Digital Press, Boston.

Peacock, Peter R. (1998) Data mining in marketing: part 1, *Marketing Management*, **6**, 4, Winter, 1–14.

Slisser, Frank (2000) *Data Mining*, Visor, Almere.

Venugopal, V. and W. Baets (1994) Neural networks and statistical techniques in marketing research: a conceptual comparison, *Marketing Intelligence and Planning*, **12**, 7, 30–38.

Zahavi, Jacob and Nissan Levin (1997) Applying neural computing to target marketing, *Journal of Direct Marketing*, **11**, 4, Autumn, 76–92.

11

Segmentation and selections

Segmentation is the dividing up of customers into various, distinct homogeneous groups for whom it can be desirable to approach in a specific way. Those within the group react in the same manner to marketing stimuli provided by the supplier. Customers within a segment have communication or purchasing behaviour and/or needs and wants in common. Differences exist between the groups.

In this chapter, we will first discuss the strategic aspects of segmentation (Section 11.1). We will then look briefly at how we can divide the market into segments, how we can describe the customers in the segments, and how the research outcomes may be used in the strategic marketing policy. Segmenting not only has strategic objectives however; it also plays a role in the selection of people and organisations that we would like to approach with a certain marketing campaign. Section 11.2 will study these tactical segmentation analyses in more depth. The topic of *selection* will also be examined: who will be approached in which segment during a marketing campaign?

In this chapter we will address the following questions

- How can we define segmentation?
- What are segmentation criteria?
- Segmentation for the benefit of strategic marketing issues:
  - How to divide the market into segments.
  - How to profile the segments.
  - How to develop the marketing service concepts per (group of) segment(s).
- Segmentation for the benefit of tactical marketing issues: the selection of people and organisations for marketing campaigns:
  - How to divide the market into segments using the RFM technique, CHAID and CART.
  - How to make selections on the basis of response gain charts.
- What are the research techniques?

Practitioner's insight

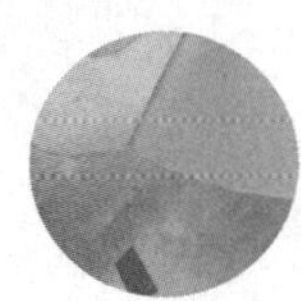

Every customer is unique. Although one-to-one marketing does justice to this fact, for many, the concept is not (yet) realisable. On many fronts, organisations seem to be experiencing problems in approaching each customer separately.[1] The reasons for this are that the capacity and customer insight necessary to do this are lacking, and the benefits do not appear to be able to justify the costs. The result is that companies must fall back on segmentation which distinguishes between groups of homogeneous customers. The organisation must decide how many and which groups to identify, and how to get to know them and whether to approach them with a standard or customised offering.

11.1 Segmentation study as input for the formulation of the marketing strategy

Segmentation criteria

Segmentation criteria are used to divide up the market. These are the indicators used as the basis to identify or assign the groups. It is important to note that the customer groups have not yet been profiled at this point; they may not yet be described as buyer, user and individual or organisation (see Chapter 5).

In consumer markets, the following are used as criteria (for example, by Kotler, 2003):

- Geographical characteristics, such as postcode.
- Demographic characteristics, such as age or sex.
- Socio-economic data such as income, social class or education.
- Behaviour, such as purchase or communication behaviour.
- Psychographic characteristics such as lifestyle and the set of norms and values.
- Buying motives and purchase considerations.

The work of Bonoma and Shapiro (1983) has gained a considerable amount of notoriety in business-to-business markets. The authors distinguish five categories of segmentation criteria:

- Demographic factors, including industrial classification, company size and location.
- Operating variables, such as technology, user status, customer capabilities, which indicate whether a customer requires a great deal of or very little support.

[1] With the exception of situations in which personal account management is applied, as this is justified by the customer's spending level.

- Purchasing approaches, which describe how purchasing is organised, the dominant position within a company, the nature of the relationships that are maintained with suppliers and the purchasing criteria and conditions.
- Situational factors which involve the urgency, the specific application and the order size.
- Personal characteristics: what are the values and norms of the employees working for the prospect or customer, what is their risk attitude and how loyal are they in general?

At the top of this list are the criteria that describe the exterior of the market; this involves data which may be easily obtained. The further down the list we travel, the more we zoom in on the interior of organisations, until finally we reach the last level and the people with whom we come into contact within the organisation.

Bruhn (2003) supplemented these criteria within the framework of relationship marketing. He makes a distinction between the normal segmentation criteria mentioned above, which he characterises as exogenous, and endogenous criteria such as customer value, customer satisfaction, recommendation behaviour, and the likelihood of retaining the customer. The organisation is incapable of exercising influence on the first category through the use of policy, yet is capable of this with the second category. It is capable of influencing customer satisfaction, for instance.

Segmentation technique

Markets may be segmented in a large number of ways. Choices must be made regarding the number and the specific segmentation criteria to be used. Do we divide the market according to age categories, light and heavy users, etc.? If we list all of the possibilities, it quickly appears that the number of alternative ways in which a market may be categorised is, or at least seems to be, infinite.

The guidelines which must be satisfied by workable and good segmentation solutions offer the only solid ground we have to go on in this segmentation process and are (Kotler, 2003):

- Measurability: the size, purchasing power and characteristics of the segment can be measured.
- Substantial: the segments are large and profitable enough to serve. A segment should be the largest possible homogeneous group worth going after with a tailored marketing programme.
- Accessibility: the segments (and individual prospects and customers) can be reached and served effectively.
- Differentiable: the segments are conceptually distinguishable and respond differently to different marketing stimuli.
- Actionable: effective programmes can be formulated for attracting and serving the segments.

In addition, a segmentation solution is bound by the requirement that it be stable; there are few changes that occur within the category over time. The migration of customers from one segment to another is limited.

Figure 11.1

Cluster solution

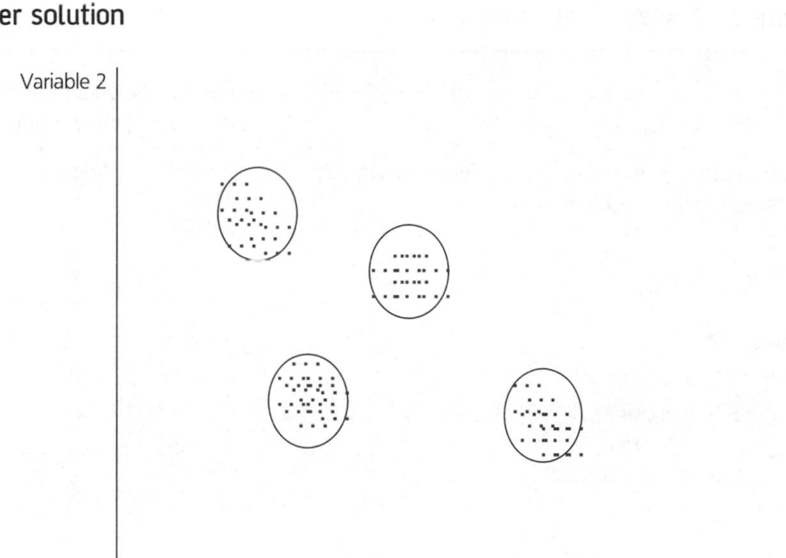

In spite of these guidelines, there are still numerous segmentation solutions possible. Within the framework of dividing the market up into segments and choosing the target groups which the supplier would like to service with a specific offering, there are various methods and techniques which have been developed and which may be of assistance. Cluster and discriminant analyses are often used in market research.

Cluster and discriminant analyses complement one another during the segmentation process. The goal of cluster analysis is to classify subjects as customers in relatively homogeneous groups, or clusters. Each customer may be placed in only one group, and there is no overlap between the clusters. The first and probably most important step in a cluster analysis is the determination of the segmentation variables. Insight is required into which variables may function as such. Figure 11.1 illustrates a cluster solution with two segmentation variables.

There are various methods available to assign the subjects to the groups. The most common is the K-means cluster analysis in which the researcher specifies the number of groups to be distinguished beforehand. Imagine that a solution using two segments must be formulated in advance. By identifying additional segments, the conditions of substantiability and actionability would no longer be satisfied. The computer will then draw two observations from the data set, completely at random, in which the first represents group A and the second group B. Next, the subsequent objects will be assigned to the group which is 'closest' to them in terms of distance. After this initial cluster solution has been formulated, an iterative process begins. The average scores for the segmentation criteria are calculated for the two groups. A new group classification is then formed on the basis of the cluster averages, and objects are allocated to the clusters for which the distance to the cluster average is the smallest. Should a new round fail to show signs of a solution or an improved solution, then the procedure stops.

The determination of the number of segments to be distinguished is arbitrary. Suspicions regarding the number of clusters and requirements for the minimum segment

Table 11.1 Classification results

Group membership (according to cluster analysis)	*Number of cases*	*Predicted group membership (with discriminant analysis)*	
		Segment A	*Segment B*
Segment A	108	85 78.7%	23 21.3%
Segment B	90	25 27.8%	65 72.2%
Percentage of correctly classified cases: 75.76%			

Source: Drozdenko and Drake (2002).

size can offer something to go on. Expectations regarding the solution can also provide guidance. In general, the recommendation is to condense the analyses for a different number of clusters. The solution that appeals most intuitively is usually the best one. Several cluster techniques more advanced than the K-means analysis have been developed which also offer a solution to this problem.

Performing a K-means cluster analysis requires the researcher to make (arbitrary) decisions. For this reason, outcomes should be treated with caution. In order to test the solution, different methods may be used. The data set may be split in two and a cluster solution may be calculated for each half, for example. If there are few differences between both solutions, then this is a sign that the outcome is reliable.

A discriminant analysis can also offer a good means of testing the cluster solution. This is a more solid technique. Executing the technique requires advance knowledge of the groups to which the individual subjects belong. It must be known beforehand whether the customer may be included in segment *a*, *b*, . . . , *n*. In addition, the scores for the (segmentation) variables form the input. The discriminant analysis is then used to develop a model used to allocate the observations to the classes. If, using the model, the customers are assigned to the groups in the same way as this occurred with the cluster analysis, then the solution may be considered reliable. A table such as that shown in Table 11.1 may be drawn up in order to gain further insight into the similarities in classification. For further information on cluster and discriminant analyses, the reader is referred to Malhotra and Birks (2003).

Profiling a segment

Easily obtainable variables which produce reliable measurements and do not vary much are used to identify the customer in the segmentation process. They only provide a limited insight into the customer as buyer, user and as organisation or person. As such, further profiling may be desirable for the realisation of a CRM strategy.

External and internal sources can supply data to enrich the profile (see Chapter 9). Postcodes, the profile of the household, the geographical environment, income and social class are all expanded upon. Outcomes from questionnaires, involving the values, needs, satisfaction and buying intentions, for example, can also help. Where these types of profiling data are not available for everyone in the database, extrapolation becomes more challenging. Is there a characteristic known for everyone in the database that correlates with the specified profiles so that the profile may also be determined for customers for whom these data are not directly available?

Qualitative research can also result in enrichment, considering the fact that it provides a great deal of insight in general terms. Many data become available from an individual respondent regarding buying behaviour, buying motives, use of services, perception of the relationship with the supplier, etc. The disadvantage is that the size of the random sample is limited and that no pronouncements may be made regarding the degree to which certain patterns will occur in the population. No concrete statements may be made on the number of people or organisations that satisfy a certain profile. It is nonetheless a challenge to attempt to make a link between these data and the quantitative market research and database data (see the example in Chapter 5 on customer knowledge).

Developing marketing service concepts for each segment

Segmentation is a research process that aids in the formulation of the marketing strategy. The goal of segmentation is to approach customer groups in a differentiated manner so that they will become more satisfied and loyal and will spend more with the supplier. Within the scope of CRM, this is referred to as designing marketing service concepts for each segment (see Chapter 8). The product range, the service, the price and the communication are determined for each of the distinct (combinations of) customer groups. Times and events are determined which offer the best opportunities to make contact to provide feedback, take advantage of cross-sell possibilities and provide service. A service concept can gain in quality if the segmentation research provides clear insight into the customer profile: who is the person or organisation behind the buyer and what motivates them?

11.2 Segmentation research used in compiling the list

The objective of tactical segmentation research is to provide input for the selection question: who do we want to approach for a certain marketing campaign activity?

Three techniques used in direct marketing have gained a great deal of notoriety. The most classic of these is the RFM, or the Recency Frequency Monetary Value, method. More recent and popular within this same sub-discipline of marketing are CHAID and CART. Each of these techniques will be discussed in the next two sub-sections. Then we will focus on the ultimate list compilation: which segments will be approached?

RFM

Direct marketers have the most positive experiences with behavioural segmentation. Behaviour observed in the past appears to be a better predictor of future behaviour than pronouncements made by customers regarding their purchasing intentions and attitudes (Spiller and Baier, 2005). Reasoning and plans seem to be less reliable than historical behaviour in estimating the likelihood of response to a specific marketing campaign at a certain time.

It has also been shown that customers who spend the most during a certain period do not necessarily have the highest likelihood of responding to a new marketing campaign. For this reason, the Recency Frequency Monetary Value model was developed to identify the most attractive prospects. By focusing on the frequency and the most recent transaction date in addition to the annual amount spent, better selections may be made and higher response percentages can be achieved. In the RFM model, an index is calculated on the basis of scores customers receive for three aspects. The determination of the score model is left more or less open:

- The last purchase date: a score of 20 will be assigned, for example, if the last transaction occurred less than three months ago; if the last purchase took place between three and six months ago, the score is 10; if the transaction was made between six and nine months ago, the score is 3; and if it has been more than twelve months since a purchase was made, then the score is 1.
- The purchase frequency: the score for the purchase frequency might be calculated by multiplying the number of purchases made in the last two to four years by four; a maximum score of 20 may be set, for example.
- The amount spent: the score may be equal to 10 per cent of the sum of the purchase amounts from the last two years, with a maximum of 20 for instance.

In order to calculate the index value, the separate scores must be weighted for their importance. The recency is usually the most important and the monetary value the least important. The weights assigned may be 5 for the last purchase date, 3 for the frequency and 2 for the amount spent. The calculation of the RFM score is illustrated in Table 11.2. Apart from the RFM points that are scored with individual transactions, the cumulative RFM score is presented which the customer obtains with all of the purchases he or she makes in a year.

The RFM approach has advantages and disadvantages. The advantages have already been discussed. First, behaviour from the past is an accurate predictor of the response to marketing campaigns. In addition, the technique employs data that are maintained in the most basic of databases, namely transaction data. The disadvantage is that time and again, the 'best buyers' are selected for a promotion, thus creating the risk that these individuals will experience an excessive 'mail' pressure. The strong transaction orientation that lies at the basis of the technique is to blame for this.

Table 11.2 RFM calculation

Customer	*Purchase*	*Recency*	*Recency score*	*Weighted score*	*Frequency*	*Frequency score*	*Weighted score*	*Monetary value*	*Monetary score*	*Weighted score*	*Total weighted score*	*Cumulative score*
A	#1	2 months	20	100	3	4	12	$30	3	6	118	118
A	#2	8 months	5	25	3	4	12	$100	10	20	57	175
A	#3	13 months	1	5	3	4	12	$50	5	10	27	202
B	#1	12 months	3	15	2	8	24	$500	20	40	79	79

Given

Recency score: 20 points if the last purchase was made less than 3 months ago
10 points if the last purchase was made between 3 and 6 months ago
5 points if the last purchase was made between 6 and 9 months ago
3 points if the last purchase was made between 9 and 12 months ago
1 point if the last purchase was made more than 12 months ago

Frequency score: The number of purchases made in the last 24 months multiplied by 4 points (maximum: 20 points)

Monetary value: Gross amount spent in the past 24 months × 10% (maximum: 20 points)

Weights: Recency = 5; frequency = 3; monetary = 2

Source: Baier (1983). Reproduced with permission of the McGraw-Hill Companies.

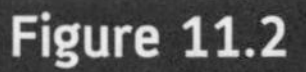
Figure 11.2 CHAID analysis

Source: Peelen (2002).

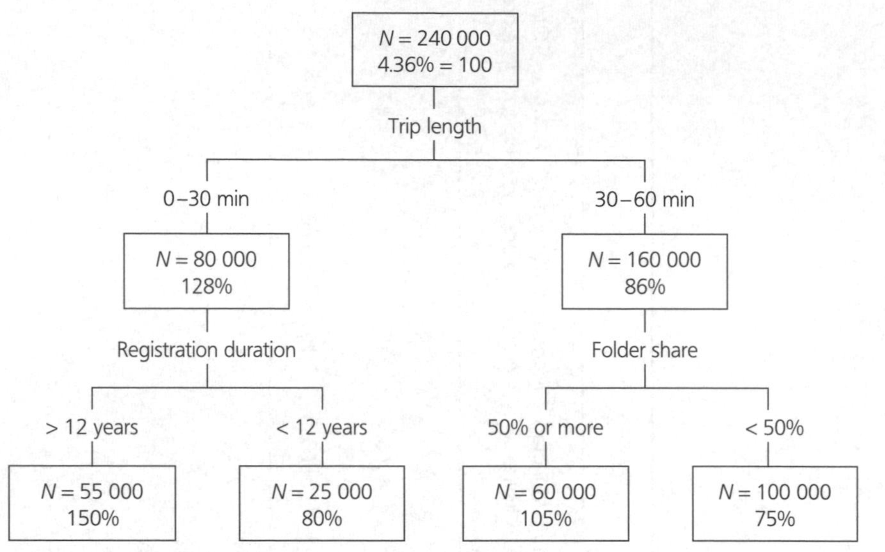

CHAID and CART

CHAID

CHAID stands for Chi-squared Automated Interaction Detection. A CHAID analysis produces a tree diagram, such as that shown in Figure 11.2. At the top of the diagram, the response to the marketing campaign(s) is shown for the entire customer database. The organisation here has 240 000 customers of which an average of 4.36 per cent responds to a marketing campaign activity (Peelen, 2002). On the level below this, these customers are split according to the most discriminating significant segmentation criterion. In this example, this appears to be the travel time from the customer to the service provider; the better customers – 80 000 in number – live closer than those who tend to produce less of a response. Customers who do not have to travel more than 30 minutes respond 1.28 times better to marketing campaigns than the average customer in the database. On the level below this one, the next most distinctive segmentation is illustrated for the *separate* segments. Customers with a short travel time may best be divided up according to length of membership, and customers with a longer travel time according to 'folder share' (which indicates which portion of the products purchased had appeared in the folder). Striking is the fact that in the less attractive segments on the first level, there are still identifiable sub-segments which nonetheless produce an above-average response to marketing campaign(s). An index of 105 is encountered.

A CHAID analysis creates a categorisation within each group until further significant division is no longer possible. If a marketer is capable of choosing from a large number of different segmentation variables, the decision tree can be quite sizeable.

The software is normally unable to process more than 40 variables, with a maximum of 15 classes per variable.

CHAID can lead to better results than an RFM analysis. The response to a marketing campaign that is obtained from the best 25–50 per cent of the respondents from the database, according to CHAID, may be higher than the response from the best 25–50 per cent indicated by RFM (Magidson, 1988).

CART

CART, or Classification and Regression Trees, is a technique that is often compared with CHAID (Thrasher, 1991). Unlike CHAID, CART is not characterised by limitations for the number of variables and classes to be included. With CART, a binary decision tree is constructed (repeatedly with two branches). In order to construct this, CART first splits the data set into two groups for each variable; segment *A* is separated from segment *B*. Next, the segmentation variables are examined to determine which of these best splits the group in two; this is the sub-division which is applied to the second level of the decision tree (see Figure 11.3). After that, segments *A* and *B* are further divided up *separately* on the level under this according to the same logic. The lowest level in the decision tree is reached if a further division is no longer useful because the size of the segments has become too small.

Unlike CHAID, CART is capable of working with a ratio scale. With CHAID, variables which are measured on a ratio scale will be returned to an interval scale (with

Figure 11.3 CART analysis

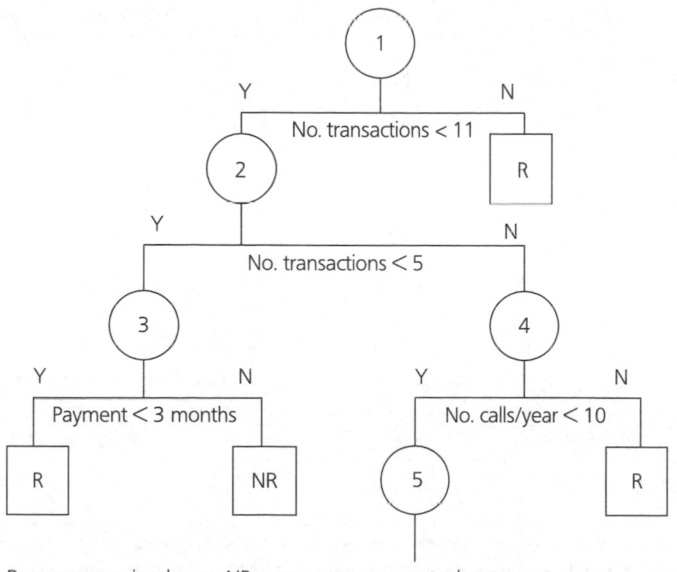

Source: Thrasher (1991). © 1991 John Wiley & Sons, Inc. This material is used by permission of John Wiley & Sons, Inc.

classes such as 1–100; 101–200; 201–500, etc.). Balancing out this disadvantage, the advantage offered by CHAID is that more than two segments may be identified for each level, whereas CART always splits the database in two.

Response gain chart and composing the list

Which people included in the data set will be approached for a marketing campaign? The objective of segmentation is to divide up the customer database into homogeneous groups, yet it stops short of selecting the prospects in a campaign. Will someone with an RFM score of 150 (see Table 11.2) still be approached? Will customers from segments from the CHAID analysis with a response index under 125 receive an offer? In short, the so-called *list* must still be compiled.

The response gain chart may be of help in this regard (see Table 11.3). Table 11.3 illustrates an RFM analysis. In order to produce the gain chart, the customer database is split into equal parts with respect to size. The database may be broken down into ten sections, for example. The top decentile comprises the customers with the highest RFM score, under these, the next 10 per cent and so forth. Next, data on the response to the current marketing campaign are gathered for the different segments. Data on the response to past campaigns may be used, but also the outcomes from a test may prove

Table 11.3 Response gain chart

Cumulative RFM score	*Percentage data set*	*Response percentage*	*Response gain*[1]	*Cumulative response %*	*Cumulative gain*
>255	9.98%	7.48	76	7.48	76
208–255	10.02%	6.38	50	6.93	63
194–208	10.00%	5.53	30	6.46	52
178–194	10.05%	5.14	21	6.13	44
155–178	10.01%	4.72	11	5.85	38
128–155	9.94%	4.42	4	5.61	32
108–128	10.04%	3.19	–25	5.26	24
96–108	10.00%	2.38	–44	4.90	15
75–96	9.98%	2.00	–53	4.58	8
<75	9.98%	1.29	–70	4.25	0
	100.00%	4.25	0	4.25	0

[1] Response gain or the response's number of percentage points higher or lower in this percentile as compared with that of the entire data set.

Source: Drozdenko and Drake (2002) (modified).

to be useful. As opposed to the historical data, the test results are specifically related to the marketing campaign(s) still to be launched and will thus – except for the random sampling error – provide a more accurate picture.

For each partition in the database, it must then be determined how many percentage points higher or lower the response is with regard to the total response percentage. Cumulative percentages may also be calculated for the first 10, 20, . . . , 90 per cent of the database (see the last two columns in Table 11.3).

It is the marketer's task to determine the cut-off point: which portion of the database will continue to be approached with campaigns and which will not? The decision on the composition of the list targeted for a campaign is not an isolated or independent one, but instead will have to be made within the context of the relationship policy. A decentile may be approached, even if the response percentage is low and the campaign is not profitable (Table 11.3 may be filled in to determine this). For example, the relationship is currently in the growth phase and the realisation of a repeat purchase is crucial in order to increase the probability of customer retention. The effect of the campaign is not profitable on a transaction basis, whereas its impact on the lifetime value is profitable.

11.3 Conclusion

Segmentation is a research process in which the market is divided up into homogeneous customer groups that respond in the same way to marketing stimuli from the supplier. The greatest challenge in segmentation is finding the most effective categorisation from the gigantic range of possibilities available to choose from. With strategic marketing problems, the effectiveness of the solution is dependent upon the question of whether or not there are marketing service concepts which may be developed for each (group of) segment(s) which result in the organisation becoming capable of developing profitable and long-term relationships with customer groups. A good profiling of the customers in a segment is essential to this so that insight may be gained into the person or organisation behind the buyer as well as his or her motives.

The input of segmentation research for the formulation of the tactical marketing policy consists of the supply of lists or selections of people and organisations which may be approached with a promotional activity within the scope of a campaign. This involves the selection of the people and organisations which have a high probability of response. Three techniques have been developed within the direct marketing field – the RFM technique, CART and CHAID – which may be employed to divide up the customer and/or prospects database into groups. The response gain chart may then be used to determine which of these groups will be selected for the promotion.

It is important to avoid viewing the selection in isolation, but instead to see it within the broader context of the relationship policy and the maximisation of the lifetime value.

Case study

Garnier, The Beauty Bank (IDM Business Performance Award 2003 – silver winner)

Banking on planning

Proving the impact of relationship marketing in the packaged goods sector requires planning and tracking. By overhauling its database and recruiting a tracking panel, Garnier was able to discover the positive impact of its new marketing strategy – an incremental increase in spending that delivered a positive return on investment (ROI) within 36 weeks. The judges described it as 'a classic example of excellent planning'.

Since 1999, Garnier had been using direct mail, but in a tactical, one-off fashion. Data was transferred onto a database, but proving that the mailings had made a positive impact was difficult – consumers in this sector are highly promiscuous and there is strong price sensitivity.

A beautiful relationship

Following a brand relaunch, Garnier appointed WWAV Rapp Collins in 2002 to develop a relationship marketing strategy. This would focus on portfolio buying and total customer value, rather than single product purchasing.

The Beauty Bank was devised as a way of segmenting, valuing and tracking customers. A database audit was carried out to identify where new records and variables were required. Using a postcode sector ranking, a national door-drop was carried out to acquire data, which generated a rise in the response rate of more than 1 per cent.

A health and beauty questionnaire was then mailed to selected prospects. A response rate of 11 per cent produced detailed attitudinal and quantitative data.

Using the data acquired in this way, a life-stage segmentation was developed to drive relevant communications. A value segmentation was also built to identify frequency and value of spend, which produced 12 groups. Scoring derived from this segmentation identified the type of communication required and the relevant use of incentives.

Each product was scored in this way, then each category, with scores finally calculated into an overall Garnier score for each customer. Responses from previous campaigns were used to understand how different segments reacted to the use of incentives such as coupons.

Understanding how marketing communications would generate incremental spending was critical. A tracking panel was recruited, which provided purchasing data every four weeks. A control panel was also established which would not receive any communications.

The highest-value customer is always right

To demonstrate the value of the data analysis, a retention campaign was mailed to the highest-value customers in November 2002. Using insights from the database, two different executions were used – one for under-35s and one for over-35s. A target of 15 per cent coupon redemption was set – actual redemption rates across six products ranged from 24 per cent to more than 30 per cent.

The database has also been used for tactical promotions of new product launches, with a Lumia campaign generating a 16 per cent response rate. From the tracking panel, it has been shown that within 36 weeks – half the target period – significant incremental spending on Garnier has been achieved, creating a positive ROI.

Source: IDM (2003).

Questions

1 How do you evaluate Garnier's segmentation approach?

2 In consumer markets where direct contact with customers is missing, it is always difficult to build a database of the best customers from different segments. How do you evaluate Garnier's database in this respect?

Questions

1. Select a market and describe the path you would like to take to arrive at segmentation for strategic marketing objectives.
2. What differences in segmentation arise between the business and the consumer markets? Explain your answer.
3. How may results from qualitative research be used to enrich the profile of individual customers?
4. Three techniques have been mentioned frequently for the purposes of compiling the list for a marketing campaign.
   (a) What are the disadvantages associated with segmentation created on the basis of an RFM analysis in the context of a CRM strategy?
   (b) Do these same disadvantages apply to the CART and CHAID analyses? Why?
5. Describe how a response gain chart may be used to make a selection of people and organisations which are to be approached with a marketing activity within the scope of a campaign.

References

Bonoma, Thomas V. and Benson P. Shapiro (1983) *Segmenting the Industrial Market*, Lexington Books, Lexington, Massachusetts.

Bruhn, Manfred (2003) *Relationship Marketing*, Pearson Education, Harlow.

Drozdenko, Ronald G. and Perry D. Drake (2002) *Optimal Database Marketing: Strategy, development and data mining*, Sage Publications, London.

Kotler, Philip (2003) *Marketing Management*, 11th edn, Prentice Hall, Englewood Cliffs, New Jersey.

Magidson, Jay (1988) Improved statistical techniques for response modeling, *Journal of Direct Marketing*, **2**, 4, 6–17.

Malhotra, Naresh K. and David F. Birks (2003) *Marketing Research*, 3rd edn, FT Prentice Hall, Harlow.

Peelen, Ed (2002) *CHAID Analysis for a Discounter*, ICSB, Rotterdam.

Spiller, Lisa and Martin Baier (2005) *Contemporary Direct Marketing*, Pearson Education, Upper Saddle River, New Jersey.

Thrasher, Rosana P. (1991) CART: a recent advance in tree-structured list segmentation methodology, *Journal of Direct Marketing*, **5**, 1, 35–47.

12

Retention and cross-sell analyses

This chapter will examine both retention and cross-sell analyses in further detail. In Section 12.1, the retention question is raised: which customers run an increased risk of ending the relationship and may be retained for the organisation if they are approached? Cross-selling will then be discussed: which customers should be stimulated to buy another product (Section 12.2)?

Attention will be placed on the definition of the analysis problem, the compilation of the set of variables and data, exploratory analyses, model development and the outcomes of the research and the interpretation of results. The techniques will be discussed only briefly. For further information on these techniques, we recommend that the reader consult the reference list at the end of the chapter.

We will examine these two example questions fairly closely, even if we do focus primarily on the user and the client commissioning the analyses. We consider it important to expand the insight into these analyses so that we are in a position to:

- formulate the right question or assignment;
- support the researcher during the process of selecting the variables, for example; and
- interpret the results.

In this chapter we will address the following questions

- How can you illustrate two popular CRM selection analyses with the objective of becoming familiar with the application of datamining techniques to the resolution of similar analysis problems?
- How to evaluate a retention analysis.
  - What is a retention analysis?
  - How to evaluate the exploratory analysis.
  - How to evaluate the variable selection for the final model (the role played by an information gain chart).
  - What do the model development and the choice of analysis technique imply?
  - How to interpret the results.
- How to evaluate a cross-sell analysis.
  - How to define cross-selling.
  - How to evaluate the exploratory analysis and the verification of the data quality.
  - How to evaluate the variable selection and model development.
  - How to interpret the results.

Practitioner's insight

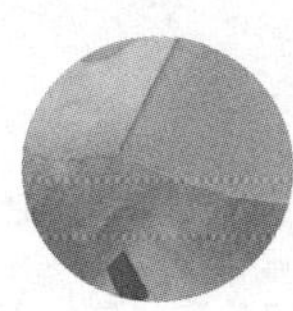

Two analyses which enjoy great popularity within CRM policy are retention and cross-sell analyses. The greatest gains may usually be realised as a result of the first type of analysis. Closing the back door costs less than luring prospects to the luxuriously designed front entrance. Furthermore, a retention analysis produces more than a cross-sell or deep-sell exercise. By retaining a customer for the organisation, the entire remaining lifetime value is 'secured'. Although the yield from cross-selling is generally lower than that gained with customer retention, the advantages of this technique must not be underestimated. With cross-selling, the direct benefits consist of the transaction profit and the indirect advantages include the boost the transaction can give to the relationship. Thanks to the cross-purchase, a supplier can reduce the likelihood of the customer ending the relationship prematurely during the growth phase, before the supplier has had the chance to earn back its investment in the customer. It gives the customer the opportunity to discover the advantages its supplier has to offer and to ease the transition to the saturation phase.

12.1 Retention

Retention, in a marketing sense, means holding on to customers. If a company becomes aware in time of those customers who demonstrate an increased likelihood of ending the relationship, then it may take action to prevent this.

In order to be able to determine this likelihood or probability, companies must arrive at definitions of former and current customers. Does someone become a departing customer at the moment he or she no longer buys a certain product; a consumer, for example, does not buy fresh meat any more at a particular supermarket but keeps on shopping for all sorts of packaged goods? Or is another level of aggregation used whereby a customer is referred to as having left if he or she does not execute any transactions with the supplier involved over a period of a year, for example? The choice for the product or organisational level is dependent upon the size of the outflow and the position of the responsible manager within the company: is he or she responsible for the product or for the customer?

Exploratory analysis

In order to determine the importance of the retention analysis, several exploratory economic analyses may be performed to gain insight into the flows of money that are leaving the organisation. Figure 12.1 illustrates the level of cash outflow for a financial institution's investment product over a period of four years. A specification is also provided for the withdrawal's destination: will the capital be invested elsewhere, saved, or will it even be appropriated outside of the company?

Figure 12.1 Outflow analysis

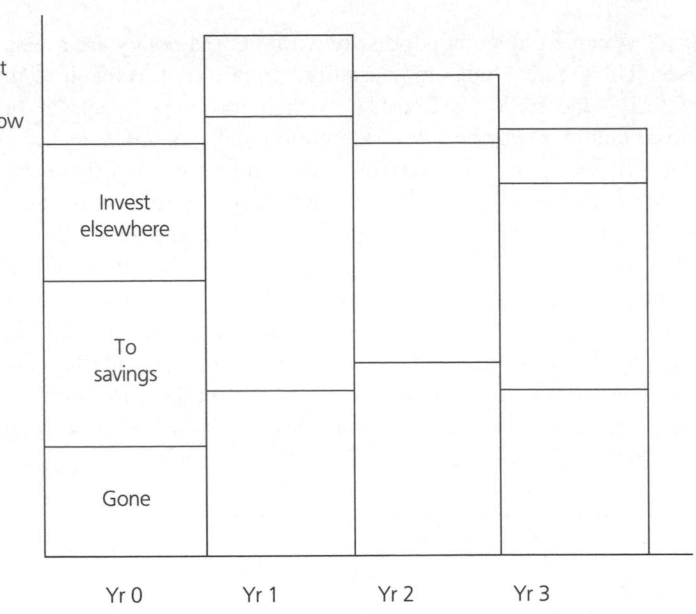

In certain markets, the external destination for the departing customers is known, allowing the creation of an origin and destination matrix. In the automobile industry, for example, this is the case because of the requirement for owners to register their vehicles. In Figure 12.2, the diagonals indicate which customers remain loyal to their brand. The origin of the current customers for a particular brand is shown in the columns, and the rows indicate the other brand to which a specific brand has lost its customers.

Which variables should be included in the final model?

An important step in the analysis process is the selection of the variables to be included (Mena, 1999). For many companies, ensuring that they have available the sorts of data that will be reliable predictors of the possible defection of a customer is a challenge. If the customer and the organisation do not interact intensively and the company only has static customer information on names, address, lifestyle, etc. available in the database it becomes harder to find data that trigger the potential customer defection. During the relationship it soon becomes important to think about the collection of data that will predict churn.

Not only is the data's availability of crucial importance, their quality also plays a role. Feeding all of the available data into the models without sufficient preparation offers little hope of obtaining a stable model with good predictive power. Within the scope of the retention analysis, an investment company will introduce the amount of the capital invested as a variable. It will focus on the different ways in which this information may be measured. This level may be gauged at the moment that someone becomes

Figure 12.2

Origin and destination matrix

New

Previous	Le	Me	Bm	Li	Ca	Ac	In	Au	Sa	Vo	Ja
Lexus	*68*	3	4	2	3	2	4	–	1	–	1
Mercedes	14	*42*	4	2	5	1	7	1	–	1	1
BMW	13	5	*43*	–	–	2	4	1	–	3	1
Lincoln	4	1	1	*64*	7	1	2	–	–	–	1
Cadillac	3	1	1	8	*54*	1	1	–	–	–	1
Acura	7	1	1	2	–	*35*	4	1	1	1	–
Infiniti	9	–	–	–	2	2	*53*	–	–	–	2
Audi	5	2	3	–	2	2	1	*16*	–	2	–
Saab	5	–	3	–	4	1	4	1	*28*	5	–
Volvo	2	1	2	–	–	2	1	–	–	*29*	–
Jaguar	18	9	6	7	9	–	10	2	2	1	*28*

a customer, at the time the level reached its peak, on the last day of the year, on the last day of the previous month, and so forth. Apart from the amount itself, the changes in the amount may also be measured. The differences may be expressed in absolute terms or as percentages. The difference between the current amount invested and the maximum amount invested may also be expressed in absolute terms, but an index number is likely to have better powers of prediction when used in a model. In addition to the rise and fall, the speed with which positive or negative developments have occurred may also be measured. For example, how much time passed between the high and low points?

Up until now, companies have focused solely on the ways in which the level of investment may be measured, and all sorts of other variables which influence customer retention have fallen by the wayside. These include:

- investment behaviour: how often does an investor modify his or her portfolio?
- the number of different products that the customer purchases;
- the financial climate;
- the earned rate of return;
- customer satisfaction;
- the customer's investment objectives; and
- the communication behaviour.

These variables may also be measured in a variety of ways.

In an exploratory analysis, those variables which discriminate the most between 'stayers' and 'quitters' will have to be removed. They will be used to develop the final model.

Figure 12.3 Information gain chart

Source: Eiben *et al.* (1995a).

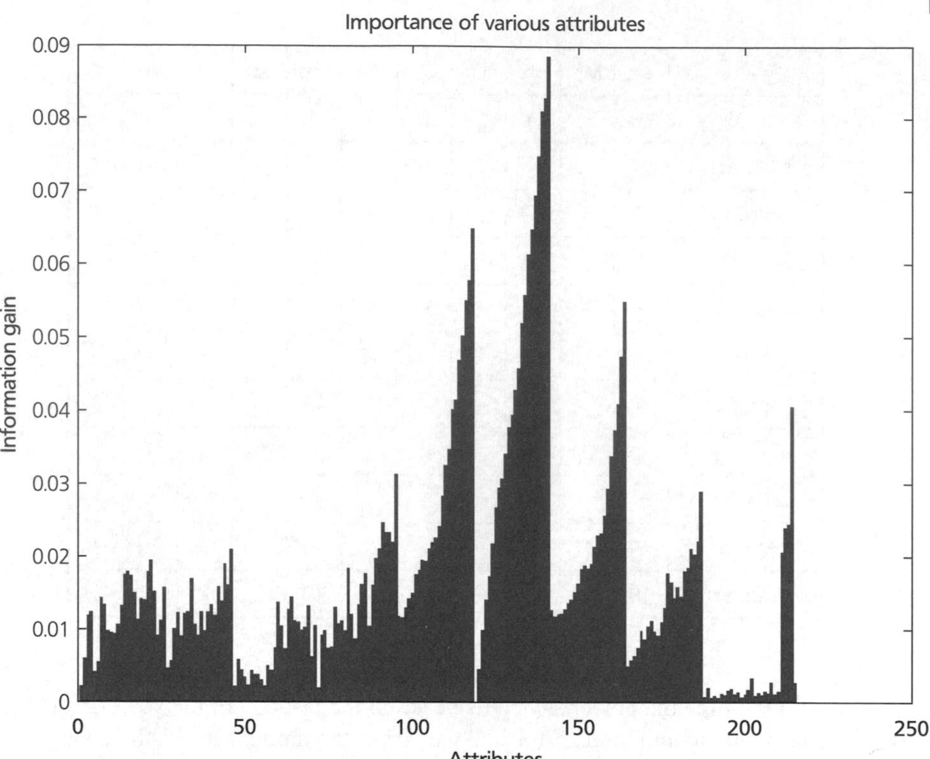

Figure 12.3 contains an information gain chart for some 220 variables. The score on the *y*-axis indicates to what degree the variable (the attribute) correlates with departure.

Model development

One of the challenges involved in performing a retention analysis is the compilation of a qualitatively good data set. The share of former customers as a percentage of the sample must be determined. If a random sample is taken from the current customer database, the share represented by former customers will probably be relatively small. Very little relevant empirical material is then available for the development of the model. If, on the other hand, a data set of exclusively former customers is created, it remains uncertain in what sense former customers differ from customers who have decided to continue the relationship. In short, a 50:50 split between former and current customers in the data set to be compiled would seem the ideal distribution since it overcomes the objections to the previously mentioned random sample draws.

In order to be able to evaluate the power of prediction of the model to be developed, it is advisable to split the data set into a training and a validation set. The first is used to develop the model and the second to test it for reliability. The developed model will be filled in for the customers in the validation set; the prediction obtained in the process

An analysis outcome

Figure 12.4

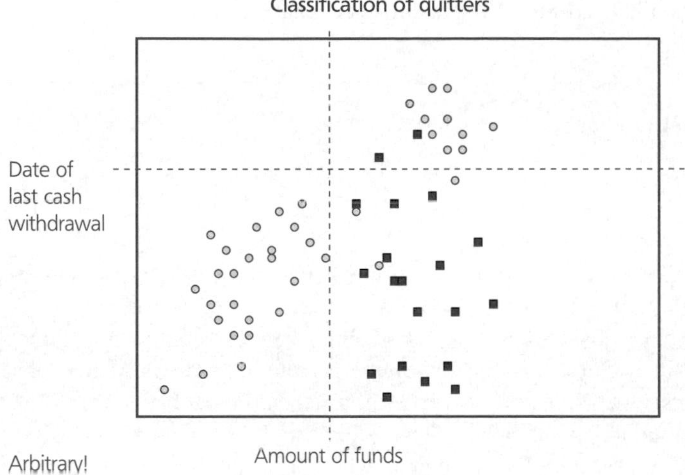

Source: Eiben *et al.* (1995b).

regarding 'staying' or 'leaving' will be compared with the actual behaviour that has been recorded in the validation set.

The decision may also be made to develop more than one prediction model. Customers from different segments do vary. For the one investor, for example, a disappointing return may be reason enough to accept his losses and seek refuge in savings, whereas for another investor this may provide him with a reason to invest even more. Furthermore, there are considerable differences between active and non-active customers. Both may be loyal or disloyal, yet the chance of departure for customers from the active group will have to be deduced from other characteristics than those used for the less active customers. There are no behaviour variables available for this last group and, as such, dynamic data are lacking and the model will have to be based on static characteristics.

In this retention study a technique[1] is used by which 'stayers' and 'quitters' may be distinguished from one another. Figure 12.4 contains an illustration showing how the two groups may be successfully separated on the basis of the date of their last cash withdrawal and the number of funds that they hold. In the imaginary situation involved, it appears that quitters, indicated by the squares, may be distinguished from stayers by:

- withdrawing money from their account after a certain date;
- purchasing less than a certain amount of investment products.

It is the researcher's and client's task to determine how the lines in the figure will be drawn. Is the intention to *correctly* classify as many observations as possible, or is it important to prevent a certain type of misclassification? It is perhaps better to be safe than sorry and to minimise the number of times that a potential former customer is characterised as such. This optimisation objective will have to be formulated in advance.

[1] Rough data modelling was used in this example.

The analysis itself will produce countless classifications like this one. A combination of classifications will have to be compiled which collectively gives the best prediction of the customer's likelihood of leaving. These outcomes may be recorded in business rules and used in CRM systems (see Chapter 18).

CRM illustration

Churn alert

It sounds fascinating. How is T-Mobile able to predict what a customer will do a few months from now? Sander van den Berg, database marketing analyst at T-Mobile explains: 'Our gift for prediction rests on two pillars: the decision model created using Omega and the independent variables. We have designated no less than 300 variables which collectively describe customer behaviour. Naturally there are also obvious variables, such as the duration of a contract. But there are also less "hard" variables such as decreasing call behaviour. Also, text messaging traffic provides an indication as does roaming. The movement from phone to phone says something about the customer's mobility. You must have this information available historically in order to be able to perform trend analyses. The advanced model with the quantity of variables guarantees that decisions will be of extremely high quality.' Van den Berg does not exclude the possibility that the number of determining variables may be reduced. 'In the beginning, it is better to have too many than too few. With the aid of the so-called Business Monitoring functionality of Omega, we can monitor the model and the systems. This way, we are able to determine whether or not the variables chosen have a true significance.'

T-Mobile has completed the first project involving private individuals with a subscription (residentials, post-paid). Reitsma: 'We can predict the expected return on new customers and decide whether or not they are profitable enough for us to take on. The credit scoring functionality of KiQ plays an important role in this regard. If they are already customers, then predictive datamining allows us to spot when they will leave far in advance. Through the integration with campaign management, you can then choose whether they will be approached via telesales and direct marketing, and if so, what we will use to do this. Besides, no two customers are alike. Sometimes your preference lies with letting a customer go if he doesn't fit the profile. You might do this, for example, if he rarely calls or is difficult about payments. The integration of the system must lead in the short term to the appearance of a "churn alert" on the contact centre agent's screen if someone from the churn risk group checks in, so that they may make a suitable offer.'

Source: Loth (2002).

12.2 Cross-selling

Cross-selling is the sale of products to current customers who are already purchasing one or more products from the supplying company (Peelen and Kowalczyk, 1999). During the growth phase of a relationship, engaging in cross-selling is of relatively great importance to guarantee the continuity and further development of the relationship (see Figure 8.4). Within CRM the interest in cross-selling arises from two different points of view:

- The product: focused on the compilation of a list of existing customers that qualify on the basis of their product history for the offering of a certain product.
- The client: when customers contact the organisation, it must be possible to establish on an individual level which products have the best chance of being cross-sold.

Cross-selling is possible in a number of ways. For the development of the cross-sell model, the appropriate form must be determined. Different forms may be distinguished as noted under the following two headings.

Cross-selling over time

- A customer who buys more than one of the same product during a contact (two life insurance policies).
- A customer who buys two or more different products during a contact (home contents and liability insurance policies).
- A customer who buys a second or third product at a later time.

Cross-selling within the product range

- A customer who buys another product within the same product category (for example, a different type of property insurance might be purchased within the product group property insurance).
- A customer who expands the products he or she buys from the organisation by buying a product from another category (for example, a property insurance product is supplemented by a life insurance product).

Cross-selling must be distinguished from deep selling, in which the goal is the sale of a product from the same category. The intention is to encourage the customer to take out a vehicle insurance policy that offers extra coverage, for example.

The cross-sell model may be developed in business-to-consumer markets for an individual or a household and in business-to-business markets for a company, the division, the business unit or the branch. It will have to be determined which level is the preferred one. In making a selection, it must be taken into consideration that there are more cross-sell possibilities available at the higher levels of aggregation than at the lower ones.

In order to determine the cross-sell opportunities from the point of view of the product, models will have to be developed for the individual product categories in which:

- the dependent variable relates to a different product category each time;
- the independent variables relate to the transaction that occurred prior to that for the product being studied (at another time and for another product), the number of products that the customer acquires from the organisation and the customer profile (see the box on the next page).

If one umbrella model is developed for all of the product categories, then predictions for the product categories with a low turnover and sales volume will be more inaccurate than those for the more current categories.

A variety of techniques may be used in order to determine the business rules. Examples are probabilistic models which indicate the probability that the relevant cross-sell will occur, or the rule extraction algorithm technique (REAT). The output of REAT consists of 'if/then' rules (business rules); *if* someone satisfies the following conditions (such as product possession and customer profile), *then* the cross-sell probability for product category *Y* is a certain percentage.

Selection of the variables to be included in the analysis

Customer profile

- Identification of customer on the basis of house number and postcode.
- Description of the household on the basis of the number of customers living at the specific house number + postcode.
- Since when has the person been a customer?
- What is the sex of the customer?
- What is the customer's date of birth?
- What is the customer's source of income?
- Does the customer rent or own his or her home?
- What is the origin of the customer?

Relationship client–supplier

- Who is the customer's current contact person?
- What is the contact history with the customer?

Product history

- How many products does the customer purchase?
- What quantity of product *X* does the customer purchase?
- For individual product categories: what is the number of articles purchased, the turnover, the date on which the product in question was last purchased?
- On the individual product level: the same data as for the categories.

If more than one product is purchased at one time, it is possible that a choice must be made in the analyses for one of these products. The choice then falls on the more expensive product.

During the creation of the model, it is advisable to exercise caution with regard to the use of data on customer contacts. One may actually expect a great connection between the purchase of a product and the occurrence of a contact. One may not deduce from this, however, that the cross-sell probability increases if a contact can be established.

Verification of the data quality

Before performing the final analyses, the data quality should be verified. In adding up the individual products to arrive at category totals, inconsistencies may occur, for instance. The sum of the individual products does not add up to the total number of products sold. Data may also be incomplete; the products may have been purchased, however, there is no known date of purchase, the transaction amount is missing, and so forth.

Exploratory analyses

Economic significance of cross-selling

In order to obtain an indication of the economic significance of cross-selling at an early stage, it may be determined how many products the current customers are purchasing (as illustrated by Figure 12.5). Calculations may be performed to determine which

Figure 12.5

Contribution to turnover made by customers purchasing one or more insurance products in the past year

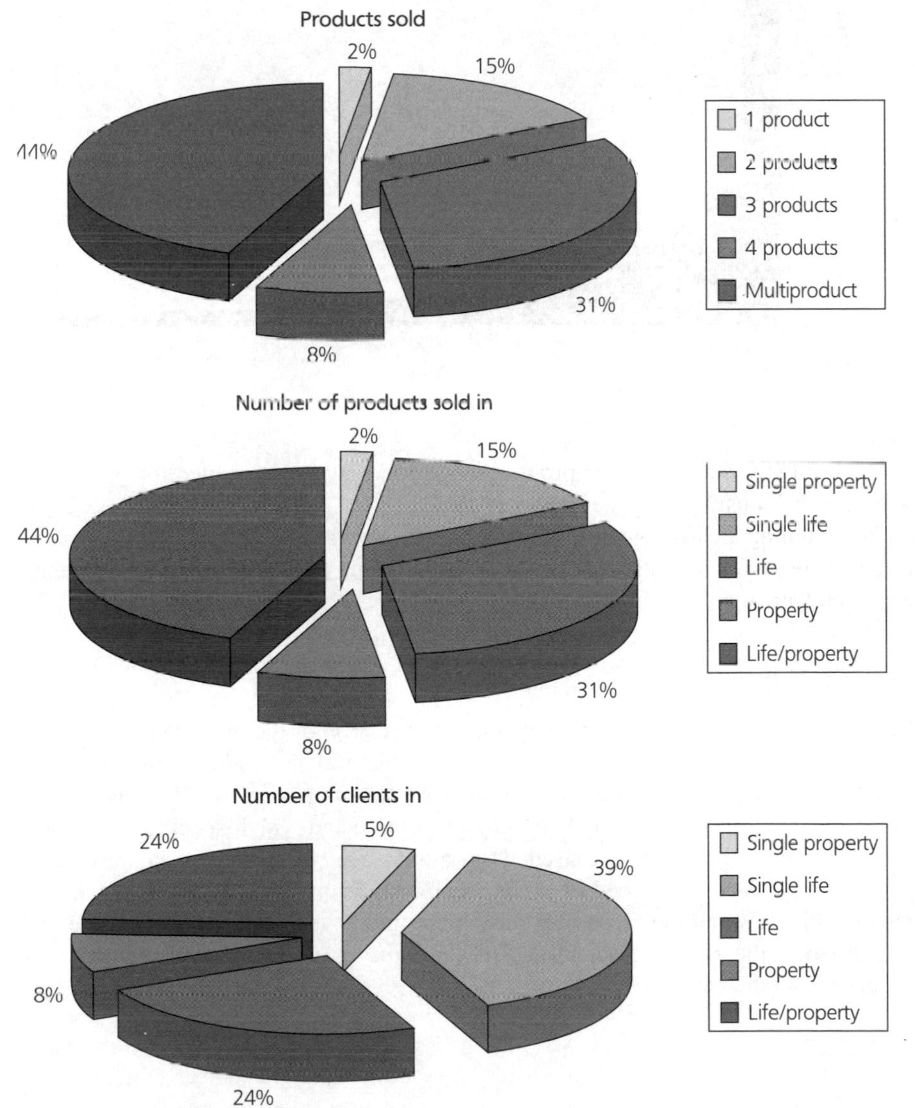

Figure 12.6 Cross-selling; the time between two purchase moments

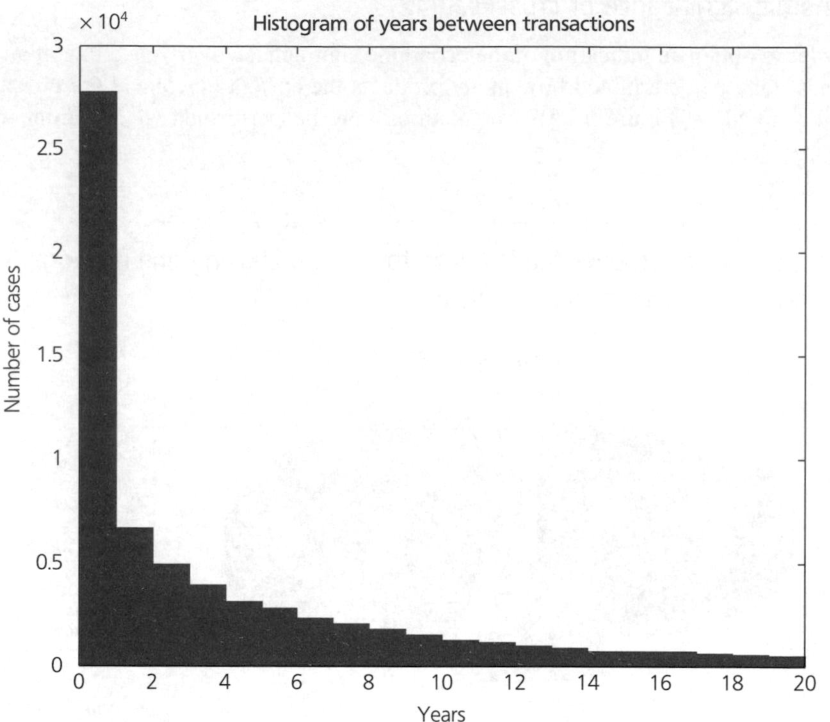

portion of the turnover and the profit contribution may be accounted for by customers who may be considered as the 'heavy users'.

Determining the average time between two transactions (Figure 12.6) is just as interesting. It provides an indication of the length of time required before a result may be expected from a cross-sell campaign.

Cross-tables

Cross-tables may also be used to gain a first impression of the most common combinations of product categories. However, cross-tables do not indicate the sequence in which the products have been purchased from the supplier. For all of the most frequently purchased products, a chain may be constructed which specifies the sequence in which the products are purchased. They are grouped according to the most recently purchased product or the product at the end of the chain. The percentages indicate the relationship between the number of customers that have purchased the three products concerned in the sequence specified, and the number of customers that have the first product from the chain.

Figure 12.7

Pareto optimal business rules

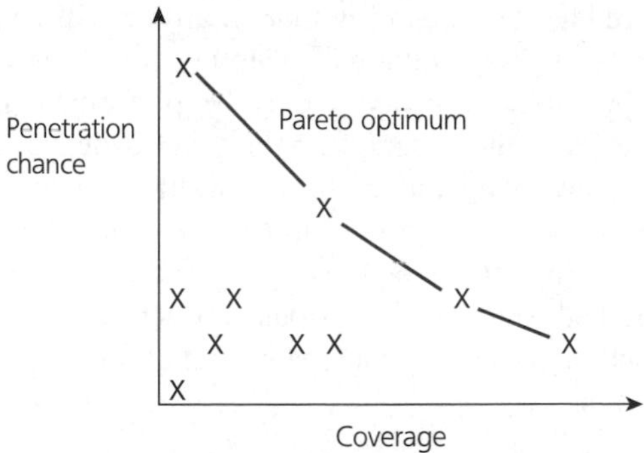

Rule extraction algorithm: the cross-sell probability of the most recently purchased product has been determined for all of the possible combinations of customer profiles and product history.

The final analysis

Vis-à-vis the product

Now the cross-sell probability for the most recently purchased product may be determined with regard to all of the possible combinations of variables such as the customer profiles and product history.[2] There are possibly thousands of business rules which may be created which indicate the probability that customers with a certain product history and a certain profile possess the product (the dependent variable).

By compiling a list of the people to be approached for the cross-sell of another product category, a choice will have to be made from among these thousands of business rules. In making a selection, two aspects should be kept in mind:

- How high is the cross-sell probability for the product category for a given customer profile and product history?
- What is the coverage: what percentage of the customers in the customer database are typified by the customer profile and product history? If the cross-sell probability is high, it is possible that only a few customers in the total database possess these qualities (profile and product history).

For each calculation rule, a graph may be used to determine how well it scores in terms of cross-sell probability as well as coverage. See Figure 12.7 for example. The business rules that form the outermost line are the optimal rules (they form the so-called Pareto optimum) and are preferred to rules that fall under this line.

[2] The rule extraction algorithm was used to do this in this example.

Cross-sell probabilities from the customer's point of view based on probabilistic models

In order to be able to determine the probability that an article will be purchased from a different product category by an individual customer who has contact with an organisation, a Bayesian probabilistic analysis may be performed. In this analysis, the probability of purchase *Ps* of the separate product categories is made dependent upon conditions $c_1, \ldots, c_n$ involving the customer profile and the product history $(Ps \mid c_1, \ldots, c_n)$. Customer A is *k* years old, lives in city *y* and has already bought product *c* and therefore the probability that he or she buys a product from product category *x* is *z*. It may also be determined which of the various product categories have the highest probability of a cross-sell; this category may be brought to the customer's attention during the contact with him or her.

Interpretation of the cross-sell probabilities from the models

Reasons why the cross-sell probabilities from the model can produce an overestimation

The cross-sell 'probabilities' that the model provides may result in an overestimation for the following reasons. The cross-sell probabilities indicate the chance that a customer who has bought one specific product has also purchased another product over the course of time. What is not specified, however, is the length of time that has transpired between the two transactions, which contacts have occurred during this interim period, how the customer's situation has changed, and which changes have been made to the supplier's offering. What is clear, however, is that between the time of the cross-sell product purchase and the product purchased prior to that, it is possible that more has happened than simply the one-time offer which is now being considered within the scope of the cross-sell activity. It is perhaps also more accurate to use the term *penetration probabilities* than cross-sell probabilities.

Reasons why the cross-sell probabilities from the model could produce an underestimation

There are various reasons why the probabilities from the model could result in an underestimation. The model is based on cross-purchase patterns which have occurred in the past, and, as such, those patterns reflect the marketing policy implemented in the past. If the organisation now focuses more on cross-selling than it had in the past, the cross-sell probabilities can increase. There are other paths chosen than those historically selected, and there are new successful cross-sell options to be discovered.

The stability of the proposed solution will have to be verified over the course of time. A simple test to determine whether or not the business rules are still satisfactory is to build a cross-table showing the frequencies (percentage-wise) with which product combinations occur. A comparison between this table and a previously created table will show whether or not important shifts have occurred in a short period of time.

Utilising the research outcomes in designing policy

The knowledge of the cross-sell (penetration) probabilities may be used in CRM policy by discussing the successful cross-sell patterns encountered with marketers so that an explanation may be discovered for the patterns found; after all, they reflect the method of (certain) marketers or agents. Marketers and agents may then exchange their successful experiences with one another. An insight may be gained into the manner in which effective cross-selling may be realised within marketing, in other words, which arguments are necessary to encourage customers to cross-purchase.

In addition, a brainstorming session may be used to discuss the cross-sell patterns which were *not* encountered, but which would be opportune nonetheless. These new cross-sell paths may be tested out in the future.

There are two ways in which cross-sell activities may take place:

1 By drawing customers' attention to another product from the range during customer contact:
   - if the 'probability' exceeds a minimum level to be determined later, it may be considered worthwhile to guide the customer's attention during the contact to the product with the best cross-sell probability;
   - the ultimate decision to cross-sell will depend, apart from the minimum level, on the context and content of the conversation (for example, if a customer's call concerns a complaint or the purchase of another product, it would not be wise to make the cross-sell offer).
2 By approaching existing customers for other products from the range (or by using another form of direct marketing communication for products):
   - on the basis of the customer profile and the product history, the 'probability' that a customer segment reacts to the product offering is determined using the rule extraction algorithm technique;
   - the customer segments are ranked on the basis of these 'probabilities'; the segments with the highest 'probability' are at the top, those with the lowest are at the bottom;
   - on the basis of a trade-off between these 'probabilities', the costs of approach and the margin on product sales, an initial list may be compiled;
   - a test may be used to determine whether or not these probabilities must be adjusted; the possibility that the cross-sell probabilities from the study are actually penetration probabilities must be taken into consideration.

12.3 Conclusion

The analysis capacity within companies is scarce. In order to achieve a maximum return from this resource, only the most crucial questions should be researched. Within the scope of making selections – that is, who should be selected for a certain offer – two main points deserve attention:

1 The retention analysis designed to identify customers with an increased probability of ending the relationship. Approaching these customers must lead to a reduction in the probability of their departure.
2 The cross-sell analysis designed to determine the probability of the purchase of another product from a different product category. Knowledge of these probabilities gives the agent in the contact centre the opportunity to determine whether a calling customer will be offered another product or not. The marketer can use this knowledge to determine which customers will be approached for a cross-sell effort. The success of this can be crucial to the maintenance and development of the relationship during the growth phase.

The following are indispensable to the success of the analyses: a careful formulation of the problem, an exploratory analysis of the problem area, a thorough compilation of the variables and the data set, an analysis that uses the most suitable techniques and a sensible interpretation of the research results. This is not exclusively the task of the researcher; the contributions from the marketer and the client are also vital.

Case study

Cross-selling within a fully automated convenience store

Background

'In the past, retailers saw their job as one of buying products and putting them out for sale to the public. If the products were sold, more were ordered. If they did not sell, they were disposed of . . . It has been described as a product-oriented business, where talented merchants could tell by the look and feel of an item whether or not it was a winner. In order to be successful, retailing today can no longer be just a product-oriented business . . . It has to become customer-oriented and a full understanding of all the customer's purchasing behaviour as revealed through his or her sales transactions will become crucial, i.e. *market basket analysis*.

'Currently, the gradual availability of cheaper and better information technology has in many retail organisations resulted in an abundance of sales data. Wal-Mart, the American supermarket, stores about 20 million sales transactions per day. This explosive growth of data leads to a situation in which retailers today find it increasingly difficult to obtain the right information, since traditional methods of data analysis cannot deal effectively with such huge volumes of data. This is where knowledge discovery in databases (KDD) comes into play.

'Today, among the most popular techniques in KDD, is the extraction of association rules from large databases . . . The rules describe the underlying purchase patterns in the data, like for instance, bread → cheese (support = 20 per cent; confidence = 75 per cent). Informally, support of an association rule indicates how frequently that rule occurs, i.e. how frequently is the purchase of bread followed up by the purchase of cheese. The higher the support of the rule, the more prevalent it is. "Confidence is a measure of the reliability of an association rule." '

Optimal assortments

'Determining the ideal product assortment has been (and still is) the dream of every retailer . . .

It is known that the optimal product assortment should meet two important criteria.

'Firstly, the assortment should be qualitatively consistent with the store's image. A store's image distinguishes the retailer from its competition and is projected through its design, layout, services and, of course, its products. Therefore, retailers often distinguish between basic products and added products. Basic products are products that should not be deleted from the assortment because they are the foundation of the retailer's store formula . . . In contrast, added products are chosen by the retailer to confirm the store's image even more and should be selected as to maximise cross-sales potential within basic products. Indeed, retailers are interested in adding items whose sales will not be made at the expense of currently stocked items but may help increase the sales of other items. For the convenience store, examples may include cigarette lighters, coffee whitener or tea warmers. This means that added products should be selected by the model based on their purchase affinity with basic products.

'Secondly, because retailing organisations are profit-seeking companies, the product assortment should be quantitatively appealing in terms of the profitability it generates for the retailer . . .'

Product selection based on 'frequent item sets'

'According to the problem situation described above, a model must be constructed that is able to select a hitlist of products, i.e. a selection of a user-defined number of products, from the assortment which yields the maximum overall profit, taking into account the background knowledge of the retailer. A simple solution to this problem, which is often used, . . . is to calculate the total profit contribution generated per product and then select those products, in addition to the basic products that have already been selected by the retailer, that contribute the most to the overall profitability. We call this the product-specific profitability heuristic. Although easy to calculate, it does not take cross-selling effects of products into account. In contrast, the PROFSET model, introduced in this study, implicitly takes into account cross-selling effects by using "frequent item sets" (purchase combinations such as bread → cheese that occur quite frequently, i.e. more often than X).'

The empirical study

'The empirical study is based on a data set of 27 148 sales transactions acquired from a fully-automated convenience store over a period of 5.5 months . . . The concept is closely related to that of a vending machine. The product assortment of the store under study consists of 206 different items . . . The average sales transaction contains only 1.4 different items because in convenience stores customers typically do not purchase many items during a single shopping visit.

'As the objective function in the PROFSET method requires frequent item sets as input, frequent item sets and association rules were discovered from the database. An absolute support of 10 was chosen. This means that no item or set of items will be considered frequent if it does not appear in at least 10 sales transactions . . . It could be argued that the choice for this support parameter is rather subjective. This is partly true; however, domain knowledge from the retailer can often indicate what level of support may be considered as relevant.

'In order to make the comparison between PROFSET and the product-specific profitability heuristic straightforward, we chose not to specify basic products in the model. Consequently, the model will be able to fully exploit cross-sales potential between items in the assortment without any restrictions – the PROFSET method also enables assessment of the sensitivity of product assortment decisions and, as a result, allows for identification of the impact of such decisions on the total profitability of the hitlist.

►

'In the final list, not all product combinations with high cross-selling potential are necessarily included. The profit contribution of the sales combination must be sufficiently high for the items to be included in the list. For instance, the item set {toothpaste, toothbrush} has an interest of 2468 over 1 (extremely high) and, according to the association rules, they are always bought together. However, the support count of the item set is equal to 11 (slightly above 10). As a consequence, the total profit contribution of this item set is insufficient to influence the product selection process.

'The impact on total profitability caused by product assortment decisions can easily be assessed by means of sensitivity analysis. When, for instance, product i is deleted from the optimal set, and it is replaced by the best product i′ outside the hitlist, its impact on profitability can easily be observed. While most product replacements have only minor profit implications (–2 per cent), some products represent major profit drivers that should not be deleted from the hitlist.'

Conclusion

'Results indicated that the study is able to identify cross-selling effects implicitly by using frequent item sets, instead of having to estimate cross-selling parameters explicitly (as is often done in product selection and shelf-space allocation models). The study also showed that a sensitivity analysis helps a retailer to quantitatively assess the profitability impact of product assortment decisions.'

Source: Tom Brijs, Gilbert Swinnen, Koen Vanhoof and Geert Wets (1999).

Questions

1 Summarise in your own words how the optimal assortment with regard to cross-selling has been defined in this study. What are the crucial elements in this study and why?

2 What are the strengths and weaknesses of this study? Explain your answer.

Questions

1 Banks have very few customers who end the relationship. People are generally not quick to close a current account. Does this mean that a retention analysis for a bank is of little use? Or do you see potential for a (variation on a) retention analysis? Explain your answer.

2 The quality of the retention model to be developed is, to a great extent, dependent upon the variables to be included. In your opinion, which considerations play a role in the creation of these types of variables and the final set of variables?

3 Why is it important when performing a retention analysis to include just as many 'quitters' as 'stayers' in the data set? Explain your answer.

4 Why should the retention model developed for active customers be different from that for passive customers?

5 How may the outcomes of a retention analysis be used in a marketing campaign?

6 Give a description of deep selling.

7 Under which circumstances will deep selling produce a more economically desirable result than cross-selling? Explain your answer.

8 Will a deep-sell analysis proceed according to the same pattern as the cross-sell analysis outlined, or do you expect differences? Substantiate your answer.

9 Why will only the business rules found on the drawn curve in a Pareto analysis be used to select the people to be approached for a cross-sell activity?

10 What limitations are associated with the outcomes of a cross-sell analysis made using historical data?

References

Brijs, Tom, Gilbert Swinnen, Koen Vanhoof and Geert Wets (1999) Using association rules for product assortment decisions: a case study, *ACM*, San Diego.

Eiben, G., F. Slisser, E. Peelen *et al.* (1995a) Genetic algoritms and neural networks versus statistical techniques: a case study in marketing, *PASE'95 Workshop Proceedings*, Mainz, 31 August.

Eiben, G., F. Slisser, E. Peelen *et al.* (1995b) Response modeling and target group selection in a business to business market, *Henry Stewart Conference Proceedings*, Amsterdam, 26 January.

Loth, Theo (2002) T-mode kent de toekomst, minder weglopers dankzij credit scoring en predictive datamining, *Beyond, Mapping, Marketing and Datamining*, November, 10–11.

Mena, Jesus (1999) Data mining your website, *Digital Press*, Boston.

Peelen, Ed and Wojtek Kowalczyk (1999) *Cross-selling at an Insurance Company*, Visor, Almere.

13

The effects of marketing activities

How can we build an understanding of the effects of marketing activities? It is relatively easy to measure the response on one specific marketing activity: how many people or organisations respond to a mailing, a phone call or an invitation on a website? The total number of people approached or visitors is known and can be related to the number of responders. One can, however, wonder what this information actually tells you about the marketing effects. The question *not* addressed is what people finally bought and what the bottom line margin was on this transaction. It is also unknown who these customers were and what the contribution of the interaction was to their lifetime value. Did the marketing activity have a positive effect on the customer value, or was contributing to building a mutually profitable lasting relationship not seen as one of its aims? Answering this last question can be seen by many as a theoretical challenge, not worth the energy of a practitioner who is responsible for the result in the market. Nonetheless, some progress has been made in the development of a method to provide an answer to this question.

Section 13.1 will look at how we might evaluate the effects of marketing activities. Since it is not only the current scoring we are interested in, but also ways to improve the situation, Sections 13.2 and 13.3 will deal with methods used to learn about the interrelations between marketing activities and results. In experiments and testing (Section 13.2) and in a learning organisation (Section 13.3) we can enhance our understanding of the effects that marketing activities have on customer relations.

In this chapter we will address the following questions

- How can we evaluate the effect of marketing activities on the customer relationship?
  - How to evaluate the sales process.
  - How effectively is the organisation targeting (selecting) its customers?
  - How do marketing activities contribute to the lifetime value of a customer?
- How to learn from previous marketing activities.
- How to construct tests and experiments.
  - What is the definition of an experiment?
  - What types of experiments are there and how are we to judge their validity?
- What is a learning organisation?
  - What are the conditions for learning and making improvements effectively within an organisation and as a team?
  - How to apply knowledge management and the learning organisation in the field of improving the effectiveness of marketing campaigns.

Practitioner's insight

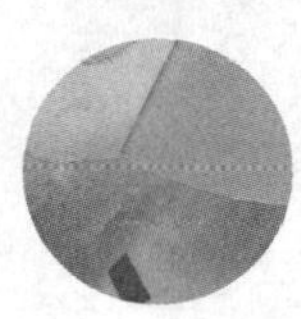

The selection of customers who will be approached for a cross-sell or retention activity is the preparation for the subsequent marketing activity. If precision is the theme during the identification of the customer or prospect, then this is no different during communication. Also, now the goal is to serve the customers as effectively as possible. This is unlikely to be achieved with a standardised marketing approach in which mass media are used, for example. The chances are improved if the communication is tailored to the market. The direct feedback that customer and supplier give one another is lacking in mass marketing activities. The customer is anonymous and market research will have to be organised in order to gain insight into the behaviour and imagination of the customer. It is difficult to determine which results specific marketing campaigns have produced. In 'micromarketing' in which the customer and supplier communicate and interact with one another, it is much simpler to determine what will and will not score. The accountability of the marketing and sales efforts is high. Efforts which do not contribute to the result may be eliminated. Priority may be placed on the improvement of those marketing and sales activities which both have an effect and are appreciated by the customer.

13.1 Evaluating the effect of marketing activities on the customer value

We will start with the analysis of the sales process and come step by step to the evaluation of the contribution of marketing activities to the customer relationship.

The effectiveness of the sales process (Mertens and Heilijgers, 2002)

Analysing the sales process has one major advantage over the evaluation of marketing activities and campaigns, combining separate marketing activities with one overall communication objective. Instead of focusing on the organisation's efforts, the sales process as regards a prospect or customer forms the subject of analysis. The subsequent steps that have to lead a relation towards the closing of the deal are monitored. Customer relationship management forces organisations to define explicitly the customer processes (Chapter 19), among them the marketing process. As such, the sales process should no longer be a 'black box', the domain of marketing and sales people who claim that, due to the intuitive nature of their work, it is impossible to define their activities.

Although the focus on the sales process reflects a transaction perspective and not a relationship perspective, it is chosen here as a start, as it helps to evaluate:

Figure 13.1 Sales process analysis

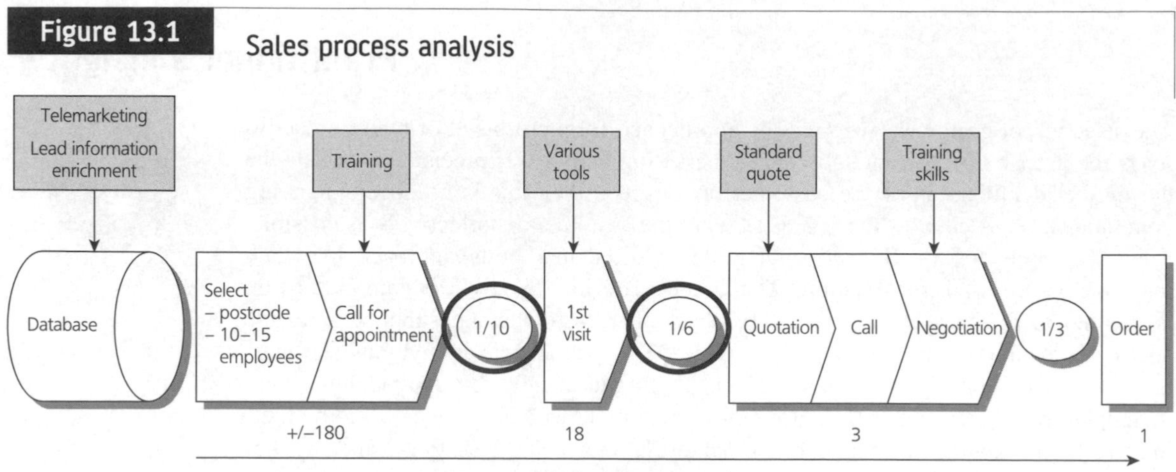

Source: Mertens and Heilijgers (2002).

- the logic of the steps in the sales process;
- the conversion between the steps through time;
- the allocation of resources to each of the steps;
- the marketing or sales costs of a transaction.

Figure 13.1 illustrates the sales process of, say, photocopiers. It starts with the selection of addresses in a database that will be approached for telemarketing activities. Agents in a call centre will call the suspects for the possible making of an appointment. During a first orientation visit the prospect and the salesperson can find out if there is any ground for doing business together. If there is, the salesperson can supply a quotation, make a call and a second visit to negotiate the deal. The analysis shows that for the closing of one order the company needs 250 prospective selected addresses. On average, ten weeks are needed to convert prospects into customers. The costs involved in selecting, calling, visiting, quoting, negotiating and closing deals can be calculated and allocated to the orders and the value they represent.

The value of this analysis can be improved by exploring methods to increase the effectiveness of the marketing and sales approach. Are there ways to shorten the throughput time of the sales process? Can we eliminate one step in order to speed up the whole process? Can we make a better selection of addresses of prospects? Will the training of agents and salespeople help to increase the conversion rate? Have we applied the appropriate channels?

The effectiveness of targeting

The sales process analysis can be brought one step closer to the relationship marketing perspective when we address the targeting issue: who do we select for a specific sales process? From the perspective of the relationship strategy, who should be approached with the offer? A cross-sell 'calendar' (see, for example, Figure 8.4), developed to

Allocation of resources

Figure 13.2

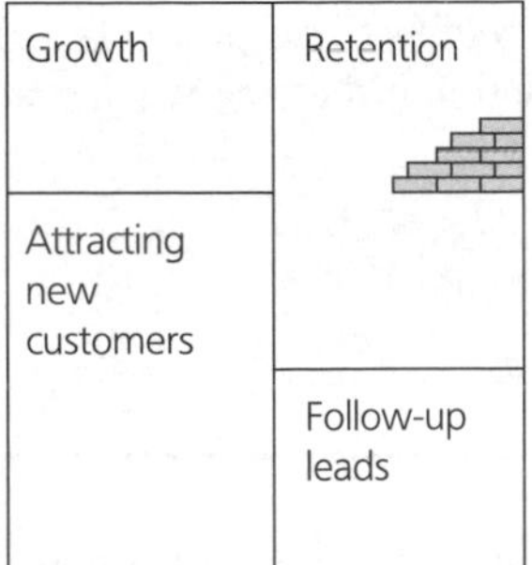

transfer relations from the exploration into the growth phase in the investment sector, may specify that new customers should receive at least three product offers in the first six months following their first purchase, and that customers in segment A should be excluded from specific product offers – as risk averse investors they should not receive a mailing for an emerging market fund. Customers behaving in a way that indicates they might end the relationship could be selected for an 'informative call', with the aim of exploring the client's satisfaction (or lack of it) and of finding ways to improve the relationship.

Effective targeting optimally builds the value that the customer base represents. The percentage of customers that cannot be approached for some reason is small and the potential of the customer base can be fully exploited. There is a balance between attracting new customers and growing the value that current customers represent. The allocation of marketing and sales resources to segments, products, the acquisition of new customers, the retention and treatment of current ones is in line with this priority setting. Figure 8.1 has already illustrated a specific example. Objectives were set for segments of current customers and new prospects: how many customers do we want in each segment and what value do we want them to represent? One further step is to set the budgets and resources needed to realise these targets.

A typical imbalance in the allocation of resources is found in organisations where too much emphasis is put on attracting new customers and where capacity to follow up first calls (see Figure 13.1) and to maintain the relationship with current clients is lacking. Both the inflow of new customers and the growth of the value represented by current customers are disappointing. This situation is shown graphically in Figure 13.2.

Contribution of marketing activities to the lifetime value

The ultimate accountability of marketing activities lies in their contribution to the lifetime value that the customer base represents (see Chapter 14). Severens from Acxiom believes in the use of Markov chains to measure the impact of an individual activity on the customer lifetime value. Each interaction takes the relationship one step further and therefore influences the future interactions and the direction of the relationship. A welcome call, a complaint, a reward for continuing the relation and a price discount during a sales week all have an impact on the value of forthcoming interactions. After a complaint there may not be any interest in a new product offer for several months and marketing activities aimed at selling these products will become obsolete. In theory, with Markov chains the interaction effects between marketing activities can be incorporated over time.

13.2 Experiments

Gauging the effects of marketing and sales efforts and learning from them occurs first in the context of analytical CRM and foremost within the framework of experimentation and testing. This involves a formal method of learning, which imposes certain requirements on the available time of the analyst and the marketer and the size of the customer database.

Experiments come in different shapes and sizes. In the classical experiment, people are exposed to a stimulus in a manipulated environment, and their response to this is measured. Given the fact that one or more groups of people are confronted with different stimuli in an identical environment, the difference in responses may be attributed to the differences between the stimuli. Two groups are often used. While the first group, or experimental group, is exposed to the stimulus, the second, or control, group is deprived of this stimulus.

In choosing an experimental setting, a balance must be found between internal and external validity. The *internal validity* is determined by:

- The degree to which the manipulation requirements are being satisfied: can differences in response be attributed solely to the stimulus and not to other disruptive factors?
- The degree to which a time sequence may be recognised: does the response measurement follow the stimulus?
- The distinguishing capacity and the stability of the measuring instruments: do the instruments determine the effect of the stimuli in a reliable way?

The external validity concentrates less on the explanation of the obtained results and more on the significance of the outcomes in practice. Is the outcome of the study of any practical use in solving policy problems? Does the research provide an answer to the question of how customers should be approached? The external validity depends on:

- the reality content of the experimental situation; and
- the degree of representativeness of the random sample, the stimuli and the response variables.

Take an experiment in a laboratory, for example. The internal validity will be positive. The researcher determines the application of the stimuli. Environmental influences that can disrupt the connection between the stimulus and the response are kept out of the study. If the research involves a study of the effects of a communication message, it may be decided to measure the unaided awareness of claims contained in the message.

To do this, an instrument is used which measures the response to the stimulus in detail. The instrument is reliable if the respondent could not previously have familiarised him- or herself with the claims made by the supplier. The unaided awareness is then the result of the communication activity. The stability of the measuring instrument will depend on whether or not changes have occurred in the measured outcome in the absence of an external cause.

The external validity may, however, suffer in the laboratory situation. A person's familiarity with the contents of a communication message may be measured, but the marketer's actual interest might be in the response (purchasing, information requests, etc.). The conclusions from the experiment will have to be translated to the actual situation.

In the reality of the customer–supplier relationship, the application of the stimuli may also not be carried out in a forced manner. The customer is not obligated to absorb the communication message. After all, a longer period of time will pass between the confrontation with the stimulus and the occurrence of the response. During this time, the customer may be confronted with all sorts of other stimuli. The environment is dynamic and influences the ultimate response.

In short, in conducting research, the proper balance must be found between the internal and external validity. Meeting the validity requirements to a lesser degree can be a practical solution. This appears to be particularly acceptable when the timeframe between stimulus and response is in practice short. The importance of the external validity increases if people are confronted with a complex problem in reality. The significance of extremely valid internal measuring instruments will be limited for this type of problem. For each situation, a consideration of internal and external validity requirements will have to be made. Various experimental settings have been developed, each with its advantages and disadvantages.

Alternative experimental settings

The experimental settings differ in terms of:

- whether or not they use a control group;
- whether or not they include a null measurement prior to the application of the stimulus;
- whether or not a manipulation takes place (forced stimulus application);
- the number of experimental groups that are used.

There are experiments in which a control group is not used and where the response is measured before and/or after confrontation.

Experimental settings also differ from one another in terms of the number of measurements that are performed per group. If a control group is not used, a measurement before and after exposure to the stimulus provides insight into the effect of the stimulus. If a control group is used, insight into the effect of the stimulus may be obtained by comparing the response in the experimental group with that observed in the control group. The significance of the measurement to the application of the stimulus here lies with the increase in the comparability of the control group with the experimental group. An equal starting position is conducive to good comparability.

The experimental settings also differ in the degree to which the stimulus application is manipulated. Experimental settings exist in which staged exposure exists; there are also pilots in which the customer decides him- or herself which elements he or she would like to be exposed to in the communication message.

Experimental set-ups may be designed to work with multiple control and/or experimental groups. The experimental and/or control groups may be exposed to different stimuli and the aim of the experiment is to compare the effects of several alternative stimuli. The number of groups may also be increased in order to perform a more accurate variance analysis. Two control groups may be identified. Two effectiveness measurements can be performed on one control group, both before and after the time at which the stimulus is applied to the experimental group. In the other control group, only one measurement is taken. The difference in response between the two control groups sheds light on the influence a stimulus has on the chance of response. The measurement, which was most likely performed during a telephone survey, can actually increase the respondent's awareness of the stimulus. Through voluntary exposure, the probability thus increases that the respondent will remember the stimulus.

CRM definitions

Examples of experimental settings

Each of the following four settings may take place with or without staged exposure. Experimental setting 3 is the most common in CRM.

Setting	Group			
Setting 1	EX:	S	E1	
Setting 2	EX:	E1	S	E2
Setting 3	EX1:	S1	E1	
	EX2:	S2	E1	
	EX*n*:	S*n*	E1	
	C:		E1	
Setting 4	EX:	E1	S	E2
	C1:	E1		E2
	C2:		S	E1
	C3:			E1

Key:

S	Stimulus
E	Effect measurement
O	Observation
C	Control group
R	Staged exposure to stimuli
EX	Experimental group

The addition of 1, 2, 3, . . . to the symbol indicates with E, for example, the first, second, third, . . . effect measurement.

In order to increase the likelihood that reliable and significant judgements may be made about the differences in outcomes between the groups, the random sample size will have to be adequate. An estimation may be made using the following formula:

$$N = \frac{R(1 - R)C^2}{E^2}$$

Here R is the expected response percentage to the marketing campaign expressed as a decimal, N is the random sample size, C is the confidence level and E is the allowed margin of error. The confidence level is the number of times that a correct indication was given that marketing campaign A led to a higher response rate than campaign B, for example. Assuming a normal distribution of the results, a confidence level of 95 per cent applies to a C value of 1.96. The accepted margin of error E (or the desired degree of accuracy) indicates the number of percentage points by which a chance of response may be incorrectly estimated. It indicates the acceptable range within which the answer lies.

Tests such as the *t* and the chi-squared test may then be used to determine whether the outcomes between the groups differ significantly. Variation analysis may also be used. For a further explanation of this topic, please refer to statistics reference books.

Within the field of CRM, numerous opportunities exist to conduct experiments – in this case *tests* – which have high external validity. Because direct *feedback* to campaigns is gathered within CRM, the response may be measured without it being necessary to carry out additional procedures. Mailings may be sent in various shapes and sizes. Scripts may be tried out in call centres. Different layouts and constructions may be tested for the website. The effect of different incentives on response and transactions may be gauged. At the same time, the internal validity may be monitored. Thanks to the customer characteristics recorded in the databases, it may be seen whether or not the groups are identical and representative of the population. Control groups may be used to isolate the influence of situational factors. The validity, however, comes into play when it comes to determining the indirect effects of marketing activities on the lifetime value, for example, or the degree of retention which must manifest itself in the longer term. In the interim, many situational effects occur which make it difficult to attribute any changes in activity to the experiment.

13.3 The learning organisation

Gaining insight into the effects of marketing through experimentation is time consuming. At the same time, even more questions arise. The number of channels has grown. It is no longer simply the effectiveness of a mailing that matters, but the dialogue that is conducted through the different channels that is important. Is something learned in this dialogue about the customers, and is this knowledge used effectively in the development of a relationship? It is not only the direct effects that attract attention, but also the indirect results that first appear over the long term. Furthermore, the time remaining to gather the answers is shorter. In the real-time market mentioned in the introduction, short response times are a precondition for success. In short, a pressing need asserts itself not only to respond but also in order to accumulate knowledge in another way and to distribute it across the marketing performance.

The need arises for a learning organisation in which know-how is expanded and deepened in all of its aspects (see the following box). Learning is the process in which knowledge is created from the experience gained.

Know- . . .

Know-how: a specific skill or procedure; knowing how to entice a customer.
Know-who: the ability to point out an individual who can aid in the execution of a specific task.
Know-what: structured patterns and knowledge, based directly on facts, data and figures.
Know-why: a deeper insight into the underlying reasons and motives; knowledge in a broader context.
Know-when: a feeling for timing and rhythm.
Know-where: a feeling for location; what is the best place for a banner?

Source: Zuiderduin (2002).

Characteristic of learning organisations is that the attention is not focused on the components of a problem or issue that screams for an immediate solution, but concentrates instead on the whole (Senge, 1990). If, for example, the number of long-term customers falls under a certain minimum, this can prompt additional acquisition efforts, by which the quality of the inflow will be negatively influenced. Prospects who became customers had been offered many incentives which weighed heavily in their decision to become customers. The interest in the organisation's core proposal becomes relatively limited as a result. This is temporarily compensated for by the additional advantages that the incentives offer, but as soon as these have 'worn off', the chance that the relationship will be terminated grows. The organisation ends up in a position in which the outflow grows and the number of customers drops even further below the minimum level. The inclination is there to become more active and aggressive in acquisition efforts and thus to become caught in a downward spiral. Time after time the outflow grows and more efforts are required to keep the customer database at its current level. The only solution is to break out of the cycle. And to find this solution, the limited view which has been taken of the problems will have to be replaced by a total overview.

Learning remains *the work of individuals*. Everyone within the organisation performs and thus gains experience. This applies to the agents in the contact centre, to the service repairman in contact with the customer, to the account manager, the marketer and the database manager. The dedication to expand upon these experiences and explain them forms the basis for a learning organisation. Although the motivation and inspiration to learn must come from the individual, it is the task of management to encourage the learning process and not to punish it. Agents in the call centre who are paid exclusively to be productive are not given the time to reflect. They are unable to convert their numerous experiences into knowledge, or share these with others both inside and outside their department.

Learning is the development of *mental models*, the construction of an image of reality. It requires us to bring the hidden image of reality to the surface, and to hold it up to the light, examining it rigorously. It will have to be opened up for discussion by individuals. The images of others should not be renounced beforehand. The perception, for example, that customers will not accept a paid service number may be discussed further. It can appear possible that customers object to this because it demonstrates the one-sidedness of the customer–supplier relationship. If a sale can be made, the supplier is available and friendly, but if it is held to its previous promises, there is no response. If this impression can be removed, the path to a paid service number is open. Then, it is the gateway to a serious and committed supplier who is ready and willing to help.

A *shared vision* may be developed from these discussions. A common answer to the underlying question of why we are doing things this way, may be formulated. Knowledge is obtained for the objective that is pursued. Meaning is given to the work that is performed; it represents the incentive to learn more, to acquire and to distribute knowledge and to excel. The service employees are not there to minimise costs and keep customers away. The goal of the salesman is not to maximise turnover, and the objective of the financial department is not limited to the reduction of working capital. Everyone has the same goal; to achieve success, together with the customer.

Team learning is then necessary to turn the visions and knowledge which were developed collectively into actions. Teams must be capable of acting collectively and learning from experience. This requires a dialogue in which assumptions are removed so that the free exchange of information and meanings becomes possible. The slow agent in the call centre that continues to try to find out the underlying reasons motivating customers to make contact should not be painted as the black sheep who fails to achieve his productivity goals and who should not be taken seriously. In all likelihood, he is the person who knows the most. In an open dialogue, his experiences could be converted into collective knowledge of the customer and the effectiveness of the way the customer is managed.

Knowledge management

Knowledge management (see Figure 13.3) can play a role in the focused creation, distribution and use of vital knowledge. Knowledge management should, however, not be identified with the systems, which is a mistake that is often made. The tool can never take the place of the product, nor are CRM systems fully capable of giving shape to CRM.

The track record of knowledge management systems is perhaps even worse than that of CRM. Major investments are made in systems and the filling of them with data, and hopefully knowledge. However, often the use of this is lacking. A dynamic link between the users of the system is absent. In order to realise this link, those involved will have to discover its relevance and value in daily operations (see Figure 13.1). The system must be built around people and the activities within the company. At the time a question appears, the system must be able to respond to this and provide knowledge that immediately proves its use. Someone in the contact centre can look up the contact history and respond to the caller's question. Supplementary information is also available. The advantages and disadvantages of a product are described, an old mailing may be retrieved, and so forth.

In addition to embedding it in the operational processes, the development of a successful knowledge management system also requires a connection to the strategic processes. After all, control over knowledge development must come from a common vision and strategy. From here, it must be indicated whether or not more knowledge is necessary in the effectiveness of the website, the segmentation and profiling, the relationship strategy and so forth.

Knowledge is developed on the basis of people's experiences. As a result, the quality of a knowledge management system is determined ►

Figure 13.3 Knowledge management

Source: Tissen *et al.* (1998).

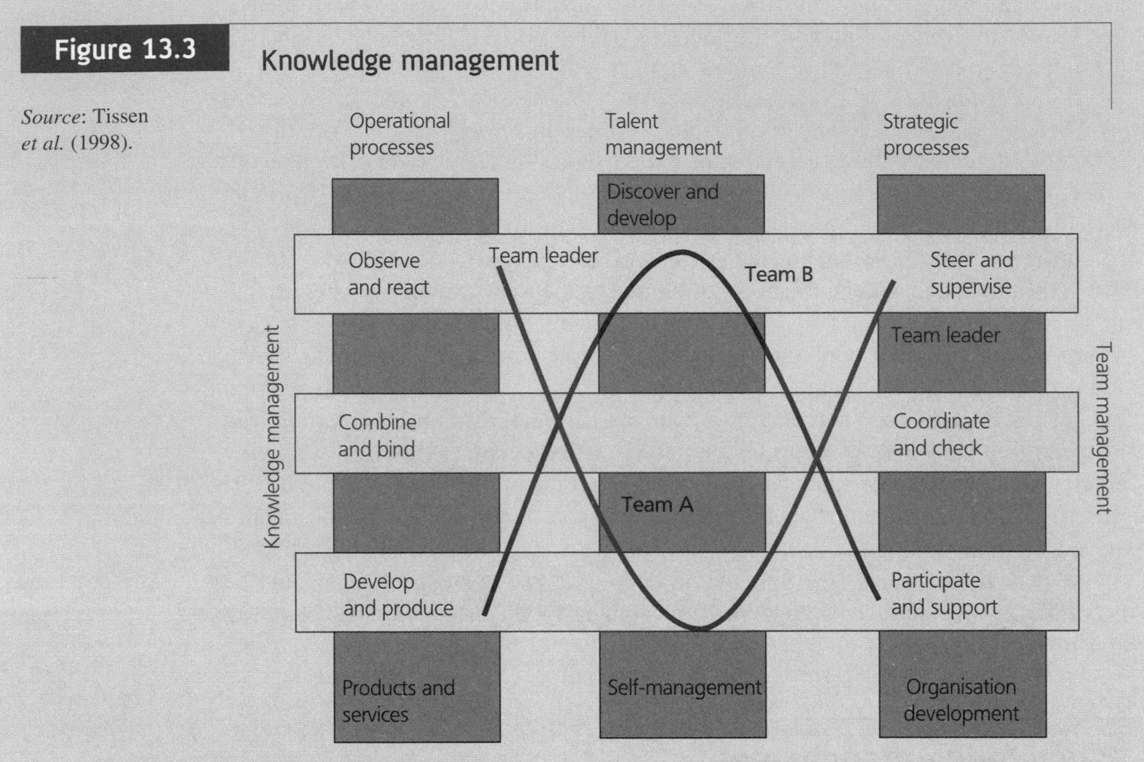

by the people who must work with it. Although the system will have to manage itself to a great extent by recording knowledge and making it available, its development may be influenced by selecting certain people for certain learning projects (teams). They are held responsible for the development, recording and the distribution of knowledge in areas such as fitting the Internet into the multichannel environment, cross-selling, personalisation, segmentation, etc. The information will have to be used to improve the operations. Account managers, marketers, agents from the call centre and database analysts develop and use a cross-sell engine, for example, and on the basis of their experiences with this tool, knowledge of it will be expanded and recorded. Those involved from different channels, experiment with different forms of personalisation and share the results. A cross-functional project team that tackles the efforts to reduce customer churn, gains experience with different retention analyses and campaigns, and ensures that these are recorded and made available. These teams may count on participation and support from management.

13.4 Conclusion

The situation in which we evaluate only the effectiveness of separate marketing activities has to be avoided. CRM's aim is to measure the impact of marketing activities on the value of customer relations. Although this may be theoretically sound, it can be hard to achieve in practice. Therefore an analysis of the activities in the sales process and their contribution to the final transaction is a first practical step to build an integral understanding of the accountability. An evaluation of targeting decisions, specifying who will be selected for a marketing activity, can place the sales analysis in the context of CRM, and for the real achievers a Markov chain can help to calculate the contribution of activities to the lifetime value.

Evaluation is one way to learn. Through experimentation and testing marketers can actively seek out the most effective marketing campaigns and activities. Extensive experience with experimentation and testing has been built up in the fields that were the precursors of CRM: direct marketing and database marketing. Individual reactions to marketing campaigns originate from customers and prospects so that the costs and returns from a campaign can be linked to one another. Analyses can be created to demonstrate which campaigns and segments produce good results. Insight can be developed regarding the communication, the incentive, the proposition, the list and the effects which may be expected from these. As long as the variation in the marketing activities is limited and a transaction is the immediate goal, an important portion of the necessary marketing knowledge can be expanded through tests and experiments.

However, when the complexity and changeability increase, the situation changes. The need arises for a learning organisation with less formal and time-consuming methods of learning. Motivation and effort from everyone is desired in order to derive knowledge from their experiences, to form a common picture of the reality, to expose the purpose behind the actions, and to gain inspiration from this in order to further develop and exploit this knowledge gained. Knowledge management systems can facilitate the realisation of a learning organisation, but it is ultimately the people who must do the work. Thanks to these systems, knowledge is made available more quickly and easily, and knowledge development is supported as a result.

Case study

Proteq Direct: testing e-mail marketing is effective

Direct writer Proteq Direct used e-mails in experiments to acquire new customers and the result is: although the response on a physical direct mailing is higher, the costs per order for an e-mailing are lower, and in combination with a direct mailing the conversion improves. Sending more than one mailing to the same address works, but is, however, expensive.

The pros of an e-mail marketing campaign – low costs, extending the market reach – will only become evident when the medium is applied in the right way. Only few companies, however, test before they send out the bulk mailing and are confronted with disappointing low response rates.

For direct writer Proteq this was the reason to organise, together with an e-mail marketing agency, a test case for a new car insurance campaign. Finding out how effective and appropriate e-mail actually is to acquire new customers was the motive for Proteq to initiate the test . . . The marketing manager at Proteq Direct: 'In traditional direct marketing it is always a trade-off. On the one hand you want to make a sharp selection to increase your response, but on the other hand you want to reach many people. We wanted to learn if with e-mailing we can increase our market reach. Besides that, an e-mailing is a lot cheaper. The economic climate and the maturity ►

level of the market are reasons for a decrease in response on traditional mailings.' Michael Bres, managing partner of the e-mail marketing agency E-Profile: 'It is the challenge to come up with a targeted offering and in the meantime to maintain the size of the mailing list. E-mail marketing can also seriously reduce the costs of an order.' Peter: 'But first we wanted to see if this was true.'

'The subject of the mailing was a new car insurance with a price that decreases when the customers' driving experience increases and therefore has fewer accidents and a safer driving style. Not only will the customer have a higher no-claim, but also a lower contribution. Prospects were private drivers without lease cars in the age categories of 29 to 65, living in areas with a high penetration of older and smaller cars up to a purchase price of €20 000.' These criteria were used by E-Profile to select addresses in the online databases of Jecomputerisjelot and Testnet. Five equal experimental groups have been formed with the help of Experian; in the online database the e-mail adresses were related to names and addresses for which segmentation profiles were available in the Experian database.

Different ways were used to approach prospects; in a one-step approach or a multi-step approach, with or without a message informing the prospect of the upcoming e-mailing and with or without a physical direct mailing followed up by an e-mail as reminder.

The proposition remained the same in all mailings. Also in all experiments the main mailing was sent out at the same time. Further, by clicking through the e-mail prospects could, in an interactive way, directly calculate their premium. Peter: 'E-mail allows you to make an offer directly when people show interest. Therefore a functional use of the medium is to be preferred.' There were three ways for people who did not want any e-mail offerings in the future to get off the list. Bres: 'You could chose to be removed from all mailings, to be removed from mailings of this advertiser, or to receive mailings on selected topics.' The sender was clearly visible on the mailing to avoid complaints about spamming. Furthermore, an e-mail address will never be used more than once or twice a month for an e-mailing. And, of course, we only mail when we have something to tell. By following this approach, the agency achieved that only 1 per cent of the receivers state they want to be removed from the list.'

E-Profile selected five equal experimental groups of 5000 consumers. Addresses were selected based upon the drivers' experience, the geographical spread, the purchase value of the car (when new) and the kilometre usage per year. Sex was not a selection criterion. Peter: 'Men have no significantly different claiming behaviour from women. Therefore it is a not a criterion. Besides that, we do not think it is a relevant segmentation criterion.' For previous Proteq Direct mailings profile analyses were made for the best responding addresses (Ideal Profiles). A part of the mailing list was formed by these Ideal Profiles.

The quality of the e-mail addresses is good as only 1 per cent of the e-mails bounced.

Results

Mailing consumers more than once will have a positive impact on the response, but will also affect the costs. An increase in the share of e-mails in the campaign will reduce the costs per order. The Ideal Profile consumers responded best (37 per cent). The one-step approach with only the digital main mailing had the lowest response (index 41) but ranked second in costs. To measure what the results would be if not 5000 but 60 000 mailings were sent out, a new calculation was made in which economy of scale effects were incorporated. The Ideal Profile remains the most profitable group with an index of 89, but experimental group 4 becomes more lucrative with an index of 60 and test group 2 with only an e-mailing, will cost less than half the average cost per policy. It is the result of avoiding the physical print and postal costs.

Conclusions

Proteq is satisfied; e-mail appears to be an effective medium to acquire new customers. Although the response on a physical mailing is higher, e-mailings are cheaper and offer opportunities to reach a larger share of the target market. The combination of direct and e-mail has synergistic effects. Approaching consumers more than once has a positive impact on the conversion, but a negative one on the costs. Peter: 'We have to experiment further. We will continue to develop and send out direct mailings and keep on learning in experiments. E-mail databases will be expanded and improved, profiles will be combined and for sure we will combine media in the future.'

Source: Filander (2004).

Questions

1 What are the pros and cons of combining a physical direct mailing with an e-mailing?

2 Why can you increase the reach of your campaign with an e-mailing?

3 What is meant by the statement that e-mailings should be used functionally?

4 How do you evaluate the sampling in this test/experiment?

5 What is the reason that the outcomes in the entire population are different from those in the sample?

6 Can you think of two other relevant experiments that Proteq might initiate in the future?

Questions

1 Different aspects of relationship marketing (the stimuli) may be tested in an experiment. Come up with five experiments.

2 Proposition: in experiments, it is recommended to modify only parts of the marketing activities, because otherwise the effects may not be easily attributable to certain stimuli.

(a) Do you agree or disagree with this statement? Substantiate your answer.

(b) Give an indication of how limiting one or a small number of stimuli would affect the internal and external validity of the experiment.

3 Learning is the acquisition of knowledge from experience. Explain this definition using an example.

4 Learning in organisations is hindered by a number of factors. List five of these and provide an explanation.

5 Describe the learning organisation for a company with a CRM strategy and CRM systems.

6 What is the cause behind the failure of many knowledge management systems? Explain your answer.

7 Within the framework of knowledge management, teams may be created (see Figure 13.1) which are responsible for the development and distribution of knowledge throughout certain areas. Formulate ten of these types of teams for an organisation with a CRM strategy and CRM systems. Indicate whether the team leader should be recruited from operations or the management team (strategy). Substantiate your answer.

References

Eilander, Elisabeth (2004) Proteq Direct: testing e-mail marketing is effective, *Tijdschrift voor Marketing*, April.

Malhotra, Naresh K. and David F. Birks (2003) *Marketing Research*, 3rd edn, FT Prentice Hall, Harlow.

Mertens, Faust and Boudewijn Heilijgers (2002) Driving sales at Daimler Chrysler, in Christian Belz and Wolfgang Bussman (eds), *Performance Selling*, Thexis, St Gallen, 142–145.

Senge, Peter M. (1990) *The Fifth Discipline: The art and practice of the learning organization*, Currency and Doubleday, New York.

Tissen, Rene, Daniel Andriessen and Frank Lekanne Deprez (1998) *Value Based Knowledge Management*, Addison Wesley Longman, Amsterdam.

Zuiderduin, Jurgen (2003) *De effecten van marketingacties*, TIAS/Postbank, Amsterdam/ Tilburg.

Zwan, Arie van der and Jan Verhulp (1980) *Marktanalyse en bedrijfsstatistiek*, Stenfert Kroese, Leiden.

14

Reporting results

In this chapter, we oscillate between the ideal and reality. In Section 14.1 we will examine the theoretically desirable definition of lifetime value, but will then quickly describe the methods which are used to calculate this value in practice. In Section 14.2, we will describe the ideal image, yet will not neglect to report the several steps that have already been taken to achieve it. Finally, the manner in which the balanced scorecard may be interpreted will be discussed in Section 14.3.

In this chapter we will address the following questions

- How to evaluate the final result of the relationship marketing activities.
- How to define and calculate the economic customer value: the lifetime value.
- What is non-economic customer value?
- What is the economic and non-economic supplier value: the value that the supplier represents for the customer?
- How to describe and construct the balanced scorecard in this context.
  - How to translate the strategy into critical success factors, their criteria and norms.
  - How to use benchmarking as a method for determining norms.

Practitioner's insight

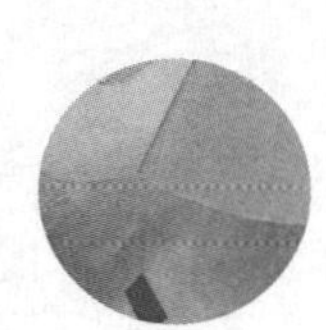

One often hears that it is no longer the transaction profit that matters in CRM, but the customer's profit contribution as a whole that is important. The ambitious term 'lifetime value' has been created for this very purpose. However, anyone who has a good look around will see that very few companies succeed in arriving at an accurate and reliable calculation of this economic customer value. It appears more difficult than once thought to attribute costs to individual customers. It seems as though years of experience with activity-based costing has failed to provide a solution to this problem. In addition, experience teaches us that companies that have succeeded in arriving at a determination of the lifetime value were too optimistic in their calculations. They have been unable to get the intended CRM off the ground. Economies and markets change and loyal customers can suddenly appear to be less loyal and less profitable. Investments in customers designed to produce future results appear to result in losses instead. And to make the challenge or disappointment even greater, we must conclude that even the companies that have succeeded in calculating the intended lifetime value have only reached a way station instead of a final destination. Companies that strive for a long-term, bilateral and mutually profitable relationship will have to address supplier value as well as customer value.

In order to be able to evaluate and guide CRM policy, more management information is necessary. Insight into the factors that bring about the final result is needed and may be provided through the use of a balanced scorecard.

14.1 Lifetime value

Definition

The lifetime value is the net present value[1] of the future contribution by a customer to the overhead and the profit of a company. The customer makes a contribution to the result if the income from transactions exceeds the expenses incurred in completing them and maintaining the relationship (Hoekstra and Huizingh, 1997).

From a theoretical viewpoint, the most accurate calculation of the contribution is obtained when all of the customer-specific incomes and expenses are allocated to each customer (see Table 14.1). Not only the expenses incurred in completing a transaction, but also those involved in acquisition and relationship management are allocated so that the most complete insight possible may be gained into the customer's profit contribution. However, this is not practicable in most situations. Incomes may

[1] One euro that someone has in their wallet now is worth more than one that is earned in the future. For this reason, it is determined what value future income and expenses represent today. To do this, the amounts are discounted to include the time value of money.

Table 14.1 Allocation of income and expenses to one customer

Customer turnover
Discounts granted (–)
Shipping costs passed on to customer (+)
Supplier's credit (+)
Gross turnover
Turnover from returns (–)
Net order sales
Costs of goods/services sold (–)
Administrative order processing costs (–)
Physical order processing costs (–)
Administrative and physical costs of processing returns (–)
Bad debt expenses (–)
Costs of acquisition and relationship management (–)
Customer's contribution to overhead and the profit of the organisation

Source: Roberts and Berger (1999).

generally be attributed to a certain customer, but this is more difficult when it comes to expenses. Companies usually have no insight into the actual expenses that are incurred for a specific customer. Calculations of standard costs should give an indication of the expenses that are incurred when efficient methods are used to acquire, serve and manage the relationship, etc. Depending upon the degree to which reliable cost estimates may be prepared, the decision may be made to allocate either more or fewer expenses to the customer or to choose to categorise them under the overhead costs. If insight into the costs of relationship management are lacking, it may be wise to include only the transaction costs in the lifetime value calculation. In this regard, reliability is more important than thoroughness.

In order to arrive at the actual calculation of the financial customer value, the customer will have to be identified. This can be more difficult in practice than it seems, perhaps as a result of working with intermediaries, direct customer contact is lacking or perhaps because there is no central registration of customer identification data. In principle, someone is a customer as soon as the first transaction has been completed. The customer value calculation will then have to incorporate all of the transactions performed during the time the person is officially a customer. The expenses will have to be determined during the period from acquisition up to and including the departure. This can involve actual realised cash flows (person is already a customer) as well as results to be obtained in the future which will have to be predicted (more transactions will be completed).

The following simplifications are made for practical reasons:

- The customer value calculation does not take place on an individual customer level but on a segment level.
- The time period to which the calculation applies is restricted. The calculation includes the expected income and expenses for only the first two or three years.

Example

In order to illustrate the customer value calculation, we will follow Blattberg, Getz and Thomas in their book *Customer Equity* (2001). They describe the situation of Buford Electronics, a company that sells $350 million worth of electronic components annually in the United States to a variety of customers. Within the framework of the acquisition and relationship management policies to be implemented, customers are segmented into groups of small and large customers. Companies that spend less than $3000 per year are categorised as small customers, whereas the larger companies spend on average between $25 000 and $100 000. In Table 14.2 in which the acquisition is described, it appears that the acquisition of large customers requires more effort than the acquisition of smaller clients. The higher amount of money spent by the larger

Table 14.2 Acquisition of customers

	Small customers (< $3000 per year)	*Large customers ($25 000–$100 000 per year)*
Starting situation		
Conversion ratio	15%	5%
Costs per sales visit	$20	$100
Number of sales visits per prospect	2	9
Turnover per customer during the first year	$1 200	$44 000
Margin on sales per customer – first year	$360	$8 500
Number of prospects approached	40 000	8 000
Financial results		
Sales expense per prospect	$40	$900
Costs to acquire a customer	$267	$18 000
Net contribution from the acquired customer	$93	($9 500)
Contribution as a percentage of the acquisition expense	13.5%	47%
Number of customers acquired	6 000	400
Initial investment in expansion of customer database	$1 600 000	$7 200 000
Net contribution newly acquired customers	$560 000	($3 800 000)

Source: Blattberg, Getz and Thomas (2001) p. 26. Reprinted by permission of Harvard Business School Press. From *Customer Equity: Building and managing relationships as valuable assets* by R.C. Blattberg, G. Getz and J.S. Thomas. Boston, MA 2001, p. 26.

Table 14.3 Customer performance from the first transaction to the present (2002)

Year	*Sales ($)*	*Gross margin (%)*	*Margin ($)*	*Marketing and service expense ($)*	*Retention percentage (%)*
Small customers					
1998	1 200	30	360	267	
1999	1 700	35	59	75	75
2000	2 300	35	805	75	80
2001	2 500	40	1 000	50	85
2002	2 500	40	1 000	50	85
Large customers					
1998	44 000	19	8 500	18 000	
1999	52 000	24	12 480	1 000	40
2000	70 000	26	18 200	1 000	55
2001	85 000	27	22 950	400	65
2002	85 000	27	22 950	400	65

Source: Blattberg, Getz and Thomas (2001) p. 28. Reprinted by permission of Harvard Business School Press. From *Customer Equity: Building and managing relationships as valuable assets* by R.C. Blattberg, G. Getz and J.S. Thomas. Boston, MA 2001, p. 28.

customers cannot compare with the additional efforts necessary to acquire the initial sale. By the end of the year, there is still no profit being earned in the large customer segment.

In order to determine the lifetime value, in addition to this first year, attention must also be focused on the other years during which customers place orders with Buford. Historical data which relate to the years which have passed since the company first became a customer may also be used. What was the churn in the segment, how much did the customers who remained customers spend and what expenses were incurred (Table 14.3)? The calculation will have to be based in part on the prediction of future behaviour (Table 14.4). Buford eventually decided only to perform an estimate for the coming five years and not to apply differentiation to the customer performance per year. The years following 2006 were not included in the calculation of the lifetime value; the future is considered to be too uncertain for this. Buford wished to prevent a situation from occurring in which an excessively high current customer value calculation stimulates too much investment in relationship development.

These basic data are then used to calculate the customer contribution for the segment for the large and small customers. These calculations are shown in Tables 14.5 and 14.6. What is striking is that the ultimate average lifetime value per customer is smaller for the large customers than it is for the smaller ones. They appear to be less loyal, demand lower prices and better service. The additional effort that Buford must expend for these customers does not seem to be in proportion to the higher amount received.

Table 14.4 Expected customer performance from 2003 to 2007

Year	*Sales ($)*	*Gross margin (%)*	*Margin ($)*	*Marketing and service expense ($)*	*Retention percentage (%)*
Small customers					
2003	2 500	40	1 000	50	85
2004	2 500	40	1 000	50	85
2005	2 500	40	1 000	50	85
2006	2 500	40	1 000	50	85
2007	2 500	40	1 000	50	85
Large customers					
2003	65 000	27	17 550	400	65
2004	65 000	27	17 550	400	65
2005	65 000	27	17 550	400	65
2006	65 000	27	17 550	400	65
2007	65 000	27	17 550	400	65

Source: Blattberg, Getz and Thomas (2001) p. 28. Reprinted by permission of Harvard Business School Press. From *Customer Equity: Building and managing relationships as valuable assets* by R.C. Blattberg, G. Getz and J.S. Thomas. Boston, MA 2001, p. 28.

14.2 Alternatives for lifetime value

The lifetime value is characterised by limitations. It is a calculation of the economic value of a customer (group) to be used by the supplier. The non-economic aspects are neglected and the value that the *customer* assigns to the supplier is completely ignored. Nonetheless, it involves aspects which are relevant within the framework of a CRM strategy. Organisations that strive for long-term, mutually profitable customer–supplier relationships should not reason exclusively on the basis of themselves and their financial aspects. Should they do this anyway, the chance that the relationship will outgrow the transactional phase will not increase substantially (see Chapter 2). They will also discover that customers with a certain lifetime value or RFM score can be extremely heterogeneous; there may be significant differences between them as buyer, user and as individual or organisation. The input that the economic customer value gives to the relationship policy is limited as a result.

The measurement of the non-economic customer value and the supplier value can be recommended, yet will not be easily performed. It is difficult enough for an organisation to allocate the expenses incurred to individual customers; for consumer households that do not keep records, this will be nearly impossible. And for non-economic quantities, it holds true that they are difficult to quantify.

Table 14.5 Customer value contribution calculation: small accounts

Small accounts: first transaction in 1998

Cost of money: 20%
Number of acquired customers: 6000
Customer value contribution first year: $560 000
Customer value contribution in the nine following years: $9 026 823
Total segment customer value: $9 586 823
Average customer value: $1598

Year	Turnover ($)	Gross margin (%)	Margin ($)	Marketing and service costs ($)	Customer value contribution/ account ($)	Discounted value contribution/ customer ($)	Retention percentage (%)	Number of accounts in year	Yearly discounted customer value contribution
1998	1 200	30	360	267	93	93	–	6 000	560 000
1999	1 700	35	595	75	520	433	75	4 500	1 950 000
2000	2 300	35	805	75	730	507	80	3 600	1 825 000
2001	2 500	40	1 000	50	950	550	85	3 060	1 682 292
2002	2 500	40	1 000	50	950	458	85	2 601	1 191 623
2003	2 500	40	1 000	50	950	382	85	2 211	844 066
2004	2 500	40	1 000	50	950	318	85	1 879	597 880
2005	2 500	40	1 000	50	950	265	85	1 597	423 499
2006	2 500	40	1 000	50	950	221	85	1 358	299 978
2007	2 500	40	1 000	50	950	184	85	1 154	212 485

Source: Blattberg, Getz and Thomas (2001) p. 29.

Table 14.6 Customer value contribution calculation: large accounts

Large accounts: first transaction in 1993

Cost of money: 20%
Number of acquired customers: 400
Customer value contribution first year: ($3800)
Customer value contribution in the nine following years: $4 188 108
Total segment customer value: $388 108
Average customer value: $ 970.27

Year	*Turnover ($)*	*Gross margin (%)*	*Margin ($)*	*Marketing and service costs ($)*	*Value contribution/ account ($)*	*Discounted value contribution/ customer ($)*	*Retention percentage (%)*	*Number of accounts in year*	*Yearly discounted customer value contribution*
1998	44 000	19	8 500	18 000	–9 500	–9 500	–	400	–3 800 000
1999	52 000	24	1 248	1 000	11 480	9 567	40	160	1 530 667
2000	70 000	26	1 820	1 000	17 200	11 944	55	88	1 051 111
2001	85 000	27	2 295	400	22 550	13 050	65	57	746 447
2002	85 000	27	2 295	400	22 550	10 875	65	37	404 325
2003	85 000	27	2 295	400	22 550	9 062	65	24	219 010
2004	85 000	27	2 295	400	22 550	7 552	65	16	118 630
2005	85 000	27	2 295	400	22 550	6 293	65	10	64 258
2006	85 000	27	2 295	400	22 550	5 244	65	7	34 806
2007	85 000	27	2 295	400	22 550	4 370	65	4	18 853

Source: Blattberg, Getz and Thomas (2001) p. 30.

Figure 14.1 Bilateral customer value determination

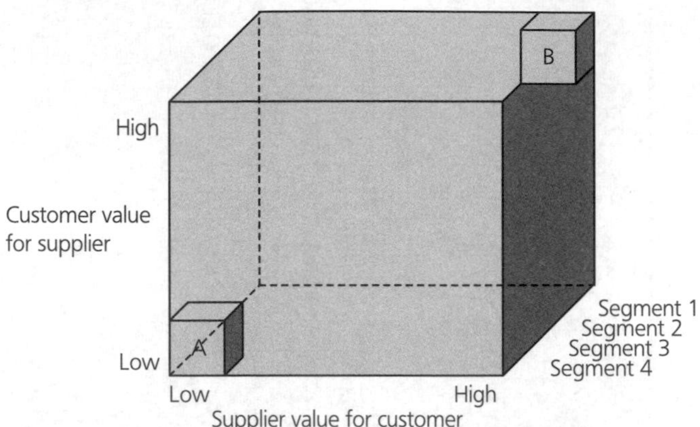

In spite of these implementation problems, there are initiatives that can place this customer value calculation in a broader perspective. The company Loyalty Profiles in the Netherlands, for example, attempts to deduce the value that customers assign to a supplier from the type of goods and services purchased, the purchase frequency, the most recent purchase date and the amount spent. A customer from a certain segment with the corresponding needs-and-wants pattern, who has not yet purchased the crucial goods and services specific to that segment, would most likely not describe that particular supplier as strategic. The non-economic customer value is thus deduced from the pattern in which the relationship develops. Does the turnover demonstrate a pattern that is characteristic of the segment? Is the cross-buying or the cross-selling path developing as expected? Can it be inferred from the development that both parties appreciate one another?

Value determination from the perspective of the customer and the supplier may be illustrated graphically. This has been done in Figure 14.1 for three different customer segments. In the cube, A occupies the least attractive position, whereas B occupies the most attractive position.

14.3 Balanced scorecard

In Chapter 4, it has already been indicated that financial data in and of themselves offer very little basis for the communication, monitoring and finalising of policy. The expansion of this with non-economic results data does, in fact, contribute to the creation of a more complete picture of customer and supplier value, yet is just as inadequate. It may be compared to attempting to fly a plane with only an altimeter and speed indicator. Supplemental data are desired which can explain how the customer and supplier value may be realised. A strategic map can indicate what these are and how they are related to one another (see Figure 14.2). The financial stakeholders' satisfaction with

Figure 14.2

Strategic map

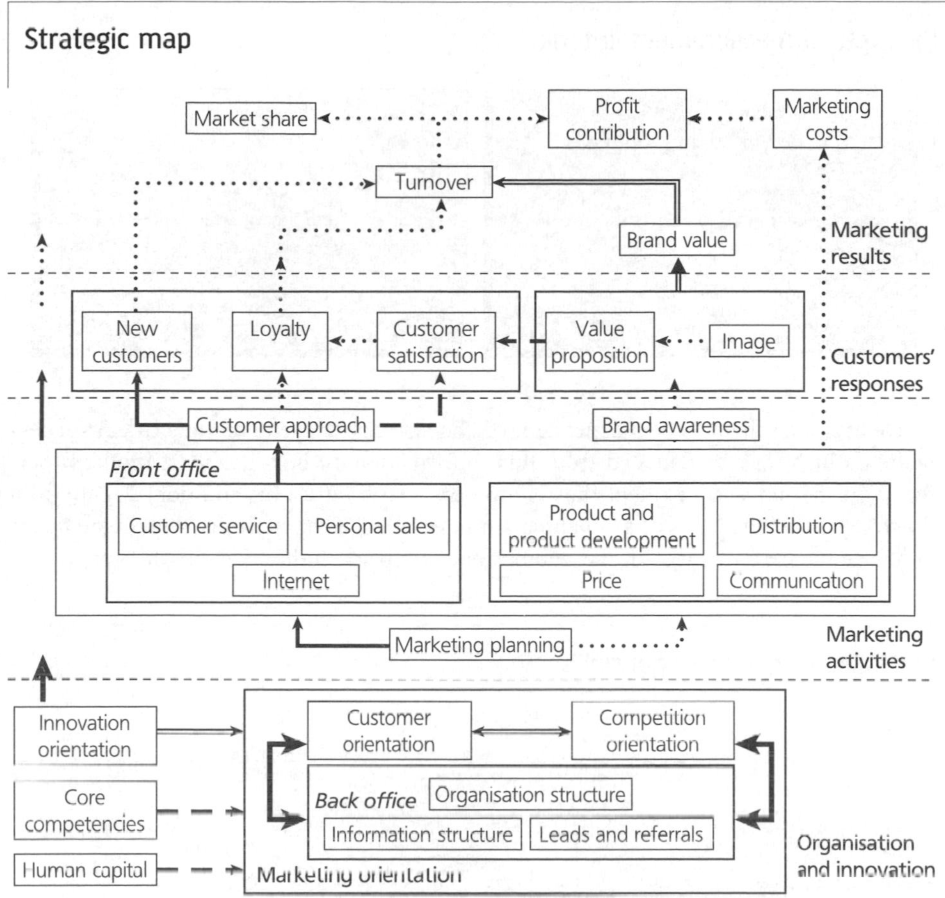

Source: Beltman *et al*. (2000). © ICSB, Marketing en Strategie, Rotterdam (2001).

the financial results – in terms of market share, profit, lifetime value – may all be related to the loyalty or customer commitment. To what extent does the loyalty contribute to the results and to what degree are they the result of the acquisition of new customers? Customer loyalty may then be associated with satisfaction. To what extent is this the result of the value position or of the customer approach, such as may be expected with a CRM strategy? The valuation for the customer approach is dependent, for example, on the processes in the front office, the marketing communication (image), the product development, the pricing policy and the distribution. Ultimately, the marketing planning and the market orientation of the organisation lie at the base of these processes.

Criteria will have to be developed to measure these data. Data from the available systems may be used as part of the data necessary for the measurement; however, other data will also have to be gathered separately through the use of surveys. The collection of some of the data also requires a great deal of effort. Dependent in part on the degree to which they are critical to the implementation of policy, the decision may be made to collect these data less frequently (see Figure 14.3). Customer satisfaction studies may be performed once every quarter, for example, whereas turnover data may be collected internally once a week.

Figure 14.3 Example of measurement criteria

- Number of monthly complaints
- Turnover per customer (group), profit contribution
- Customer segments' share of turnover
- Introduction of new products
- Accounts receivable
- Profitability per:
  - segment
  - channel

- Detours from the planned path of growth
- Developments in the market share
- Number of departing customers
- Availability of contact centre
- Realisation and follow-up to marketing activities according to planning (deviations)

Determining the norms is dependent on the strategy chosen and the critical success factors which may be deduced from this. Information on how the 'best-in-class' performs in the industry segment may, however, also be a useful addition. Figure 14.4 illustrates how the results of a benchmark are recorded. The outermost web in the figure indicates the performances of the number one company in the financial market.

Figure 14.4 Benchmarking in the financial sector

Source: Beltman *et al.* (2000).

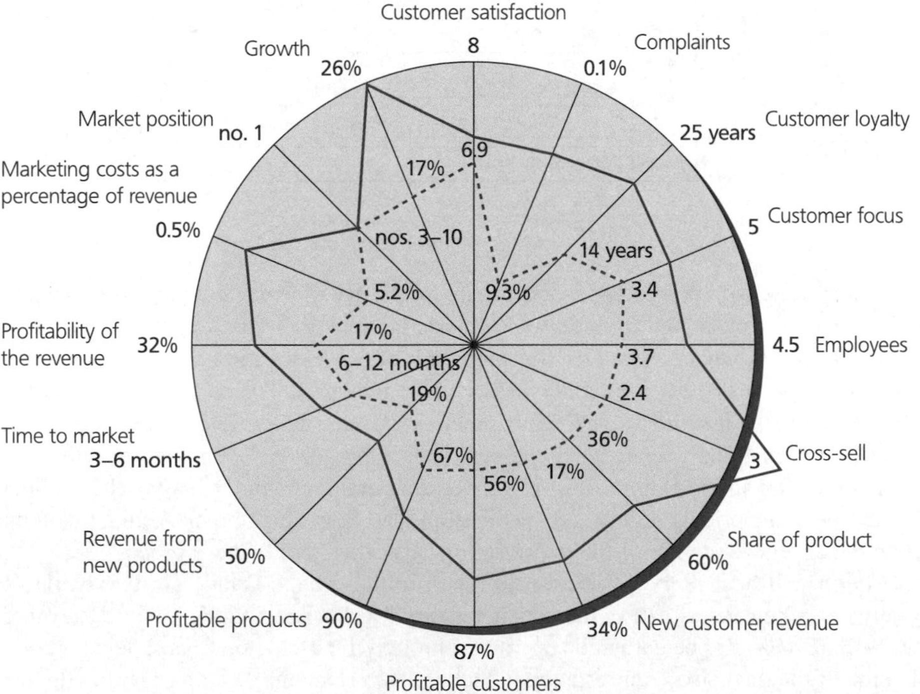

14.4 Conclusion

A CRM strategy focuses on the development of the relationship with a customer and thus the customer value. The idea is that keeping customers and developing relationships with them is ultimately less expensive and more profitable than attracting new ones. The consequence of this is that the transaction profit loses its value as management information. A customer is an asset that represents value. The lifetime value is an indicator of this; it specifies what the customer's cash contribution is to the profit and the overheads of an organisation. In practice, its calculation is dependent on the availability of data. In how much detail may costs be allocated to customers and, as such, be deducted from overheads? To what extent may a prediction be made of the future turnover?

The calculation of lifetime value has its flaws. Organisations that truly strive for long-term mutually profitable relationships with customers will have to calculate the supplier value to the customers in addition to the customer value. Furthermore, they will also have to pay attention to non-economic aspects in their calculation rather than focusing exclusively on economic factors.

Management information is necessary for more aspects than the (non-) economic customer and supplier values alone. Using a balanced scorecard, insight will also have to be gained into the factors that are responsible for the results.

Case study

A different ending to the end-of-year promotion of fitness centre Yacht

Fitness centre Yacht is one of the most modern fitness centres in Rotterdam. John Upstream bought it five years ago from the previous owner and has fully renovated it. The old, baroque, but rather poorly maintained building has, despite its architecture, been transformed into a fitness centre that reminds us of ancient Greece. Since its opening the centre has attracted many customers and is highly profitable.

In total, the centre was visited by approximately 200 000 customers last year. On average the guests spend €35 on which a profit margin of 15 per cent is made. Some of these customers visit the fitness centre on a regular basis; but the clientèle also consists of people making one visit or participating during the summer or a training or slimming period. Companies also organise events in which a visit to Yacht is part of the programme.

The facilities contribute to Yacht's success, but there is more. The employees and the marketing activities also have an impact. The marketing manager, the brother of the owner, Michael Upstream, initiated several successful campaigns. He found that 30 per cent price cuts had the best results. Yearly, he initiates five to six campaigns, which in total represent 10 per cent of the annual turnover.

At the beginning of 2002 Michael invested in a new marketing system. His contact person at the system integrator took care of the implementation and besides that was helpful enough to present him with a database of names and addresses of people that previously visited a fitness centre in the neighbourhood of Yacht. This was an exceptional offer that Michael could not resist at the time, but which later on he would regret intensely. The list appeared to come from ▶

a competing fitness centre from a nearby town that also hired the services of the system integrator. The employee perceived the reselling of the list as a nice supplement to his regular income.

Although the guilty party was the employee of the system integrator, Dunhill, the fitness centre in the neighbouring town, sued Yacht. The list of relationship data contained several dummy names and addresses. When Yacht sent out a mailing at the end of 2003 with a 30 per cent price cut to the people on the list, it became obvious to Dunhill that their customer database had fallen into the hands of their rival.

As part of the preparations for the upcoming lawsuit, Dunhill hired an adviser who estimated the damage of the unapproved usage of their database. In his report the advisor mentions a loss of approximately €271 000.

Yacht hired a solicitor to defend themselves and on his advice *you* are hired as a CRM expert to make an independent estimate of the value of the illegitimate use of the database. As input for your advice you will find information on the report of Dunhill's adviser and a report produced by Yacht's accountant with a calculation of the number of customers that visited Yacht because of the end-of-year promotional campaign.

Summary of the report produced by Dunhill's advisor

In his report, Dunhill's adviser has taken the following approach. The damage that results from the theft and illegitimate usage of the customer database equals the lifetime value of the customers Dunhill could have acquired if they had executed the promotional campaign. Dunhill's customer database contains 40 000 names and addresses. The experience with earlier highly targeted promotional campaigns is that around 10 per cent of the addressed persons respond. Considering the economic circumstances, the advisor forecasts that the response will be 10 per cent less at present. Visitors to Dunhill normally spend €50, on which a contribution margin of 35 per cent is realised. The contribution margin is calculated by deducting the variable costs from the turnover. An initial visit will normally be followed up with repeat visits. To calculate the value that these visits represent in the context of the measurement of the lifetime value, the adviser uses retention data that were available for the sector. He states that:

- During the upcoming season 50 per cent of the initial customers will repeat their visit.
- The season thereafter 25 per cent will still come.
- Thereafter 15 per cent of the customers will remain.
- And after a further year 10 per cent will visit the fitness centre.
- In the end 5 per cent will keep on visiting the centre; they will become part of the regular clientèle. A capitalisation factor of 3 is proposed to estimate the value this group represents.

The damage can then be calculated as shown in Table 14.7. According to the adviser this is a realistic estimate of the damage.

Accountant's report on the end-of-year action

Yacht asked their accountant to check the administration and to calculate how many people responded to the end-of-year campaign addressed to people in the database Yacht hired from the system integrator's employee. Tracing back the visitors that responded to the particular action was possible since they had to hand in a blue coupon to claim the 30 per cent discount. In the end 2035 customers handed in this coupon. In total 33 000 were mailed and therefore the response rate for this campaign was 6.17 per cent. Not all persons in Dunhill's database were selected; further analysis showed that only 11 000 names and addresses were used and that 22 000 cases originate from Dunhill's database. Besides that, Dunhill's database did not amount

Table 14.7 Damage calculation

Period	*Response*	*Visitors*	*Value (€35)*
4th season 2003 (100%)	10.00%	4000	140 000
1st season 2004 (50%)	5.00%	2000	70 000
2nd season 2004 (25%)	2.50%	1000	35 000
3rd season 2004 (15%)	1.25%	600	21 000
4th season 2004 (10%)	1.00%	400	14 000
5% remaining (capitalisation 3)	0.50%	600	21 000
Total missed contribution margin			**301 000**
Correction for economic climate (–10%)			**270 900**

to the previously mentioned 40 000 names and addresses, but only to 27 000.

Questions

Michael Upstream and brother John have some specific questions to ask you as an advisor. First of all they want you to produce an independent report as an expert; they do not want to direct its contents. The underlying idea is that it will then be accepted as evidence during the lawsuit. Nonetheless, they would like to ask you to attend to the following questions:

1. What does the privacy legislation state on this issue?
2. Is Yacht guilty?
3. Is the approach of Dunhill's adviser correct; is it appropriate to work with the lifetime value of a customer?
4. What value does this list represent on the market? How much would a list broker charge you for it?
5. If Yacht is guilty, how would you estimate the damage they caused Dunhill?

Questions

1. What does the discount rate depend on?
2. Why is it difficult to allocate the internal expenses to individual customers?
3. What is the difference between costs and expenses? Does a net cash value calculation work with costs or expenses? Explain your answer.
4. The lifetime value is often calculated for a so-called annual echelon (per segment). Can you provide an explanation of this?
5. What criticism could you provide for the calculation of the lifetime value performed by Buford?

6 Develop a method for determining the supplier value for a customer for a company of your choice.

7 Prepare a strategic map for an arbitrary organisation.

References

Beltman, Rob, Ed Peelen and Philip Waalewijn (2000) *CRM, de klant centraal*, Samsom, Alphen aan den Rijn.

Blattberg, Robert C., Gary Getz and Jacquelyn S. Thomas (2000) *Customer Equity: Building and managing relationships as valuable assets*, Harvard Business School Press, Boston, Massachusetts.

Hoekstra, J. and E. Huizingh (1997) Lifetime value measurement methods, working paper, RU Groningen, Groningen.

Roberts, Mary Lou and Paul D. Berger (1999) *Direct Marketing Management*, available for download at www.marylouroberts.info.

Part IV

Operational CRM

The topic of operational CRM is the contact cycle. The contact cycle is initiated with the target group, new customers are welcomed in, initial contacts are followed up and the dialogue between customer and supplier is expanded upon. Communication takes place via different channels, and at different times and locations. The relationship strategy which has been designed is implemented through a learning dialogue in which both parties learn from one another continuously and make use of the knowledge gained. Problems are spotted and solved and customers who threaten to leave the organisation are won back, if this is both possible and desirable.

Operational CRM forms a substantial part of the CRM system. The CMAT model, which is illustrated in Figure IV.1, is used to describe it. Although it is not an academic model, it is often cited and should not be missing in a CRM textbook. In the centre of the figure the contact cycle is shown in the block 'Customer Management Activity'. The contacts form a process in themselves, the communication process, and will have to fit in closely with other processes in the organisation so that goods or services purchased may be managed, produced, purchased, supplied and serviced. An accurate definition of these processes is determinative for the reliability of the CRM system, but just as crucial is the quality of the people and the manner in which they organise themselves in order to carry out the activities. They are dependent on the underlying (IT) infrastructure (see bottom of figure) for their success.

During the contact process between customer and supplier, the right proposition will have to be made to the right customers (see left side of figure). By conducting a dialogue, companies will have to determine what customers would like in a certain form at a certain time so that the right experience may be created and a competitive advantage may be realised (see top of

Figure IV.1 The contact cycle

Source: © QCi Assessment Ltd 2004.

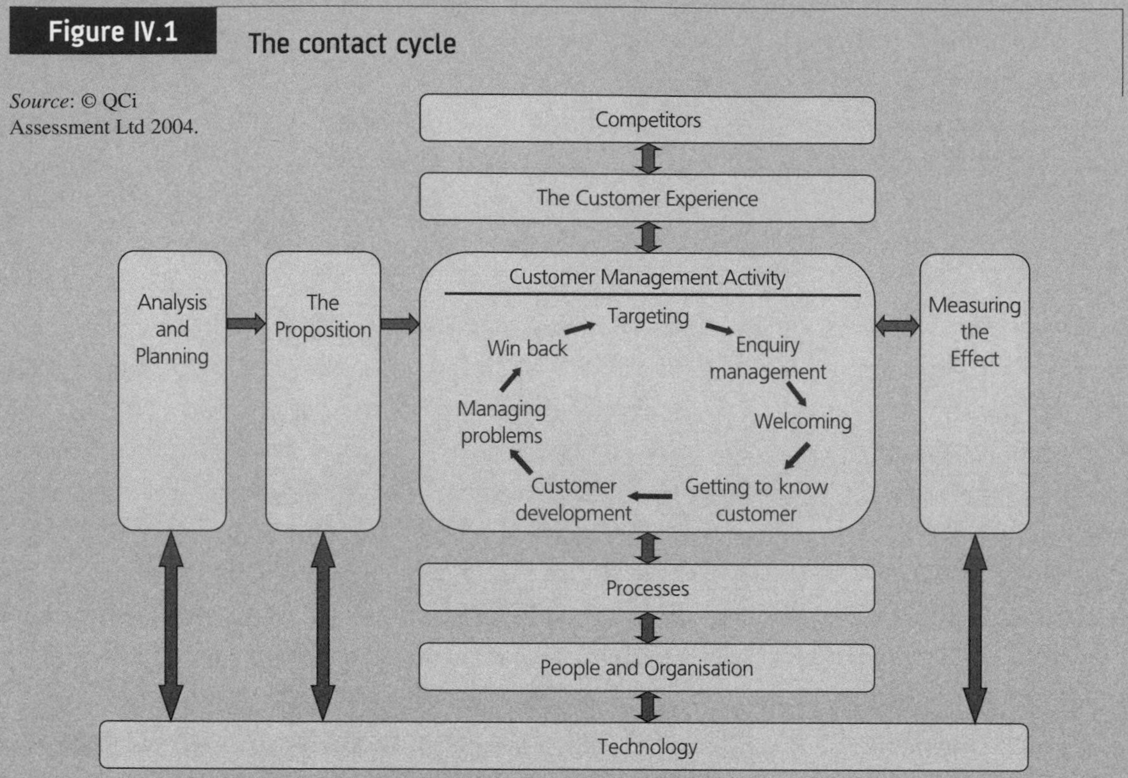

figure). Continuous measurement of the contacts is desirable in order to learn from the effectiveness and efficiency of one's own behaviour and the customer preferences (see right side of figure).

In this part of the book, we examine the manner in which the contact cycle may be organised and managed. First, we will focus on the call or contact centre, from which telephone contacts and now also e-mails are managed. Next, the website and the Internet will be treated and we will describe the place this 'channel' occupies in the dialogue. Finally, a description of the contact cycle would be incomplete without an analysis of the classic 'mail' tool.

The description of the technical systems that support the contact cycle are not covered in this part but will instead be handled in Part V, CRM Systems and their Implementation.

15

Call centre management

The express courier sector happens to be an industry in which call centre management is well developed. It must, however, be noted that the management of the business telephone contact traffic between customers and suppliers continues to grow in its complexity. The demands of customers increase. People tend to grab the telephone more quickly than they used to and use it for asking direct questions to which they expect a prompt answer from suppliers. In a culture in which time is scarce, many people experience the pressure of time, the level of 'laziness' is high, and customers expect a great deal from suppliers. In many cases, the level of accessibility and the supplier's availability by telephone should be high. People should expect and be willing to communicate with customers for many hours per day, be capable of gaining quick insight into the customer situation and be able to provide customers with solutions – in an efficient, and also in an empathetic and communicative manner! This is all arranged in the call or contact centre.

This chapter examines call centre management. First we provide a description of a call centre (Section 15.1) and analyse a critical factor determining the success of a call centre: the human resources (Section 15.2). In Section 15.3 we will then focus on the service level that we would like to offer customers and prospects by telephone. We will then discuss how this level may be realised. In Section 15.4, we explain capacity planning which is determinative for the aspect of availability. Managing the quality of the contact follows, and Section 15.5 deals with the specific opportunities and challenges involved in fax and e-mail transactions. In Section 15.6 we describe the key performance indicators which may be used to measure and control the performance of the call centre.

In this chapter we will address the following questions

- What is the definition of a call centre (contact and service centres)?
- What are the elements of a call centre?
- What are the role and importance of human resources for the quality of a call centre?
- How can we determine the (desired) service level for a call centre?
  - What should the accessibility be?
  - What should the quality of the contact be?
- How can we plan the capacity and achieve the desired availability?
  - How can we predict the workload (in- and outbound telephone calls)?
  - How can we deduce the staffing needs based on the workload?
  - How can we route calls to the agents?
- How to manage the satisfaction with the telephone contact.
  - What can monitoring, training and technology mean?
  - Should we be involved in cold prospecting and should we outsource the contact centre?
- How to manage the satisfaction with the contact through other channels.
  - How to deal with the privacy issue (opt-in).
  - What are e-mail marketing tips?
  - How to organise follow-up for contacts.
- How can we measure the call centre's performance?

Practitioner's insight

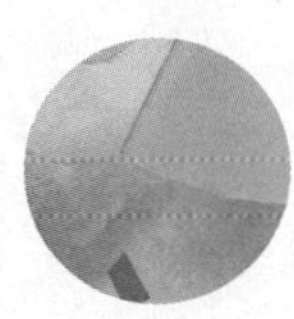

The tension is rising. Before the final contract may be drawn up, the prospect would like to see a hard copy of the new version of the contract. The contact person would like to ascertain that the modifications which have been discussed will actually be implemented. He would like to receive the adapted version by tomorrow to present it to management. As account manager, you call the express courier's call centre and struggle through the lines traced out by the voice response system to reach an agent. You indicate in which language you prefer to communicate by pressing the right number. In this way, you make it known that you would like to place a shipping order and are then placed in the queue. You listen to pleasant yet not exactly restful music and discover after several minutes that somehow the cycle has started all over again. You are asked to specify which language you speak and what you expect from the organisation . . . Although the call is free of charge for you, your time and that of your company is most definitely not . . . You would have preferred a rapid response, a listening ear and a tailored solution . . . Not that you expect the telephone to be answered on the first ring, after all, this would only catch you off-guard again . . .

15.1 Call centres described

A call centre is the 'place' where a large number of people handle the incoming as well as outgoing telephone conversations of a varied nature with their customers and/or prospects (see Figure 15.1). The centres are supported in these efforts by a switchboard equipped with call-centre functionalities such as automatic call distribution (ACD) and call queuing facilities. They can also input the caller's details into the system and may (via scripts) receive support in their dialogue. Depending on the functionality of the call

Figure 15.1

Possible contacts

Telephone sales
Information supply
Making an appointment
Service
Entertainment
Making and evaluating contacts
Fund-raising drives
Market research
Credit control

Source: Huijnen (1997).

centre, IT will play either a small or a very large role in the daily operations (Van den Brink, 1999).

Call centres are undergoing major development. Not only has there been a considerable increase in the number of calls, but the demands placed on the centres are increasingly high. Companies are becoming customer-oriented instead of product-oriented and are investing in CRM. They are interested in developing their relationship with their customers in terms of telephone contact as well. Not only do they want to sell and provide product information, but they would also like to be able to actually identify, get to know, and be of service to customers. Furthermore, people working at the call centres are aware of the fact that the telephone is not the only customer entrance to the business. Alternatives such as e-mail, voice-over-IP and fax have been integrated within the call centre and have led to the existence of new centres.

CRM definitions

Call centres in different forms

Call centre: collective term for a telephone interchange.

Customer care centre: an in-house call centre whose objective is to supply the specific customer group of a company with information, advice and service. Often uses free numbers or service numbers.

Contact centre: large customer care departments which handle a combination of incoming and outgoing telephone, e-mail and fax traffic, produce correspondence in which information and service are provided and commercial options are utilised.

E-centre: collective term for centres specialised in the processing of e-mail.

Source: CallCom Group.

Henceforth we will use the 'classical' term 'call centre' even if we are referring to that 'location' where contact is orchestrated through a multichannel system. A call centre consists of the elements detailed in Figure 15.2. *Manpower* (human resources) includes the recruitment and selection, hiring and training of personnel. Manpower perhaps represents the most important element in a call centre; after all, it is the people who are responsible for the quality. Reduction in staff turnover and absence due to illness are important challenges for many call centre managers.

The *telecommunication* module comprises the telephone switchboard, the systems used for routing the calls to the proper persons and voice response systems (see Chapter 19). The organisation of rescue and relief operations during emergencies is also considered to be part of this element of the call centre; this involves the organisation of temporary solutions for emergency situations in which the switchboard is out of operation due to computer failures, fire and the like. The choice may be made to have the calls handled by an external call centre or to relocate this operation to another location where a substitute call centre may be set up within a short period of time. Or the company may choose to answer the telephone and assist callers as much as possible, to manually register data and, in many cases, to call back at a later time.

Figure 15.2

Elements of a call centre

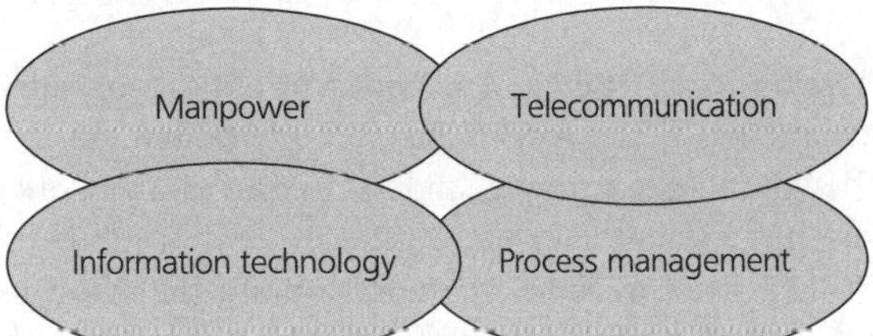

Source: Belloni Business Consultancy Contact Centers.

The *information technology* component (see Chapter 19) must make it possible to:

- identify callers;
- register customer contacts and payments in the database;
- gain access to information within the right time period and at the right workplace;
- organise the fulfilment: the automatic electronic generation and issue of documents such as order confirmations, appointment confirmations, etc.;
- manage the workflow: manage processes and issue the status (for example, what is the status of the processing of an order?);
- generate management information on the productivity of the personnel, the number of calls completed, the realised turnover, etc.;
- record quality measurements and to distribute them;
- provide the back office with information on the processing of orders and the like;
- give electronic training programmes;
- support control activities involving the information system.

Process management focuses on the management of the contact cycle. Important points of attention include capacity planning and quality management. The first must ensure that a call centre can handle the volume of calls; the subject of the second is the quality of the contact. In this part of the book dealing with operational CRM, we concentrate on the process management, and technology and manpower are a given.

15.2 Call centres and human resources

The ultimate quality of a call centre relies to a large extent on the quality of the workforce (van den Brink, 1999). It is not the technology, but the people that work with it that make the difference. Call centres face several challenging human resource issues. Many are known for rather high illness and labour turnover rates; it seems to be hard to bind people to the organisation and the work in a call centre for more than one to three years. In circumstances in which the scripts are detailed, there is a continuously high workload and the receivers are not always pleased with the conversation, the work in a call centre will become dreadful in due course and drive agents away (see the case study at the end of this chapter). The consequence is that a lot of effort has to be put into the hiring and training of people; investments are made that have to be earned back in a short timeframe.

Rather than accepting these effects, it is better to put efforts into offering perspective, pleasure and challenge in the work. This already begins during the hiring phase. Solicitors have to be able to get a proper understanding of the work in a call centre; it is a way to avoid disappointment later on. Furthermore it has to be clear from the start what competencies they need to have or build; among them the service orientation, communication and listening skills and the discipline to update the communication history. Management has to invest in the proper training and education, the enabling technology and workplace as it contributes to the agent's satisfaction and productivity (Heskett *et al.*, 1994).

Further, call centres managers should give priority to building an appealing team spirit, allowing for personal initiatives and the development of agents. It is known that agents that can use their knowledge of the customers and the products in the conversation build more pride in their work. They feel and perceive their contribution to the success of the organisation and the satisfaction of the customers. Together they can form a strong team of individuals that is allowed to learn and to share their best practices.

Several companies also have positive experience with involving the agents in developing the performance measurement system. In this way they are actively involved in the process of evaluating and improving their work. They are addressed as professionals in whose opinion the company is interested and they are made responsible, together with management, for improving the quality of their work.

15.3 Determining the service level

What determines the quality of the contact?

Availability

The quality of the contact is, to a great extent, dependent on the organisation's availability by telephone. It seems to be a simple concept, that, upon further examination, has more facets than one would think upon first glance. It is more than simply the percentage of telephone calls that are answered within *y* seconds. First, making a distinction between *customer groups* can be desirable, for which different levels of service are created. Then, attention is prescribed for the callers who get a *busy signal* and cannot reach the call centre at all and for those callers who decide not to wait and break the connection prematurely (call abandon). Calls falling into this latter category are referred to as 'lost calls'. In general, callers decide right after the establishment of the 'technical' connection whether they will wait or not. Should they decide to wait, then the chance is high that they will remain until the end. Finally, the *average response time* provides an incomplete picture. If we use a graph to indicate which frequency results in a certain response time, we will usually discover a skewed distribution. A small percentage of callers must wait much longer than the average amount of time.

Practitioner's insight

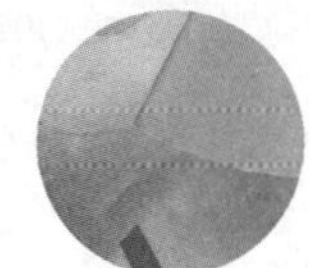

For a service level of 80 per cent answered within 20 seconds, roughly 30 per cent of the callers will end up in the queue, the longest waiting time will be approximately 3 minutes and the average response speed will lie between 10 and 15 seconds.

Source: Cleveland and Mayben, according to Erlang C program (1999).

Quality

In addition to the availability, the service level is naturally also dependent on the quality of the contact itself. Critical points involved in determining and measuring of the level of quality are:

- Are customer wishes being interpreted correctly?
- Are details being noted correctly?
- Are customers not being angered?
- Is the customer prevented from having to call back?
- Are opportunities just being missed and is valuable feedback being picked up?
- Has the transaction been completed or the complaint resolved?

An insufficient level of quality has consequences for productivity. Agents have to cope with customer irritation, and lose time, energy and the motivation to do their job. Furthermore, staff turnover and absenteeism grow as a result.

The impact of different aspects of the telephone conversation on customer satisfaction is shown in Figure 15.3. Only a limited number of aspects have a positive influence on the caller's level of satisfaction. How polite the agent is does matter, yet this has only a slight influence on the satisfaction. Their product knowledge, friendliness and ability to offer 'real' solutions allow agents to exercise a great deal of influence on the satisfaction. Aspects which may be considered hygiene factors and which must be of high quality may be found in the lower right quadrant. This involves availability, following up on promises, putting customers through and the recognition of a customer.

Determining the service level

The desired service level will have to be a derivative of the strategy. With a customer intimacy strategy, the quality level of the telephone contact should be higher than that found with an operational excellence strategy. By translating the customer intimacy strategy into service requirements for the call centre, there must be just as much attention dedicated to making sure that customer intimacy is not seen as a synonym for servitude. Customer orientation and customer friendliness are desirable, yet must not deteriorate into altruism and self-sacrifice. Commercial skills must guarantee that fulfilling customers' wishes is profitable and satisfying for both parties. Determining

Figure 15.3 Impact of quality on satisfaction

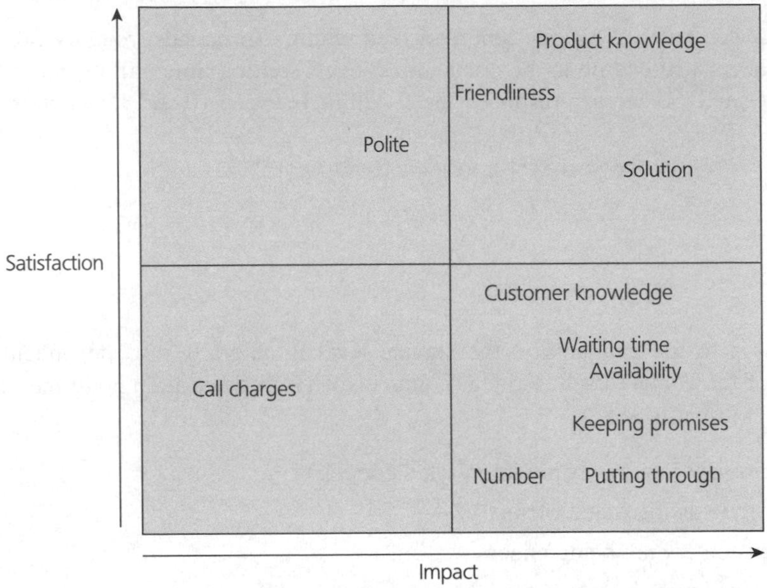

Source: *Call Centre Magazine*, no. 5 (1999).

Product knowledge
Friendliness
Polite
Solution
Satisfaction
Customer knowledge
Waiting time
Availability
Call charges
Keeping promises
Number
Putting through
Impact

CRM definitions

What is a high-quality telephone conversation?

- The caller is satisfied.
- The data have been input correctly.
- The conversation was necessary.
- The agent gave the right answers.
- The caller received the correct information.
- The agent received all of the necessary and useful information.
- The caller is not put through a countless number of times.
- The caller is not rushed.
- The caller has the feeling that the conversation was effective.
- The call centre has completed its task.
- Unsolicited information from the customer has been noticed and recorded.
- The caller does not feel it is necessary to enquire, check or to call back.
- Other employees can correctly process the customer's order.
- The agent is proud of his or her work.
- The caller did not get a busy signal.
- The caller did not have to wait in the queue too long.

Source: Cleveland and Mayben (1999).

the desired level of service also requires weighing costs and returns against one another. Service has its price!

Table 15.1 illustrates how an optimal service level may be determined for a call centre whose task it is to take orders by telephone. The optimisation decision

Table 15.1 Analysis of the increasing marginal return

	Agents on the telephone	Scheduled personnel (× 1.3)	Calls answered < 20 sec. (%)	% lost calls (estimate)	% calls permanently lost	Hours lines are in use	Answered calls	Gross turnover/ average call ($22.25)	Labour costs ($)	Line costs free number /15 min.	Net turnover	Increasing marginal return ($)
	25	33	45	26	7.80	14.6	184	4103	244	218	3641	0
	26	34	62	12.5	3.75	12.2	193	4293	254	182	3847	206
	27	35	74	6.5	1.95	11.2	196	4363	263	167	3933	85
	28	36	83	3.5	1.05	10.7	198	4403	273	160	3971	38
Optimum →	29	38	89	2.0	0.60	10.4	199	4423	283	156	3985	14
	30	39	93	1.5	0.45	10.3	199	4430	293	154	3984	(1)
	31	40	96	1.0	0.30	10.2	199	4437	302	152	3982	(2)
	32	42	97	0.5	0.15	10.1	200	4443	312	152	3980	(2)

Source: Cleveland and Mayben (1999).

concentrates in this case on the determination of the number of agents to be deployed for the completion of a given number of incoming telephone calls. How many direct and indirect individuals (columns 2 and 3) must be scheduled to answer the calls (column 7)? Which service level will then be reached? Or how many calls will be answered within the norm of 20 seconds? How many callers abandon? How many of these quitters try again later and which portion have we 'lost for good' (columns 3 to 5)?

Next, the turnover that may result from the customer contacts may be determined (column 8). This return may be used to counter the call centre costs which are linked to the workforce size and the use of the telephone lines (columns 9 and 10) in order to determine the net turnover.

Finally, the 'increasing marginal return' of the use of an extra agent in the call centre is calculated in the last column: how much extra net turnover is earned through the use of an extra agent? It appears that the optimum is achieved with 29 agents and that, after this amount, the extra costs are no longer offset by the growth in net turnover.

15.4 Capacity planning

Realising the desired level of availability is dependent upon the capacity planning. At any given moment of the day, the right number of agents should be available to handle the telephone contacts.

In call centres where incoming as well as outgoing telephone calls are processed, the work pressure is more or less manageable. Outgoing calls may be conducted at times when there is very little incoming call traffic. Nonetheless, we must also realise that the timing of the outbound calls is of importance for their effectiveness. For example, an agreement has been made with a customer that he or she will be called back at a certain time and the chance of reaching a prospect is higher at certain times of the day than at others. The result is that capacity planning remains necessary. From a prediction of the number of calls, the number of staff needed will have to be deduced.

Prediction of number of telephone calls

In predicting the number of telephone calls, long-term patterns are usually translated into half-hour periods. Figure 15.4 indicates how the number of telephone calls may be predicted for a half-hour block of time. To do this, a step-by-step decomposition takes place for the aggregated prognosis. In this way, the annual forecast is successively translated into a half-hour prediction. Fluctuations in the call traffic for certain seasons, weeks and days are also taken into account. Figure 15.4 gives an explanation of the calculation concerned.

There are call centres that base their capacity planning upon sales forecasts. On the basis of the average transaction amount, the expected turnover may be converted into the number of transactions to be completed. Next, it will be determined how many telephone calls are necessary to be able to complete this number of transactions. This number is multiplied by the average call duration and the completion time required in determining the final call centre capacity.

Capacity planning

Figure 15.4

Source: Cleveland and Mayben (1999).

Dissection of a forecast

720 000	calls this year
× 1.12	12% growth expected for this year
806 400	estimated number of calls for the coming year
× 0.071	ratio for January
57 254	calls in January
/31	operational days in January
1 847	average number of calls per day
× 1.469	index factor for Monday
2 713	calls on Monday
× 0.55	ratio for period from 10:00 to 10:30
149	Forecast number of calls from 10:00 to 10:30

Remarks

1 To calculate the operational days, count the days that the call centre is open

2 To calculate the index factor for the days of the week, divide the ratio for that weekday by the average ratio for that weekday.

Example: January						
Su	Mo	Tu	We	Th	Fr	Sa
		1	2	3	4	5
6	7	8	9	10	11	12
13	14	15	16	17	18	19
20	21	22	23	24	25	26
27	28	29	30	31		

Example	Ratio	Avg. ratio	Index factor
Monday	0.210	0.143	1.469
Tuesday	0.170	0.143	1.189
Wednesday	0.165	0.143	1.154
Thursday	0.165	0.143	1.154
Friday	0.150	0.143	1.049
Saturday	0.095	0.143	0.664
Sunday	0.045	0.143	0.315

In predicting the necessary capacity, the influence of campaigns on the work pressure of the call centre must also be factored into the equation (Bontebal *et al.*, 2001). Which activities have been planned at which times? How much conversion is expected? Campaigns may cause trend breaks in the size and composition of the call traffic. If this is not taken into account, it can lead to a drop in the level of service and a loss of turnover. In order to be able to accurately estimate the influence of these marketing activities, good communication between marketing departments and the call centre is a top priority. The most preferable situation is that in which the activities calendar is created in consultation between the two. If marketing determines the calendar contents unilaterally, an unnecessarily high number of peaks in the call traffic may occur. The opposite situation is no more desirable, in which the call centre and the postroom (fulfilment) are calling the shots. The optimum activity calendar will be one that is born out of a weighing of commercial against operational interests. With regard to modifications in the calendar, discussions will also have to take place regularly and in a timely manner.

In order to be able to make an accurate prediction of the call traffic, the organisation will then have to develop insight into the response percentages to marketing activities. Which response is achieved from a similar mailing at a similar time? How many people call in reply to a direct response advertisement or commercial? What will be the effect of a marketing activity incentive?

Predicting staffing needs

In order to calculate the staffing requirement, Erlang developed a much-used yet difficult C-formula back in 1917 (Cleveland and Mayben, 1999). Given the fact that Erlang C is built into many software packages for workforce management, the complexity is no longer a problem. In order to calculate the minimum staffing figure, four parameters must be filled in:

1 The average conversation time in seconds.
2 The average completion time in seconds.
3 The number of calls.
4 The desired service level in seconds (number of seconds within which the call should be handled).

In Table 15.2, the staffing needs have been calculated using the Erlang C formula for an inbound call centre with the following parameter scores:

- Average conversation time: 180 seconds.
- Average completion time: 30 seconds.
- Number of calls per half hour: 250.
- The desired service level in seconds: 20.

The computer program indicates in this case that the optimum workforce size is 34 agents. This calculation is based on the assumption that the unanswered 'calls' wait and do not hang up. This assumption, which lies at the basis of the Erlang C formula, generally results in an overestimation: the actual number of telephone calls to be handled is lower owing to the lost calls. In determining this optimum, the law of diminishing returns applies. Increasing the number of logged-in agents has a diminishing effect on the service level. A degressive increase in the percentage of callers that are handled within 20 seconds occurs. This is why achieving a top service level places demands on the personnel budget.

An alternative to the Erlang C formula for predicting staffing needs is simulation. A computer program may be developed in which call traffic spread out over the day, the week and the month may be simulated. Variations may be built into the call duration as well as the probability that callers in the queue will abandon the call and call back. The service and cost levels may be calculated for various staffing levels in the call centre, thus allowing the determination of the optimum workforce size.

In predicting the staffing requirement, special attention must be placed on the effect of lengthy calls and peak traffic on the service level. A disorganised effect can be the result, and may extend over a longer period of time. The completion activities can come under pressure and the quality of the contact can decrease.

The influence of the workforce size on the line occupancy rate will also have to be reviewed. The more agents that are deployed for a certain 'call load', the more the line occupancy will decrease. The opposite is true as well. If fewer agents are available to handle a certain call load, the occupancy of the lines will increase because the speed of answer has increased. If the supplier provides customers and prospects the opportunity to call free of charge, its line costs will rise.

Table 15.2 Erlang C for inbound call centres

Call centre for incoming telephone calls

Average conversation time in seconds: 180 | *No. of calls per half hour: 250*
Average completion time in seconds: 30 | *Service level in seconds: 20*

No. of agents required	*P(0)*	*ASA*	*DLYDLY*	*Q1*	*Q2*	*SL*	*OCC*	*TKLD*
30	83%	209	252	29	35	24%	97%	54.0
31	65%	75	115	10	16	45%	94%	35.4
32	51%	38	74	5	10	61%	91%	30.2
33	39%	21	55	3	8	73%	88%	28.0
Optimum → 34	29%	13	43	2	6	82%	86%	26.8
35	22%	8	36	1	5	88%	83%	26.1
36	16%	5	31	1	4	92%	81%	25.7
37	11%	3	27	0	4	95%	79%	25.4
38	8%	2	24	0	3	97%	77%	25.3
39	6%	1	21	0	3	98%	75%	25.2
40	4%	1	19	0	3	99%	73%	25.1
41	3%	1	18	0	2	99%	71%	25.1
42	2%	0	16	0	2	100%	69%	25.0

P(0) probability of a waiting time longer than 0 seconds
ASA average speed of answer for a call
DLYDLY average delay for all of the calls that are not answered immediately
Q1 average number of calls in the queue (all calls are included in the calculation, even those calls which do not end up in the queue; the designation is misleading as a result)
Q2 average number of calls in the queue when all of the agents are occupied or when there is a queue
SL service level, in this case the percentage of calls that must be answered within a certain number of seconds
OCC % of agents that are working on the processing of the calls (call and completion time)
TKLD the line occupancy rate in hours: (conversation time + ASA) × no. of calls per hour

Source: Cleveland and Mayben (1999).

Routing

The effectiveness and the quality of the call traffic increase if the calls take place between the right people. The regular customer will speak to his or her regular contact person, or if he or she is either absent or unavailable, to his or her replacement (the *fallback scenario* or the *second-line back-up*). The French-speaking customer will be assigned to someone who speaks his or her language. The person interested in a specific product will be put through to the product specialist and the person filing a claim will be helped quickly and appropriately. To do this, the call traffic will have to be routed. The first- and second-line agents will have to be specified in the system for the different types of contacts and customers. The effect of this 'skill-based routing' on the necessary workforce size most not be overlooked.

15.5 Managing satisfaction using telephone contact

Once the call centre's availability has been taken care of, the focus may be shifted to conducting an *efficient and effective dialogue* with prospects and customers. Figure 15.2 contains the previously mentioned elements from the customer contact which determine satisfaction.

CRM illustration

You have to make sure that the call centre does more than just answer the phone. Ultimately, it is an important encounter between customer and supplier; the flow of customers who call is also an inexhaustible source for market research. You have to try to make customers happy during calls and to surprise them with your service.

Source: Wassing, during the Second National Call Centre Congress (1999).

One of the most important negative influences on satisfaction appears to be the call charges. This raises the question: which costs may be charged to customers and prospects for their use of the call centre? Should the customer be able to call at the expense of the supplier, or may a fee be charged to him or her? Research has shown that customers are in principle prepared to pay a price for after-sales service by telephone which goes beyond the telephone charges themselves, provided they receive proper assistance quickly from a capable individual. It is worth the money to customers to reduce waiting time and to prevent the situation in which they are put through to the wrong person time and time again. There is a general preference for services in which a fixed price is charged per call instead of a variable charge.

One other point of particular interest is the use of ICT (information and communication technology) in the dialogue with customers. To what extent may voice response (VRS) and voice recognition systems be used? The following statement made by a call centre manager offers something to go on: 'The efficiency of telephone contact is determinative for the pleasantness of the conversation and the costs. Any technology that may aid in this is welcome.' In other words, for customers the telephone is primarily a communication channel which may be used efficiently to obtain an answer to a specific

CRM illustration

The supporter . . .

Voice response systems are a generally accepted tool. Some target groups will not always want or be able to make use of VRS, such as the elderly or foreigners. The barrier to communicating via a VRS may even be lower than that for personal communication, because people can remain anonymous.

The opponent . . .

Voice response systems are irritation tests for customers . . . Using agents can contribute to a 40 per cent increase in turnover.

Source: Second National Call Centre Congress (1999).

question. Voice processing systems help to increase this efficiency and convenience, particularly when it comes to answering frequently asked questions.

Managing the satisfaction and the quality of the call traffic with customers demands attention to the privacy issue. In other words, to what extent is it wise to call customers at the most annoying times when the chance of reaching them is the highest? Outbound call traffic to non-customers is generally not approved of by companies who implement a CRM strategy. Cold prospecting is associated with an active and perhaps even aggressive acquisition method that does not fit within relationship marketing. On the other hand, making a service call to welcome new customers is appreciated. It is a chance to express the company's appreciation for the customer and to determine if everything is satisfactory. Following up previous contacts via outbound calls at agreed-upon times is also one of the possibilities. However, in general it may be said that call centres at companies implementing a CRM strategy must process more inbound than outbound calls. The customer is more likely than the supplier to initiate contact by telephone.

A good conversation is characterised by a certain structure. The two parties identify themselves and determine the goal of the conversation. Several remarks may be made to positively influence the tone of the conversation from the outset. Next, information may be gained so that a solution may be devised and communicated. Finally, the conversation will be completed and follow-up appointments may be made.

The satisfaction with the conversation being conducted is furthermore influenced by the agent's conversation and listening skills, the directly accessible customer and product knowledge and the time the agent has available. The agent's competency is a determining factor for the quality of the conversation. Is he capable of uncovering the question behind the question? Someone who calls a financial services company and asks for the interest rate does so for a reason. It may be interesting to determine the motive behind the call and to use it to deepen the conversation, providing a recommendation if desired, or making a product offer. The computer monitor can aid the agent in conducting this conversation. It may contain information about favourable cross-sell opportunities, complaints which have arisen in the past, certain characteristics specific to that customer, an indication of the preference *not* to receive mailings, newsletters and the like. Sales arguments or the status of an order may be called up.

However, these same screens may also hinder the agent in conducting the conversation. This may be the case if the conversation is set out in scripts from which the agent may not deviate. On the one hand, these texts may have already proven themselves and can benefit productivity, on the other hand, they may prevent the employee from getting a feel for the customer's unique situation. The human element of the contact then suffers and this can have a great impact on a CRM strategy in particular.

Practitioner's insight

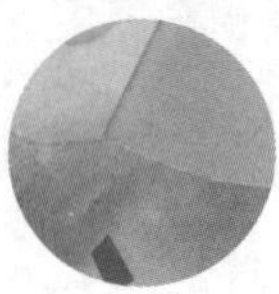

Inputting personal and contact data during or after a call can be experienced as aggravating and irritating. It goes without saying that updating and filling the database is nonetheless essential to CRM. It is therefore important to motivate employees to perform this task with care and to make it clear to them that this will benefit them in future contacts.

The competency on the part of the agents in conducting a certain conversation is naturally dependent upon their previous education, training, attitude and motivation. In order to achieve an optimal match between customers and agents, many companies divide the call centre up into sections, each staffed by specialised employees. The adverse effects of this segmentation on the capacity planning, the productivity and the availability of the call centre are considered to be fewer than the advantages. Agents specialised in certain customers, products or customer questions are capable of raising the quality of the customer contact and thereby developing the relationship and increasing turnover. With a financial services company for example, the relationship managers may opt for customers from a segment with which they feel they have the most affinity.

Advanced (voice) recording techniques make it possible to structurally monitor agents' performances, both quantitatively as well as qualitatively, and to analyse, compare, combine and process research data simply and in any manner desired to create insightful and valuable management reports. Insight is gained into the quality and the productivity of individual employees and in the call centre as a whole. Thanks to these data, management can support and guide its personnel in a more targeted manner. Some advanced monitoring techniques even make it possible to register an agent's entire screen behaviour.

Within many call centres, the quality of the contact moment is still evaluated personally. This is done by logging in and listening in on an agent or through the recording of conversations on tape. Standard evaluation criteria are used to grade the contact. Afterwards, the team leader, mentor or coach will evaluate the agent's contact. Agents are evaluated on the basis of the following aspects:

- The result of the conversation: is the customer satisfied?
- The use of guidelines.
- Telephone conduct.

- Executing cross- and up-sell activities.
- Structure and content of the conversation.
- Attitude towards the customer.
- Providing the correct information.

15.6 Managing the quality of contacts through other channels

As was indicated earlier, telephone contact is not the only channel managed from the call centre. Written, faxed and e-mailed correspondence may also be handled by the agents in the centre. It is the call centre manager's choice to work with specialised agents who can handle contacts through a communication channel, or with generalists who are versatile and may be employed everywhere. The ultimate decision may be dependent upon the following:

- The effects, and on the productivity of the activities that are necessary in order to manage the contact and make good the promises made.
- Agents' ability to learn to work with more than one channel; often it appears that an agent with good oral communication skills is less skilled at writing texts, and vice versa.
- The positive effects on motivation that may result from introducing variety into the agents' duties.
- The possibility to generate a stable workload by placing employees in various communication channels.

In managing the quality of these contacts, a number of aspects should be examined. Outbound fax traffic should be monitored to prevent irritation on the part of prospects and customers. Complaints may be submitted if the recipient must incur printing costs for unsolicited and unappreciated advertisements, and must make its fax equipment available for these advertisements.

The most problems arise, however, with regard to e-mail traffic. With *outbound* e-mail, just as with outgoing fax traffic, the company will have to prevent any violations of privacy. It must take steps to ensure that the messages are not considered to be 'inbox pollution' or junk mail or spam. This only irritates the customer and can lead to blocking digital post from the organisation in future or even demonstrating rebellious behaviour by bombarding the sender with enormous files, for example. By asking customers' permission beforehand whether they would like to receive the messages in question (opt-in), this situation may be prevented. It is also recommended that the company should always clearly indicate how recipients may exempt themselves from these kinds of messages in future (opt-out).

Practitioner's insight

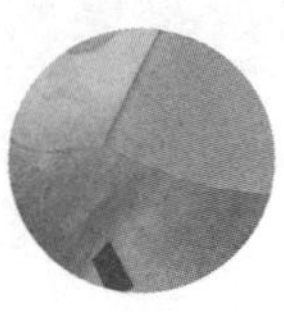

Effectiveness of e-mailings under pressure

'One-quarter of the two-and-a-half billion e-mail messages that were sent in 2002 was spam, and unfortunately there is still money to be made on this', according to e-mail pioneer Cin Crosbie, president of Digital Deliverance.

'The result is that the click ratio has dropped from twelve to three per cent.'

Source: *ITCommercie*, no. 6 (2002).

Practitioner's insight

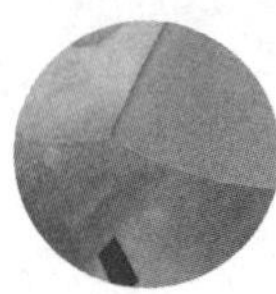

New European Directive

On 12 July 2002, a directive was established on a European level to increase clarity regarding commercial e-mail. This directive requires all of the member states of the European Union to bring their legislation and regulations into line with this directive before 31 October 2003 in order to impose restraints on the unsolicited distribution of commercial e-mails. Among other issues, it was determined that the sending of e-mail for direct marketing purposes will only be permitted if sent to persons who have provided prior permission for this. A so-called opt-in regime was chosen (e-mails may only be sent if the recipient agrees) and not the opt-out option (e-mails may be sent until someone indicates that they no longer wish to receive this type of e-mail), in spite of the lobby by trade and industry for this last option.

One exception has been made for individuals and companies who receive e-mail addresses from their customers within the framework of supplying of products and/or services to these customers; these individuals and companies may use these e-mail addresses for direct marketing of similar (thus not necessarily equal) products or services, provided their customers are clearly and explicitly given the opportunity to object to the use of their e-mail addresses easily and free of charge.

The regime of the directive as described above applies not only to e-mail but also to other 'automatic calling equipment' and faxes. From the considerations included in the directive, one may assume that text messages also fall under the scope of this regulation.

Source: Broos (2002).

Outbound e-mail traffic is used for various purposes, including newsletters, advertisements, alerts/reminders and market research. The advantage of e-mail is, for the most part, a financial one. Sending physical mailings is accompanied by high printing and postage costs. These are more or less non-existent on the Internet. Furthermore, e-mailings are extremely suitable for a customised offering. If the message links contain websites, invitations for other forms of contact, or contain pages which make direct interaction possible, the chance of customisation and bilateral contact increases. The content of the communication may be geared towards the recipient's interests.

Practitioner's insight

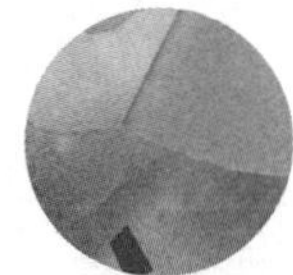

Ten e-mailing tips

1. Stop sending general information.
2. Use sophisticated, clean databases. Don't use a blunderbuss approach. Make sure you have opt-in addresses: people who don't mind being approached with commercial messages.
3. Produce concise, tailored reports.
4. Approach your potential customer intelligently; don't push your product too hard. The customer is no fool.
5. Try starting a one-on-one dialogue with the customer.
6. Create reports. Keep track of how often you have approached a customer, in which stage of contact you are at the moment; don't send the same e-mail twice.
7. Notify the recipient. Provide information on the reasons why he or she has received the e-mail.
8. State the sender's name on the e-mail.
9. Indicate clearly what the recipient must do in order to stop future e-mails.
10. Always send to personal e-mail addresses. Never send to sales@ . . . nl, info@. . . . nl, etc.

Source: Vlam (2003).

The handling of *inbound* e-mails also involves challenges. In the early stages of this method of communication between customers and suppliers, the latter underestimated how much work the processing of these messages would entail. It appeared that an agent was able to complete many fewer e-mails in one hour than telephone calls. At the same time, with such a medium as 'fast' as the Internet, customers expect a prompt answer. Response times which are accepted with physical post are unacceptable in the digital world. Customers expect an answer to their question within a day or even a number of hours.

Since sending an e-mail is a low-threshold, anonymous means of communication for Internet users, there are many companies in the start-up phase which are also caught off guard by a larger number of inbound e-mails than they had expected. If we add this to the fact that the processing of e-mails is time consuming and that the capacity in a call centre in the start-up phase is rather limited, then we may conclude that the chance that incoming e-mail messages will pile up is high. With many companies, this has even led to a situation in which agents never got around to answering e-mails. The reliability of this form of communication has been (temporarily) harmed by these types of events. Customers who doubt whether or not they will receive an answer to their question might start calling, thus causing even more communication traffic and incurring additional costs.

People also had rather high expectations for systems which generated fully or partially automatic answers to the questions asked. However, the initial experiences have taught us that many dialogues are complex and may not be automated within a short timeframe. Nonetheless, positive results were achieved; within various call centres, it was possible to answer some 60 e-mails per hour.

The experiences with inbound e-mailing have provided many organisations with a reason to undertake activities to 'hold back' the flow of digital messages. By making over-obvious references to the frequently asked questions section, these companies have attempted to answer customer questions in a less labour-intensive yet customer-friendly way. There is less appreciation within the context of a CRM strategy for companies who 'hide' their e-mail address in the website so that the visitor has a much harder time sending an e-mail.

15.7 Key performance indicators

The availability and the quality of the call centre may be measured through the use of key performance indicators. The following were identified by Cleveland and Mayben (1999):

- Average value of a call (for turnover-generating call centres), to be calculated as the total turnover divided by the number of calls.
- Customer satisfaction.
- Availability.
- Percentage of abandonment: the number of people who hang up, callers who get the busy signal.
- Costs per call: the total costs for the call centre during a specific period divided by the total number of calls; the development of insight into the factors which influence the level of costs.
- Errors and work that must be redone. Using the database, it may be determined how often customers must call back, how many problems remain unsolved, and how many errors are made during data entry.
- Forecast call load versus the actual situation.
- Scheduled personnel versus practice.
- Schedule discipline.
- Average handling time (AHT): the sum of the average conversation time and the average completion time.

15.8 Conclusion

The call centre is the place where the message traffic is managed and handled as it passes through different channels. In an efficient yet effective manner, attempts are made to conduct dialogues with prospects and customers via telephone, fax and the Internet. An optimal balance is sought between technology and manpower. On the one hand, technology will have to ensure efficiency, convenience, reliability, and information on products and customers; on the other hand, it will contribute to a reduction in costs and an increase in productivity. However, and this is certainly the case with a CRM strategy, people will remain indispensable for lending a 'human touch' to the contact. At crucial moments, they will have to 'show their faces', allowing themselves to be supported by technology.

The quality of the call centre depends to a great degree on the organisation's *accessibility*. Professional capacity management must ensure that there are enough personnel available at the various times for the completion of the communication. In addition, the quality is determined by the *quality of the contact*. Telephone contact involves questions such as: are the agents capable of listening and do they have the desired communication skills and knowledge to provide customers with solutions? Are they sufficiently well-equipped to make good on their promises and can they rely on the back office? Have they had enough education and training? Is there room to learn and make improvements and be able to focus on the customer's wishes? In e-mail traffic, the quality is primarily dependent on the respect for the customer's privacy. High quality may be offered if customisation is supplied in the e-mails and answers are provided promptly to customers' questions.

Case study

Life of a novice call centre agent

These days, more and more young people entering the workforce are applying for jobs at call centres. Since Asia is at the heart of the growing call centre industry, the Philippines have become one of the biggest providers of this service, along with India and China. But how attractive is the job of a novice call centre agent.

Gracious accommodation. Pilipinas Teleserv Inc., the company that takes care of the NSO Helpline Plus and DFA Passport Direct Service, among others, was gracious enough to accommodate me. Malou Bermio, operations head and HR and training manager, took charge of my training and job performance. Since a few hours of training would not sufficiently prepare me for the more difficult jobs, I was assigned to the order processing area for a food outlet.

Waking up early one Wednesday morning, I went to their headquarters in Quiapo. Taking the elevator to the fourth floor, I was greeted by the sight of a pool table. At least it's not just all work and no play, I thought. And so my tutelage in the world of customer care began. Although training depends on the type of service the company ►

offers, it usually covers four essential skills: phone ethics, phone skills or verbal communication, customer service and phonetics.

Your tone of voice must match the script to be delivered, and you must learn how to project a professional telephone image. Trainees also learn the military alphabet, since spelling needs to be accurate. A good part of the training, at least in the order processing service, has to do with learning the company background. The history of the company, the pioneers of the company and the decisions that were crucial in making the company attain a certain competitive advantage are all taken up. I also had to study the food outlet's menu.

Amazing system. When the battle officially began, I was led past the busier areas of a wide carpeted room, where every station had a customer care officer (CCO) catering to the needs of the customer. The least busy part of the room was where I found myself. But it was no reason to slack off. This was, after all, my first (and only) day on the job. After Malou led me to my station, I was introduced to their computer system. As the CCO enters the customer's particulars, the computer tells him whether the person is a new customer or not, and what branch will deliver his order. Then, the CCO simply uses the mouse to click on the customer's order by scrolling down the menu, which is conveniently classified into sizes and flavours. The bill is also automatically displayed. It's no wonder, then, that placing delivery calls now is much shorter and has less chance of getting the orders mixed up.

About an hour later, after learning the program options by heart, or so I thought, I was introduced to a pleasant girl by the name of Jasmin – my buddy for the day. While waiting for my turn at the headsets and watching Jasmin take calls, I decided to invent a name for myself (Tammy). In a way, this job is a bit like having another side of yourself show through.

First blooper. The first call came from a computer shop. Jasmin and I put on our headsets – she was assigned to listen in on the conversation in case I forgot something in the script. Noise filtered in from the caller's background, so the speaker could not hear himself, or me for that matter, very well. My first blooper was rattling off the standard greetings: 'Good afternoon, this is Tammy speaking, may I have your telephone number?' without releasing the 'mute' button. But during the rest of the call, Delusional Me actually thought I did okay, taking the customer's order, thanking him and even remembering to inform him of the new loyalty programme that started that day. I ended the call, feeling relieved and strangely accomplished, and turned to Jasmin for her verdict. She was laughing as she took off her headset. 'You forgot to recap the order!' she said.

Rats. Well, so much for breaking the ice. And yet as the hours wore on, the calls became easier and the waiting time in between made me fidgety and impatient. Since distractions such as reading materials or music are prohibited to enable the CCOs to focus more on the job, just staying put was something I had to get used to. The waiting time between the first and second calls was a bit torturous for me, so the ringing of the phone was like the tinkling bell of an ice cream cart in the middle of summer.

Bad luck. From the noise in the background, I could tell this call was coming from a guy in a bowling alley. Another noisy call: I was getting anxious at the thought that this was a streak of bad luck. But I managed to finish the call. When working intensely on a task, you become more aware of the things you use the most. Here, I became conscious of how my throat felt dry after taking a call. I periodically needed to sip water and warm up my voice to make sure I could still speak. You also need hand–eye–voice coordination; the voice to keep talking to the customer, and the hands and eyes to enter all the information in the computer system. You need to break some habits when it comes to the phone; I could never end up saying 'Thank you for using [name of company] delivery service; please order with us again' as a parting shot. Despite being glued to my station for most of the day, to say that the job was mind-numbing and sedentary is largely inaccurate. Flexibility is essential, especially in the mental aspect. You need to be alert all the time. Two other skills required are diplomacy and confidence, since the ability to interact with people is hard to fake when dealing with irate customers.

Although I don't think anyone would recommend doing this job for a lifetime, it does address the big problem of unemployment in our country. Whether you are taking the job because you want a break before graduate studies, or you want to earn to help your family or you've simply no idea what to do for now, working at the call centre may prove to be an enjoyable and fulfilling experience. Not only will it keep you in the workforce, you also get to help people with their needs.

At the end of the day, like most jobs out there, it's good money for an honest day's work.

Special thanks to Raffy David and Malou Bermio, Call Pilipinas Teleserv Inc.

Source: Young (2004).

Questions

1 What are the pros and cons of outsourcing call centre activities to countries such as the Philippines, India, etc.?

2 The quality of a contact depends to a large extent on the people working in the call centre (and, of course, on the resources they have). How will you evaluate the quality of the workforce here? Mention positive and negative aspects. What are your recommendations to improve the quality?

Questions

1 What type of message traffic between customer and supplier do you consider to be particularly suitable for processing in the call centre? Explain your answer.

2 Do you consider a call centre belonging to a company that implements a CRM strategy to be more of a cost centre than a profit centre? Explain your answer.

3 Under what circumstances would you choose outsourcing for the call centre?

4 Name four reasons for the growth in the size and complexity of the work performed in call centres.

5 What are the five subjects to which a call centre manager at an organisation that employs a CRM strategy must pay special attention in order to be able to conduct an efficient and effective dialogue with customers? Substantiate your answer.

6 The quality of capacity planning is a direct influence on the call centre's availability. What are your recommendations to a call centre manager who is unable to make an accurate prediction of the size and composition of the in- and outbound message traffic via the telephone and the Internet?

7 Contact a number of different service providers in a specific market and compare the quality of their call centres.

8 Name five measures that you could take to improve the quality of telephone contact.

9 In which sort of real-life situations do you consider the chance for a successful application of a semi-automatic e-mail answering function to be high? Give four examples.

10 If too many companies send unsolicited e-mails to companies and consumers, this effective communication tool can gain an unfavourable reputation and its efficiency can suffer as a result. What can you do as a commercial company to prevent this from occurring with your customers? Illustrate your answer.

References

Bontebal, Sven, Coby Oudhoorn and Ed Peelen (2001) Vermijd de dolgedraaide direct-marketing klok, *Customer Base*, 1, 26–28.

Brink, Marion V. van den (1999) *De opzet, implementatie en organisatie van een call center*, F&G Publishing, Amersfoort.

Broos, Lesley C.P. (2002) Analytische CRM versus anti-spam wetgeving, *Beyond Mapping, Marketing and Datawarehousing*, December, 10–11.

Cleveland, Brad and Julia Mayben (1999) *Call center management, in volle vaart vooruit*, F&G Publishing, Amersfoort.

Elias, D.E. and H.E. Panbakker (2000) *KwaliTijd, onderzoek naar quality management en quality management tools in het call center*, Nyenrode University/KPN, Breukelen.

Forrester (1999) *New Affiliate Marketing Models*, Forrester Research Inc., October.

Hendrickx, H. (2000) *CRM systemen*, Cap Gemini/E&Y, Utrecht.

Heskett, J.L., T.O. Jones, G.W. Loveman, W.E. Sasser Jr and L.A. Schlesinger (1994) Putting the service–profit chain to work, *Harvard Business Review*, March–April, 164–174.

Huijnen, R.L.M.E. (1997) *Het starten van een call center; een multidisciplinair proces*, Nijmegen Business School, Nijmegen.

ITCommercie (2002) Effectiviteit e-mailings in gedrang, *ITCommercie*, 6, October, 10.

Nippa, Michael (1999) Call center strategierecht organisieren, *Harvard Business Manager*, 6, 86–93.

Vlam, Peter (2003) Marketing of spam?, *Emerce*, March, 60–61.

Young, Catherine (2004) On the other side of the phone line, *Philippine Daily Inquirer*, 9 June.

16

Internet and the website

The contribution that the Internet and the website in particular can make to the dialogue to be conducted between customer and supplier is the subject of this chapter. We will complete the contact cycle (Figure 16.1) and start with the generation of traffic in Section 16.1. Which basic assumptions must we satisfy in order to ensure that the visit meets the customer's expectations in a reliable and comfortable manner (Section 16.2)? How should we design the site, the pages and the content to achieve this goal (Section 16.3)? If the role of the Internet in the communication cycle extends beyond the simple supply of information, attention will also have to be focused on the receiving and completion of transactions. The subject of retention may not escape our attention either and will be discussed in Section 16.6. Finally, we will examine the measurement of performance and evaluation of websites in Section 16.7.

The contact cycle on the Internet **Figure 16.1**

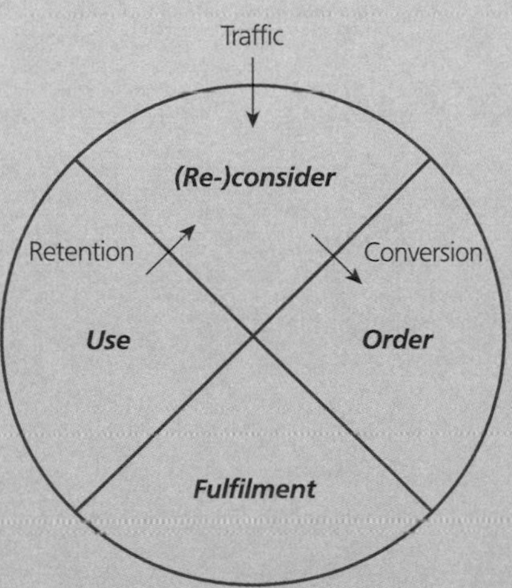

Source: Capgemini Nederland B.V.

In this chapter we will address the following questions

- What is the role of the Internet and the website in the contact cycle?
- How to build traffic applying on- and offline methods.
- How to measure the quality of the site visit.
  - How can companies capitalise on visitors' expectations?
  - What direction should the development of the website's functionality take?
    - various functionalities of websites;
    - the influence of the context and the type of website on the determination of the desired functionality.
  - How to increase the quality of the web visit.
    - How to improve the design of the page, the content and the website.
  - How to convert visitors into buyers: how to entice visitors to buy.
    - How to handle transactions by means of order-taking and payment systems.
  - How to follow-up on a transaction by making the delivery: the costs of e-commerce.
  - How to retain customers according to the Peppers and Rogers method: the identification of customers, distinguishing between customers, interacting with customers and offering them customisation.
  - How to measure the results achieved through the website.

Practitioner's insight

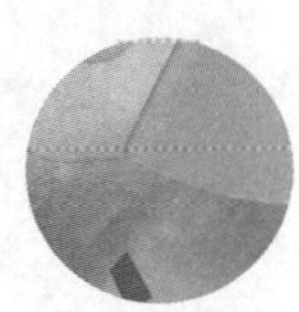

The lyrical days of the Internet are over. The time when Internet success stories were like raindrops that fall out of a cloud onto the Earth has ended. Dreams about the disappearance of distances, free and readily accessible information that would give the consumer power and result in a flourishing service economy have come to an abrupt halt. The expectation that the Internet would turn the world and the corresponding economies upside down has perhaps been realised, although rather differently than was expected. At the moment, realism reigns supreme. The fact is that the distribution and use of the Internet is growing steadily throughout broad layers of society, and not only when it comes to looking up information, but also for placing orders. The role of the network is growing and deserves a place in the marketing communication policy that can help it live up to this role.

16.1 Traffic building

Visitor traffic to a website may be stimulated online as well as offline (Niks, Plasmeijer and Peelen, 2000).

Practitioner's insight

How is the use of the Internet developing within Europe?

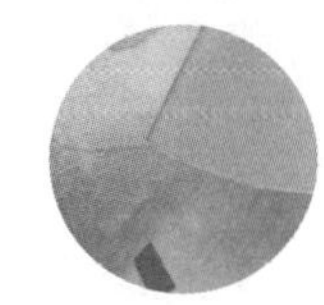

From the Internet International Key Facts investigation conducted by IP into Internet use in Europe (2001 through 2002), it appears that the growth has dropped significantly: 10 per cent growth versus 25 per cent the year before. This means that, at present, some 130 million Europeans use the Internet. Of all European households, 46 per cent have a computer but only 39 per cent of these have an Internet connection. There is thus a considerable potential for growth among these users. An indication: in the United States, 56.5 per cent of the households own a computer, but 59 per cent of these have an Internet connection. The European market is still divided into four blocks when it comes to Internet connection: Scandinavia and Denmark (where the penetration is more than 60 per cent), the Anglo-Saxon countries of Great Britain, Germany, Austria, Switzerland and the Netherlands, with penetration of 40–60 per cent), the 'up-and-coming' countries (France, Belgium, Italy, Iberian Peninsula: 20–40 per cent), and Greece and eastern Europe (less than 20 per cent).

Source: *Marketing International* (2003a).

CRM illustration

More intensive surfing

The existing users have started surfing a bit more intensively . . . The explanation is quite obvious: more and more people have broadband connections (cable or ADSL) . . .

Broadband access is becoming widespread more slowly than was expected.

Source: *Marketing International* (2003b).

Online traffic building

Suppliers may make use of a large number of opportunities the Internet has to offer to draw the attention of prospects and customers to their site. There are a variety of approaches available. They may start from customers' particular areas of interest. Finding an association with a virtual community is one example of this pull strategy. Another angle is more offer-oriented: bringing the offer to potential customers using intensive 'webvertising', or what is known as a push strategy.

In order to apply structure to the possibilities, they are categorised into the cybermediaries on the one hand, which allow suppliers the opportunity to profile themselves, and the marketing tools required to promote one's own site, on the other hand. This categorisation is not exhaustive.

The optimum mix of instruments is different for every supplier and is dependent upon the competition and the offering, among other factors.

Cybermediaries

Cybermediaries are Internet initiatives, used by customers, which supply them with a limited to comprehensive added value. These involve portals, affiliate marketing programmes, virtual communities, integrators/malls, comparison sites, mobile agents and consumer aggregated buying sites.

A visit to the Internet often begins from a regular departure point. Portal sites offer surfers a home base amidst the enormous offering on the Internet with a well-organised classification of topics and sites. By offering a broad range of services, such as search engines and free news, portals attempt to bind as many people as possible to their site and to be the first site people use when surfing the Internet. Within the framework of traffic building, it is important to seek affiliation with an organisation that generates sufficient high-quality traffic and matches the image, topic and look of the supplier's own site.

Jupiter Communications makes a distinction between primary and affinity portals. The former are large portals which strive for the most complete and broadest offering possible, varying from, for example, sports, weather and investments to current news and online dating. These horizontal portals generate a great deal of traffic, high costs for a partnership yet relatively few return visits to the company's own site. Affinity portals or vertical portals focus more on a specific area, a niche in the market, for example food and drink, gardening or another hobby. A partnership with these types of sites most likely produces less traffic in terms of numbers. The audience for affinity portals is a specific target group for which the chance of conversion is higher. Moreover, the costs of a contract with this type of portal are generally lower.

A portal deal is often linked to an affiliate programme. With this form of cooperation, the turnover from sales of products is shared with partners. Portal sites receive a percentage of the sales that are made or initiated via their sites in the form of commission: revenue sharing. Strong brands or suppliers of attractive products offer other partners a spot on their site. A sort of 'shop within a shop' arises as a result. By clicking through using banners, for example, the visitor may be led to the supplier's site. The advantage of this for the organisation is that, without any investment, a number of branches may be added to its offering, and in this way it may approach a target group that is extremely small and specific.

A virtual community (see also Chapter 2) consists of a group of people with a common bond, who are dependent upon a physical location and a physical interaction in order to maintain this bond. Virtual communities are formed on the basis of areas of interest, age and background. An organisation may generate traffic through these communities and thus come into contact with its target group. It is important that focus is first placed on the members' needs: the organisation will need to win appreciation and inspire confidence. By listening, it will be able to increase its customer knowledge. The emphasis is not on the sale of the product, but on building the brand and relationship development.

Integrators/malls are sites where many suppliers are gathered together, usually with a common characteristic. This characteristic may be the location region, the type of product or customers' particular area of interest. Malls in the retail trade may be considered as a sort of shopping centre where a number of suppliers have gathered. The added value that these cybermediaries supply is in:

- creating an overview;
- inspiring confidence and independence;
- promoting competition between suppliers.

Malls also often claim to perform a portal function. Not only is the offering classified, but related products are also offered. A successful American example is autobytel.com.

Comparison sites make it easier for buyers in the pre-transaction phase to compare the available offering. In the previously mentioned malls, suppliers are brought together in one location so that visitors may get a good overview of what the suppliers have to offer. Product comparison sites go one step further; the customer can compare different products and services with one another in real-time here. This may be a comparison based on price, but also on the basis of other qualities such as delivery time and/or shipping costs. For a supplier, it is crucial to be rated favourably in the comparison; often only the top 5 or 10 companies or products are shown. When the organisation is not included in this group, the buyer will not even see what that company has to offer. On Travelocity.com, a visitor can compare various travel offers with one another. After the search has been completed, a list of suppliers, their offerings and prices appears. The order may be booked online with the hotel or airline.

Consumer aggregated buying sites give customers the opportunity to bundle their buying power. The customers organise themselves in a buyers' cooperative and are able to exact price reductions owing to their purchase volume. Initiatives in this regard were expected to be quite promising, yet usually produced very little result.

Mobile agents consist of knowledge systems that support buyers in finding their way around the Internet. They are personal assistants that work both in and outside of the user's computer and can perform a variety of tasks (Jonkers, 2000). By downloading software, a personal assistant may be sent out into the web on an extensive specific search. On the basis of the information the buyer gives to the mobile agent and information it has gathered during prior search activities, the agent will look for specifically requested information. These agents are learning knowledge systems in which frequent use leads to better search results. Even when the computer is not online, the mobile agent is working on its search. For the time being, the role of the mobile agents is limited.

Online marketing tools

In addition to the use of cybermediaries, the organisation can also stimulate the routing of traffic to its site through its own efforts. Online advertising is one way to attract attention. Banners and buttons are the most common means. A banner is a sort of billboard displayed on an Internet page that refers the visitor to another page. A button is a smaller round or square advertisement. In addition to these, there are interstitials, which are pop-up advertisements or windows that come up on top of the original window. The effect of online advertising has decreased considerably. Creativity is crucial to achieve any kind of substantial results.

It is important that online marketing tools (banners, buttons, etc.) are integrated in the marketing policy. Additionally, there are a number of other relevant issues:

- the advertisement must be placed on the sites visited by the target group;
- the message must be geared towards the wants and needs of the target group;
- the content and the design must correspond to the company's intended image or the product and should not conflict with other marketing tools;
- the message is obviously important; an attractive offer is a requirement.

Often companies contract out advertising on the Internet. An advertising network is a group of websites with the same banner server. The banner server is operated by a sales organisation that is responsible for the commercial handling and reporting of the results. An advertising network is specialised in the focused dissemination of certain advertisements among a given target group. An example of an advertising network is DoubleClick.

An effective way of generating traffic is to ensure a good ranking with *search engines*: after all, a very large portion of the traffic goes through search engines. A search engine may be described as the 'software that indexes the worldwide web and on the basis of the key words entered, searches for the URLs of the pages in which the relevant key words may be found in the index and displays these to the user' (Haarman and Peelen, 2000).

Practitioner's insight

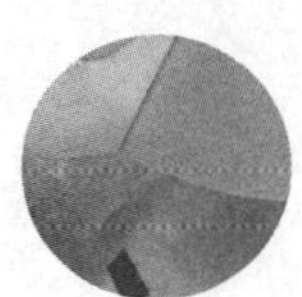

Search engines are often evaluated on the basis of the size of the index and how current the information is that it produces. In order to rank well in the numerous search engines, it is advisable to consult a number of cybermediaries. Rankthis (www.rankthis.com) and positionAgent (www.positionagent.com) provide insight into the ranking of a site for ten popular search robots when certain search terms are entered. They also provide information on the criteria that the different search agents take into account in determining the ranking. Registering with a number of different search engines may be done via a special service offered by Microsoft: www.submitit.com. With some search engines, positions at the top of the list of search results may be purchased. It is also possible to relate banners to the search terms that are used in search engines. If, for example, someone enters the search term 'car audio', a banner appears for a supplier of car audio products.

A supplier may also approach customers directly with an e-mailing. From the database, the company's own customer database may be approached or new potential customers may be approached via permission e-mail providers.

Offline traffic building

Traditional media continue to play an important role in the promotion of the site visit. Although the significance will decrease as the penetration of the Internet grows and customers become more experienced Internet users, at the moment it is still quite high. Advertisements on the radio, television and in magazines and newspapers, outdoor advertising, information on packaging and bills, free publicity, word-of-mouth advertising, flyers, brochures and so forth are all responsible for a substantial portion of the flow of visitors.

Practitioner's insight

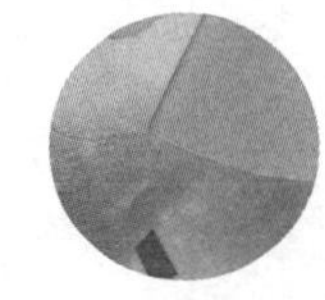

In the United States, nearly 67 million households or 62 per cent of the American population had an Internet connection at the end of 2002. In terms of media use, the television still ranks at the top (15 hours per week), but the Internet (14 hours per week) is advancing fast and has overtaken radio (11 hours), books (6 hours), newspapers (3 hours) and magazines (2 hours) by leaps and bounds. The American consumer sees on average 554 pure marketing messages – and this figure is expected to climb to 836 over the next five years. Of the total advertising expenditures, 3 per cent of these are spent on the Internet ($5.6 billion) and this is expected to reach 6.1 per cent ($14 billion) within five years.

Source: Marketing International (2003c).

The effectiveness of offline promotion is dependent upon the manner in which the URL addresses (see Section 16.2) are communicated. Companies must prevent addresses from appearing too briefly or too small in television commercials, for example, and must not forget or neglect to communicate what customers may expect to find on the site. Of the communication tools, packaging lends itself particularly well to communicating the address and the benefits of the website, and particularly those types of packaging that last longer have a good yet inexpensive communicative power (Van der Schans, 2001).

Practitioner's insight

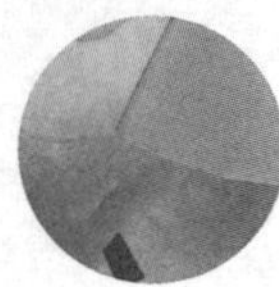

The addressing

The success of traffic building activities is also partially influenced by the choice of URL address.

Marketers can purchase a generic address or a brand address. Generic addresses are named after a product category, for example (such as detergent.com or are named after a key word such as beauty: beautiful.com). A brand address is an address that is named after a brand such as persil.com. In the start-up phase of the Internet, people assumed that surfers would be in search of information about certain product categories and not the brands. At the moment, this does not always seem to be the case. Nonetheless, it can be wise for a brand or company to register several addresses so that the chance of a hit and the likelihood of a high position in the search lists increases.

A brand can have a different brand identity and associations from one country to another. A consumer in France will find a different sort of Danone than he or she would in the Netherlands. It used to be that customers only encountered other brand associations when abroad. The arrival of the Internet has ensured, however, that the borders can also be crossed in the virtual world. This can lead to so-called *spillovers*. A site such as persil.com, which is destined exclusively for the English market, can also attract visitors from other countries. Because these people are exposed to a different identity for a brand which is familiar to them, confusion and – as a continuation of this – aversion can occur. They may be confronted with product variants and offers which are not available in their own country.

This spillover may be prevented by setting up a sort of passport control facility. Visitors will first be asked for their nationality and will then be led to the site that is applicable to their home country. But also by forgoing one address for all countries and regions and by working with local addresses, this effect may be reduced. In particular, organisations with a .com address can experience this problem if they geographically differentiate their marketing policy.

Source: Van der Schans (2001).

16.2 Starting points for providing quality during the visit

Provide what the visitor expects

The quality of the visit is above all dependent on the visitor's expectations. The site must offer the visitor what he or she is looking for, allowing it to be easily found. The visitor must not encounter features on the site that are *not* necessary. Someone who is only looking for further information about the organisation and the supplier's products does not need to be offered the option of completing a transaction. The interactivity of the site may be limited; offering entertainment may be unnecessary. Investments in expensive features on the website may not be needed.

A distinction may be made between four types of online (buying) visits (Moe and Fader, 2000, in Swinkels, 2001):

1. Visits with the intention of making a purchase: the visitor is in search of a product or service and is prepared to make an immediate purchase.
2. Visits designed for buyers, for orientation and evaluation of the product or service: prompted by a planned purchase, the visitor studies the offering and the conditions; he or she tries to optimise the choice and considers making a purchase in the near future.
3. Hedonistic visits: electronic window-shopping occurs, purely for recreation and pleasure; the shop visit does not take place with the intention to purchase; any purchase made is an impulsive one.
4. Visits with the aim of gathering knowledge: the visitor browses and learns more about the marketplace or products; the increase in knowledge as a result of the online visit can influence future purchase behaviour.

This classification system focuses on visits that take place before and during the purchase, and may be supplemented by also distinguishing the visit that will take place after purchase and which involves after-sales service.

Decisions regarding the expansion of the features of a website should be based on a consideration of:

- the value that the customers and prospects assign to the aspects involved; in particular those functions which are valued and distinctive with regard to the competition are those which deserve attention;
- the complexity of and costs involved in realising the features.

Functions which represent high value and are distinctive and simple to implement are the first to qualify for implementation (Bügel, 2000). In the long term, work can be done on the realisation of complex valuable functions. Figure 16.2 illustrates how an estate agent can systematise the selection problem graphically. Easy-to-realise functions which can significantly increase the distinctive capacity and valuation of the agent's site seem to be related to providing visitors with the possibility of making an appointment online to view a property and to providing statistics and prices as well as

Figure 16.2 Site functionality and visitors' expectations

Source: Bügel (2002).

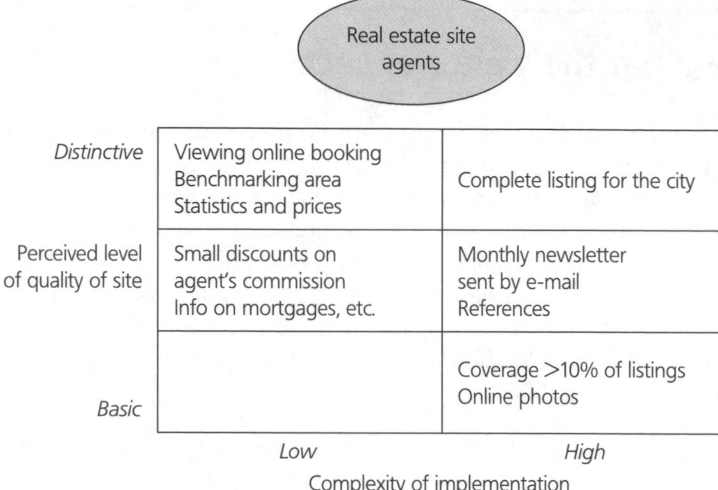

information on the attractiveness of the location. Basic functions which must be satisfied involve the coverage and offering visual material. If less than 10 per cent of the buildings which are for lease or for sale for a specific geographical area are offered on the site, the site will lose its purpose: it does not provide a useful overview of the offering in the market. The other functions which can contribute to the value of the site are illustrated in the other cells shown in Figure 16.2.

Visitors to the website must have confidence in the features that the supplier offers on the site. The Internet is still a relatively new medium and one where it is known that the expectations of customers and prospects can be violated, for example, there may be no response to questions asked in e-mails and booked transactions may not be completed as agreed.

The type of site and the web context (Van der Schans, 2001)

Marketers do not always have to opt for a website for their own brand or their own organisation straight away. Depending on what visitors seek and expect from a website, they may also choose a broader context or web environment than the so-called individual site. They may not limit themselves to their own 'advertisement, service or sales space' but instead use a larger portion of the web. They elect to use a portal, a community or perhaps a promotional or microsite.

Procter & Gamble and Unilever develop their respective portals targeting women, such as women.com and ivillage.com (which have now merged). In this way, women's needs on the Internet are better addressed and a context is created for the spreading of messages.

Communities (see Chapter 2) form a place where people can gather to exchange information and experiences. This can involve a brand community, which is created around a brand and where brand fans get together. Brands with a strong image and a high degree of involvement which are publicly consumed and have a rich and extensive history are the most suitable for building a community. Also, brands which are threatened by the competition can benefit from a community. The united brand fans can strengthen the bond between them and stand up to the common enemy.

The communities may be set up by the marketer or by the customers themselves. The situation in which marketers challenge their customers' communities because they are not official should be prevented. Coca-Cola, for example, challenged the site Cocacolavintage.com belonging to brand loyalists because it was afraid the site would be broadcasting the wrong brand messages, but ended up arousing the disdain of its loyal customers. It is advisable to involve the ambassadors of the organisation in the creation of the community sooner rather than later. They sometimes claim to be even more aware of the brand's status than the marketer and in a better position to keep watch over the brand capital.

In addition to these initiatives on the part of fans, there are also communities which are focused on destruction such as the ihate*brand*.com or *brand*sucks.com sites (such as ihatecocacola.com, for example). On these sites, consumers can share their negative experiences with the brand in question. These brand haters can go yet a step further by taking on the form of brand terrorists who spread negative rumours on these types of sites. Marketers can attempt to prevent these types of initiatives by buying these addresses in advance.

Communities are also regularly formed around users of a product who would like to exchange experiences among themselves. A good example is the Microsoft Certified Software Engineers who have set up their own community. They all work with Microsoft software and encounter the problems involved in it on a daily basis and help one another to solve these problems. It is a successful community from which Microsoft initially distanced itself, but which it now – unsuccessfully – has tried to buy.

In contrast with the portals and the communities, microsites are limited in size. They concentrate on a specific aspect; for example, they are dedicated to a certain brand association.

Marketers can utilise promotional sites to give direct sales a boost. On this sort of site, coupons, samples and savings programmes are the focus. On a former site named 'street breakfast', consumers in the Netherlands could participate in a contest to win breakfast for their street, for example. On one of Kellogg's sites, virtual points may be collected and on veryfine.com, coupons may be printed out in the store for discounts on the purchase price of soft drinks.

Creating trust

The development of trust in the Internet and the website takes place through a dynamic process. Six factors have been identified with which a supplier may gain the trust of its customers (Cheskin Research, 1999):

1 The brand and the reliability of the organisation. The brand must inspire trust and make clear what the company stands for. Not only the company's own brand can

prove to be important, but also those of affiliate partners and the supplier's other relationships.

2 Presentation: the content, layout and design of the site must disseminate the organisation's objectives.
3 Navigation: the ease with which visitors can find what they are looking for.
4 Seals of quality: symbols that inspire confidence such as Webtrader, Visa and VeriSign can ensure trust in the organisation, the level of service and the computer network.
5 Technology: the technical functioning of the website (speed and functionality).
6 Fulfilment: how simple is it, for example, to buy a product, gain insight into the process involved in order processing and establish contact with the organisation in the event that problems arise? It is also important to indicate what the customer's data will be used for and to ask permission to do so.

Offering convenience

In comparison with an offline environment, there are already immediate advantages to a website that are worth mentioning. There are no traffic problems, there are no queues to wait in, it is possible to compare products and prices, and the customer can communicate from any location without having to take opening hours into consideration (Swinkels, 2001). However, these benefits do not offer the visitor enough of a guarantee that they will retain a positive feeling about their online buying experience. More is necessary to achieve this. Three factors that determine the convenience of a website are the user-friendliness and utility of the site, the degree of self-service and the speed with which the visitor can execute the intended tasks.

Organisations must continually work on the ease with which visitors can find what they are looking for. The navigability of the site influences the user-friendliness of the site to a very large degree. Customers also have a requirement for self-service: they want to log in, look up information themselves, place orders, track packages, maintain their account, and all at any time and on a 24/7 basis. Self-service saves time and gives people the feeling that they can exercise control over their environment. It increases the utility of the site. The speed with which answers may be found to questions influences the convenience as well. Customers have little time and patience. They do not want to waste their time filling out long forms and going in search of forgotten passwords. They are not prepared to wait too long before a page has been fully loaded. They expect immediate and clear results in performing a search task on the site (Swinkels, 2001).

Personalisation

Websites offer access to data that are stored elsewhere. The data originate from underlying information systems or files kept on file servers. Making optimal use of the available data takes place by linking these databases to offer the customer a personalised environment. He or she can then look for products within this personalised environment and easily make a selection. To facilitate this process, the user's profile may be maintained in a profile database. This database is used to store the visitor's data and to personalise the following pages. Within the framework of the personalisation, a distinction may be made between 'moment-to-moment' marketing and 'one-on-one' marketing. The former focuses on the moment itself: if a customer has placed a printer in his or her shopping cart, a promotion for ink cartridges will appear on the next screen. 'One-to-one' means that the company knows that the customer has a preference for a certain clothing label, for example, so that the offering may be tailored to this preference. This requires a good match between the profile and the end user, the content on the site and the products from the offering. To do this, a link is necessary between the profile database, the content database (texts, promotions, banners, photos) and the product database (list with products). Linking the data from the three databases occurs with the aid of business rules. These record that a user with a certain profile must see a promotion for a certain brand and a slogan with a specific composition or choice of words (Niks, Plasmeijer and Peelen, 2000).

16.3 Creating quality during the visit (Swinkels, 2001)

In the previous section, the quality of the visit was said to be dependent on the degree to which an interactive system, in this case the website, allows the user to complete the desired task within a given environment and in an effective, efficient and comfortable manner. This involves the usability or the utility of a website. The interaction between man and computer is vital to this aspect and is determined to a great degree by the design of the website.

There are two meanings to the concept of design. The first is the artistic ideal to express yourself, and the second is a design ideal to solve problems for the user. Design as it is used in this context involves the latter meaning. If a team designs a product, it attempts to endow the product with those characteristics which people need to perform tasks. The team tries to present these features in such a way that people intuitively grasp at these features and experience them as being efficient for long-term use. They also try to eliminate the potential for design-related errors and to give the product qualities which will cause people to take pleasure in using the product (Wiklund, 1994, in Swinkels, 2001). Analogous to the design of a product, these aspects should also all have to apply to the design of a website. The design of a site must be optimised to meet user criteria so that the user's satisfaction is guaranteed. Websites that attempt to control and manipulate the user do not satisfy this basic assumption and have little chance of success. The short attention span of surfers should be taken into consideration. If a visitor cannot find the desired information quickly enough, he will disappear. The tolerance for complicated designs and slow sites is low. Users are not prepared nor are they motivated to learn how to use a website. Keeping a site as simple as possible, however, does not mean that the site is lacking when it comes to functionality. It implies that the fewest possible necessary concepts are being implemented to meet a need. A steep initial learning curve and a limited number of tasks or concepts that the user has to understand are taken into account.

Recommendations are given in the following sections for the three aspects involved in the design of websites, specifically, the page, the content and the site.

Page design

The design of the page is the first aspect with which a visitor comes into contact and is also immediately the most visual portion of the entire design of a site.

- The loading time for a page should not exceed five or six seconds. Popular sites load twice as fast as others.
- The download size of the pages should be geared towards the allowable loading time.
- The page size must be consistent so that the visitor will retain his or her confidence in the site. If some of the pages are small and load quickly and others are large and slow to download, the visitor no longer knows what to expect and loses his or her sense of control.
- If graphics are used, they should be small yet recognisable. The reuse of graphics is not recommended. Once present in the browser's cache, these files should not need to be reloaded.
- The page should be designed so that it meets the user's needs. Even if the structure seems logical to the design team, this does not necessarily translate into a situation in which the intended user can get around the site easily.
- There are different browsers (and versions), hardware platforms, image sizes and bandwidths with which users operate. The pages must be designed so that they may be viewed under all of these different circumstances.
- The use of frames is not recommended. They create confusion, causing the visitor to quickly become disoriented.
- The visitor to the site is there of his or her own free will and does not have to be held captive. This is far from polite and ultimately does not work. If links to other sites are included, it should be clear to the visitor that clicking these links will mean leaving the current site.

Content design

The reason users ultimately visit a site lies in the content. The entire site must be designed to offer the visitor easy access to the desired, valuable content.

- The content must be short and clearly laid out. Internet users read text on a monitor approximately 25 per cent slower than on paper. They also actually read much less on the web, scanning pages instead.
- Does the page contain visual clarity? The use of headings, boldface type, tables and other visual supports make it easier for the visitor to scan the page. It must be quickly clear to the user what he or she can do on the page in question.

- Spelling errors, grammar mistakes and errors in the content reduce the site's credibility. All of the content must be carefully checked before it finds its way on to the web.
- The public benefits from understandable content offered on the site. Not all of the visitors are experts in the field of the Internet and many find extensive help functions an advantage.
- A clearly designed structure with many hyperlinks ensures that visitors obtain access to the desired information without having 'to sift through' too much irrelevant text. Therefore, it is not necessary to place an overabundance of topics on one page.
- Page titles must be clear, meaningful and unique. This will help the visitors to determine where they are on the site, even if they did not enter the site through the digital main entrance. Page titles can be saved under the favorites or bookmarks function.
- The legibility of a monitor is promoted by using sans serif fonts (such as Arial or Verdana) and by using high contrast colour schemes.

Site design

In setting up a website, sometimes it is the individual pages that get the most attention. Besides, users usually only see one page at any given moment. The entire site is never seen explicitly displayed on the screen. From a design standpoint, the design of the entire site is, however, often more difficult to achieve and is more important than that of the pages itself. The following aspects are key in determining the success of the site design:

- Every page on the site must indicate clearly and consistently the site that is being visited and what may be done on this particular individual page. The company logo at the top left (or in any case, at a consistent location) is the most broadly accepted way of accomplishing this.
- There should be a portion of the homepage that contains links to the most important sections of the site. This section involves the global site navigation. Roughly 20 per cent of the users are link-dominant: they try to browse to find their way around websites. Naturally clear and concise descriptions of the links are a must.
- Approximately half of all Internet surfers are search-dominant. They try to obtain all of the information they are looking for via the search function. For this reason, every page should contain a search function.
- The homepage is a suitable location to place announcements regarding changes, new products and services, press releases and so forth. The condition, however, is that the content supplied is refreshed on a regular basis.
- There are three questions that are important in order for a visitor to determine his or her position on the site:

- Where am I?
- Where have I been?
- Where can I go?

- The skeleton or the structure of the site must have meaning for the user. A site without the proper architecture can lead to chaotic situations and create frustrated visitors.
- A site should be designed according to dominant conventions on the web. Users have become accustomed to certain patterns and the use of site design and navigation.
- A site may not contain links to incomplete sections. The classic 'under construction' message is not telling visitors something they want to know.

16.4 From visit to transaction
(Niks, Plasmeijer and Peelen, 2000)

Although not all websites ultimately strive to take an order (see Section 16.1), this functionality should be offered if customers expect and desire it. The contact cycle therefore does not end on the Internet with the collection and processing of information, but goes beyond this.

CRM illustration

Queues at amusement park are ancient history thanks to e-tickets

Customers never have to become annoyed again with the long queues at Bobbejanland, a popular amusement park in Belgium. Starting in July of this year [2002], they can buy entrance tickets to the Belgian park online and then print these out immediately themselves. The bar code on the e-ticket will be scanned upon arrival at the park, after which the entrance ports will open. That a need existed for this service became evident from the fact that, without a corresponding advertising campaign, Bobbejanland sold thousands of e-tickets in the first two trial weeks via the Internet site. The e-ticket solution for Bobbejanland is being supplied by These Days interactive service in Antwerp.

The transport company Noordned will also start with electronic tickets this autumn. For one bus line between Dokkum and Veenwouden in the Netherlands and three Frisian train lines in the north, travellers may order their tickets via the Internet or telephone and then receive the tickets by SMS text messaging in the form of a code. The conductor in the bus or train will receive this same code on his or her hand-held computer for verification. Noordned has involved various partners in this effort in order to make e-ticketing possible.

Source: *ITCommercie* (2002).

In order to be able to process the transaction, a decision will have to be made about payment systems. Various aspects play a role in this process. To what degree is the system safe and easy to use, for example? If a buyer must purchase and install additional software, this can influence the progress of the interaction. Furthermore, it is important for the company to weigh developing the payment application itself against contracting out payment facilities to a service organisation. A large number of parties are active in the supply of payment systems and options such as:

- credit card companies;
- banks;
- Internet service providers;
- computer suppliers;
- telecoms companies;
- payment service companies.

True clarity on the best Internet payment system is still lacking. For the time being, most payments in the business-to-business market proceed in the same manner as they did previously, and in consumer markets, credit cards and giro slip payments are used. In classifying Internet payment options, the moment of payment is crucial. This moment can occur before, during or after the transaction, during which e-commerce companies usually offer the customer a choice of the following:

- *Pay before*: the buyer pays with e-money from an open electronic wallet that must be replenished prior to the purchase transaction. Examples include e-cash and Millicent.
- *Pay now*: during the purchase transaction, the buyer will gain direct access to his or her bank account balance. This occurs for example with PIN payments, authorisations and COD payments.
- *Pay later*: after the completion of the transaction, the payment will be deducted from the buyer's bank or giro account. This occurs, for example, with credit card transactions and giro slip payments.

The Internet payment options may thus be classified as described under the following headings (and see Figure 16.3).

Credit systems

Credit payment systems are the most popular. Most Internet transactions take place using a credit card. The customer keys in the number of the credit card and the expiry date and a purchase transaction may be initiated. Still, the lack of security makes people jittery when it comes to using this form of payment. In contrast to the traditional credit card transaction in the physical world, the possibility of verifying the authenticity of the cardholder is lacking in the virtual world. The credit card is missing, as is a signature. The openness of the web makes it possible to intercept credit card data. Two methods, with different protocols, have been developed to make credit card transactions safer, namely: Secure Sockets Layer (SSL) and Secure Electronic Transaction (SET).

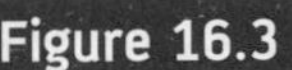
Figure 16.3 Internet payment systems

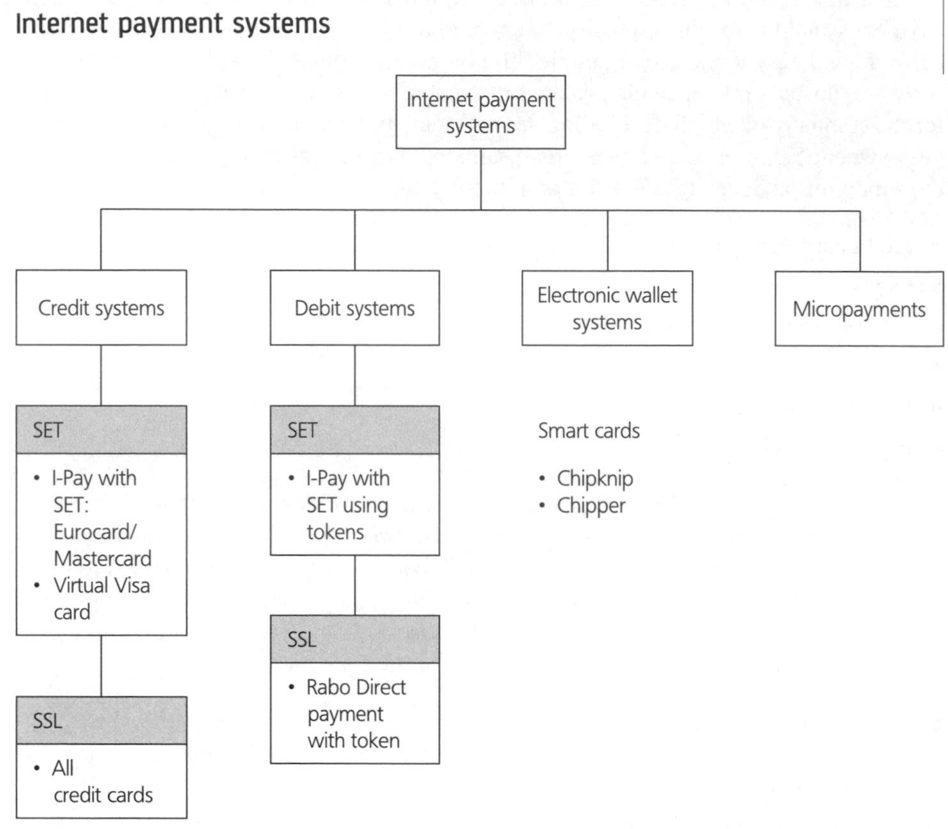

SSL is a simple protocol in a network protocol layer on top of TCP/IP (visible from https:// instead of http://) which may be used to protect many applications on the Internet. The data are encrypted during the transmission in such a way that it becomes difficult to decipher them. The protocol, originally introduced by Netscape, uses cryptographic functions to protect the data traffic between the buyer's browser and the e-commerce company's webserver. The certainty regarding SSL's reliability has not yet been sufficiently proven.

With the arrival of SET, measures have been implemented to increase the reliability. This protocol, originally developed by Mastercard and Visa, other financial institutions and IBM, has been adopted by all of the major credit card companies worldwide. SET is an agreement, a protocol.

With this protocol, the e-commerce company receives an account from the bank or credit card company prior to the commercial process, and the identity and the credibility of the shop are verified; after approval, the shop receives SET payment software with a certificate that is issued by the certification authority.

The customer performing a transaction sends the credit card data in a digital envelope with the aid of SET software. The supplier, who cannot read the credit card data and therefore is unable to misuse them, requests authorisation and approval for the payment from the affiliated bank or credit card company. The reliability and integrity of the data sent and the authenticity of the parties involved is guaranteed thanks to SET.

The limitations attributed to SET include complexity during installation and management as well as the heavy demands placed on the customer's computer. Moreover, the e-commerce company must pay a commission to the credit card company (of 3 to 4 per cent).

Debit payment systems

With debit payment systems, the purchase may be charged directly to the account during the transaction process.

After installation of the software, the buyer of a product has access to a consumer wallet. This wallet may contain data about one or more credit cards as well as data for a debit card. With the corresponding certificate from the bank, payments may be charged directly to the buyer's bank account. The e-commerce company will also have software (with SET) installed to support the buyer's payment. During payment, a hardware token is used to verify the account holder's authenticity.

Electronic wallet systems

Smart cards (a pre-payment facility available to debit card holders) are examples of an electronic wallet system. These open electronic payment systems are primarily suitable for payments of smaller amounts and help speed up the payment. The buyer must have a secure smartcard reader with corresponding software in order to be able to perform online payments. With this system, another barrier to the penetration of this payment form online has been removed.

Micropayments

Micropayments are primarily intended for payments of small amounts (up to several euros). They are especially convenient for digital services and products such as stock market information. The most well-known original initiatives are Digicash and Cybercash.

Payment via the Internet service provider

Payments may also be executed via the Internet service provider (ISP). The ISP will then adjust the monthly account in the Internet subscription payment amount on behalf of the seller. The disadvantage to this is that an e-commerce company would have to enter into agreements with all of the ISPs.

Payment via payment service providers

Another solution for supporting different payment systems is making use of the services of payment service providers (PSPs). PSPs offer a multitude of payment options.

The seller pays an amount for each transaction, from several euros per transaction to several eurocents for thousands of transactions or more. Examples of these kinds of intermediaries include Bibit, Online Transaction Systems and Interpay.

16.5 From transaction to delivery (Niks, Plasmeijer and Peelen, 2000)

One of the important aspects in the e-commerce timeline is the processing of the orders, including the delivery of the products. The promise of the online supplier, for example two-day delivery, is tested during this phase. Physical distribution and fulfilment have a major impact on customer satisfaction and the degree to which the customer will be back in the future.

In order to inspire confidence, it is advisable to set up a tracking and tracing system that will keep the customer informed of the progress of the transaction. FedEx was the first company to offer the possibility of following the progress of the shipment via the Internet. At the time the order is placed, the customer receives a number. This number may be used to track the package's location.

The logistical process of e-commerce companies can be accompanied by enormous problems. The Internet is seen as a rapid medium; for this reason, the quick and efficient delivery of goods is extremely important.

One of the problems with regard to distribution is related to the integration of the front and the back office. The new front-office systems which are set up for the real-time processing of a variety of orders from visitors must be integrated with the older legacy systems which usually process orders in a safe, stable manner by batches (see Chapter 18).

Another complication can be one of a financial nature. Fairly high logistical costs may be associated with the delivery of e-commerce orders in consumer markets. For products or orders with high value on which a substantial margin is earned, this is usually a manageable problem. Whether the costs are paid by the customer, the supplier, or both, this involves an amount that constitutes only a small percentage of the purchase price, the turnover or the profit. This is, however, different with orders comprising low-value, low-margin items; an example would be the daily purchases one makes in supermarkets. Calculations have shown that the direct costs of an e-commerce order in the fast-moving consumer goods category have more than doubled (Van der Laan, 2000). A sharp increase occurs because customers previously came to select and collect their products themselves. Now this must be done by the supplier. Only when there are minimum sales requirements to be met and/or demarcations made in the assortment, delivery area and the delivery time zones, is it possible to limit the costs. This obviously has a major impact on companies' logistical systems.

In Table 16.1, average logistical costs are shown for different distribution scenarios. For comparison purposes, the costs of the traditional retailer are mapped out. The numbers are the costs per activity shown as a percentage of the transaction value. The table shows that the costs for online activities in the food sector are approximately twice those of the traditional retailer, owing primarily to the costs for home delivery and

Table 16.1 Example of cost structures in the food sector

Activity	*Traditional retailer*	*Online purchases supplied from store*	*Online purchases supplied from warehouse*	*Online purchases supplied from satellite station*
Overheads warehouse	1.20	1.20	4.50	6.00
Receipt and storage warehouse	0.5	0.5	0.5	0.5
Warehouse order picking	2.20	2.20	7.50	7.50
Transport to store	0.90	0.90	–	0.80
Overheads store	2.40	2.40	–	–
Receipt and storage store	1.50	1.50	–	–
Stocking store shelves	3.00	3.00	–	–
Consumer order	–	3.20	3.00	3.40
Order picking in store		5.00		
Sales point	1.20	1.20	1.20	1.50
Transport to home	–	5.00	8.50	5.50
Returns	1.20	2.00	1.80	2.30
Customer service	0.90	1.90	2.50	3.00
Total	**15.00**	**30.00**	**29.50**	**30.50**

Source: *Cost/profit Analysis Marketing and Logistics* (2000).

(warehouse) order picking. The issue of the return flows is also relevant. Offering the opportunity to return items is an important legal condition as well as being necessary to the preservation of the relationship. Buyers must have the opportunity to express complaints easily and to refuse and return faulty deliveries.

16.6 From delivery to retention (Peelen and Esterik-Plasmeijer 2001)

Commitment is also important on the Internet. Customers only have a few favourite sites that they visit on an intensive basis. For suppliers, it is possible to reduce the pressure from the competition if they ensure that their site is in the customer's mindset; then in the long term, they stand to earn a great deal of money from this customer. After all, it holds true that 'today, loyal shoppers visit their favourite sites far more frequently than they would any brick-and-mortar store'.

Figure 16.4 **Functionality of transactional websites in the stages of one-to-one marketing**

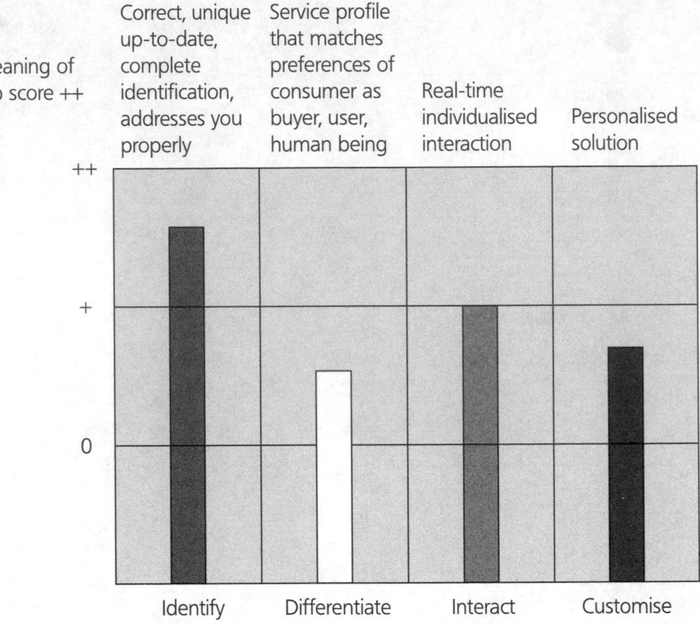

On the basis of research among transaction-oriented dotcom companies,[1] Peppers and Rogers were able to determine which functionalities are important to being able to enter into long-term relationships with customers (see Figure 16.4). These functionalities have been described in terms of the four phases of one-to-one marketing:

- First, identifying customers by recording customer data: *identify*.
- Second, determining the differences between individual customers on the basis of the analysis of customer data: *differentiate*.
- Third, entering into a dialogue with individual customers on the basis of knowledge of the customer: *interact*.
- Finally, proactively offering customised products, services and information on the basis of the needs of the customer: *customise*. In doing this, insight is obtained into the interaction with customers.

An organisation receives a score of '0' if its site has the minimum basic quality. A '+' score is awarded if it has an advanced quality, and a '++' if it has reached the supreme level of quality.

The results showed that none of the companies studied scored the maximum score on all of the points. Some of them were better in supplying customisation, such as suppliers of garden tools and the like. Others were better at making a distinction between

[1] Please note that the outcomes are different if the customers are unable to complete transactions online.

customers from different segments, such as car hire companies, or in the interaction with customers such as online investment institutions with good advice modules and transaction possibilities.

During the identification phase, recognising individual customers and protecting their privacy plays a central role. The highest level was found in sites that recognise customers both off- and online. It can even be determined whether someone is online from their place of work or if he or she is visiting the site from a private address. The person in question is not only recognised by his or her bank if he or she is surfing on the site of the financial services company for business purposes, but also if he or she is there for private money matters. Not only does the supplier stress that it guarantees the customer's privacy, it also takes sufficient measures to ensure this (strong data protection). Furthermore, it guarantees the situation not only within its own company, but also for the partners with whom the supplier collaborates.

During the differentiation phase, this goes a step further than in the identification phase. Customers are not only recognised by name but also classified into (small) groups with certain features and preferences. Thanks to this customer knowledge, sites may be set up in such a way that they are geared towards the customers' specific wishes. Questionnaires or order forms may be filled in partially or fully automatically which makes it easier for customers to do business with this supplier. The customer knowledge may be used at the highest level to ask the right questions to the particular customer. A site that helps customers to lose weight, knows, for example, exactly which aspects of the eating and drinking habits it must ask about in order to provide customised weight-loss recommendations.

Recognising and getting to know visitors can be useful in the interaction phase when a potential transaction is completed. In order to facilitate this further, as many barriers as possible will have to be removed. The number of actions that will have to be performed to place an order may be reduced with a one-click system for example, such as that developed by amazon.com. Increasing the trust in online buying by offering the possibility to return purchases, offering effective service and a tracking and tracing functionality are all comforting to customers. Organisations that also know how to ask the right question at the right time ('drip irrigation questioning') and have devised effective methods to encourage customers to make their purchases on the Internet score above average (++). Offering real-time online support is also only found with the advanced players. A book site is in a position to make real-time suggestions regarding interesting books during interactions on the basis of the purchase history and the current surfing behaviour of the customer and patterns encountered with other customers.

A basic level of customisation is present if customers are able to request and retrieve their order history on the Internet, pay using a variety of methods and receive their order in different ways. Completing the transaction in a customised manner is what is essential. A higher level of customisation is achieved if a customer can configure his or her product online and his or her specific wishes are taken into account as well, regardless of the supplier of the product or service; it is irrelevant whether the product originates from the supplier itself or one of its service partners. The 'supreme' quality level is achieved if the organisation supplies personalised products on- or offline and can automatically refill customers' stock levels if desired (replenishment). A supermarket, for example, fills a regular customer's refrigerator back up to a level agreed upon in advance.

16.7 Measuring results (Niks, Plasmeijer and Peelen, 2000)

Measuring the results of Internet activities is of vital importance to the evaluation of:

- the effectiveness of measures designed to stimulate, facilitate and realise online transactions;
- the way in which relationship marketing has been implemented on the Internet.

An overview has been created by Forrester Research with data which may be used in designing this type of evaluation. The research firm has also specified how companies may obtain the data and how they may be used.

Forrester's overview focuses on four questions:

1 Who is the customer? *Customer identity*.
2 What has he or she purchased? *Transaction*.
3 How did the system react? *System throughput*.
4 Where have the visitors come from and where did they go? *Basic traffic*.

Although the questions do not cover the full customer interaction cycle, the system may be seen as one of the more extensive evaluation regimes and is deserving of consideration.

In terms of *customer identity*, data involving name, address, city, customer number, demographic data, interests and purchase history are important. These are data that may originate from different sources and may be used to more accurately target customers in marketing activities. The effectiveness of bannering may be increased in this way, priorities may be set within campaign management among the various activities, and selections may be made with regard to direct marketing efforts. *Purchase registration* is simple if the orders and the deliveries (software downloads) take place online. Should the ultimate purchase take place offline and perhaps even anonymously, then indicators which led to the transactions will have to be found. An example of this would be filled-in certificates of guarantee (or other registration forms). These involve data which may be collected in transaction databases or with the aid of servers and which are used to determine the effectiveness of marketing activities: how effective was the advertisement, help desk, expansion of the product line, and so forth?

The *system throughput* primarily specifies the operational reliability of the website. Have there been error reports, how fast is the system and where does it freeze up? Server files, network packet sniffers and system software can all aid in gathering these data. They may be used to remove bottlenecks in the system and manage the capacity.

Finally, *traffic management* is designed to measure visitor numbers; where do they come from, how do they enter, what do they see and from which point are they exiting the site? This involves data that may be gathered in part along the same route as the data on system throughput and which may be used to improve navigation, the effectiveness of online advertising and improving content, among other aspects.

The success of Internet analyses does not lie in the gathering or analysis of the data, but in the ability to apply the knowledge that rises to the surface in these analyses effectively. Every discipline in the relationship-oriented organisation has its own angle and responsibility. For example, top management would like to know to what extent the Internet has contributed to the profitability, and marketers are interested in the effectiveness of the content. The ICT department is wondering if the server can handle the volumes. By gathering, registering, analysing, interpreting and using this information, a 'learning' organisation develops that is capable of improving its performance on the web.

16.8 Conclusion

The Internet and the website are maturing. The use of both continues to grow although youthful ambitions to develop and exploit the maximum possibilities that information technology has to offer are disappearing. The Internet is gaining its permanent position in the network of communication channels which is expected to facilitate the dialogue between customer and supplier. It should attract customers and visitors and offer them what they are looking for. Questions will be answered with ease and confidence on the website in the most effective context. In a community, on a portal and a micro-, brand or organisation site, the customer is served in a personal way. If it suits the visitor's objective, he or she may also be encouraged to make a purchase. The site will take the order in a trustworthy and informative manner, facilitate the payment and keep the buyer informed regarding the status of the transaction. Insight into the logistics costs of the delivery of the e-commerce order prevent the supplier from being (unpleasantly) surprised. An organisation with a well-integrated front and back office also contributes to a reliable delivery. The positive interaction between customer and supplier on the web must contribute to a further development of the relationship. In order to strengthen the bond between the two, it is advisable to implement (elements of) one-to-one marketing. The more successful sites have a system in which they are able to determine how they identify, differentiate, interact and serve their customers on the Internet in order to reinforce the relationship so that it becomes a mutually profitable one.

The design and set-up of a successful Internet site requires a great deal of effort, and should be monitored regularly for efficiency and effectiveness. The focus here should not be placed exclusively on the commercial aspects, but also on the technical factors which are related to the system.

Case study

Wolters J. Thomson and the Internet

Wolters J. Thomson (WJT) is a leading publisher in the world, holding a strong position in the legal, medical, educational and business markets across the globe. For many years WJT has been very successful in selling subscriptions of loose-leaf products (subscribers receive every period a new set of articles/chapters/updates that can be placed in the folders). For this product, accountable for approximately 45 per cent of revenues (2004), the company receives up-front money and is relatively sure of future revenues. Also the margin on this product is very good, since WJT is operating in a niche market where quality prevails above price. Loose-leafs, however, have entered the declining stage of the product life cycle. Over the past three years it has become more difficult to attract new customers and to have them continue their subscription. Other products that the company markets are (academic) journals, books, CD-ROMs, government publications and websites.

Furthermore WJT is facing increasing competition. New entrants have entered the market with novel business models. Government, for example, is providing free information on the Internet. Schools and universities slowly manifest themselves as publishers. Consultants provide free information on the Internet and even in physical journals to attract new clients, not just among the major organisations, but also among the small and medium-sized enterprises.

IT technology has had a major impact on WJT and the industry. Apart from the new entrants, established publishers are also investing heavily in the development of new products and value propositions. VNU, for example, sold its traditional magazine business and transformed its organisation into an information broker; it invested heavily in customer databases. Reed Business Information invested in product databases; it developed a register in which you can find almost everything on a particular legal subject. Others try to build a successful business around portals or communities.

One positive trend is that with the evolution of the Internet an increasing number of people and organisations believe information of good quality on the Internet deserves to be paid for.

To hold its leading role in the selected market segments (legal, medical, business, education) WJT faces tremendous threats and opportunities. To prepare for the future it has formulated a new strategy: it plans to become a solution provider for professionals in the legal, medical, educational and business disciplines. It wants to increase its added value by delivering high quality content that helps professionals improve their business. New products will have to be developed to realise this ambition.

Questions

1 Currently WJT has problems in realising a profit with publishing products that are sold via the Internet. Most successful are marketing campaigns in which print and Internet products are sold together as a package for one price. In cases where Internet products are sold separately it is still hard to get a good price for the delivered content. Can you recommend three ways to increase revenues through the Internet? Give arguments.

2 To add more value to customers WJT wonders how it can 'integrate into the workflow of their customer'. A physician, for example, may, during the day, diagnose several patients, prescribe medicine, perform administrative activities, look up specific diseases, and so on. WJT looks for ways to support these activities with ICT and content. Can you recommend in what way WJT, as a publisher, can realistically provide added value to customers in the prescribed way?

Questions

1 How may traffic to a website be generated? Select a particular supplier and study the methods it employs to achieve this.

2 When does *spill-over* occur with a company whose URL address ends in .com?

3 How can a company that supplies durable consumer goods best get started if it is interested in creating a community around its users?

4 Visit a website of your choice and evaluate the design using the criteria that have been named under page, content and site design. Formulate recommendations for improving the design.

5 How may an organisation ensure that more visitors will ultimate make purchases both on- and offline?

6 Characteristic of the Internet is that users are sitting in the driver's seat. Attempts to change this generally lead to frustration and resistance on the part of customers. Think of five situations on the Internet in which consumers put up resistance when they lose control over their surfing behaviour.

7 Why do the logistics costs involved in completing an e-commerce order for the last two alternative forms of distribution shown in Table 16.1 (from the warehouse and from the satellite) differ only slightly from those involved in the second distribution form (delivery from the store)?

8 Visit a website of your choice and try to establish how well the company behind the site scores in terms of Peppers and Rogers' one-to-one marketing criteria (as illustrated in Figure 16.4).

9 What are the most important website performance criteria for a marketer implementing a customer intimacy strategy?

References

Bügel, Marnix (2002) *Klantenloyaliteit, over ongelijke behandeling in het digitale tijdperk*, Pearson Education, Amsterdam.

Cheskin Research (1999) *E-commerce Trust Study*, January.

Eilander, Elsbeth (2004) E-mail marketing testen werkt, *Tijdschrift voor Marketing*, May, 32–35.

Forrester (1999) *IT View Report*, September.

Haarman, Jordi and Ed Peelen (2000) Improving the accessibility of web sites by a higher ranking in search engines, *Proceedings EMAC Conference*, Rotterdam.

ITCommercie (2002) Wachtrijen pretpark verleden tijd met e-tickets, *ITCommercie*, 5, September, 11.

Jonkers, Menno (2000) *Computable*, 20, 49, Tryllian.

Laan, J.W. van der (2000) The future of on-line food retailing, *Food Personality*, January.

Marketing International (2003a) Hoe ontwikkelt het internetgebruik zich binnen Europa, *Marketing International*, **38**, 3, March, 16.

Marketing International (2003b) Intensiever surfen, *Marketing International*, **38**, 3, March, 16.

Marketing International (2003c) De blabla voorbij in online reclame, *Marketing International*, **38**, 3, March, 17.

Moe, Wendy W. and Peter S. Fader (2000) Which visits lead to purchases? Dynamic conversion behavior at e-commerce sites, in Mitch Betts, Turning browsers into buyers, *MIT Sloan Management Review*, **42**, 2, Winter, 8–9.

Niks, Wouter, Pauline Plasmeijer and Ed Peelen (2000) *E-commerce, transactiemodel voor internet*, Samsom, Alphen a/d Rijn.

Peelen, Ed and Pauline van Esterik-Plasmeijer (2001) *Marketing in de kennis- en netwerkeconomie*, ten Hagen & Stam, The Hague.

Peelen, Ed, Tom Dolkens and Paul Winnubst (eds) (2001) *Klantentrouw via internet, e-loyalty*, Kluwer, Deventer.

Peppers, Don and Martha Rogers (2000) *OnetoOne Manager: Real world lessons in customer relationship management*, Capstone Publishing, Oxford.

Rietdijk, J.W. (2000) Oplossingen voor veilige e-commerce transacties, *Informatie*, January, 6–15.

Schans, W.M. van der (2001) *Consumentengoederen en merkcommunicatie op internet*, Erasmus University, Rotterdam.

Swinkels, Hans (2001) *Web usability bij de Nederlandse e-tailers, een onderzoek naar de bruikbaarheid van vijftien Nederlandse e-tailers*, Erasmus University, Rotterdam.

Wiklund, Michael E. (1994) *Usability in Practice: How companies develop user friendly products*, AP Professional, Boston, Massachusetts.

17

Direct mail

It is impossible to cover all contributions made by academics and practitioners in the field of direct mail marketing through the years. Thousands of studies have been done and published. The aim of this chapter is only to summarise the headlines and to give an overview. For further information we refer readers to the trade bodies such as the Direct Marketing Association and the Institute for Direct Marketing. We will begin this chapter by reviewing the developments which have taken place in the field of direct mail. We will then focus on the process in which the direct mail pack is developed, produced, distributed and followed up. Finally, indications will be provided to point out those areas deserving special attention in the development of 'the package'.

In this chapter we will address the following questions

- What is the role of direct mail in the dialogue with prospects and customers?
- What is the power of communication of direct mail as compared with other communication instruments over the years?
- How to manage the direct mail system.
  - What are the risks and points of special interest?
  - What are the stages in the process of designing, producing, sending and following-up direct mail campaigns?
  - What are the marketing brief, creative brief, traffic, fulfilment and evaluation?
  - What are the characteristics of effective direct mail messages?
  - What are the effects to be achieved?
  - What are the characteristics of effective letters, envelopes, brochures and reply cards?

Practitioner's insight

New transport and communication infrastructures have a major effect on economic structures. This influence is not reserved exclusively for the recent diffusion of the Internet, but had already been felt during the time of the emergence of the railways and the postal services. Activities such as consumption and production were able to take place at different locations. After all, it was now possible to bridge distances. Mail order companies were able to deliver products to remote areas. Correspondence by letter allowed people to share their lives with one another.

The adoption of a new infrastructure always has consequences for the old one. The new version has the upper hand in many respects: it is faster, easier, of improved quality, etc. Novelties also exert a certain power of attraction on a certain segment of society. In short, the old infrastructure is overshadowed by the new. The group of veterans that remains loyal will ultimately decrease in size. One only has to see the fate that has befallen the letter, correspondence and direct mail. Many books on CRM will not even address the topic of direct mail; it is considered passé. This is unjust, considering the fact that direct mail is still used on a large scale and once stood at the foundation of CRM. To some extent, the lessons learned from experiences with direct mail will not fit within the CRM strategy, yet will nonetheless prove in part to be extremely valuable.

17.1 The position of direct mail

Direct mail refers to the delivery of an addressed message by post. One of the strengths of direct mail is that it offers flexibility in terms of planning. The supplier determines when the mailing will be sent out. It is not dependent upon the publication dates of magazines or the broadcast frequency of radio or television. It is also not necessary to send the entire mailing all at once or to send the same pack to all of the addresses. The sender only has to take the preparation time into account that is necessary to design and produce the mailing. For this reason, direct mail was seen as a communication tool which could be used to capitalise on the current circumstances in the (personal) environment. With the arrival of the telephone and Internet, this argument lost a great deal of its persuasive power. Although the relative advantage with regard to mass media remains intact (to a certain extent), the Internet does score higher in this respect (Baier, 1983; Roomer, 1987; Berger and Roberts, 1989).

On the other hand, direct mail is and will remain a penetrating medium. Direct mail makes it possible to approach the customer at times when he or she will not be distracted. The prospect or customer is free to choose, without having to make too many preparations in advance, when and where he or she would like to 'absorb' the message, as it were. This may occur at a time and/or place where he or she is isolated from others. In this way, the medium possesses a high degree of confidentiality.

The personal addressing and the design of the envelope will have to encourage the customer to inspect the contents. However, even if the letter is not opened, the customer or prospect can still be affected by the envelope. For this reason, it can be advisable to place a portion of the message here. This medium offers a quick cumulative coverage.

After opening the envelope, the customer may be confronted with a letter with a personal tint, if desired, as well as any enclosed folders or catalogues. A large quantity of information may be transferred to the recipient which may be specifically geared towards his or her needs. Direct mail can also be used in a thematic way to a certain extent; a company's image can be communicated using text and pictures.

However, direct mail is less skilled at providing evidence of the promises made. In the customer's eyes, basically anyone is capable of sending out a mailing. For this reason, a mailing does not represent a guarantee that a reliable organisation is behind the effort. Physical contact with the product is lacking. A need can arise to support direct mail with other media.

In addition to reliability and image building, integration with other tools has to be accomplished to stimulate a response. Within this framework, the integration between direct mail and sales promotions is relevant. The sales promotion may be displayed on the envelope, for example. Although this causes the incentive to be noticed directly, which can arouse interest, this can also lead to the packet immediately being perceived as an advertisement and thus thrown in the bin. Tests will be necessary to indicate what will produce the best response.

Developments in direct mail

In spite of its age, there are still many extremely interesting technological developments taking place within the field of direct mail. Two examples are given here.

Personalisation

The possibilities for printing letters and brochures geared towards individuals are coming increasingly within companies' reach. Various texts and images are stored in databases. On the basis of these components, brochures and letters are being composed for individual customers. Someone who receives an offer for property insurance, for example, sees objects which he or she is known to own and which are valuable. On the basis of the customer profile, a suitable price quote and incentive are then created for this customer. The production costs of these personalised mailings are decreasing and the effect on the response is promising for professional direct marketers.

Media-dependent content

Content that was automatically sent by post to third parties previously is starting to qualify more and more for distribution via another channel. It will therefore become interesting to make content suitable for multimedia distribution. Using standards such as XML for recording text is becoming important, as is becoming skilled in the use of tools that place messages in the layout that correspond to a certain channel (document management). This trend is seen particularly among companies that prefer to send their invoices electronically ('electronic billing').

The high level of penetration offered by this medium is counterbalanced by the high costs for each contact. In general, the effectiveness of direct mail is decreasing – particularly as a result of the junk mail factor – while the Internet offers new, cheaper alternatives. The Internet may, after all, be used to send e-mailings which can surpass the communicative power of direct mailings. The message may be tailored to the personal situation even better by e-mail; the sender can have the undivided attention of the recipient and the opportunity for the recipient to respond has been made even more accessible.

We also see a shift towards the new mix of communication methods (Peelen *et al.*, 2000). Instead of sending in a coupon, people are using the telephone. And a message sent by e-mail can often take the place of a phone call. It is striking that people generally do not skip a generation in communication; the number of people that will abandon using coupons and make the switch to sending an e-mail instead is very low.

17.2 The process of developing, producing, sending and following-up direct mailings

The organisation of the direct mailing process deserves a great deal of attention. The process consists of numerous steps in which different people, departments and even companies are involved. Harmonised coordination of these sub-activities is influential for the timely and satisfactory development, production, sending and follow-up of mailings. Preventing delays is important in order to ensure the preservation of the link with other communication processes and to be able to approach prospects and customers at the most suitable moment. Having to make up for lost time later in the project may lead to the creation of additional, somewhat unnecessary expenses and the sacrifice of quality. Companies often have to settle for certain creative designs or printing proofs sooner than was desired or planned.

Managing this direct mail process is becoming an increasingly important skill. The trend for gearing communication more and more to the individual and his situation has led to mailings with a greater degree of variety and a decreased need for the production and distribution of large quantities. Usually, the time span allotted to these activities has decreased. The dynamic in markets and organisations is increasing and demands a shorter time-to-market. In addition, our demands are increasing because we have become accustomed to the speed with which the Internet may be used to respond to individual customer desires and situations.

For organisations with a high level of mail production, this is a reason to standardise the direct mail process to a greater degree. The term 'the factory' is used to illustrate how the reliability and speed of the mail process may be increased. The processes involved in the creation, production, sending and follow-up are accurately described. There are documents which describe the activities involved in a process, how these must be performed and documented, and how to obtain approval for important decisions, and people have become specialised in performing one or more of these processes.

A distinction is made between 'the factory' – with the more complex and all-encompassing mailings – and the smaller projects. Each may be organised in an appropriate manner. Included in the first are the campaigns involved in the introduction of a new product or the development of relationships with customers from a segment during the growth phase (see Chapters 2 and 8). Different mailings are included in the campaign as well as other communication activities. Under the latter we include the more one-off incidental activities. Examples of these might include the announcement of a sale in a department store, an offer of a discount to customers who had placed an order earlier that month, etc.

In order to accelerate the process, companies can consider the use of ICT. It is also advisable to exercise caution here at crucial moments. Organisations that choose to receive printing proofs digitally instead of having them delivered by courier run the risk that they will not be able to assess the colours properly. Additionally, a glance at the physical printwork lends itself better to making an accurate evaluation of the proof.

The outsourcing of parts of the process will not automatically lead to the reduction of the existing bottlenecks. Organisations that experience problems in printing letters and compiling the mail packet will not be able to solve them by outsourcing if the cause of delays and errors is not related to the capacities and abilities of people and machines, but arises instead from the actual delivery of the work. A third party will also experience difficulties. The thought that this party will have to find its own way around these problems and must keep to the agreed prices can offer reprieve. However, in the long term, the service provider – the fulfilment house – will resist and might even terminate the collaboration if there is no prospect of a mutually profitable cooperation.

For a supplier, the direct mail process may be divided up into the following phases (see Figure 17.1):

- marketing briefing;
- creative briefing;
- traffic;
- fulfilment; and
- the evaluation.

The *selection* of people and organisations to which the offer will be made runs parallel to this process. A test may also be built into this process, if desired. Prior to distributing the final mailing to its total circulation among the target group, different versions of a test mailing will first have to be sent out. Based on the response, the final version will be chosen and/or adjustments will be made.

During the *marketing briefing*, the marketer, or customer, segment or product manager specifies the assignment to the direct mail specialist. This will contain a description of the objective, the target group, the proposition (including premium), the brand image to be conveyed, the market opportunities and threats, the marketing communication plan and the role of direct mail with respect to other communication channels. An indication is given of the intended contribution direct mail must make to the 'big picture': what is the intended response and how will this be incorporated into the call centre's activities, for example?

During this briefing, attention is also dedicated to the financial aspects, the room used for testing purposes and market research, and the method to be employed should

Figure 17.1

The DM process

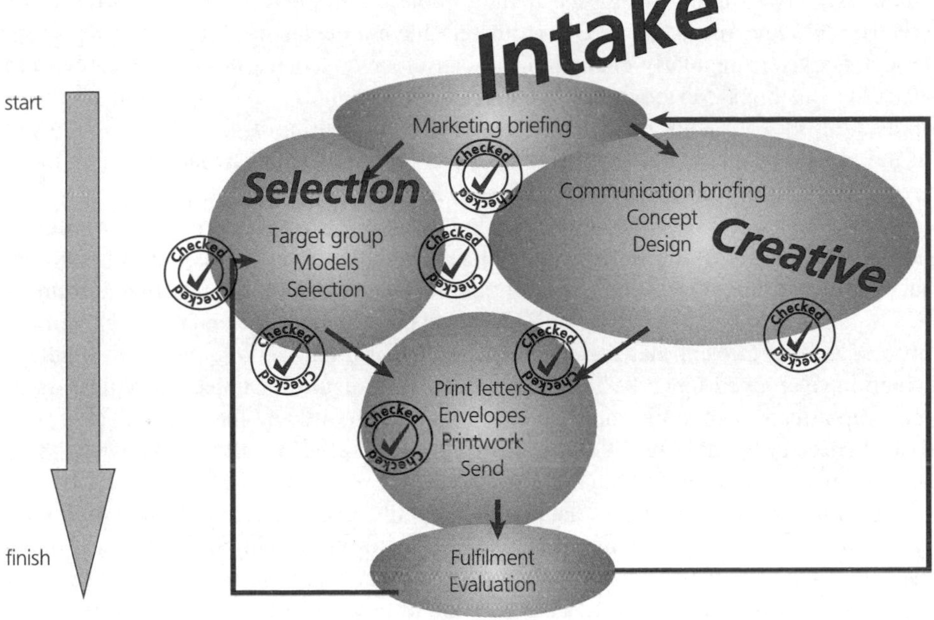

Source: Zuiderduin (2003).

the results turn out differently from planned. A plan is then drawn up for the activities to be undertaken.

After this briefing has been drawn up and communicated, the actual direct mail process may begin and a *creative briefing* may be set up which is destined for the internal or external advertising agency. This is a formal description of the message that the organisation would like to communicate to the target group and the communication objectives that it hopes to achieve. As a result of the briefing, the copywriter and other individuals involved in the creative process can put themselves in the recipient's position and think of the best way to approach him or her. Insight will be gained into the customer's problem, the proposition, evidence for the effectiveness of the solution offered and the manner in which this may be launched on to the market. Important topics such as the supplier's brand personality will also be treated in this process.

It is not recommended for the marketer to get involved in the creative process taking place during the briefing of the creative team. This can lead to conflict and diminished creativity. In evaluating the creations, the marketer will have to be careful not to allow any personal value judgements to play a role in this process. The crux of the matter is whether or not it works and what the recipient will think.

In order for the process to proceed properly, it can also be useful if the creative team – via an account director or alone – follows a number of steps in working towards a final creation, holding off confronting the client with a solution straight away. By first presenting several concepts from which to make a selection, ideas and expectations may be geared towards one another. Offering room for adjustment in the elaboration of the chosen concept also serves this purpose.

Corporate identity plays an important role in this creative process. Corporate communication departments often demand that communication messages satisfy the rules of the house style. A uniform brand identity must be conveyed through all of the channels. Copywriters view this as an undesirable limitation of the space within which creative solutions must lie and can ultimately have a negative effect on the response. Direct marketers regularly champion the cause for added freedom. Noticeably, less attractive mailings can often catch the reader's eye more easily and lure more responses. Justice may not be done to the specific proposition if the rules are followed to the letter. Dark blue and yellow company colours only hinder marketers aiming to create a beautiful, sunny, special vacation offer!

Once the creation is approved, the *traffic* stage begins, which runs from the duplication all the way up to the actual shipment. At the same time, traffic makes the necessary further arrangements with the fulfilment department or the external fulfilment house. The traffic department becomes involved only towards the end of the direct mail process and, as a result, has the disadvantage that it often has to contend with delays which have cropped up earlier along the route. It is regularly subjected to pressure to make up arrears despite the danger of a sacrifice in quality and the fact that additional disturbances occur as a result of the rush. A good traffic department knows how to handle pressure and carefully monitor the process.

The *fulfilment process* begins the moment that the response arrives or that follow-up calls must be made, for example (Baier, 1983). Tailoring the shipment to the available capacity in the call centre for the follow-up is critical for the ultimate effectiveness of the mailing. If the capacity to be able to respond in time to the interest that has been aroused is lacking, the company runs the risk that it will miss sales opportunities.

The final phase in the process involves the *evaluation*. There is a risk that this activity will fall by the wayside; new activities are already being scheduled and looking back does not seem very useful. As a result, the power of direct marketing is lost on many as it has always been based on extracting knowledge from the experience.

17.3 Effective direct mail messages

Testing almost seems to have been invented by direct marketers. For years, variations in the selection, the message, the design, the incentive, the time of shipment and so forth seem to have been the subject of tests. What is the effect of adding a 'P.S.' to the letter? What is the importance of the header and what is a good structure for the text of a letter? Is it better to write in the first or the third person? How do people view letters: where is the eye drawn to first and in which direction does it move next? Is it best to underline, colour in or italicise important remarks? Is it effective to repeat important points and/or to place them in the margin? Each of these, and many other aspects, and their effect on the response have been measured. The experience gained has been retained, passed on and used in the continual sharpening of the communication message.

However, one should be careful in applying these lessons to an organisation with a CRM strategy in place. The experience with direct mail has mostly been obtained in a transactional setting in which the main goal has been to elicit a response and receive an order.

Realising the desired effect from direct mail communication (Lumley, 1986)

Realising the desired effect from direct mailing campaigns requires first and foremost a good interplay between copy and design. Copy refers to the text that is supposed to convince the recipient of the value of the proposition. It is the words that are designed to give customers the feeling that you care about them. Design involves the visual presentation and influences the eye movements: is the attention being drawn to and are the eyes looking at the right things?

Within direct mail, the seeing or reading process that recipients participate in is divided into four stages (see Figure 17.2). During the first stage, customers or prospects scan the message for several seconds to determine if it is relevant to them. They look at the headers, images, postscript and/or the possibility of replying. Before a mailing is discarded, people do actually read and look at it. If the recipient gets through the first stage, then a process begins in which customers look for reasons to stop reading, as it were. This is why we must develop a visual 'road map' which guides them to those subjects which interest them. In the last phase, those readers who have not yet given up reach the confirmation stage.

Each of the elements of a direct mail pack proves its value during one or more of these phases. The envelope plays a major role in the early stages, while the brochure and letter will have to be convincing in the appropriate manner later.

Figure 17.2

Stages of reading

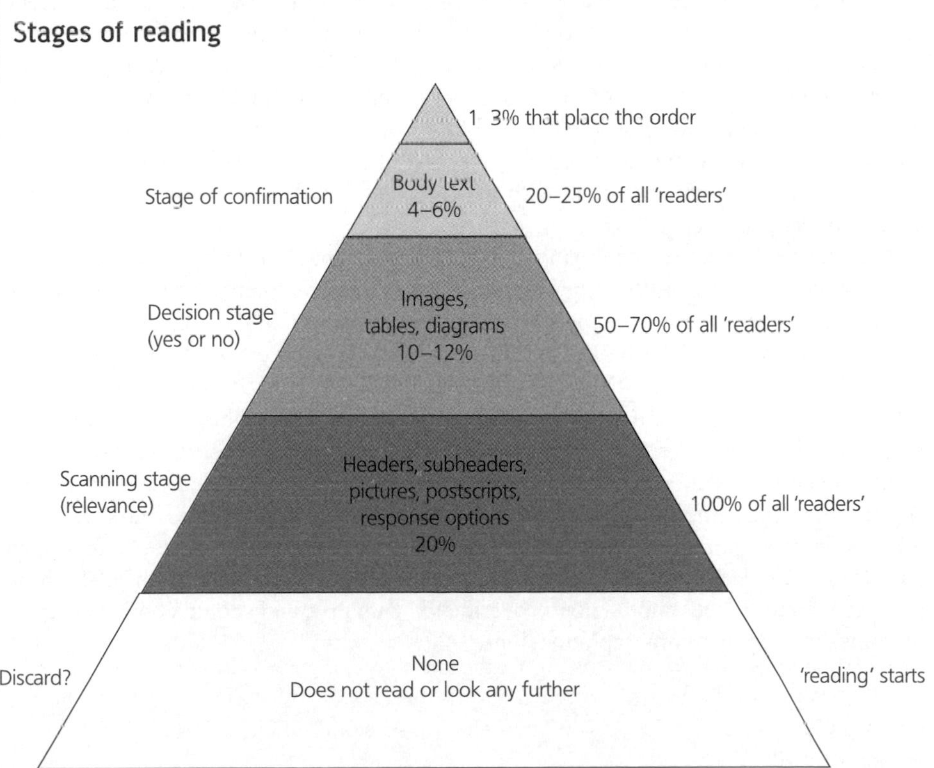

Source: Lumley (1986). © 1986 John Wiley & Sons, Inc. This material is used by permission of John Wiley & Sons Inc.

The letter

The copywriter's job may be compared with that of the relationship manager or salesperson who finds him- or herself 'face-to-face' with a defensive prospect or customer. The ultimate goal of the copywriter is to make sure the recipient makes a positive decision. To do this, he or she will have to spark interest, remove risk, provide proof, and have an emotional effect on the respondent. The arguments will have to be communicated in a focused, comprehensible and convincing way. Only those benefits that appeal to 'readers' who have made it to the interest stage and who have not 'quit' beforehand are the ones that deserve to be communicated. The primary advantages are those which express what the product does for the customer. You can make ice in your refrigerator with a flick of the wrist! Bake a fresh loaf of bread within an hour using grain! In addition to these primary advantages, secondary benefits will also have to be stated which are related to the product features. They support the message and sell the promise. Testimonials may also be used to lend credibility to the message. The primary advantages should be repeated in headers, in summaries and in graphic images. The secondary benefits, on the other hand, should never appear in the headers.

Barriers must be removed which delay any positive decisions which may have ultimately been reached. If a choice has been made, the 'reader' will have to be encouraged to take action.

The final text will have to be written for the 20 per cent of respondents who are interested and have reached the decision stage. It is pointless to try to reach everyone. It is recommended that the copy is written in a positive style and provides reasons to purchase or respond. Never turn the text into a sales pitch. Do not negotiate with prospects either and try to avoid reacting to arguments involving why they should not respond. Be careful about telling a story or a 'teaser'; after all, it is no longer necessary to attract their attention. Also, the use of humour is not recommended; it distracts from the real message. Use details to reinforce the credibility of the message. Avoid copy in which the focus lies on the company's organisation or staff; the reader is not interested. Write in such a way as to create a bond with the recipient. Finally, avoid tiring language as well as fillers and clichés.

It is not the appeal or the creativity of the subject that determines the quality of a letter. A good design on the other hand will invite the recipient to read the text and guide him or her towards the reply device. 'Boring' colours and an inadequate contrast between the colour of the paper and the text must be avoided. Different paper sizes should be used if necessary to attract attention. The right type of paper will be used in order to make the texts and images legible and to leave behind the desired impression of quality. Headers are printed in the proper dimensions and right fonts. Important arguments are emphasised because it is known generally that bold or slanted texts are less striking than underlined texts. Handwritten remarks in the margin, for example, can be used to focus attention on important aspects. The use of graphic images is functional and designed to help readers make a decision. They also draw attention to the more important topics. Pages should not be overloaded with text, and should contain adequate margins, spacing and paragraph divisions.

CRM illustration

The sales letter – *a bad example*

Sales Management
FAO: Mrs M. Krol
Postbus 23
7400 GA Deventer

Enschede, 7 December 2001

Re: Improvement of results through a successful Internet strategy

Dear Mrs Krol,

What is the added value that the Internet brings to your organisation? Have you incorporated this medium into your strategy? Which advantages does it offer your organisation and target groups?

At XXX, we believe in the Internet. By using Internet applications that help organisations to improve their results. We have proven this to our customers and with our approach.

XXX offers you **strategic advice** and **results-oriented management** in the area of e-communications (primarily, Internet, intra-, extranet). We work with organisations that are ranked at the top of their sector, and have more than five years of experience and work **independently of** computer experts, advertising agencies and site builders.

Have a look at XXX.nl. Where visions, models and practical cases come together. Where our customers share their results and experiences with you and describe the possibilities that can also apply to your organisation and your target groups. We are convinced that, using our knowledge and experience, we can also help you to improve your company results using the Internet.

We assume that you will appreciate this gesture, and will contact you in the near future to make an appointment to discuss how to incorporate the Internet into your company strategy.

Kind regards,

YYYY

PS. XXX works with the following:
Profit: Company Y, Z, X, . . . , **Semi-/non-profit:** Institution Y, Z, X, ...

Evaluation

- Unclear sender.
- Many questions, few answers.
- Third paragraph does not fit in with the previous paragraph.
- Argued from the standpoint of the writer (we) and ensuing use of presumptuous language ('we assume that you appreciate this gesture').

Source: Andriesse (2001).

Brochures

Brochures will have to spread the same message as the letter, yet must avoid repetition. The role of the brochure is to provide a reason why the customer should remain a customer. By adding new material, such as technical information and specific details, the message may be supplemented in the brochure. Testimonials may provide additional evidence. There is more room for a longer header which may be used to describe the proposition and the benefits.

As with letters, the design is geared towards attracting and retaining the audience's attention. The most important elements are usually placed in the centre of the first page. Through the use of photographs, the reader may be encouraged to read further, to turn the page. Photos will have to depict the users and people generally in an advantageous setting. Illustrations and figures prove their worth when it comes to explaining technical details. Using sub-headings as reference points, attention may also be held further into the brochure.

Checklist

The checklists under the following four sub-headings include aspects which should be attended to in the creation of a direct mailing (Roomer, 1987).

The envelope

- Is a standard envelope used or a custom-designed envelope?
- Does the envelope's exterior arouse interest? Or does seeing the envelope lead the recipient to discard the packet?
- Will the envelope be stamped with a regular postage stamp (is more personal) or with a 'postage paid' stamp?

The letter

- Does the letter entice the reader to read it?
- Does the letter appear pleasant at first glance?
  - Are there a minimum number of different fonts used?
  - Is underlining not used too often?
  - Are there a minimum of comments placed in the margin?
- Does the first paragraph contain the crux of the message?
- Is the main message point repeated further on in the letter?
- Are the consequences of a positive or negative (non-) response described?
- Is there sufficient 'evidence' provided with regard to keeping the promise?
- Are there, in addition to the most important communication, other aspects mentioned that can convince the customer of the truth of the supplier's promise?
- Is it completely clear what the recipient must do?
- Have all the barriers to respond been removed?
- Have alternative methods of response been offered?
- Is it necessary for the recipient to keep the letter, and have measures been taken to ensure this?

- Is the personal nature of the letter sufficiently convincing for *all* of the groups from the target group, or would the intention be better communicated if different groups were to receive different letters?
- Does the closing contain a legible name, title and even telephone number?
- Does the company realise that a 'P.S.' scores high when it comes to attention-value?

The enclosed folder, newspaper, brochure and information leaflet

The letter may be seen as the introduction given by a presenter at a film or theatre performance. The folder, newspaper, brochure or information leaflet may be seen as the performance itself.

- Has the most important promise been described in the clearest manner possible?
- Has a proper balance been achieved between the textual and the visual sections?
- Is the description completely truthful?
- Has a full description been given of what must be communicated?
- Will the printed materials be opened in such a way that the message will be read in the logical sequence?

Reply card/reply envelope

The primary function of the reply card is to facilitate and stimulate an immediate response to the mailing.

- Does the reply card look interesting (valuable) enough to prevent it from being discarded?
- Is the card easy to fill in? Is there enough room to answer all of the questions completely?
- Have the supplier's name and address already been filled in?
- Have the questions been formulated in such a way that the recipient can answer them by simply ticking 'yes' or 'no' boxes, or are the questions too complicated, or has the term 'strike out whichever is not applicable' been used?
- Is the purpose of the card an expression of approval, or have you asked for a signature?
- If the information to be provided on the reply card is at all confidential in nature, has a reply envelope been included as well?
- Has a reply envelope been enclosed into which the reply card fits easily without requiring any annoying or complicated folding?
- Is it necessary to enclose a document that the recipient may keep as proof that he or she has responded?
- Is the deadline for response indicated clearly?
- Is the reply card/envelope supplied with a stamp or freepost number?

17.4 Conclusion

The popularity of the oldest addressed communication channels is under pressure. More and more attention is being placed on the newer channels such as the telephone and the Internet. Even the customers and prospects are starting to make more frequent use of the alternatives to direct mail. Nonetheless, direct mail continues to play an indispensable role in the contact process between suppliers and customers. Although it is a relatively expensive tool, it retains advantages when compared with other forms of mass media, and even with respect to the Internet and the telephone. Very few preparations must be taken to read or look at something, and reading the printed word always remains a point of reference for the valuation and legibility of texts found on the Internet.

In order to employ direct mail effectively in the contact process with customers, careful management of the direct mail process is a requirement. Within a shorter time span, an increasing degree of variation must be designed, produced, distributed and followed up in mailings. In order to complete this task successfully, many processes must be standardised, described and organised. The communication between different specialists, such as marketers, direct mail specialists, copywriters, account directors, traffic managers and fulfilment departments must be orchestrated. Everyone will have to know what is expected of them in a timely manner and they will have to ensure that they are equipped to perform their specific task.

In addition, it goes without saying that it is vital to evoke the right effects in recipients by creating a good interplay between the design and copy used in mailing packets. The copy must convince and the design must attract attention so that the proper response is elicited from the largest possible portion of the recipients.

Case study

Pampers: relationship building using multiple channels (IDM Business Performance Award 2002: bronze winner)

The disposable nappy market in the UK is worth £480 million per year. However, the Pampers marketing team faced threats to their traditional brand dominance from a new, impressive rival. Huggies challenged their hitherto unquestioned leadership. Huggies were perceived as the innovator in the marketplace because they were constantly creating new products. The new brand had also managed to develop close relationships with mothers using interactive marketing techniques.

A less direct threat came from a growing independence among mothers, particularly first-time ones. Their use of widely available information from diverse sources to make decisions challenged traditional purchase patterns and reduced brand loyalty. Direct marketing gave Pampers a chance to cut through the marketplace 'noise' and re-establish trust and loyalty with mothers, one-to-one.

Market background

The disposable nappy market is a highly lucrative one. There are approximately 750 000 births in the UK each year and nappies are usually worn for three years. For Pampers this represents a relatively short customer lifetime.

In 1991 Huggies' arrival challenged Pampers' traditional dominance of the disposable nappy market. By 1997 Huggies had gained 17 per cent of the market. This had almost doubled to 30 per cent by 2000. Huggies continued to take share through a combination of competitive pricing and product innovation. The benefits of Huggies were promoted aggressively using TV and their Mother and Baby Club. Growth pattern projections showed that Huggies would be the market leader by Autumn 2001. Focus groups reflected the growing strength of the Huggies brand. When mothers were interviewed many assumed that Huggies was the market leader and there was much discussion about Huggies' latest news.

Consumer research and trend analysis revealed two key trends affecting Pampers' impact on the marketplace. The growing independence amongst UK mums in the way they make decisions and the traditional reliance on advice from parents and health professionals was being replaced by the most up-to-date information from friends, the Internet or print. The proliferation of information channels forced Pampers to explore a new approach to cut through the background noise to reach prospective customers.

One-to-one communication strategy

Pampers decided to introduce a one-to-one approach in addition to their traditional TV-driven campaigns. New channels were appropriated and existing ones enhanced. Pampers launched their one-to-one communication strategy in August 2001.

The mailings are targeted using data captured by Bounty Euro RSCG. Bounty work with midwives and hospitals to obtain unparalleled, almost total, coverage of all mothers-to-be at the three-month check stage and in hospital shortly after the birth. Bounty packs are delivered directly to the mother. The packs include incentives such as free samples and money off coupons.

Pampers decided to send a direct mail communication to mothers at eight key points in the mother and baby's life; three pre-birth and five post-birth. Research had revealed the importance of building a relationship with the mother prior to the birth. Mothers are most keen to research and absorb information during their pregnancy. The emotional moment at the first three-month check-up is the initial point of contact.

Communications are designed to bring the baby's experiences of life alive for the mother. For example, one item of interest concerned the little known fact that babies develop favourite tastes as early as three months post-conception. A baby's swallow rate increases with varying levels of sugar in the amniotic fluid. The booklets are designed to be more contemporary than many other sources of information. The communications included collectable booklets written by top baby care experts, built around the theme of the 'senses' as they develop. The booklets contain a wealth of information touching on most key aspects of baby care and development. Pampers recognised that their credibility as an information provider on subjects other than nappies was somewhat doubtful. Advertising and information from non-competing relevant major brands, such as baby food and medicine, was included in the booklets. Two CDs were also sent to mothers-to-be. One CD gives an insight into how babies experience the world while still in the womb. A post-birth CD of baby massage music was also sent. Appropriate nappy samples and discount coupons to encourage first purchase were included as well.

Online communication benefits mothers

Forty per cent of mothers are now online so the Internet couldn't be ignored as an opportunity for interactive communication. These communications could be viewed at a time convenient for the mother and are personalised using data collected regarding the baby's age. A vast library of in-depth information can be delivered in this way, without being overwhelming. Pampers.com sees a spike in traffic in the early hours of the morning, circa 2 a.m., at a time when phoning a friend for helpful advice is usually out of the question. Parents can opt-in to receive a monthly newsletter that updates them about the development of their baby.

Pampers.com is built around three areas covering the aspects of childhood development that are of most interest to parents: learning, playing and sharing. These areas include unique, interactive elements so that the parents can see the world through a baby's eyes. The areas are structured by age. The learning centre includes information from baby care experts around the world. The play centre provides ideas for developmental games. The sharing centre provides tips for parents divided by age and stage of development.

All website information is verified by baby care experts to ensure that it is of a high standard. The depth, diversity and reliability of information available for parents has established the Pampers website as a channel of choice for this target market. Pampers has used the opportunity for personalisation to encourage parents to register on the website. Being able to find the information you want is critical for the success of any website, and never more so for parents with young children. Their free time is in short supply and they often need to find information quickly. Research had identified that parents only log onto the Internet when they have a specific question that needs answering.

The iTV future

Trend analysis has identified it is likely that this emerging channel will become the preferred interactive device in the home. By 2001 more homes had interactive TV connections than the Internet, so this channel could not be ignored. Forrester research showed that Internet connections had reached a plateau as consumers have opted for interactive TV instead. Pampers saw interactive TV as an opportunity to extend brand leader communication. A channel cannot be ignored if this is where your customers are looking for information. Interactive TV was used as a bridge, combining the emotive strength and visual quality of traditional TV advertising with the depth and personalisation available through the Internet. Interactive TV offered the opportunity to develop consumer relationships over time, using TV e-mail to send profiled newsletters. The Internet and iTV complemented each other as there was only an overlap among 20 per cent of homes, and people use the services at different times of day and in different ways.

Data was captured via a request that viewers register to receive a newsletter. The newsletter can be e-mailed to a TV or PC, or posted. Parents were offered the chance to see themselves and their babies on TV in the baby gallery or in the video area talking about baby development issues: 'real babies, real mums, real tips'. Consumers were also offered the opportunity to give feedback and visit a frequently asked questions area.

Results

Latest qualitative consumer research showed that there has been a turnaround in the perception of the brand and the way in which mothers relate to Pampers. Market share has risen and a clear market leadership position has been established. AC Nielsen's *Top 100 Grocery Brands* survey showed Pampers ranked 14th compared with rival Huggies at 34th. Consumers consistently give positive feedback, showing that the right messages are being communicated. Focus group research among parents with babies of different ages showed that the interactive TV experience was positive and useful. They particularly liked being able to contrast opinions of experts and parents together. Feedback suggested that loyalty had improved towards the Pampers brand. Loyalty was measured using frequency and depth of contact between Pampers and parents. The provision of free information using a choice of interactive media also provided positive feedback. Pampers' interactive TV technology won 'best use of interactive TV' in *Marketing* magazine's 2001 Connection Awards.

Source: The Institute of Direct Marketing (2004).

Questions

1 Pampers' campaign is highly effective because it addresses the consumer's situation quite extensively. Describe and evaluate the way they analyse the consumer and the way they act upon it in communication.

2 What is the role of direct mail in relation to the other channels used in communicating with mothers? Do you think this role has changed since the rise of the Internet and interactive television?

3 Why is relationship marketing effective in the market for nappies and other baby products?

Questions

1 Analyse why the relative advantage of direct mail decreases with regard to other media. Give five reasons.

2 Under what circumstances does direct mail remain the preferred communication tool? List five situations.

3 A well-organised direct mail process is a requirement for the timely development, production, distribution and follow-up of direct mailings. Where are the critical moments in this process that require additional attention from management? Illustrate your answer.

4 The direct mail process is relatively complex; many activities must be performed and there must be coordination between many people, departments and companies. Think of three methods which may be used to simplify the direct mail process.

5 Which requirements must an effective creative briefing to an advertising agency or creative team satisfy?

6 Describe the role of the text and the design in a direct mail pack.

7 Which criteria must an effective direct mail pack satisfy? Name up to ten.

8 Think up an effective header for a letter for an imaginary situation. Substantiate your solution.

9 Write a letter for a direct mail pack for a company of your choice.

10 Collect three direct mailings and analyse the design and the text for their effectiveness. Provide reasons for your judgements.

References

Andriesse, Freek (2001) Verkoopbrief, *Sales Management*, 7–8, 14–15.

Baier, Martin (1983) *Elements of Direct Marketing*, McGraw-Hill, New York.

Berger, Paul D. and Mary Lou Roberts (1989) *Direct Marketing Management*, Prentice-Hall, Englewood Cliffs, New Jersey.

Lumley, James E.A. (1986) *Sell It by Mail: Making your product the one they buy*, John Wiley & Sons, New York.

McDonald, William J. (1998) *Direct Marketing: an integrated approach*, Irwin/McGraw-Hill, Boston.

Peelen, Ed, Arnout van der Swaluw, Wilfried Hutten, Frank Slisser and Erik de Vries (2000) *Multichannels, de inpassing van ICT ondersteunde kanalen in het contactproces met consumenten*, KPN Telecommerce, Den Haag.

Roomer, J. (ed.) (1987) *Handboek Direct Marketing*, Kluwer, Deventer.

Stone, Bob (1997) *Successful Direct Marketing Methods*, 6th edn, NTC Business Books, Chicago.

The Institute of Direct Marketing (2004) www.theidm.com

Zuiderduin, Jurgen (2003) *Het direct mail pack*, Postbank/TIAS, Amsterdam/Tilburg.

Part V

CRM Systems and their Implementation

Customer–supplier relationships are as old as the road to Rome; however, we have IT to thank for relationship management coming within reach of organisations which serve many millions of customers. Technology makes it possible for individual customers to be recognised and known, for them to be able to interact with the organisation on an individual basis, and allows them to rely on customised solutions. In principle, the deployment of personnel and costs may be kept within limits. However, we are not there yet; many companies still have a long way to go. Strategic questions have not yet been answered, leading to vagueness about the goals companies hope to attain with this technology. As a result, investments in IT are improperly guided; situations can arise where technology takes a leading role instead of being a tool to help achieve the organisation's goal. Embedding the applications in the organisation fails to run smoothly. The project management for the innovative multifunctional CRM projects is already complex, and is now suffering from inadequate guidance. In addition, organisations are often product-oriented and not prepared to think and act in a customer-oriented way.

Aspects such as strategy and organisation have been covered extensively in the previous parts of this book. This part focuses on CRM systems (Chapter 18). Insight is first provided into the different sub-systems that can support the CRM strategy and processes. The front and so-called mid-offices are discussed; special attention is paid to the call centre, the website, the campaign management system and the data warehouse.

We will then examine the implementation of CRM systems in Chapter 19. The road map used to develop CRM systems is discussed, based on the strategy. The rules of good project management are also set out.

The book is concluded in Chapter 20 with a glance into the future.

18

CRM systems

Insight into the most important CRM systems is indispensable in order to identify and use the possibilities offered by information technology. The utilisation of technology will also have to be customised under all circumstances to suit the strategy and the organisation on the one hand (Part I), and the relationship policy to be implemented on the other (Part III).

This chapter briefly discusses the most important elements in the CRM system. The final section looks in particular at the suppliers of CRM software packages that form part of such a system.

In this chapter we will address the following questions

- What CRM systems are there?
  - What are the tasks of a CRM system?
- What is partner relationship management?
- Which components and/or features are distinguished in the call centre?
  - How do the features in the call centre evolve over time?
- How to use the Internet and websites.
  - What are the components?
  - What is an intranet and an extranet?
  - What are security issues?
  - What is e-commerce?
- What is a data warehouse and a datamart?
  - What types of data warehouses and datamarts are there?
- What is a campaign management system?
  - What are the features of a campaign management system?
  - How to select the supplier of a campaign management system.
- What are content management systems?
  - What is their significance and what are their features?
- Who are suppliers of CRM software packages?
  - What are the advantages and disadvantages of different suppliers?

Practitioner's insight

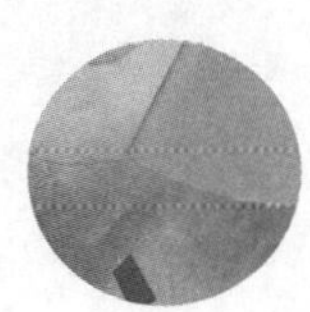

A CRM system that does not make use of IT is practically unthinkable in this day and age. As soon as organisations and (larger groups of) customers are required to maintain contact with one another on a variety of levels, hope to be quickly available to one another and would like to supply customisation to one another, IT will start to play an important role. It will support or take over entire contact processes through different channels. It will contribute to the maintenance, analysis and availability of customer data. The possibilities are numerous. Thanks to voice recognition and voice response systems, the computer is able to conduct telephone conversations. Automatic e-mail response systems can ensure that customised responses will be sent to questions submitted. Campaign management systems are capable of (developing) sending and evaluating hundreds of campaigns in a single day. Thousands, if not millions, of people can be reached in a period of 24 hours without a direct human contribution being necessary.

18.1 Overview of CRM systems

Customer relationship management has been practised since the abolition of economic self-sufficiency and the arrival of the division of labour. The role of information and communication technology (ICT) is to bring CRM within reach of a larger group of organisations and customers. It is now conceivable to develop relationships with customers in situations in which it was previously impossible organisationally and economically to do so. Thanks to the technology, even large groups of low-spending customers are personally recognised and known; and they, in turn, conduct a dialogue with, receive customisation from, and, to a certain extent, develop a relationship with the supplier. The technology can also prove its value even for parties who had already been practising CRM. CRM systems make it possible for the members of decision-making units for both parties to easily find one another and remain informed about the communication between them. Salespersons or account managers can maintain their customer and visit profiles in the system and use them for the planning and evaluation of their work. The placement of orders may be simplified, to the extent that this had not already been arranged in another manner.

Even in markets where the contact with the end user is lacking because distributors are used, CRM systems can prove their utility. The system offers suppliers and intermediaries the possibility of collectively developing a clear customer profile and creating and implementing a customised, mutually beneficial relationship strategy. The realisation of this is naturally dependent upon the trust and the relationship that the supplier and distributor have with one another. Mutual distrust usually prevents both parties from wanting to share their customer knowledge with one another.

The *primary task* of CRM systems consists in supporting or performing the activities involved in customer contact processes. Customer contact processes may involve the exchange of information, the placement of orders, the invoicing, payment, provision of service and so forth. They consist of the contacts and, to a certain extent, the actions arising from these contacts. An accurate definition of the different processes is an important point of departure for CRM implementation; if this is lacking, it is difficult to program and automate. The CRM system supports the employees during their contacts with customers; in the case of self-service and customer–machine or machine–machine interaction, the customer contact is also fully taken over by the system.

The *secondary task* is related to facilitating the primary task, and involves providing customer information and management information, among other information. It involves data which may be used to improve the efficiency and effectiveness of the customer processes.

Practitioner's insight

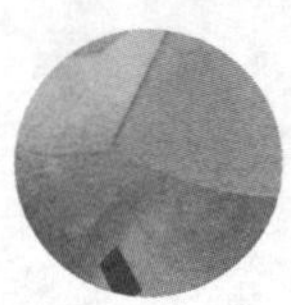

In the report *CRM Insights 2002*, IDC observed 'considerably lower growth figures than in previous years': compared with the €102 million from last year, the investments this year only grew to €121 million. In order to convince the market, expertise in a vertical market is a good way of meeting suppliers halfway in their need for specific solutions for their end users, according to IDC. The expected growth in the market – IDC expects on average 19 per cent growth rates until 2006 – will be witnessed primarily in the utilities sector, government organisations, and the health care industry.

Source: *ITCommercie* (2002).

A variety of CRM sub-systems have been developed for the performance of these primary and secondary functions in the front and back office and linking activities between the two. Characteristic of the systems that support the front office is that customer data must be easily retrieved and modified. For example, within several seconds, insight may be gained into who the person is on the other end of the telephone line. In the back office, this is generally not the case. It is difficult and takes a long time to see which products the customer has purchased in the past. In order to be able to retrieve and adjust data from the back office in the front office, a link between the two is necessary. Recently, we have seen that it is possible to make direct links between front and back office applications. In many situations, companies use what is known as middleware to achieve this, which also coordinates activities that take place through different channels. Figure 18.1 shows the different systems. From left to right these are as follows.

The front office

- The salesforce automation or the sales information system that supports the salesperson or account manager during face-to-face sales and relationship management activities.
- The partner management system which is geared towards providing support to the intermediaries (distributors) in the joint approach to the end user market.

Figure 18.1

CRM system

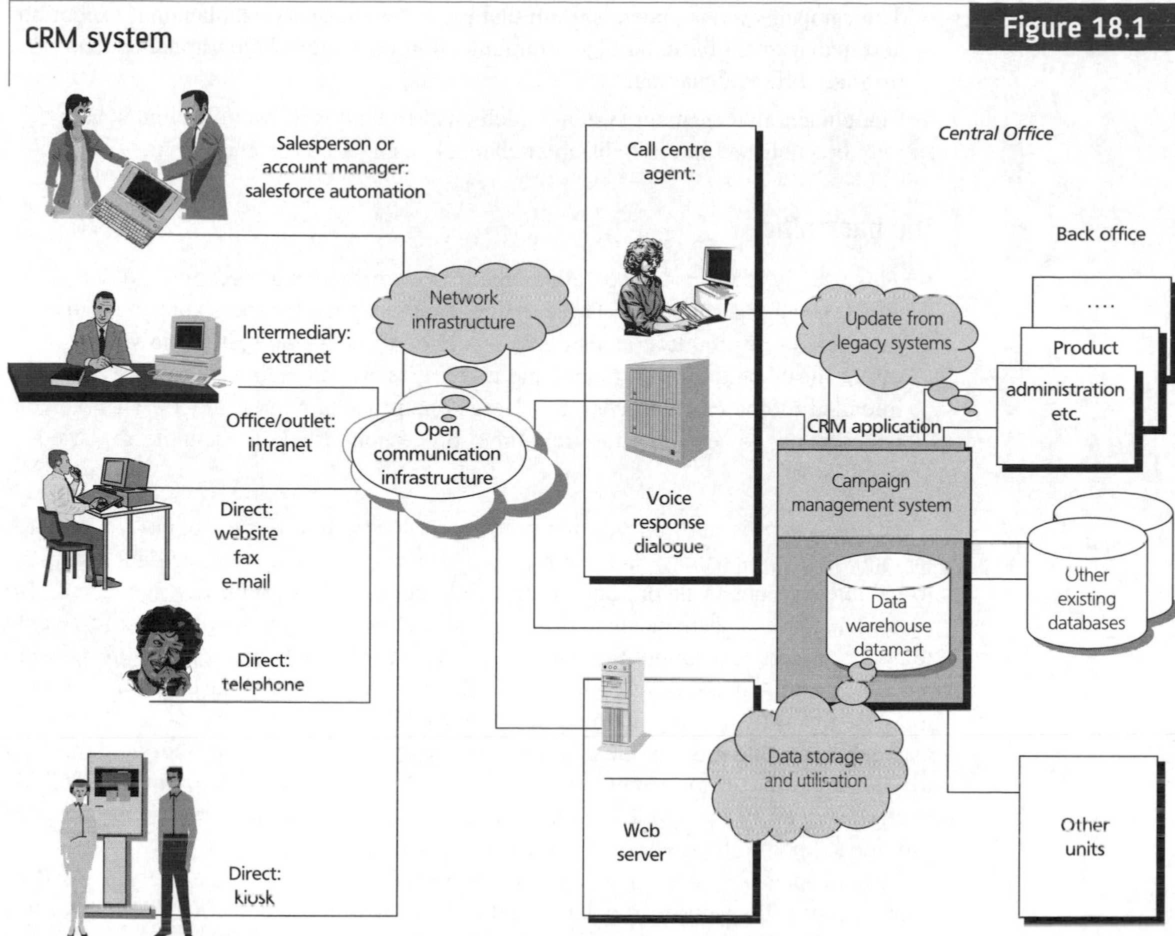

Source: Hendrickx, Capgemini E&Y.

- The call or contact centre, where incoming and outgoing traffic by telephone, fax and the Internet (e-mail) takes place; even the written correspondence with customers may be (partially) handled here.
- The website.
- The kiosks; examples would be information pillars (points of information) or point-of-pay terminals where customers are capable of helping themselves on location.

Middleware

- The data warehouse or the datamart, in which data originating from different sources are compiled to obtain a clear and better customer profile.

- The campaign management system that produces the analysis, planning, execution and management of marketing communication campaigns being implemented through different channels.
- The content management system which ensures that data from different sources may be published through different channels using a consistent design.

The back office

- This usually involves the so-called legacy systems which are generally older and have a longer lifespan. These systems are designed for the management of transactions or products; an example would be the separate systems in which motor, health and life insurances and mortgages are maintained. They are intended for the batch processing of large quantities of similar orders. They are not suitable, however, for the 'real-time' processing of a large quantity of varied small orders.

Every system is built up out of a number of layers. In order to support or perform the activities in a process, data are required. An example would be the data necessary to be able to route an incoming call in a call centre to the appropriate agent, but also those data that the agent needs in order to conduct the conversation. In order to be able to store, process and supply these data again later, databases and application software are necessary. A network of computers with operating systems must then be installed to allow this software to function at the preferred locations and times.

Insufficient attention to one of the aspects of the system will, without a doubt, lead to problems during implementation. This can lead to a network failing to provide enough support to the application or a situation in which the data required to actually provide support to the customer process are missing.

This chapter only examines several typical CRM sub-systems, namely the call or contact centre, the website, the data warehouse, the campaign and content management system. The CRM module partner management is covered briefly in the following box. For a more detailed description, please see the literature available on information systems.

CRM illustration

Partner relationship management

Customer relationship management is an accepted term within organisations and the realisation continues to grow that entering into and developing relationships with individual customers is a necessity to survive. While the emphasis in CRM lies on companies' own processes, culture, organisation and direct customers, a new opportunity has revealed itself: the indirect channel.

Partner relationship management (PRM) is the continuous and systematic entering into and development of relationships with partners in the indirect channel in order to achieve and retain mutual advantages.

IT organisations, financial institutions and telecom companies that offer complex products and services online have an increasing need for partners. They know the products and services, how to reach customers and can supply added value to customers as well as the organisation. In the IT sector alone, 60 per cent of the sales go through the indirect channel.

The partners, however, experience difficulties in the area of communication with and getting information from their supplying partner. They see an extensive website where information and materials that they require in order to sell their supplier's products cannot be found. In addition, marketing managers still have a bad feeling about the indirect channel due to a lack of insight. Lack of insight into the partners' processes, or feedback on generated leads and success, or lack thereof, of marketing campaigns are likely to mean that investments are made in the wrong area and in the wrong partner.

In short, the relationship between organisations and partners is not optimal while it is precisely this channel that offers so many possibilities. In 1999, Hewlett Packard demonstrated that special programmes and projects had increased partners' profitability considerably. This was due to better and more efficient inventory management, lower administrative costs, automatic stocking, process simplification, better forecasting and demand-generating activities.

There are already many tools available on the market to support PRM (campaign management, salesforce automation, e-commerce, etc.): as a separate module or integrated into a total solution. As a standalone, PRM can supply high added value for the indirect channel. However, it may also be included in a larger whole, often under the name CRM . . .

Source: Stuurman (2000).

18.2 The call centre (Van den Broek, 1998; Van den Brink, 1999)

The call centre may consist of a relatively large number of components, as detailed under the following sub-headings.

Switches, computers and connections

An indispensable component of the call centre is, of course, the telephone switchboard or switch. The switches available today are nearly entirely independent; all of the hardware and software required is located in the switch. In addition, computers play an important role. By means of the automatic call distributor (ACD), the computer first distributes the incoming calls to the various employees. The application may be programmed in such a way that if it gets too busy for a certain group of agents, the overflow of calls may be automatically routed to another team or even an external call centre. The ACD also registers the number of incoming calls, the average call duration and the number of calls that have been abandoned. Second, the computer or the computer network plays a role in the storage, processing and supply of data.

These components will have to be connected to one another via physical links, modem connections and the like. Protocols must be established to regulate this communication between the machines.

Calling-line identification

Thanks to the calling-line identification, the telephone number of the caller will be visible, provided the caller has not prevented this.

Automated outbound dialling

The computer is used to select the numbers to call and then make the connection. With preview dialling, the agent chooses a telephone number from the list on the screen and then manually calls via the keyboard. Power dialling means that the system calls at the time the agent is available. Predictive dialling is an anticipatory system; before a call is terminated, it initiates a new call, ensuring that agents are constantly operational.

Voice processing[1]

With voice processing, the digitisation of speech is the focus. Included in these types of products are interactive voice response (IVR) systems, which are used to answer telephone calls automatically. Speech recognition is an important component of IVR. An example of this would be an ordering line.

Voice mail and voice messaging also fall into this category. This involves a non-interactive form of communication between the sender and the right recipient of a recorded or typed-in message.

Computer–telephone integration (CTI)

CTI becomes important in cases where there is a need to integrate the call and data traffic. The integration of telephone and computer result in many additional application options.

CTI applications include (Van den Broek, 1998):

- On-screen dialling: telephone calls are initiated and monitored by the computer. As a result, the calling process is accelerated and supported.
- Intelligent routing: calls are transferred to the right person or department. Repeated transfers are kept to a minimum.

[1] Voice processing is not considered to be part of CTI (computer–telephone integration) because the link between the systems is not controlled by the switch.

- Call-based data selection, in which the caller's relevant information appears on the agent's screen at the moment the telephone is answered, or even before that point. The agent, for example, no longer has to ask customers to identify themselves.
- Voice and data call association: this provides for the simultaneous transfer of telephone calls between agents in the call centre, as well as the corresponding data.

Thanks to CTI, it is possible to reserve agents' time for the important elements involved in the contact. At the same time, gains in efficiency result in cost savings. Customers can also experience advantages in that they are served more quickly and accurately and do not have to be transferred as often.

The database

A database is required first and foremost in order to record customer data, so that customers may be identified and so that their contact history may be known. Additionally, it is desirable to gain insight into data from transactional systems: what has the customer purchased and during which stage was the transaction completed? Is the customer creditworthy? Product information, knowledge of marketing activities and media preferences are also important if the agent is to develop customer contacts to the customer's satisfaction. Call centres will often have their own datamart at their disposal (see Section 18.3) which may be used to manage these data and to make them accessible in real time and to process them. A current copy of the relevant data from the back office systems may be kept in the datamart as well as the product records (see Figure 18.1), so that these types of data may be retrieved immediately. Changes that the agent would like to make to the data are then processed on a batch basis in the legacy system.

Telebusiness software

The following tools may be used specifically for the call centre:

- A scripting tool. While conducting the dialogue, the agent is 'supported' through the supply of standard texts that he or she may read aloud. This way, goals of treating customers and prospects in a consistent manner may be attained and balanced texts may be used. The disadvantages are that it is less motivating for agents and that the dialogue conducted with the customer is less natural.
- Trouble ticket software. Call centres with a help-desk function may create a database using this application which supplies all sorts of solutions to problems that customers experience. The solution to the problem as well as the procedure for handling it is described. Questions or problems which qualify as being complex may be referred to the so-called second or third line. In this way, the first line is spared from having to spend too much time on problem solving.
- Workflow management system. This is a system that provides insight into the status of the underlying work processes, so that the operator may see whether the requested information has already been sent and, if so, on which date.

- Documentation information systems (DIS) or content management systems, which make it possible to digitally scan and store written information. In this way, agents gain simple and up-to-date insight into brochures and other mailings that have been sent to customers and may lead to questions.

CRM definitions

New contact centre techniques . . .

The classic call centre uses primarily mature and trusted applications. In the call centre development cycle illustration (see Figure 18.2), these are the type C solutions. The design consists of a switch for automatic call distribution and options for interactive voice response. Computer telephony integration has also since become a trusted technique.

A new generation of call centres – type B – implements the virtual call centre. A virtual call centre allows a company to make optimal use of the knowledge that it has available. Specific customer questions will go via the call centre directly to the employee with the knowledge and experience required to answer them (skill-based routing). This employee may be located at any random place either inside or outside of the company. Another form of customer contact that is very much on the rise right now yet is still being developed, employs the E-mail Response and Management System (ERMS).

The true trendsetters in the call centre field – type A – apply two techniques which are closely related to the Internet and which are still in the developmental phase: the Universal Queue – a queue for all of the incoming traffic, regardless of the form – and Web Chat. These are the forerunners of the multi-channel contact centre. Two very promising techniques which have since become available are Web Collaboration and Web Call Through. Using Web Collaboration, the remote caller and the agent can browse a web page together or fill in the details on that page. Web Call Through makes it possible to initiate a

Figure 18.2 Call centre development cycle

Source: Gartner Research (2003).

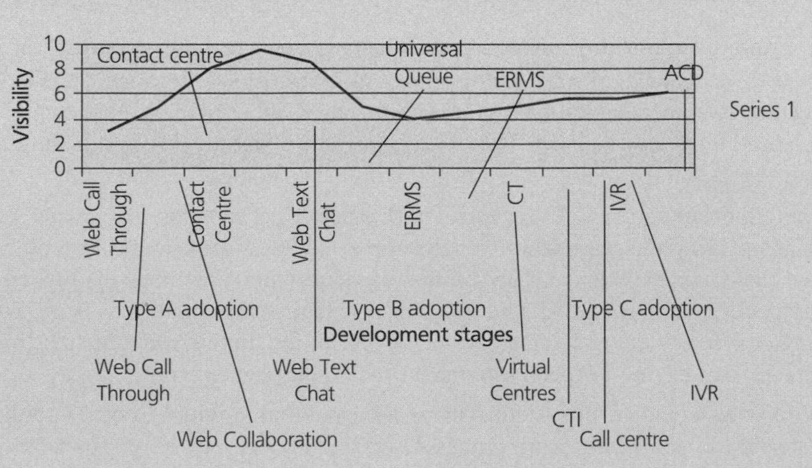

telephone call through the Internet and then to conduct this call using a normal telephone or a webphone.

A call centre may only call itself a multi-channel contact centre if a combination of at least two of the following media types is being used: speech, e-mail and web applications (Web Chat, Web Call Through, Web Collaboration, and the like). All of these media may be combined on the agent's computer screen. Using advanced software, the agent can then see at a glance how many telephone calls, e-mails and web contacts are waiting in the queue.

Source: Sybrandy (2003).

18.3 The Internet and the website (Fuller, 2000; Watson *et al.*, 2000)

The Internet is a worldwide network of computers, each of which may independently consist of different computers, terminals and other equipment such as mobile telephones and digital personal assistants which users may use to gain access to programs, data and information. The computers and the aforementioned peripheral equipment may communicate with one another and thus make use of a common communication protocol; in other words, they speak the same language. The protocol used on the Internet is *Transmission Control/Internet Protocol* (TCP/IP). The TCP in TCP/IP is responsible for splitting the message into separate packages with unique numbers which are then regrouped into the appropriate sequence again upon receipt so that they form a logical message. These packages may actually take different paths along the Internet and can reach their final destination independent of one another and at different times. Each package traces out the best route and in this way avoids as much 'congestion' as possible. This differs from the telephone network where exclusive capacity is reserved for the transmission of data or the sound from the sender to the receiver before a connection is made. The method used for splitting leads to a better utilisation of the available transmission capacity.

Messages may only be sent if the servers on the Internet have a unique address; this is the IP address (a 32-bit number). Because the numerical display of the IP address is difficult to remember, names such as Marriott, Hilton, etc. may be linked to these addresses. A domain name server makes sure that the IP address 128.193.73.60, for example, is linked to Hilton.

One of the most well-known segments of the Internet is the World Wide Web (also known as the abbreviation www). The web is a system which is used to store information in web pages that may be called up. Webpages that are generally accessible are called websites. A webpage is a hypermedia file that belongs to a certain website and may consist of a combination of text, images, sound and video. Connections, or so-called hyperlinks, with other websites and other webpages may also be set up. Browsers are used to look for websites and other necessary information. A specific language is used on the web, the HyperText Markup Language (HTML) or the eXtensible Markup Language (XML).

Intranet, extranet and internal computer networks (Niks, Plasmeijer and Peelen, 2000)

The intranet is a computer network that is based on the same technology as the Internet, yet is protected and thus accessible only to those within an organisation who have authorisation to use it. An example of this is the closed system in a hotel that allows guests to view their bill electronically via the television.

An extranet is designed also to grant access to external parties to the computer network such as customers and suppliers so that their activities may be better co-ordinated with one another. Tour operators and travel agencies may also gain access to the reservation system of a hotel or an airline company, for example.

In general, a different language is used on intra- and extranets and the Internet from those used within an organisation's internal computer networks. These latter are usually older and have been constructed with another goal in mind than that of communicating with customers. They are used for administrative purposes, for example, or to plan production. In many of these systems, it is even difficult to identify or recognise customers; it is only the transactions that are registered.

In order to be able to support the total contact cycle so that, in addition to information exchange, transactions may also be completed, payments may be made, and goods and services may be supplied, a link from the Internet to these internal computer systems is also desirable. How may potential hotel guests get information on the availability of rooms otherwise? And how else may reservations be processed, loyalty programmes maintained and check-out procedures simplified?

In addition to compatibility problems, safety considerations may be one reason to forgo integrating the two systems. It may be undesirable to grant 'strangers' access to the internal systems upon which the planning and control of the organisation depend.

In order to obtain an acceptable integration level, a 'mid-office' with data warehouses and datamarts may be created (see Section 18.4), in which data are registered and structured which may be crucial to the communication and support of the interface between the customer and the organisation. Data may be available on the services of the organisation, the prices, the available capacity and stocks, the completion of the transaction, the customer profile with data on the customer identification, purchase history, satisfaction and complaints, payment behaviour, etc.

Security

The security issue is a two-sided one. First of all, not only does the stored data require protection, but the transport of the data must also be protected. The Internet is an open system that provides people with information from a distance. This same technology, which lies at the base of the Internet, may also be used and abused by hackers.

Control over access starts with verifying the authenticity of visitors. They will be granted access provided they can supply the customer number, the password, and/or the IP address. Different authorisation methods may be used simultaneously. One or more firewalls may be placed between the internal computer network and the Internet. A visit to the website, or to certain sections of it, may be made conditional upon pre-specified IP addresses. However, more advanced screening methods may be used to arrange access.

Coding or encrypting techniques may be used to protect the transmission of messages. Digital signatures may play a role in the verification of someone's identity. Traffic involving payments in particular must be protected (see also Chapter 15).

Electronic commerce

The Internet is suitable for more than simply the exchange of messages. Transactions may also be initiated, paid for and completed using the Internet and that is where e-commerce comes in. E-commerce is defined as the process of buying, selling, transferring, or exchanging products, services and/or information via computer networks, including the Internet (Turban, King, Lee and Viehland, 2004). E-commerce applications are based on different technologies which collectively form a layered, integral infrastructure. The description under the following sub-headings summarises the integration with internal computer networks.

Information infrastructure

All of the traffic must be sent via one or more communication networks which comprise the information infrastructure. Examples include cable television networks, the telephone network, the Internet and computer networks.

Message distribution infrastructure

This level consists of software used to send and receive messages and ensures that messages go from the server to a client. For example, an HTML or XML file is sent from the webserver to the client who uses Internet Explorer.

Electronic publishing infrastructure

The content on the web is organised on this level. Three elements play a role in this:

1 A uniform resource locator (URL), which is used to indicate the server's identity in a unique way.
2 A network protocol to obtain access to and mobility on the Internet and to search and send data.
3 A structured markup language, HTML or XML to build a webpage, for example.

This level still involves the addressability and the common language on the network.

Business services infrastructure

The goal of this level is to support company processes. The secure transmission of credit card data is supported here thanks to encryption and identification techniques. Search machines can be helpful to the user in finding the information he or she is looking for.

Figure 18.3 The levels of e-commerce infrastructure

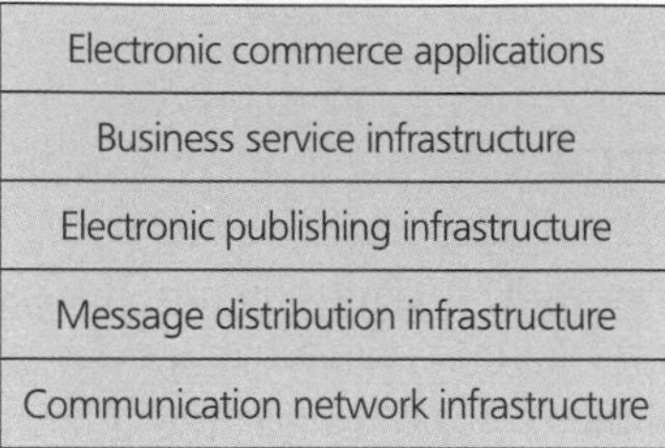

Electronic commerce applications

As shown in Figure 18.3, we find the e-commerce application as the top level of the e-commerce infrastructure. For example, the hotel with information on room availability, price information, reservation options and the status of the customer's loyalty programme.

18.4 Data warehouse and datamart

There are several definitions of a data warehouse in circulation. The following description may be inferred from the definitions cited by Jonker (1997):

A data warehouse is an isolated environment,

- destined for the support of management information systems/executive information systems/decision support systems, without placing an additional burden on the operational systems;
- that contains data that make it possible to gain a clear, topic-oriented view into the organisation's history;
- in which users may obtain access to information in a quick and useful manner which allows them to better support their decisions.

In the mid-1970s, the need began to arise among managers to extract additional information from the existing computer systems (Jonker, 1997). This appeared to be a desire that could not be met in the short term by the IT available at the time. Given the database structure, it was difficult to use the computer for answering ad hoc questions. This required the development of complex software by specialists. The mainframe also put up barriers. Incorporating these programs occupied a great deal of time and disturbed operational systems upon which primary company processes depended. The completion of 'tasks' in batches by the mainframe also appeared to be less suitable for another reason. This led to too much time being wasted in finding and restoring errors in the software whose objective was to answer the ad hoc questions.

The need arose for a retrieval system (Jonker, 1997):

- which could store large amounts of data which related to a certain period;
- which could answer complex ad hoc questions relatively quickly;
- which did not result in a disturbance of the operational processes.

This demand led to the development of relational databases and SQL. With the arrival of the PC, many of these files were stored and maintained locally. However, this solution quickly proved to be limited. Analysing large quantities of data was very time consuming, and SQL appeared to be a laborious solution for answering complex questions. It also appeared to be difficult to maintain data at various locations and to maintain a clear definition of data. Many data fields were left incomplete or were not kept up to date, and different definitions and methods of calculation for certain variables such as profit began to circulate.

CRM definition

SQL or Structured Query Language is the standard programming language that is used to approach relational databases.

The consequence was that people formulated additional wishes which the ideal retrieval system was supposed to satisfy, namely:

- the computer system must be able to keep up with the growing quantity of data and increasing number of users;
- the data stored in the retrieval system must be a concise presentation of the concepts used within the company;
- the design of the database must be adapted to the usage;
- the querying of the database must be made relatively easy, enabling it to be done by a non-specialised computer user.

These are wishes that a data warehouse can fulfil. Data in a data warehouse originates, for the most part, from operational systems that are usually set up as OLTP (online transaction processing) systems. These OLTP systems are primarily designed to process and store many smaller transactions. The design of the databases in OLTP systems is targeted to the rapid processing of small transactions so that the response time of the operational systems is as short as possible. The data warehouse, on the other hand, consists of one or more computer systems which are able not only to quickly answer questions that require large quantities of data but also to store data efficiently (Jonker, 1997).

A distinction may be made in data warehouses that are more or less centrally maintained and the degree to which they are updated. For the databases to be built locally for a certain function, the name *datamart* is used. In contrast to the 'real' data warehouses, these may be installed in a shorter period of time and less expensively. The

Figure 18.4 Four types of data warehouses

Source: Jonker (1997).

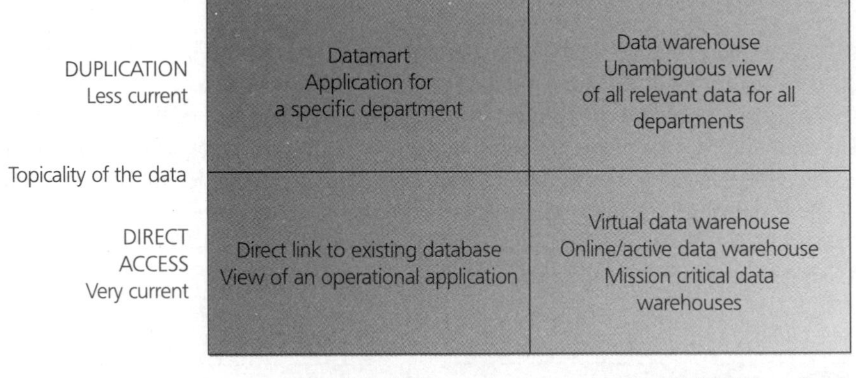

investments vary greatly and are dependent on the size of the (customer) database and the quantity of data to be recorded, among other factors, as displayed in Figure 18.4.

A direct link with an existing database is chosen if a certain department would like to consult a single operational system on a regular basis for questions that are not too extensive and complex. Should there, however, be a preference to have these types of questions answered, then these queries may be processed on a batch basis outside of office hours. If a department wishes to run complex queries on data from one or a limited number of operational systems, then a datamart may be installed.

An online/active data warehouse is continuously being supplemented with the newest data. Over the course of just one day, the company is capable of discovering trends and responding to them. In order to prevent the connected operational systems from being interpreted in a specific way in each datamart, it is preferable to feed the datamarts from a central data warehouse. This way the view of the data remains clear and thus also the degree to which they may be maintained.

The application of CRM often requires a data warehouse to be set up, as well as several datamarts. Usually a separate datamart or data warehouse is installed for the contact centre in which supplementation with the newest data occurs once every 24 hours, for example. For marketing purposes, a data warehouse is kept with data on customer identification and the further profiling, and a separate active datamart is used for the website.

Answering questions from the data warehouse

Queries are created for answering questions. A query is a question which consists of a combination of choices and criteria as these have been compiled by a user, the objective of which is to search for and find data in a database. For example, customers who have purchased product X, Y, Z more than three months and less than two years ago in the regions A and B.

In answering these questions, OLAP, or online analytical processing, is often used. This is the generic name for a generation of end-user tools, usually operating under Windows, which make it possible to compile complex queries easily and to run them on a database that is usually maintained on another platform. Normally the database is implemented in the form of a data warehouse and thus contains large quantities of historical data. It involves a read-only application so that changes may not be entered into the files. An OLAP tool may be used, for instance, to gain insight into the turnover, the profit contribution and the communication frequency of customers from different segments during a variety of periods of time. These indicators may easily be decomposed in various ways. The decomposition may be adjusted time and again in order to expand the insight into the customer database step by step. The results may be presented in a variety of ways: in simple tables, or in pie charts, graphs, spiderweb diagrams, etc.

In addition to OLAP tools, software which supports statistical or datamining analyses may be used to answer questions. This topic was discussed in some detail in Chapter 10.

18.5 Campaign management systems

Origin

Back in the old days of direct marketing, campaign management referred to the planning and execution of *a single* marketing campaign, which made use of the telephone and/or the postal services. The preparation time for this type of campaign amounted to several weeks if not months. Nowadays, within the framework of CRM, campaign management encompasses the multitude of campaigns that are planned and executed through different channels so that a continuous marketing communication flow is created. Sometimes these campaigns are devised in the morning and executed that very afternoon. By continuously measuring the effect of every contact (*customer touchpoint*) and making adjustments, the dialogue may be continually refined. This puts the organisation in a better position to market its goods and services and develop relationships with the right customers. The goal of campaign management is to interact with prospects and customers at the right moment, with the right offering and the right message communicated through the right channels.

Functionality of campaign management systems

Campaign management systems (see Figure 18.5) are developed to achieve the aforementioned goal. Data warehouse tools such as OLAP only satisfy part of this requirement. They help provide an answer to a selection question, but do not support the entire contact cycle. They help find an answer to the question of who should be approached for a specific campaign. Campaign management systems, on the other hand, are characterised by the following functionalities:

Figure 18.5 Campaign management system

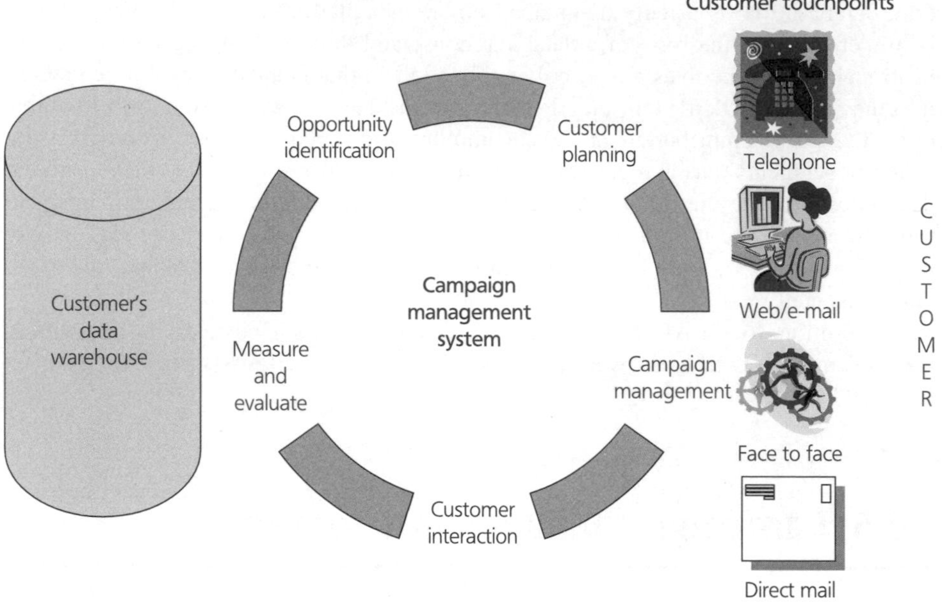

- Opportunity identification: the identification of contact opportunities on the basis of events involving the supplier, the customer or those occurring in the environment.
- Relationship planning: indicating how the relationship with customers should be further developed in terms of the communication.
- Campaign management: the selection of contacts, the development and the implementation of the campaign.
- Customer interaction: supporting the contacts that follow the sent messages.
- Measuring and evaluating: what are the effects of the campaign and do they satisfy the goals?

Within the framework of the *opportunity identification* an analysis is performed to determine who should be approached at a certain time with a certain marketing communication message. Are the (potentially) most profitable customers the ones to be approached? Are certain events involving the customer to be played upon; will customers who are going to move be approached with a mortgage offer, for example? Or is the introduction of a new product the occasion for the contact? For example, a new model of a certain car has just become available, and the manufacturer would like to give the owners of the current model (provided it is two years old or more) the first opportunity to see it when it is presented in the showroom. Or perhaps a cruise line would like to make a special offer to regular customers who live less than 50 kilometres from the harbour for the cruise set to sail that next week which is not yet fully booked.

CRM definitions

Four types of campaigns

1 *Single shot campaign (one-step approach).* The most traditional contact strategy; this involves a campaign in which the intended effect is achieved in a single contact; the activity is usually planned and prepared months in advance.

2 *Wave campaign.* This involves a multiple-step approach in which a direct mailing might be followed up by a telephone campaign, for example.

3 *Triggered campaign.* In this type of campaign, the time schedule is not determined by the marketer but is made dependent upon the customer's behaviour. For example, someone will receive a message 60 days before the expiration of his or her telephone subscription or will receive an offer within a few minutes of clicking on to a certain site.

4 *Longitudinal campaign (communication calendar).* This campaign takes place over time and its goal might be to acquaint the customer with the supplier and thereby develop a relationship. An example would be the communication calendar that a company creates to encourage new customers to 'cross-buy' during the first two years and discover the supplier's range of products.

The *relationship planning* functionality demonstrates many similarities with opportunity identification. Contact opportunities are now also placed within the context of relationship planning. It will be determined what the opportune time is to approach a customer with the particular offer. The cruise line wants to exclude customers who have already taken a trip in the previous two months. The salesperson who is involved in negotiations might consider it desirable if no further offers for comparable or different types of products are sent to the prospect during the period concerned. And the organisation that has created a communication calendar to reinforce and perpetuate the relationship with the customer during the first two years prefers only to deviate from this within certain limits.

Within the framework of *campaign management*, the campaign is designed. Ready-made templates are used to generate the campaign. The system supports the development of different types of campaign, varying from the 'single shot' to the 'wave', and to the 'longitudinal'. The progress of the contact cycle may be shown in an easily created tree structure. This tree indicates who will receive a reminder, which channels will be used to receive the response and how this will all be followed up. Selections may be entered and the company may determine how many people satisfy the criteria. Using certain instructions, arrangements may be made so that people who satisfy certain criteria are selected real-time for a certain period. In order to prevent a person or organisation from receiving more than one communication message at a certain time, rules may be set up for prioritisation and exclusion. These rules indicate which campaign is considered to be important and which may be sent in a specific situation and which may not. In addition, customers who have indicated that they do not wish to receive any information from the supplier or those with a history of delinquent payments may be excluded. The addition of several control addresses may prove useful for being able to monitor the execution of the campaign.

For each of the selected groups, it will be specified which communication message they will receive. It is also determined how the response will be measured.

The goal of the customer interaction functionality is to initiate and support the contacts which follow the communication message. The system can arrange for the recipients of the message to be called or to arrange for those recipients who are interested to contact the call centre themselves, on their own initiative, and make sure that they will speak with an agent who is well informed about the campaign and the fact that the caller has been approached.

The results of a campaign are *continuously* measured thanks to the *measuring and evaluation functionality*. In this way, a good insight may be gained into the progress of the campaign. The actual results may be measured against the goals at various times throughout the campaign. For different channels the response and the conversion[2] may be illustrated, for example. It is also possible to compare several campaigns with one another to determine their effectiveness. Which campaign generates the most traffic and which has the highest conversion ratio?

Input for campaign management

The link between data warehouses, datamining and the campaign management system forms an important point of interest. Opportunities, the selections and the like become apparent from the customer data and the analyses performed on these data. Suppliers of CRM systems use terms such as *predictive marketing* to indicate their datamining tools in this area.

Selection of a campaign management system

Campaign management systems are sold on the market by various suppliers. Whereas one system might be adept at generating campaigns on the web 'real-time', another may be more capable of supporting processes in the call centre. Functionality – and prices – vary. In selecting a system and a supplier, the following elements should be taken into consideration (Verduin, 1999):

- Functionality of the system:
  - Can the system support different types of campaigns?
  - How does the system support different aspects of the campaign management?
  - How does the system link up to the data warehouse and the customer touch points?
  - How does the system link up to the back office?
- User friendliness: how much training is necessary to use the system and how much time is needed to develop and send a campaign?
- Market position of the supplier: does the supplier belong to the category of companies which will still be around five or ten years down the line?

[2] Conversion is the number of respondents who end up placing an order, for example.

18.6 Content management system

CRM illustration

Do you need a special system for that?

It can be helpful. Up until the year 2000, websites were generally maintained 'by hand'. The positions of webmaster and editor were often integrated, and websites were edited directly in HTML. With time, the quantity of information on websites became larger, and a need developed to directly link the website to internal documents and other information. In short, organisations had to exert increasingly more effort to maintain their websites. The need arose to automate the management of web content, and the software packages that became available for this purpose were called content management systems, or CMS for short. You could say that content management is a more intelligent form of document management.

Source: Dekker and Hiemstra (2002).

Content management is interesting for companies with a great deal of content (Dekker and Hiemstra, 2002). Publishers have large quantities of information that they would like to distribute and reuse on the basis of target groups and perhaps even of personal needs. Since the 1980s, they have invested in data structures. Even production companies such as Philips or Sony have large quantities of content with instruction manuals, background information on artists and so forth. Nowadays, they would also like to publish this documentation via different media.

A content management system makes it possible for web publishers to maintain their websites easily and in a structured manner.

Finally, it offers advantages to those companies who wish to manage all data and documents in a structured way, organisation-wide and make this information available through different channels. Business plans, brochures, sales texts, reports and annual reports are very accessible thanks to 'enterprise content management'.

The functions that a content management system should fulfil are (Dekker and Hiemstra, 2002):

- Authoring: adding and changing content in an automated digital environment.
- Workflow management: management of the steps that are taken between authoring and publishing. For example: who has to have viewed and approved a certain block of information before it may be published, and which blocks of information will be published on one page or in one brochure?
- Storage: placement of content in a digital warehouse.
- Publishing: publication of the content. This usually occurs in HTML websites, but PDF documents, WAP pages etc. are also becoming more common.

A content management system makes it possible for data from different sources to be combined, while the publications receive a consistent appearance. To achieve this, a strict separation between content and design is ensured.

In order to ensure careful management of the data, management procedures and authorisations must be established. Old versions of documents must be saved in order to be able to trace unwanted changes and reverse them. Metadata will have to be automatically retained during the input of new data. Content managers will have to be able to implement changes without having knowledge of Internet technology. The application will have to support the cooperation among several people in different departments at different geographical locations.

18.7 Suppliers of CRM systems

The developments in the market for CRM systems occur rapidly. The application software is further developed and geared towards market demands, all at a high speed. We see a further concentration occurring in the market. Players, particularly local ones, disappear, are taken over and continue together. The market leader with the most expensive applications witnesses its share of the market decrease in favour of suppliers of less expensive applications. Medium-sized and smaller businesses have also shifted to making investments in CRM systems and are opting for less expensive solutions with fewer functionalities.

The suppliers may be divided into five categories (Hardeveld, 2001; Gartner Research, 2004):

1. *Suppliers of integrated ERP applications, such as SAP, Oracle, Navision, Intentia and J.D. Edwards.* Initially, most of the ERP suppliers built a module themselves in order to offer CRM functionality, but in the past few years, several companies stopped doing this and either acquired a CRM package or have started to collaborate.
2. *Suppliers of CRM suites, such as Siebel, E.piphany, Onyx and Pivotal.* These are systems that support most CRM functionalities; they enable the building of a total solution.
3. *CRM frameworks (Chordiant, Graham, Pegasystems)* which, in contrast to the suite, offer more freedom to the organisation in building its application. Frameworks offer the room to design unique, distinctive processes and thus look for the enabling technology.
4. *Best of breed (Allegis, NCR, Selectica, Unica).* Companies go in search of the best application software for different CRM functionalities. The systems used for the contact centre may be different from those used for the data warehouse, campaign management system and the website. For the time being, smaller players offer a narrower range of functionalities, but can offer better products than the market leaders when it comes to niche applications. If an organisation elects to look for the best software among the different applications, then the challenge to

integrate the different systems increases. It becomes harder to create a whole from the sum of the parts, as it were.

5 *Building own applications (with help from IBM, Oracle, Sun, etc.).* The advantages to companies who choose to build a CRM application themselves are that they obtain customisation and avoid the substantial investment in suppliers' own systems. There are, of course, disadvantages as well. What originally seems inexpensive can become expensive in the end as a company wishing to develop applications itself can also find itself having to make many investments. It also appears to be difficult to keep up with the speed of development achieved by suppliers in the market, and the risk arises that companies will trail behind competitors who use the ready-made systems.

The expectation is that the market share of CRM applications integrated into ERP will grow in the years to come. The number of companies that build systems themselves and look for 'best of breed' will decline, however. The CRM suite suppliers will experience tough times and see their share decrease as well.

The current differences between suppliers of CRM suites continue to decrease. Even if they have a history with the Internet, call centres or sales information systems or with a certain industry segment – such as the construction world, financial services or the pharmaceutical industry – most functionalities have since been developed in a generic manner (Koenders, 2001). The result is that companies should not look for the differences among the leading packages in terms of the generic functions, but in the details. The depth to which a certain function is supported can differ.

Practitioner's insight

The details . . .

Other than logistical processes for example, marketing, sales and relationship management processes are generally not thought out and designed beforehand, but instead evolve over time. Every employee adds his or her own contribution over the course of time, and interprets activities in his or her own way. The result is that there is often a lack of concrete processes which may be monitored and managed, but instead an interplay of daily activities. In order to provide support to these in daily practice, it is important to know not only *what* the package does but also *how* it does what it does. A generic example is the creation of selections . . .

Think of a situation in which a quotation must be created. This always requires the registration of many data. Often ten or more screens must be brought up and filled in first, and it is often unclear how the filled-in data ultimately come together in the quotation. If the decision is made afterwards to grant a discount, this can be a good way to test the accessibility of the package functions.

Source: Koenders (2001).

18.8 Conclusion

Developing relationships with a large number of different customers may only be achieved if information and communication technology are used. Different systems have been developed to support CRM or to implement it. In the front office, we first encounter the technology required for the call or contact centre and the website. Possibilities exist to orchestrate the telephone or written contacts from one central location. Systems are put in place to ensure the timely establishment of the right connections, making (customer) data available and processing changes in this data. They can even take over parts of the communication process from people who then have more time for the truly important contact moments.

In order to supply the front office with customer data, the creation of middleware is a necessity. Part of these data must actually come from the back office which is usually set up to be able to handle the processing of large quantities of similar tasks in batches. Many of these legacy systems are organised to focus on products or functions and not on customers. In order to supply the front area with the necessary customer information, data are compiled from several different sources and input into data warehouses and datamarts, from which customer data may be retrieved and changed, if necessary, in a simple manner.

In order to facilitate the continuous communication flow with customers, more than just a data warehouse is necessary. The campaign management system satisfies this need and supports the contact cycle from the time the name–address–city files are selected, during the determination of the communication timeline, planning the campaign, sending the messages up to and including follow-up and evaluation of the campaign. And a content management system can be of support to manage the digital content to be presented through a diversity of outlets and channels.

Case study

Canada Post delivers on its CRM strategy

Background

'Canada Post Corp. (CPC), a Canadian Crown enterprise, is Canada's national postal service provider. With 66 000 employees, it is also the country's fourth largest employer. It serves 30 million residential customers and more than 1 million commercial customers, delivers more than 10 billion pieces of mail annually, and maintains relationships with more than 24 000 retail sales points for CPC products and services.'

'CPC recognised that its future depended on having customer processes and support systems in place . . .' with customer expectations rising and the ongoing emergence of the Internet. 'To demonstrate its commitment to change, CPC launched an enterprise-wide business transformation initiative to redesign all processes and employ innovative technological solutions to create customer and employee value.' In the new situation 'every process must add value for the customer, the employee or the corporation'.

'Each process was reviewed to ensure that it was customer-focused, process-driven, self-service-oriented and could withstand the scrutiny of measurement with assigned accountability.

'In the past, customers' experience with CPC were often complicated and frustrating. A customer could call three or four times about the same issue and receive different responses from call center agents. Customers can now take control, tracking their own parcels and placing online orders, as well as having 24/7 ability to satisfy their postal needs.

'The new system has also improved the internal employee experience. The former systems were standalone and didn't integrate customer and call information. Now, when a customer calls, there is a history of the cases related to the customer, and the system can reference frequently asked questions [FAQs] from the CPC solutions database. These provide an integrated view of the customer – from prospect to the placement of orders and accounts receivable.'

Realisation

'CPC implemented the new system through extensive change management that involved process and organisational redesign . . . Change was communicated through traditional methods, and through a network of "readiness teams", using leadership coaches, area project managers and local implementation coordinators. Implementation involved two years of process design and system stabilisation. This included a team of CPC employees plus systems integrators from SAP, Accenture, EDS, and interactive voice response telephony suppliers . . . People readiness was addressed through more than 50 000 participants-days of learning delivered to employees during the implementation year . . . Externally, a take-to-maket team made advance contact with many of CPC's largest customers and communicated changes directly to some 145 000 commercial customers. For post-launch fixes and stabilisation activities, customer-facing issues were treated as the first priority.'

Using the built-in processes defined by its application provider SAP, CPC changed its business processes to leverage what it believed to be the best practice inherent in the software. Package tracing, rate calculations, service standards and an online business center were redesigned to be technology-enabled by SAP modules, such as case management, order taking, Internet sales and Internet service. Each of these provides CPC with the functionality to enable the transformation, as well as the integration of back and front end processes.

The Internet service application provides customer-service agents and delivery supervisor with details of customer transactions (including inquiries, complaints, claims and orders) from a single screen. It provides customers with online access to a comprehensive solutions database for self-service query resolution. Internet sales integrates processes with mySAP Retail Online Store to provide customers with online access products. These processes are tightly linked with the back office SAP R/3 system to provide a single customer view and a single face to the customer.

Six customer databases were combined into one, as were three case management databases. Since all parts of the enterprise now have a single view of each customer's activities, every interaction is more productive.

CPC also launched a business warehouse reporting functionality from CRM. The ability to analyse the information from sales and customer cases enables proactive responses to customers' needs and change processes to better serve customers.

CPC deployed technology in a phased program plan. In launching the CRM initiative, the first three components were as follows:

- A new CPC website . . . It quickly climbed to a position as Canada's most visited website.

- Electronic shipping tools: enhancing and combining two existing online tools, these are available to commercial customers in both desktop and web-based versions that enable them to place orders directly and create all shipping documents.
- New telephone tools: CPC deployed mySAP CRM to nine contact centers that handle 5 million calls annually across numerous time zones. Using SAP Phone, CPC supports queuing for customer inquiries and enables fax, e-mail and voice-back options for customers and supply agents.

'Implementing the CPC systems required some 400 individuals. As it configured and integrated the components, the team replaced more than 80 legacy systems.'

In a little more than two years the implementation was realised. 'The most significant technical implementation challenges included understanding the fully integrated back-end and CRM processes from an organisational perspective and testing.'

Conclusion

'CPC's CRM program supports the way the enterprise wants to operate . . . It supports its strategic priority for customer-centricity and operational excellence . . . It defined its vision, strategy and business processes choosing an enterprise resource planning/CRM application suite. More importantly, CPC has achieved its business goals by defining and using a CRM strategy as the core of its overall business strategy.'

Source: Eisenfeld (2002).

Questions

1 Why is process redesign so important for CPC's success?

2 Describe the way CPC redefined its processes. Illustrate your answer with three examples.

3 Analyse the CRM systems that are in place at CPC. In what way do they enable the processes?

Questions

1 Voice processing has its proponents as well as its opponents. Both sides are capable of shedding light on the pros and the cons from the perspective of the customers as well as the supplier.

(a) Name two advantages of voice processing for the customer as well as the supplier.

(b) Name two disadvantages of voice processing for the customer as well as the supplier.

2 Think of four technical measures which may be used to shorten the access time for customers calling a call centre.

3 Indicate three differences between the Internet and a closed computer network for a company.

4 Name three methods which may be used to protect critical company data while still facilitating the interaction between customer and supplier on the Internet as much as possible.

5 What is the difference between a data warehouse and a datamart?

6 What are the reasons for setting up separate datamarts for call centres and for websites? Substantiate your answer.

7 What are the objections to giving visitors to a website direct access to the legacy systems?

8 Think of three recommendations designed to improve the security of your critical business systems in a multichannel environment.

9 In the text, references were made to a cruise line. Customers of a cruise line have a large number of 'customer touchpoints' with the carrier.

(a) Name fifteen of these touchpoints.

(b) Create a possible campaign for each contact point.

10 Name five reasons why the implementation of a campaign management system can fail. Substantiate your answer.

References

Brink, Marion V. van den (1999) *De opzet, implementatie en organisatie van een call center*, F&G Publishing, Amersfoort.

Broek, Robert van den (1998) *Call centers en databasemarketing*, Beerens Business Press, Woerden.

Dekker, Hans and Femke Hiemstra (2002) Content management, *Emerce*, September/October, 62–66.

Eisenfeld, B. (2002) Case Studies, CS-16-7100, *Research Note*, 12 July 2002, Gartner Inc.

Fuller, Floyd (2000) *Getting Started with Electronic Commerce*, The Dryden Press, Fort Worth.

Gartner Research (2003) *Overview of CRM Trends*, February.

Gartner Research (2004) Gartner Business Intelligence Summit, Royal Lancaster Hotel, London.

Hardeveld, Gert van (2001) CRM: typen en trends, *CustomerBase*, **7**, 1, 30–33.

ITCommercie (2002) Gebuikers eisen verticale expertise, *ITCommercie*, 6, October, 10.

Jonker, Jack (1997) *Datawarehousing en daarna*, Kluwer BedrijfsInformatie, Deventer.

Koenders, Christiaan (2001) CRM-pakketten, steeds meer me-too's?, *Tijdschrift voor Marketing*, April, 16–20.

Niks, W., Pauline Plasmeijer and Ed Peelen (2000) E-commerce – *Transactiemodel Voor Internet*, Kluwer.

Stuurman, Bart (2000) PRM zorgt voor grip op het indirecte kanaal, *CustomerBase*, 6, 29–32.

Sybrandy, Arno (2003) Nieuwe contact center technieken, de hype voorbij?, *Beyond, Mapping, Marketing and Datawarehousing*, **8**, I, March, 17–19.

Turban, Efraim, David King, Jae Lee and Dennis Viehland (2004) *Electronic Commerce: A managerial perspective*, 3rd edn, Pearson Prentice Hall, Upper Saddle River, New Jersey.

Verduin, R. (1999) *Customer Relationship Management*, Kluwer.

Watson, Richard T., Pierre Berthon, Leyland F. Pitt and George M. Zinkhan (2000) *Electronic Commerce: The strategic perspective*, Dryden Press, Fort Worth.

19

Implementation of CRM systems

The step-by-step development of the CRM competencies of an organisation is covered in this chapter. First we describe the aspects which must receive attention during the implementation of CRM. Then we will provide a scan which a company may use to determine its position: how does it score with regard to the various aspects of CRM? A comparison of this assessment with the strategy provides insight into the CRM initiatives to be taken. These are divided into programmes which are then developed into different projects.

In this chapter we will address the following questions

- What leads to satisfaction with CRM (systems)?
- What causes disappointing results from CRM (systems)?
- How to implement CRM and how to form a relationship-oriented organisation.
  - What is the scope of CRM?
  - What projects are needed to implement CRM and to form a relationship-oriented organisation?
  - How to determine the status of the organisation: *assessment* and *quick scan*.
  - What is the CRM readiness: have the necessary conditions been satisfied for implementing CRM?
  - How can companies grow from the current situation to the desired one: how can they translate the strategy into programmes, projects and business cases?
  - How to specify the objectives (per phase in the CRM process) that an organisation would like to achieve in a CRM project or programme.
  - What are the characteristics of good CRM project management?
    - What are points of special interest for successful implementation?
  - How to evaluate international or cross-division CRM projects.
    - What is the desirability of a globally standardised approach?

Practitioner's insight

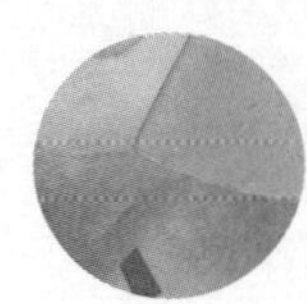

Many a CRM project fails to lead to the intended financial results or even to make it to the finish line. Companies report struggling with CRM projects; it seems no one knows for which functionalities a need exists and in which order these should be realised. This not too optimistic situation is the consequence of the hype with which dreams were sold. By implementing CRM systems, it appeared to be possible to realise a customer intimacy strategy. However, we now know better and many companies have experienced the implementation of CRM as sweat, hard work and plugging away. The idea has spread that the implementation of CRM can take a long time, and that it is better to talk about it in terms of a process and programmes rather than as one or more projects. Moreover, we have experienced that there is not one type of CRM. CRM means different things to different organisations. Every organisation will have to discover what CRM can mean for it specifically as both a strategy and a system. By using an assessment, it can determine where it stands: how far removed is it from the ideal that it currently strives to attain? A growth path will have to be traced out, along which the CRM competencies may be developed, step by step.

19.1 Causes for disappointing results

A study conducted by Gentle (2002) revealed the following causes of the disappointing results obtained with CRM:

- Lack of a business case with clear objectives: it is unclear what the company hopes to achieve with the CRM project and whether this will produce a positive 'bottom line' result. The relationship between the efforts and the result is not clear.
- The organisation was not ready for CRM: various pre-conditions had not been satisfied; the integration of the front and the back office was still lacking or the quality of the customer data was still insufficient.
- Poor data quality led to a failure to customise the dialogue being conducted through the different channels to the relationship, and discouraged agents left behind in the call centres.
- The scope of the project was too broad: the company wanted too much at once.
- The lack of active sponsorship from top management.
- The project was IT-driven and the focus on technology was too strong.
- Insufficient attention for change management: after the implementation of the CRM system the company was not finished; a relationship-oriented organisation had still not been created.

Table 19.1 Satisfaction among companies with CRM results (in percentages)

Sector	*Satisfaction*
Fashion	13%
Energy companies	15%
Insurance companies	24%
Logistics/transport	24%
Publishing/media	32%
Telecommunication	35%
Banks	35%
Office furniture	38%
Mechanical engineering	38%
Chemicals/oil	39%
Consumer goods/retail	42%
Consumer electronics	44%

Source: Berger (2002).

- Customers and others involved in relationships with the company do not react positively to the system: an incorrect assumption has been made that customers want a relationship and appreciate the new possibilities for contact.
- The misconception that CRM may be contracted out to system integrators. The problem is shifted outside of the company and the idea is that a third party can offer a ready-made solution. CRM is, however, too company-specific to place entirely in the hands of others.
- An international approach to CRM that results in additional complexity and is difficult to justify business-wise. The head office imposes the choice of a system on the organisation, and dictates the speed with which the projects must be realised.
- A bureaucratic approach to project management: too much focus is placed on the writing of project plans and reports, leaving too little attention for the 'real' thing.
- Resistance from the IT department: the organisation of horizontal processes around customers has consequences for the functionally-oriented IT department.

Table 19.1 itemises the satisfaction with CRM according to different industries.

19.2 An initial exploration with CRM and how companies handle this

CRM is a container concept which everyone may interpret in the manner which best suits their situation. One person may apply it to the website, while for another it may involve the campaign management system and a third person may be concerned with one-to-one marketing. Giving CRM a clear meaning is an initial action that will determine its success. In addition, it is recommended the organisation stop and consider the manner in which it is currently dealing with customers. What is the customer knowledge? How is this used during customer contacts? Is a conscious effort being made to develop the relationship with good customers? Is customisation being supplied? How customer-oriented is the organisation?

Various 'scans' have been developed to help organisations get a first impression of how they may design CRM. They also provide recommendations on the way in which CRM may be developed further.

The scan developed by the ICSB is shown overleaf. Using this, companies can score their performance on the various components of CRM. A total score is calculated for each component, which may then be displayed in a spider diagram such as that shown in Figure 19.1. The points in the diagram show the average scores for Dutch businesses in 2002.

Figure 19.1 CRM quick scan plot

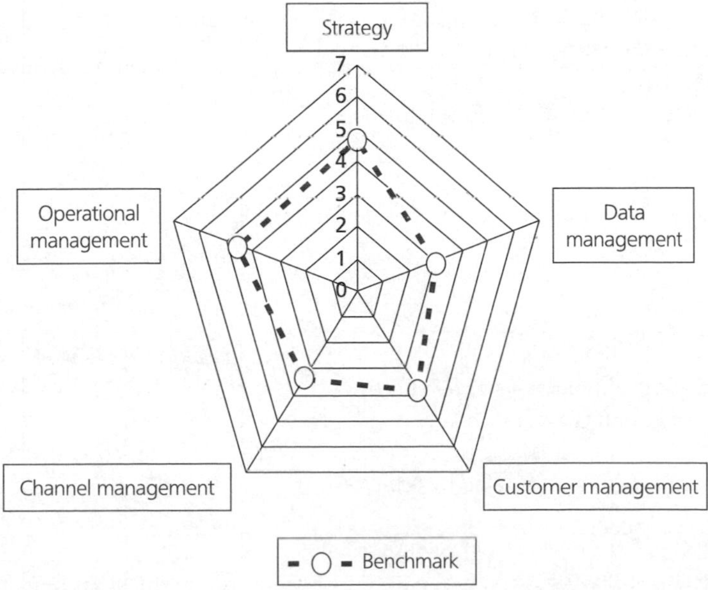

Source: ICSB, (2002).

Quickscan customer relationship management

Organisational strategy

		Disagree	*Neutral*	*Agree*
1	In our mission, our customers are the focus, not products or processes.	☐	☐	☐
2	Our mission clearly describes how we would like to treat our customers.	☐	☐	☐
3	Customer satisfaction is one of the main goals of our organisation.	☐	☐	☐
4	Empathy for the customer is extremely important in our organisation.	☐	☐	☐
5	Employees are given the space to satisfy customers' wishes.	☐	☐	☐
6	The management team spends half of its time on activities that involve customers.	☐	☐	☐
7	We do not evaluate our company's performance solely on the basis of financial results.	☐	☐	☐
		…× 0	…× 0.5	…× 1
		Total score =		

Customer management (the relationship strategy)

		Disagree	*Neutral*	*Agree*
1	We have insight into the way that relationships with our customers develop.	☐	☐	☐
2	We are able to spot when a relationship is developing in the wrong way before it is too late.	☐	☐	☐
3	We build enough moments into the relationship which are positive and not only operationally oriented.	☐	☐	☐
4	We are capable of engaging in marketing activities at strategic moments.	☐	☐	☐
5	Customer information is structurally and consistently shared between departments which have contact with the customer.	☐	☐	☐
6	Our employees' performances are determined in part on the basis of their degree of customer orientation.	☐	☐	☐
7	Employees with customer contacts have an affinity for information systems.	☐	☐	☐
		…× 0	…× 0.5	…× 1
		Total score =		

Channel management

		Disagree	*Neutral*	*Agree*
1	We have insight into our customers' communication preferences.	☐	☐	☐
2	There are objectives for different customer contact moments included in the communication plan.	☐	☐	☐
3	The mix of communication channels is not dominated by technical possibilities.	☐	☐	☐
4	We are able to identify the customer during each contact moment and have full customer knowledge at our disposal.	☐	☐	☐

		Disagree	Neutral	Agree
5	Our service and that of our partners* is flexible enough to satisfy our customers' needs.	☐	☐	☐
6	Partners* are cooperation-minded and voluntarily share customer data with us.	☐	☐	☐
7	We know exactly how customer-oriented the partners* have positioned themselves.	☐	☐	☐
		…× 0	…× 0.5	…× 1
		Total score =		

* Partners are third parties that are contracted by the organisation such as distributors or service providers (transport companies, etc.).

Data management (customer knowledge)

		Disagree	Neutral	Agree
1	We have a clear strategy for processing customer information.	☐	☐	☐
2	Acquisition of customer data is an important component of our company processes.	☐	☐	☐
3	All of the data that are necessary to implement the strategy are available.	☐	☐	☐
4	Employees are familiar with the available data and actively use these.	☐	☐	☐
5	Data are protected (both in terms of privacy issues and security) and this is guaranteed for external parties.	☐	☐	☐
6	Available data are relevant, up to date, accurate, complete and consistent.	☐	☐	☐
7	People employed in the IT department also have an affinity for marketing.	☐	☐	☐
		…× 0	…× 0.5	…× 1
		Total score =		

Operational management (supplying customisation)

		Disagree	Neutral	Agree
1	We can offer customers various elements of our services tailored to their needs.	☐	☐	☐
2	The quality of our products/services does not interfere with our relationship with the customer.	☐	☐	☐
3	In all of our operational activities, the customer's comfort and ease are high on our list of priorities; we do not automatically choose efficiency above all else.	☐	☐	☐
4	Customers are involved in the development of new products and services.	☐	☐	☐
5	During Recruitment and Selection and Training, there is plenty of focus on customer-orientation.	☐	☐	☐
6	The organisation is capable of identifying future needs of individual customers and of addressing these needs.	☐	☐	☐
7	Employee satisfaction (on all levels) is extremely important to the organisation.	☐	☐	☐
		…× 0	…× 0.5	…× 1
		Total score =		

19.3 The CRM road map

The range of CRM

CRM can have an extremely large range. Figure 19.2 presents a summary of projects which may be performed within organisations under the CRM umbrella. In order to transform a product-oriented organisation into a customer-oriented one, many sub-projects are necessary. Investments must be made in the *front office* in order to facilitate contacts by telephone and the Internet, among other activities. The *style of communication* will have to be adjusted. The persuasive style will have to be replaced by the dialogue form; instead of selling, we will now have to help prospects make purchases. This involves an adjustment that cannot take place without the implementation of *cultural and organisational structural changes*. Knowledge of customers will have to be developed and *used* in the development of a relationship. The manner in which initial contacts are expanded to become close relationships will have to be *planned*. A policy that had targeted the stimulation of transactions will have to make room for relationship marketing. Promises that have been made within that framework will have to be followed up in a reliable way (*fulfilment*). Plans to invest in the ability to supply *customisation* will have to be tailored to the relationship policy. Ultimately the activities will not be without consequences for the *business model*. By supplying customisation and having

Figure 19.2 Overview of CRM projects

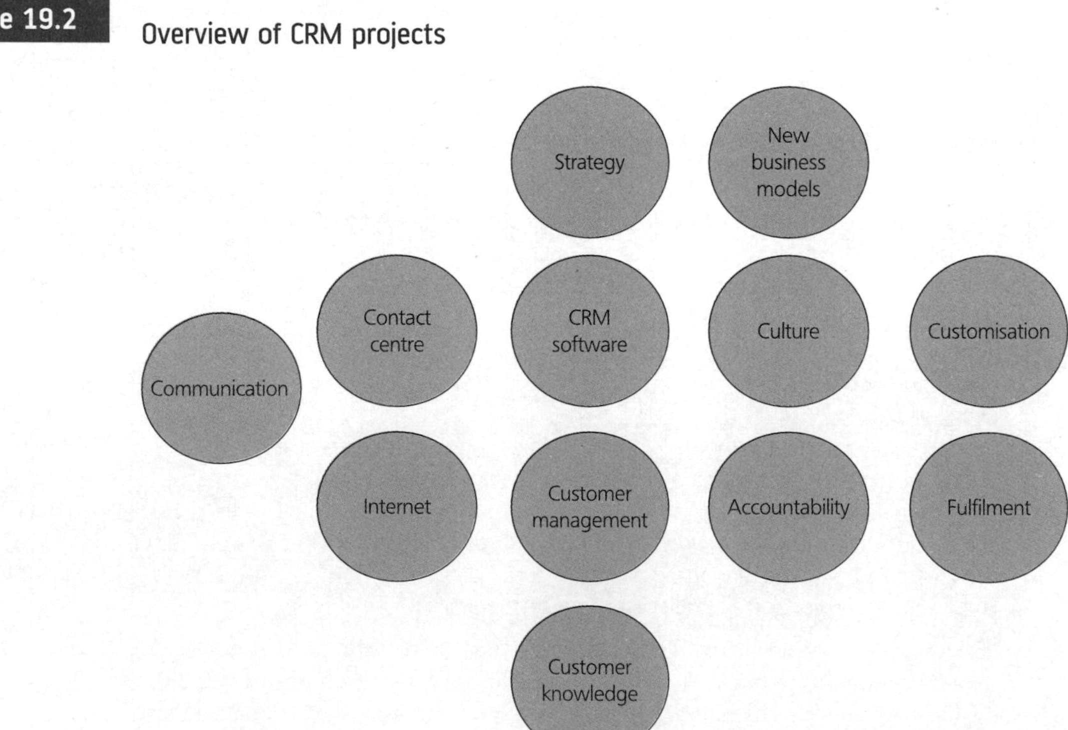

the intention to develop relationships, charter agreements become more popular, the urgency to experiment with 'pay-per-view' price models grows, etc.

In the meantime, the return on the activities and investments (the *accountability*) will have to be monitored. The transition from a product- to a customer-oriented organisation with a customer intimacy strategy can be plagued by difficulties. In the transitional phase, the influx of new customers can decrease from the moment the communication style changes. The advantages that customer retention and relationship development are expected to bring are also not immediately forthcoming. After all, investments have been made in the future of the relationship. The management that bears the financial responsibility can run into problems as a result. Pressure may be placed on these individuals to deviate from the planned path and to seek safety once again in transaction marketing, as a result of which the CRM strategy dies an early death. Longer-term commitment from the top is, as such, indispensable.

Each of the items shown in Figure 19.2 can represent a variety of projects. The result is that we should not be surprised if a large organisation reports that it has initiated more than 50 or even 100 CRM projects over the years. It is also not surprising that companies indicate that they have struggled with the possibilities involved in CRM.

The CRM vision

Formulating and disseminating a vision of CRM is crucial to avoiding getting lost in this expansive field. A vision will reflect the organisation's ambition: how will it ultimately deal with customers? It reflects the final situation that the organisation strives to achieve and to which it is committed, due in part to its pattern of values and norms. It may involve a vision of an investment fund to make financial markets accessible for private individuals with limited knowledge and ability to invest. It may be its ambition to support customers and guide them in the way they prefer in the management of their capital. By being the best listener among the service providers, it can utilise its expertise to help private customers become stronger in a turbulent financial climate.

CRM strategy

The realisation of a CRM vision requires a strategy that provides an indication of the concrete goals and how these are going to be realised. The choice of strategy provides a direction to the CRM functionalities that a company would like to develop. An organisation with an operational excellence strategy that invests in CRM systems will not supply customisation nor will it expend efforts to develop customer knowledge. Its customer strategy will also demonstrate more characteristics of transactional than relationship marketing. The contacts will have to be efficient yet effective; self-service solutions are therefore likely to be encouraged.

The concrete (financial) objectives constitute part of the strategy. The careful specification of these objectives can contribute fowards the success of a CRM project. It requires the organisation to lay a clear link between the efforts and the results to be achieved. A compulsion arises to search for possibilities which allow benefits to be derived from CRM during the interaction with prospects and customers. The company which employs the operational excellence strategy will have to specify in concrete

Figure 19.3

Relevance of CRM projects in the context of an operational excellence strategy

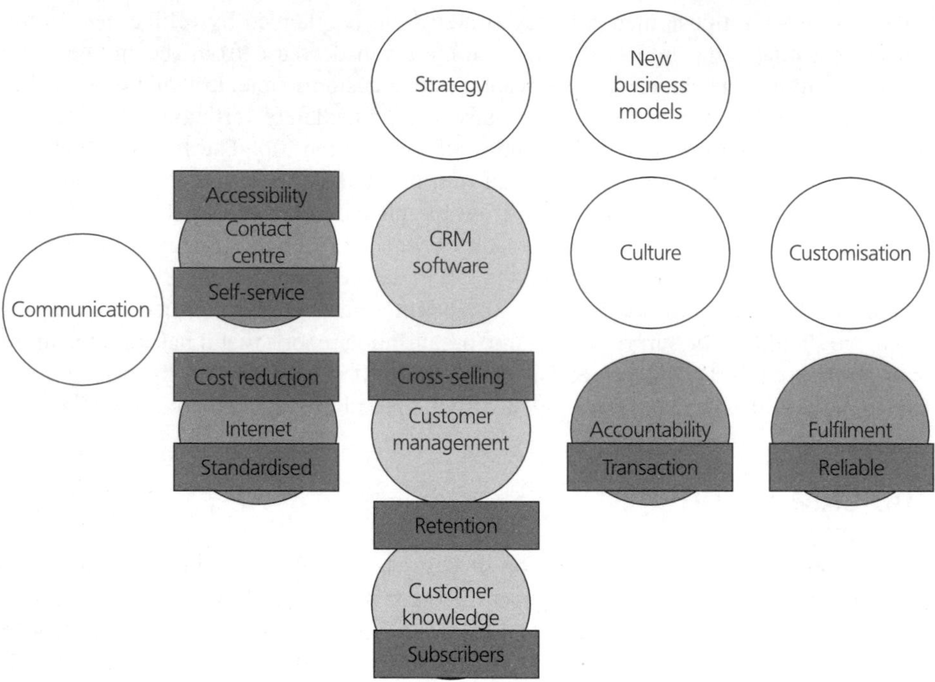

terms how the costs of order processing, resolving complaints and the like should decline over time. The desired revenues which are to be generated from cross-selling and the increase in turnover per customer will also have to be specified. During the CRM project, it will have to be monitored whether the efforts yield the desired results for the costs budgeted for this purpose.

Figure 19.3 depicts the effect of the choice of an operational excellence strategy in global terms for the different CRM sub-topics and the results to be achieved by them. If the circle is lightly coloured, this means that the importance of that topic is limited. Darkly coloured circles on the other hand indicate areas of special interest relevant for CRM.

Start at the beginning

Making the strategy work implies translating it to the operations, the processes. It is important to focus the projects on those processes involved in acquisition, delivery and after-sales service (relationship management) which are important to the organisation. Placing attention on the cross-selling process is not very interesting for a company that is operating in a growth market in which the level of penetration for its products is still quite low. It would be better to place the priority on addressing the defined acquisition processes.

The scope of the projects should not become too large as this can result in a riskier situation. Not only does the chance of a successful end decrease as a result, but the degree to which a failure is acceptable is also reduced: there is too much at stake.

The business case will have to demonstrate that the CRM project involved in this process will lead to positive results within a predetermined period of time. Appropriate to the CRM strategy will be an indication of how the project will ultimately pay for itself. What is the profit that will be obtained by reducing customer churn and how much will improvements in efficiency lower costs? How much will it cost to develop the CRM application? In budgeting, it is important to review all of the costs: those involved in the network, the application software and the data as well as the expenses related to supplier support and possible system integrators.

Usually, *initial CRM projects* will lead to a reduction in costs. It becomes less expensive to develop a catalogue, to reproduce it and to distribute it. The costs of the call centre may be lowered through the introduction of self-service concepts. Customers are assisted by voice processing systems or search for the answer to their question on the Internet in a 'frequently asked questions' section. During *a second phase*, the justification of projects is supplied by an increase in turnover. The acquisition and relationship management processes are defined and supported by ICT and may now be further optimised. Customer data may be used in approaching prospects in a more targeted way with offers, and cross-sell initiatives may also be geared towards customers' desires with a greater degree of accuracy.

Phased expansion

In further charting out the line of march for the longer term, the balanced scorecard from Chapter 4 (Figure 4.5) may prove useful. For the short, the medium and the long term, the *objectives* to be achieved may be defined for the different areas of CRM (Table 19.2). In financial terms, an indication may be provided, for example, of whether it is important to achieve a growth in turnover in the short term or an increase in the lifetime value for the long term. From the customer's point of view, the focus will initially be on increasing customer satisfaction, and later on improving the commitment. The attention shifts from satisfaction with the transaction to the bond between supplier and customer. During this same time span, the company will transform itself from a product-oriented organisation into one in which the customer is central. The market is no longer divided up into products but into market segments and ultimately even customer groups. And, the one-way communication makes room for a dialogue conducted through various channels. Business units no longer communicate independently with the customer, but gear their activities to one another.

Embedding in the organisation

Achieving the relevant objectives is dependent upon the proper embedding of CRM in the organisation. CRM has far-reaching effects for the organisation. Ultimately, the structure and the position of many managers change. Horizontal connections between departments and business units are created in order to arrive at a customer-oriented organisation. The IT department comes to fulfil a more infrastructural function and will

Table 19.2 Objectives of the CRM process within the four perspectives of the balanced scorecard

	Current situation	*Medium term*	*Long term*
Financial perspective	Turnover	Cumulative turnover over total period of custom	Lifetime value (profit contribution of the customer during period of custom)
Customer perspective	Average customer satisfaction	Individual customer satisfaction	Individual customer commitment
Process: communication	Primarily one-way; from business unit	Communication attuned between business units	Dialogue conducted through multi-channels
Learning and growing: customer knowledge	Customer knowledge distributed within organisation	Shared customer information	Integrated customer knowledge; everyone has the same image of the customer
Learning and growing: organisation (1)	Product-oriented	Market-oriented	Customer-oriented
Learning and growing: organisation (2)	Market is divided up into product groups	Market segments are identified	Individual customers and customer groups are identified

integrally support the business processes. Knowledge of individual customers must be built up and exploited. Experiments are employed to find the most effective and efficient relationship strategies. Resistance to setbacks must be built up to prevent the slightest disappointment resulting in a detour from the chosen path, which can lead to the impression that the efforts taken were fruitless.

The necessary long-term management commitment may originate from steering committees (Gentle, 2002). An important aspect is that the involvement in CRM on the part of this senior management concerns the entire process and not only the individual projects. They must be convinced of the importance, magnitude and reach of CRM and must be committed to it. They have a long-term orientation and overview, recognise the importance of a healthy business case, but realise just as much that a delay or short-term loss may not be allowed to endanger the overarching objective. Within the steering committee, individual members may take responsibility for the specific areas within CRM. One might focus on the financial aspects, for example, while the other sets his or her sights on the communication and development of the channels, and still another concentrates on the customer or the implementation of the CRM systems after a careful definition of processes has taken place.

It is common for the members of steering committees to find that their time is limited. This problem may be overcome via core teams. In these teams, professionals with authorisation operate from the top; they have responsibility for developing the organisation's CRM competency. A division of labour may now also take place by which one person will concentrate on the customer knowledge, and others on change management, external communication and the systems.

19.4 CRM project management

The separate projects may ultimately be professionally managed. It might seem to be a redundant statement, but experience has taught us that the contrary is true. Various initiatives even receive the label 'project' without a project organisation being set up or a project being defined, planned or evaluated. In other projects, those involved work strictly according to the handbooks, in which the procedures seem more important than the people who must do the work (Van Putten and Peelen, 2001).

The successful completion of a project is dependent upon various factors. A good project description is desirable, one which includes the assignment and the objectives to be realised. The project description should not be exhaustive or become too long; in practice this often leads to reduced usability, lack of interest in the document and, as a consequence, a greater chance of the project's detailed description not being implemented at all. The objectives should also preferably be SMART (specific, measurable, actionable, realistic, timely).

Project descriptions in which the selection and implementation of the software package are central are never going to win first prize in a beauty contest (Gentle, 2002)! In these types of project, the focus is usually on subjects which are unlikely to affect the success of the project. Additionally, the outcome of these projects is predictable; none of the standard packages will satisfy all of the wishes and demands and thus a solution remains forthcoming for the time being. What is important, however, is to realise that the project result is dependent on the degree to which the company is capable of defining processes from the customer's standpoint which are supported and improved by the use of information communication technology and which bring the realisation of the strategy one step closer. The business case will have to be developed from this angle in the project description.

Practitioner's insight

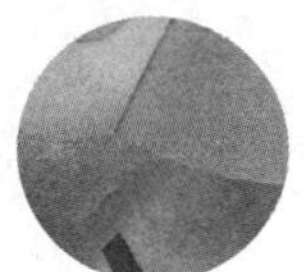

Processes consist of a succession of activities which logically follow one another (Davenport, 1993). Following the identification of an incoming telephone call thanks to caller ID, for example, someone will have to determine if the customer can be found in the customer database. If he or she is included in the database, then it may be determined to which segment he or she belongs and the telephone call may be routed to the responsible agent in the call centre. If the customer is not to be found in the database, then the call will have to be assigned to another agent who is capable of handling the input of the personal details in the customer database. If the caller ID has been blocked, then the call will have to be sent to an agent who will first ask the caller to identify him- or herself.

Flowcharts may be used to describe the processes in differing degrees of detail. On the most detailed level, the process descriptions are input for programmers. The example described here is characterised by a relatively high degree of detail. On an abstract level, it is the organisation and recognition of different contact processes that are involved, and the value that these can represent to customers. This involves a major challenge, all the more so because marketing processes are described in a less accurate way than production and logistical processes, for example. Various marketing activities are not even viewed as processes. Data for various officials, for example, are seldom approached from a process perspective. They are viewed as information and not as incoming data (input) which should be evaluated in terms of quality, stored and protected and which must prove their value in throughput processes.

In addition, the nature of the project will have to be identified. Is this a project that may be characterised as 'business as usual', or is it a complex and innovative one? (Van Putten and Peelen, 2001). If the latter is the case, then a careful risk analysis is all the more important. By recognising risks promptly, they may be more easily managed or it may be determined beforehand that the project should not be started at all. Another danger with innovative projects is that it is difficult to define the project beforehand. Many aspects are new and may not be described in advance. Insights regarding the objectives may change along the way, but the ideas on the project feasibility may also change as well as those regarding the quantity of work involved in the project. The scope of the project may then change as a result and represent a major risk for the project's chance of success.

The chance of a positive end result is furthermore determined to a greater degree by the people who are involved in the project. The inability to find qualified and motivated people who can work together in a team is reason enough to prevent a project from being started. Characteristic of many CRM projects is that people from more than one discipline must act in concert with one another. There are many situations in which IT professionals, marketers, salespeople and account managers, database specialists and/or call centre managers will have to work together to complete a project successfully. There is no room for bias and communication barriers will have to be overcome. Those involved will have to learn to speak one another's language even if that requires effort.

As was previously indicated, embedding the project in the organisation represents another point of particular interest. The project must have the aforementioned sponsor at the upper level of management who is convinced of the importance of the project and is responsible for the final result. In the event he or she appears to have insufficient time available for the project, he or she must provide a solution beforehand. He or she will have to delegate a suitable substitute who has the responsibility and sense of responsibility and with whom direct contact is maintained.

At the same time, there must be sufficient budget available in order to perform the various project activities. In addition to the purchase of the application software, the adaptation of the network, the integration of the systems and training for the staff, room will also have to be made to perform a pilot run of the system before the final rollout, and time and money will have to be provided for the evaluation phase so that people may learn from this project for the future. Financial means will also have to be made available in order to feed the system with data. A campaign management tool without customer data is, after all, not very useful. *There is the tendency in practice not to appoint enough means for the data aspect.*

It is also recommended that a pilot is organised in which the project can be tested out in a live environment over a period of several months by a selected group of users (Gentle, 2002). The goal of this is to validate the business case and to increase user acceptance. Opponents of a pilot resist this because a shadow system is maintained during such a period which places an additional burden on staff and is accompanied by extra costs. The advantage, however, is that there is a better chance that a complex and innovative project will be completed successfully. System integration issues should preferably be kept separate from the pilot. These issues should not even be an integral part of the first phase of CRM implementation, so it is especially important to separate them from the pilot.

Proper preparation for 'going live' with the project is crucial. The users must be trained and the data migration must be arranged. There is nothing worse than a user who does not know how the system works, let alone one who is confronted with a non-functional application.

Finally, the last phase of the project management must not be skipped. The project will have to be evaluated and lessons will have to be learned from it for the future.

After the completion of the project, the company must consider how and when the realisation may be raised to an even higher plane so that customer data and channels may be optimally exploited and realised. It may be considered whether changes in the organisation are desirable with a view to the transformation of the company from a product-oriented to a relationship-oriented enterprise.

19.5 International or cross-division projects (Gentle, 2002)

Expectations versus reality

In large organisations with activities in different countries and divisions, there is a good chance that the head office will 'adopt' CRM and pursue a standardised approach. The general idea is that this type of centralised approach has many advantages. It offers prospects for a professional approach. The best staff members are charged with the CRM task and they will have a sufficient budget at their disposal. Cost savings seem feasible through the centralisation of the purchase of CRM systems and by preventing the wheel from being reinvented at different locations within the organisation. By sharing best practices with one another, better performances may be achieved, quicker and at a lower cost. IT divisions, as champions of standards, are generally also proponents of a central approach.

The *actual* practice of international and/or cross-division projects is normally not a reflection of these initial expectations. The national organisations and separate divisions do not necessarily embrace the initiative. Their perception is that their local reality is being neglected. Their customers set specific demands which are not supported by the system. Their company division differs significantly from the others and thus deserves a different approach. The system with which they now work satisfies these requirements and they have the impression that the new one will probably perform worse rather than better. For them, being forced to adhere to the international standards feels like a punishment. Whether the response from the national organisations and divisions described here is justified or not is usually not even relevant. The perception is determinative for their cooperation with the initiative from the head office and the perception that 'everything that comes from the head office should be viewed with suspicion' is the subjective reality.

It must be recognised that in various situations the implicit (assumed) economies of synergy and scale of a central approach are also lacking. The cumulative quantity discount of the system supplier appears to give hope; however, this ultimately proves disappointing. If we compare this discount with the sum of the individual price reductions from the systems purchased locally, then the latter is often higher than the former. Additionally, the costs of hardware and software usually amount to only 50 per cent of the total costs involved in CRM projects and many more hidden costs emerge. Coordinating all of the activities appears to be more difficult than was expected and is accompanied by the requisite travel. It is also difficult to learn from mistakes. The political interests are great on all levels with a standardised approach. Mistakes are more likely to be hidden or camouflaged than with local projects because the failure of even a part of a prestigious project presents major difficulties.

Even if the central approach leads to a satisfactory solution, the negative consequences for flexibility will have to be recognised. Changes and renewal are not easy to implement quickly. Signals are received more slowly and less adequately; people do not realise that there is a need in certain segments of the organisation to change in order to better address the customer's needs, nor are they capable of estimating the importance of the desire for innovation.

When should a standardised approach be taken?

In overseeing the risks of the standardised approach, the question arises whether it is even useful in certain company and market situations. The answer is heavily dependent upon the degree to which cross-border or cross-division activities are being undertaken by the organisation:

- Are there corporate clients who maintain a relationship on a central level and acquire products from different national organisations and divisions?
- Are there cross-border or cross-division services being performed? This is the case with express couriers such as DHL; they collect a package in country A and deliver it in country B; telecom companies that set up international connections and banks that transfer funds from one country to another.

If an affirmative answer may be given to one of these two questions, then an integral system is desired on a *transactional level* and a standardised approach to CRM can be legitimate.

CRM illustration

One company, one database. The Economist Group integrates thirty databases into one system: View360

Four-fifths of the readership database of *The Economist* (circulation 830 000) is located outside of England; one-third of this segment lives in the United States. In spite of this, the numerous possibilities that the enormous database offers for the cross- and up-selling of different products and services of The Economist Group remains unutilised. Cause? The five business units employed more than thirty incompatible databases with different criteria and platforms.

The solution? One *customer view*, or one coherent picture of all of the customer segments that works globally and unites all of the data sources in the form of a *customer data solution*. In order to accomplish this, View360 was developed, a system that supports cross- and up-sell marketing activities, simplifies the integration process by collecting customer data from multiple sources and reprocessing these for sales and marketing purposes. The integration of all of the customer data and channels of the group was not achieved without a struggle, however. Everyone had to be convinced to share data with others and all of the international data had to be moulded together with different (address) structures to form one whole. But the result has proven that the efforts were worthwhile. The group now has access to a consolidated database, with details on 4.5 million (opt-in) customers with purchase histories of up to 12 years. The data are used for activities such as prospecting, analyses, cam-paign selections, optimisation of the advertisement offering and direct mail activities. And successfully. The turnover rate for data collection was drastically reduced, the number of orders rose, customer activities increased and office costs dropped 45 per cent.

Source: *Marketing Direct*, November (2002).

Other arguments for a standard approach should be viewed with suspicion, as has been shown above. Only the advantages offered by standardised international reporting deserve any attention. It is a considerable advantage for everyone to report in the same manner on his or her financial results, customer satisfaction, processes and innovations. The possibility of formulating norms and assigning meaning to the presented results grows significantly. Comparisons between divisions and national organisations become possible. The situation in country A may be very similar to that in country B several years prior and as such, it is easier to evaluate developments in that area more accurately. The fact is that this represents only a secondary benefit of a standardised CRM system, and may never serve as the reason to implement this type of approach. The choice for a uniform approach will have to be dependent upon a consideration of the pros and cons on a transactional/operational level.

Areas of particular interest in managing these types of projects

The successful management of the international and/or cross-division CRM projects requires attention to the relationship between head office and the local units. It is important to prevent users from getting the impression that the system is being forced upon them. Obtaining their acceptance is a project in and of itself for which time and means must be made available. Users deserve to be able to participate and have a say, and must be involved in all stages of the standardised project and not only during implementation. Members must be recruited from the specific countries and business units to become part of the project team. The final team will have to consist of members who have international experience and who are capable of assessing the situation in different countries. The requirements for the system will have to be determined collectively and agreement will also have to be reached collectively when it comes to the selection of the package and the solution. Investments in meetings should also not be avoided.

A sensitive issue in the relationship between head office and the units involves access to local data. This is seen as an undesirable invasion of privacy to which there is a great deal of resistance. The fact that head office will have access to information on customer churn, lead times, complaints, etc. is viewed as a wholly undesirable attempt at interference which may well to have a counterproductive effect. Insisting on access to these data will have to be avoided as long as it remains a sensitive issue. The chance that it will have negative consequences for the commitment to a project is very high, whereas it does not necessarily have to be crucial to its realisation. There are, after all, other workable solutions.

The success of these comprehensive projects is furthermore dependent to a great extent on the restriction of their complexity. Requests for separate versions in a specific language and/or separate functionalities will have to be examined with caution. This usually implies higher costs than were originally expected, and, in the beginning, simplicity is extremely critical for the success of the implementation. It is only in situations in which implementation is otherwise not possible that these requests should be honoured: for example, if a translation is indispensable to those in the front office for the interaction with customers; or if the agents do not understand English (the language used by the software package), and thus cannot work with the application. The initial architecture should also be kept as simple as possible. Knowledge of the specific situation is required to evaluate whether a central, mixed or decentralised architecture is preferred. In any case, the situation should be prevented in which the chosen solution becomes too risky, or delays the progress of the project and becomes a source of irritation during the development and initial phase of operation.

Finally, the actual implementation and use of the CRM system will have to be adapted to the local circumstances. The training will have to be provided in the local language and the first-line help desk will have to be able to assist users in their native tongue. For more complex questions that are referred to the second line, this is not a precondition, however.

19.6 Conclusion

Many CRM projects continue to fail. They do not produce the desired result; management struggles with the possibilities offered by CRM. In order to put an end to this situation which offers little reason for optimism, a careful CRM change and implementation project is essential. Companies will have to base their reasoning on the strategy and not the packages. An assessment of the current situation in comparison with what is desired from a strategic standpoint will have to provide insight into the direction CRM development will take with regard to the different areas of focus such as customer knowledge, the channels and the communication, the relationship strategy, the organisation and the culture, etc. Long-term commitment will have to be obtained within the organisation for this path of change and development. Senior management will have to take responsibility; because their time is so limited, they will have to delegate and appoint authorised professionals. Projects will then have to be defined. The focus should not lie on the package selection. It is more important to focus attention on the processes, the manner in which these may be supported and improved with the use of ICT, and how they will help realise the strategic objectives. A proper manning of the projects, good budgeting, timely involvement of the users and the like should all lead to a smoother implementation of the systems.

Finally, caution is called for in situations in which a standardised approach of cross-border or cross-division projects has been adopted. Potential economies of scale and synergy may be missing, while the additional costs of coordination are higher and more resistance must be overcome.

Case study

Shell and CRM: one database for 20 million customers

Interview by Peter Olsthoorn with Ruud van Munster, European Loyalty and CRM Manager for Shell

'Using overly expensive IT-driven CRM projects, other companies paved the way for Shell,' is one of the opening remarks made during an interview with Ruud van Munster, Shell's European Loyalty and CRM Manager. The oil company has learned from its failures and has chosen not to implement CRM on a Europe-wide scale, but instead to take a step-by-step approach.

A country-by-country basis

Shell has elected to expand its CRM programme on a country-by-country basis and is currently (2004) active in nine out of seventeen targeted countries. Munster: 'We first want to prove that something works on a small scale before we invest in something huge. There are too many CRM failures in the world. There are already too many projects in which the IT focus is too strong. Companies stare at huge CRM systems with abundant possibilities for which they have no sound application. If you do not know how to use them to create customer and company value and just climb aboard the CRM train, you will not succeed.'

According to van Munster, too many companies have also implemented a call centre without first formulating a proper business case. 'In our organisation IT follows and we only install a call centre if we are convinced it will improve sales. We spend as little as possible on operations. Besides, a European CRM system is not necessary in our organisation since there are only a few customers that fill up their cars across the border and those that do are normally less brand loyal.'

Shell currently maintains its own Shell (Club) Smart programme in thirteen countries and a 'coalition programme' in four countries: Air Miles in the Netherlands, Happy Days in Belgium, Thrumf in Norway and Smiles in France. The fuel card that may be used to pay for the fuel may also be seen as a loyalty programme and is in use in the Scandinavian countries.

Shell has created a three-layered CRM organisation:

- A loyalty competency centre in Hungary with IT and CRM knowledge. Van Munster: 'Hungary is known for the quality of its IT people, in addition to being one of the most successful countries for the Shell loyalty programme.'
- A European team of CRM experts; each of the team members has strategic responsibility for a cluster of countries.
- The local loyalty and CRM groups in the countries, who implement the programmes and have succeeded in creating value.

Van Munster: 'Centralisation has absolutely paid off. It was here that we developed our standard building blocks that we can apply to the countries. A few years ago we needed one year per country to implement a programme; now we do it in three months.' If it is up to van Munster, CRM applications will be further simplified and standardised in 2004, making implementation easier for local CRM teams. 'Practical efficiency is the goal. Perhaps it will become possible at some point to produce a single European or even global catalogue instead of national versions, and the articles can be sourced at lower cost.'

Facts

Is this approach typical for a follower? No, if we ask van Munster. 'You have to find out what does and what does not work on a step-by-step basis. You have to remain pragmatic. We sell fuel and cannot innovate CRM theory.' At present, Shell has a database of 20 million customers in Europe. This database is filled country by country and is currently operational in seventeen countries. The relation and transaction data are known and it is possible to identify customers and to send them correspondence or products. It is possible to look into the database to find out how active they are, how frequently they cash in their loyalty points, determine their fuel purchasing behaviour and evaluate the value that they represent. Van Munster likes facts: 'Not many consumers will admit that loyalty points influence their choice of a fuel brand, but practice has proven otherwise. I attach more value to information I get from the database than to the results obtained through traditional market research. There is a difference between what consumers say and what they actually do.'

Shell actions

Crucial within Shell is the accountability for a campaign. Control groups are used, for example, to show the value of a campaign. 'In France we noticed a significant difference in customer revenue. Campaigns pay off and add approximately 10 percentage points. We had campaigns with a 50 to 60 per cent response rate, which is extremely high. The road warriors in particular, the group that drives a lot and buys plenty of gasoline, responds quite well. They love to reach the individual target we communicated to them.' The example here is England where key customers received eight to ten e-mails during the summer with the offer of increasing their loyalty points by buying additional litres of fuel. They saw it as a game and took on the challenge.'

E-mail has become a favourite, although Shell will continue to send physical mailings as well. 'In three hours' time you can invent and create an e-mail campaign; in a regular direct mail process this will take much longer. I do not want to abandon traditional direct mail, as it is part of the multichannel approach and complements the other channels, but the Internet is gaining ground.'

Intranet

In England, the entire CRM operation, including the call centre, is outsourced to Carlson. Shell's competence centre, however, remains to be in charge and manages the relationship with Carlson. The future of outsourcing depends on several factors. 'In England, Shell has made good progress with CRM, the wages are high and there is a wide range of service providers. But taking on the challenge in-house also has its advantages as has been proven in Hungary, a country with 2.2 million cars and 2 million Smart customers in Shell's database. Smart customers can cash their points in at McDonald's and this makes the loyalty programme attractive for many. Success depends to a large extent on the efforts and spirit of the local organisation,' according to van Munster.

Crucial to the organisation of CRM is the communication among the three layers and it is here that the web is useful. Shell has a European portal, an intranet, which functions simultaneously as a knowledge base, a communication vehicle and the beginning of e-mail campaigns. Van Munster: 'Nearly everything we know about the 20 million customers may be traced on the intranet. Target groups in the seventeen countries and the success of campaigns are described in detail. If Turkey wants to copy a British campaign, they first read everything on the intranet and then get together for a face-to-face meeting to further develop the campaign. Each country has access to the available information. But only the local people have permission to access relationship data.

This online tool is for us the basis for guiding CRM. You can do as much with it as you want. You can select customers for your campaign, based upon their lifetime value or transaction profile and you can approach them whenever you want.'

Conclusion

The CRM targets differ per country and are defined using terms such as retention, reactivation and share of wallet. Van Munster: 'If we realise a retention rate of 68 per cent in the experimental group for the high value customers and 58 per cent in the control group, you can say that CRM is a success.'

Source: *Tijdschrift voor Marketing*, April 2004.

Questions

1 What are key factors determining the success of Shell's CRM approach?
2 How would you formulate Shell's vision and strategy towards CRM?
3 Reconstruct Shell's CRM road map.
4 Formulate Shell's CRM business case(s).
5 How useful will a standardised global CRM approach be for Shell? Why?

Questions

1 Describe step by step how a CRM change and implementation project may be designed.
2 Why do so many CRM projects fail? Name ten reasons and explain your answer.
3 CRM systems may be employed for companies which implement an operational excellence strategy. In this case the demands placed on the CRM system are different from those found in companies which implement a customer intimacy strategy. Indicate the differences between the two in the various areas of CRM,

namely customer knowledge, channels and communication, the relationship strategy and the supply of customisation.

4 A comparison with the strategic ambitions and the current situation should provide insight into the direction the development of CRM will take. Indicate how these can differ for companies involved in business-to-business and business-to-consumer sectors with direct or indirect distribution. Provide more detail using four company and market situations.

5 Obtaining a long-term commitment from top management for CRM projects is vital. Formulate the so-called 'elevator pitch' for a company of your choice. (This is the situation in which you are standing next to the CEO in the lift and have one minute to make your case for the topic and see that it gets put on the agenda.)

6 Defining processes represents an important part of CRM projects. On an aggregated level, provide an indication of the processes that you would like to define within an energy distribution company.

7 Explain how you would evaluate the following method of approach. In order to increase the chance of success of the CRM project in the contact centre, users (agents) are asked about their specific preferences. On the basis of their answers, the demands are then determined for the system. In your answer, describe the pros and cons of this method of approach.

8 Name several criteria that a good CRM project description must satisfy. Explain your answer.

9 Under what circumstances is it profitable to approach CRM projects in a cross-border and/or cross-division manner? Explain your answer.

10 How can you increase the local acceptance of a standard CRM package that will be implemented throughout the entire organisation in different countries and divisions? Explain your answer.

References

Berger, Roland (2002) CRM moet worden opgevolgd door CMR: customer managed relationships, *Tijdschrift voor Marketing*, December, 18–20.

Davenport, Thomas H. (1993) *Process Innovation: Reengineering work through information technology*, Harvard Business School Press, Boston, Massachusetts.

Gentle, Michael (2002) *The CRM Project Management Handbook: Building realistic expectations and managing risk*, Kogan Page, London.

ICSB (2002) *CRM scan*, www.icsb.nl.

Marketing Direct (2002) One company, one database. The Economist Group integrates thirty databases into one system: View360, *Marketing Direct*, November.

Van Putten, Willem and Ed Peelen (2001) *CRM Project Management*, Nyenrode, Breukelen.

20

The future

The future is uncertain. Extrapolations in which trends from the past are extended further into the future do not provide a reliable prediction if there are too many changes taking place in the environment. We start paving the road to the future the moment we take a step into the future and acquire experience. On the basis of our findings with CRM, we can also make several pronouncements on the continuation of the CRM journey.

In this chapter we will address the following questions

- How may we justify pronouncements regarding the future?
- Which factors influence the future of CRM?
  - Technology, buyers, the IT sector, user experience.
- What is 'the' future of CRM?
  - What is the selective suitability of the CRM strategy?
  - What will be the follow-up to operational CRM: what happens when CRM is implemented well operationally in the majority of the organisations?
  - How will interest in analytical CRM evolve?
  - How will organisational culture change?
    - The blurring of the borders between customers, suppliers and competitors.
    - Real-time marketing.

Practitioner's insight

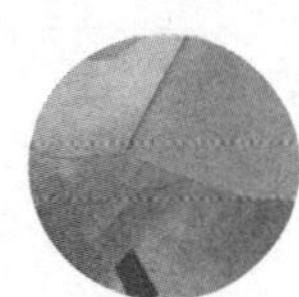

The experiences with CRM are not yet promising. The question is, what are the consequences of this for the future? Like e-business, do we place CRM in the commemorative cabinet with the other props which remind us of a time in history in which dreams possessed a great power of persuasion? Should we sound the alarm and warn others of a premature death of relationship marketing? All of the ideas that have arisen since the middle of the 1980s which have focused on the development of long-term customer–supplier relationships were embraced with a great deal of enthusiasm initially, only to prove difficult to implement and incapable of producing the desired results. So why should it be any different now, in the year 2005? Or do we have the right to be a bit more optimistic: has CRM just become purely marketing, just as e-business has become just business? Or can we really start thinking positively and say that we will overcome the current setback? It is a question of experimentation and learning so that we do not get led astray by appealing scenarios, but instead gain insight into the possibilities of the systems, the implementation and change projects, and most importantly, the ways in which the strategy may be supported.

20.1 Factors which influence the future of CRM

The continuation of the 'journey' is influenced primarily by the factors noted under the following sub-headings.

Technological progress

Technology is described as an autonomous factor that determines progress. It is difficult to undo inventions as long as no superior substitutes have come along to take their place. This applies to the invention of gunpowder, the steam engine, electricity, but may just as easily apply to the Internet and the telephone as well. It is therefore difficult to imagine a society without the Internet; even if it had been developed by coincidence or with completely different intentions from those for which we are currently using it.

Consumers change

Consumers are becoming more critical and independent, but also place higher demands on convenience. Organisations should be available for their customers and answer their questions at the time and place of the customers' choosing. Many waiting periods are quickly considered to be long and annoying. Questions to which people used to look for answers in product descriptions, brochures and the like, are now expected to be answered via a single telephone call or Internet visit. Many organisations have witnessed a substantial growth in the information exchange with their customers and will at the very least have to develop facilities to meet this growing need efficiently.

Customers in the business-to-business and government markets change

The changes taking place when it comes to customers' needs and demands are not limited to the consumer markets. In the business-to-business markets, there is a call for an orchestrated customer-supply approach in which members of the decision-making units at the customer's, supplier's, and involved intermediary's organisations are constantly apprised of their contacts with one another and gear and integrate their business processes to those of the others. Governments also strive to improve their relationships with their citizens and to make the governmental apparatus more accessible.

CRM illustration

Use of online government services sharply increases

The highest incidence of use of online government services was found in northern European countries, including Sweden (57 per cent; indicating that 57 per cent of the Swedish people have used online government services at one time or another), Norway (56 per cent), Denmark (53 per cent), the Faroe Islands (52 per cent) and Finland (49 per cent). Singapore is the only non-Scandinavian country in the top six (53 per cent). These figures originate from a study conducted by NIPO Interactive in conjunction with Taylor Nelson Sofres.

Source: *Insight* (2002).

Commitment from the industry

System integrators, consultants, CRM software developers and users have invested a great deal in CRM systems. Many millions, perhaps even billions, of euros are involved. The survival of large, established companies is dependent upon the successful use of the systems. The commitment from the parties involved is large as a result; they will do whatever it takes to achieve success.

Realism is on the rise

The hype is now over and realism is growing. The number of managers that proclaim that people should 'participate in CRM' in order to remain on top of the latest developments is decreasing. Declarations will be made in a more studied manner on the basis of business cases, strategies, and change and implementation projects.

Experience is growing

In recent years, we have watched the knowledge of CRM grow at a rapid rate. Insight into the factors that cause failure has grown as well. Lists containing the pitfalls from the early days of CRM are outmoded and signify the obvious in the eyes of CRM veterans, having made room for new pitfalls which are hopefully not destined to live very long. The experiences of CRM innovators, for instance, with the integration of the back and front offices are being recorded. Best practices are being created to prevent newcomers from making the same mistakes.

Speaking in more general terms, we are able to gain insight into an organisation's CRM readiness. We are arriving more and more often at a well-considered and concrete definition of the CRM strategy. The insight into what exactly is involved to achieve this is growing. We know that more is involved than simply a CRM system. The system can only be successful if we have qualitatively good data to develop customer knowledge and are capable of exploiting this during the development of the mutually profitable relationships with customers. We are reading into the organisational implications of CRM and the demands that a CRM strategy places on the level of customer orientation, the control model, the structure and the culture of the organisation. We also realise that we have to supply customisation in order to be able to fulfil our promise to the customer. And above all, we develop more insight into the manner in which we must accept this comprehensive challenge step by step in order to bring it to its proper conclusion.

On the basis of the irreversibility of technological innovations, the involvement of stakeholders as well as the customers, the IT industry, the organisations that use it and the growing experience, we can, in all likelihood, conclude that CRM will not disappear from management's agenda any time soon. Perhaps the term 'CRM' will gradually disappear, but this will hardly affect the direction that has already been taken in terms of thoughts and actions.

20.2 The continuation of the journey

CRM strategy is not for everyone

In the year 2005, many claim that apart from being a system, CRM is also a strategy, the implementation of which has organisational consequences. Insight into the concrete content of this strategy still has some growing to do. The confidence that there is profit to be earned in the long run by developing long-term relationships with the right customers is dwindling. The number of situations in which companies have succeeded in seeing a return on their investments in customers in the long term is fairly low. The current spirit of the times is dominated by the impression that the commitment from customers should not be overestimated. They have proven to be easily enticed, are fickle and have very little value for a relationship with a supplier. Previous calculations of lifetime values performed by Reichheld (1996) appear to have lost their evidential value. The manner in which these current experiences are analysed demonstrate, for us, some degree of having jumped a little too quickly to conclusions. The interest is limited in the discovery of the reasons why success has not been achieved and under what circumstances people may be justified in hoping for success. We must realise that the current CRM projects do not yet proceed as smoothly as everyone might hope. Successes have been achieved with regard to certain aspects of CRM; however, there has yet to be an organisation that has achieved the final ideal. The ultimate achievable result may thus not be found in the current cases. Elusive success cannot thus qualify as a reason to reject relationship marketing as being an economically useless strategy. The results of current experiences are most likely negatively influenced by the fact that companies aroused certain expectations in customers and were unable to live up to them. The implementation of CRM prevented this, customers' wishes were not properly understood, and the organisation forced itself on customers too much, showing too little empathy or being too bent on achieving its own profit objectives. Customers were not yet accustomed to the discriminating approach that is part of CRM, were still offended every now and then and had the feeling that they had to make do with what they had. The result was that they were unable to place their complete trust in the supplier.

In future, the strategic implications of CRM will have to take shape even further in practice. The realisation will have to grow that a customer intimacy strategy is essentially a niche strategy that is not ideal for every organisation. A selective acquisition policy must be made part of this strategy; the goal is to attract customers who truly desire a relationship with the supplier. In other situations in which CRM systems are developed and implemented, the system's connection to the strategy will have to be better guided. In this regard, a great deal may be expected from customer value management (CVM); this is a possible candidate as the successor to CRM. In CVM, the supply of value to the customers plays a central role; processes may be defined that result in the supply of this value and CRM systems may be designed which support this. With this, the superiority of the value proposition then shifts to the centre of the (marketing) strategy; it determines the long-term competitive position of the organisation. It is ultimately the goods and services that the organisation supplies that matter; it is here that the company must achieve a high score. Companies that succeed in effectively and efficiently customising their offering to the context and the processes of individual customers are those which approach or achieve the customer intimacy strategy.

An end to the pre-eminence of operational CRM?

In the current growth stage of CRM, most organisations tend to focus on operational CRM. Efforts concentrate on developing the communication channels in such a way that they support the contact cycle in all of its phases; from the moment that the contact opportunities are identified, the contact is made, the conversation is conducted, and the data are recorded, up to and including the follow-up and evaluation of the campaign. It goes without saying that companies engaged in personal sales activities are quite successful in these efforts. The telephone channel usually also comprises a closed contact cycle; however, the Internet – this is not limited to the mobile applications – involves yet another challenge when it comes to the interface between marketing and IT.

Additionally, in the dialogue with customers, not all of the parties are involved yet. In the year 2005, the suppliers of CRM systems place priority on the involvement of partners in the communication network. Initiatives are developed to create applications and to implement them so that intermediaries such as agents, middlemen, advisors and wholesalers form part of the CRM system. The integration of the communication channels is also far from being a *fait accompli*.

As long as the operational system in its rudimentary form is not yet 'finished', this will continue to detract attention from analytical CRM. On the one hand, justifiable or not, topics related to this field come across as being issues of luxury for the future when there is enough time to work on the specification of the marketing. On the other hand, they exert very little power of attraction. The significance of a subject such as data quality is insufficiently recognised in many cases. It does not sound innovative enough, appears to involve a detail and, at first glance, does not seem to cause very many insurmountable problems. The fact that this is not the case in practice should not come as a surprise. In spite of all sorts of advanced communication systems, if a company makes the mistake of failing to recognise or know its loyal customers, then it has a major problem.

To date, the earlier experiences with datamining have been unsuccessful in increasing the interest in analytical CRM in the first half of this decade. In the 1990s, datamining was very popular thanks to the rise of artificial intelligence. But the most important conclusion which has remained after a great deal of experimentation is that it is harder than people originally wanted to believe. The hope that the datamining application would expose hidden patterns which the marketer could use in his or her marketing efforts, without the need for numerous preparations and input on the part of the researcher, appears to be unfounded. The proper preparation, clean, good quality data, an accurate statement of the problem, and the experience to develop and refine a model are all indispensable to the performance of a thorough analysis. And even then, we must realise that possessing customer knowledge is not the same as datamining.

Nevertheless, analytical CRM will play a more dominant role in the long run. We are already seeing indications of a more standardised approach to this field. Modules which may be 'plugged' into the campaign management system have been developed to perform retention and cross-sell analyses, to identify opportunities and so forth. They support the user in creating (high quality) databases upon which analyses may be performed. In addition, they make it easy for the analyst to record the results in the campaign management system.

A new culture

During the hype, it was one of the merits of e-business: the customers are at the controls. The reality was a disappointment. Nonetheless, one, albeit slower, development occurred from which a changing division of roles and/or positions between the customer and supplier may be concluded. Customers, in particular the 'lead customers', are more actively involved in the development of new products. People know that these customers place demands on the products that will ultimately result in attracting many other customers and satisfying them. By introducing all sorts of self-service concepts, customers can not only easily help themselves, but can also gain access to parts of the supplier's organisation that were previously closed to him or her. Insight into the tracking and tracing system can tell the customer if the delivery is progressing without a hitch. One glance into the stocking system is like taking a stroll through the warehouse. An online meeting with another customer is facilitated by the supplier and communication on the supplier's performance may take place without limitations. The result of this trend is that the traditional lines between the customer's household and the supplier become more blurred (Prahalad and Ramaswamy, 2004).

This blurring of borders is not exclusively the result of the customer's 'visits' (McKenna, 1995). In reverse, we also see that companies are making a point of studying customer processes in greater detail to determine how they can make their value proposition fit in with these. They are broadening their customer knowledge; they learn how their customers use their products and how their success is influenced in part by this. Collaborations with complementary and even competing companies are not avoided if they appear to be opportune. The payment of financial benefits by an insurance company thanks to the cooperation with auto repair, car rental and telecom companies is converted into custom solutions for mobility problems which are related to the insured car. One company profits from an increase in its market range and the other from an improvement in its value proposition: more quality is offered at a lower price.

This all requires another culture in which to do business, one in which there is no competition between companies, but between networks in which cooperations take on changing forms. The classical relationships between customer and supplier appear to become somewhat blurred within this context. Perhaps a customer-oriented approach is making way for customer cooperation and customer facilitation.

20.3 Conclusion

Where the journey will take us, remains a surprise. In all likelihood it will not be the destination that is important, but the journey itself and the experiences gained along the way. As such, the final objective of customer intimacy or the network organisation and the modified relationships between customer and supplier may never be achieved and will shift along as we gain insight. In the meantime, inspiration has been provided and a successful learning curve has been set in motion in which useful innovations are brought to a proper conclusion. A great adventure awaits companies which are not well prepared and/or cut out to handle it. If this is the case, CRM investments can cost companies a great deal of money and produce very few positive learning experiences. A balance between the vision, strategy, culture, the organisation and the competencies within the company remains desirable. This balance prevents CRM from remaining simply a matter of dreams, empty policy pronouncements, frustrations and/or escalating conflicts.

Questions

1. The experiences with CRM have proven to be disappointing. Many companies have reported dismal results and terminate projects prematurely. Which arguments can you provide to anticipate CRM still having a long life ahead of it?
2. Using your own experiences as a customer, list a number of positive examples of companies which apply CRM.

3 Where will the focus within CRM lie in the next several years? Explain your answer.

4 How will organisations have to adapt themselves strategically, organisationally, and commercially in order to cope with the potentially changing relationships with customers? Explain your answer.

5 What is meant by the statement in Section 20.3 to the effect that 'the journey is more important than the arrival at the final destination'?

References

Insight (2002) Gebruik on-line overheidsdiensten neemt sterk toe in Nederland, *Insight*, 5/7, 7.

McKenna, Regis (1995) Real-time marketing, *Harvard Business Review*, July–August, 87–95.

Prahalad, C.K. and Venkat Ramaswamy (2004) The customer as collaborator, *Business Today*, February, 18.

Reichheld, Frederick E. (1995) *The Loyalty Effect*, The Free Press, New York.

Tissen, Rene, Daniel Andriessen and Frank Lekanne Deprez (1998) *Value Based Knowledge Management*, Addison-Wesley, Amsterdam.

Index

Note: page numbers for **chapters** are emboldened.